BARGAIN HUNTING
IN
CENTRAL OHIO

A Shopper's Guide to Savings and Values

BY DEBBIE KERI-BROWN

LOTUS PRESS
WESTERVILLE, OHIO

DISCLAIMER

The information contained in this book identifies prices, brand names and other details which were evident at the time of my visit to the business. Other references were extracted from advertisements and additional sources. Whenever possible, management was spoken with in order to gain further insight into the business's operation. Listings in this book, regardless of how worded, do not necessarily imply nor state an endorsement nor agreement with philosophies presented therein, by the author, Lotus Press nor its employees nor assigns. Businesses/services have not paid a fee to be listed in this book, and listings are not necessarily with the prior consent nor knowledge of the business/service. Listings reflect the opinions and observations of the author. While every attempt has been made to ensure accuracy and provide current, objective information, neither the author, Lotus Press nor its employees nor assigns will be held responsible for any nor all omissions, typographical errors nor erroneous information. As business/service policies, hours of operation, type of stock, etc. have a tendency to change as needed, I strongly recommend that you call ahead to those places you intend to patronize.

First printing, 1996.

Library of Congress Cataloging-in-Publication Data

Keri-Brown, Debbie, 1953-
    Bargain hunting in Central Ohio : a shopper's guide to savings and
values / by Debbie Keri-Brown.
       p.   cm.
    Rev. ed. of : Bargain hunting in Columbus. c1992
    Includes index.
    ISBN 0-9629590-7-3 (pbk.)
    1. Shopping--Ohio--Columbus Region--Guidebooks. 2. Columbus
Region (Ohio)--Guidebooks. I. Keri-Brown, Debbie, 1953- Bargain
hunting in Columbus. II. Title.
TX336.5.032C655 1996
380.1'45'0002577157--dc20   96-12969
                                                         CIP

DEDICATION

This book is dedicated to my parents and grandparents who started me on my journey. To my Aunt Marilyn and other relatives who unknowingly became a source of inspiration. To my children, Jason and Janelle, for whom I shopped to find all the necessities that kids need, and in so doing, unearthed many of the treasures for this book.

To my husband, Dave for his love, support and encouragement through my many sleepless nights, rooms full of papers and dinners on the corner of the kitchen table. And to God for providing me with the insight and perseverance to accomplish this enormous task.

ACKNOWLEDGEMENT

I would like to thank my editor, David St. John, for his assistance. In spite of my frequent requests to cut corners, he kept me on track and encouraged me to write the best work possible. To John Bailey for his eye-catching cover art. To my editorial assistant, Janelle, who pulled together many loose ends and set up our Bargain Hunting In Central Ohio site on the world wide web. To Maria Velalis for her expert word processing skills. And to the many businesses and services in this book, without which there would not be a Bargain Hunting In Central Ohio.

ABOUT THE COVER ARTIST

John Bailey is a 1982 graduate of the prestigious, Art Institute Of Pittsburgh. He has been working as a graphic designer for the last thirteen years and specializes in caricatures/cartoons. He is the featured cover illustrator/cartoonist for Hoot, Columbus' Humor Newspaper, and an editorial cartoonist for Business First Of Columbus. John is the recipient of numerous awards and distinctions for his work including the local Columbus chapter of the Society Of Professional Journalists and the Press Club Of Cleveland. The artist is happily married and the father of two sons, George and Ben. The male pictured on the cover of this book, is actually the artist, John Bailey. He is currently booking caricature engagements, freelance projects and accepting all kinds of nutty assignments! John can be contacted at (614) 231-6432.

TABLE OF CONTENTS

PREFACE

As far back as I can remember, I have always loved to shop for bargains. I recall the frequent exhilaration I felt as a child every time I came across an unexpected "find" and it still continues. I have many relatives who are somehow connected to the New York garment center district, and this is how my interest in shopping began. My dad, an accountant, still maintains his practice which includes many Korean owned manufacturers as well as others. In fact, he is was the executive director of the *Greater New York And New Jersey Korean Garment Manufacturers' Association*. In recent years, he was described by the New York Post as the "spokesman for the economic trends in the garment industry".

My grandfather helped to set up many of the prominent garment manufacturers by selling them industrial sized sewing machines. He also owned and operated several garment factories. My grandmother was a stylist for an international design house and as a benefit, she received many couture clothes for free. In fact, she owned so many formal clothes that she used to wear cocktail dresses when she went to the grocery store! Numerous other relatives have been involved in the New York garment center district in other capacities. As I was growing up, my dad frequently took my sisters, mom and I behind the scenes to the manufacturing operations where the garments were made. It was a thrill to see the workers in action and the rows upon rows of finished garments awaiting shipment to the retail stores. My dad pointed out that, "this manufacturer makes clothes under such and such designer labels, and he also makes other merchandise for lower priced lines". "Hmm, an interesting fact I thought." I acquired a wealth of knowledge and many additions to my wardrobe from those frequent factory visits. The lively conversations I had with my relatives also provided me with food for thought.

My aunt Marilyn always delighted me with her stories of how she frequently travelled to New York City by bus from Wilkes Barre, Pennsylvania as a personal shopper for some of the more affluent residents of that city who wanted special baked goods and other items which were not available in their home town. She really enjoyed those shopping experiences. It's no wonder that she was supportive of my idea for a book on shopping!

My mother always made certain that my sisters and I had new clothes when school began each September and intermittently throughout the year. After I came of age to shop on my own, my parents would give me money to buy clothing and I would come home with a shopping bag full of things for a mere $20, unlike my sister, Bonnie, who would only buy one or two items. She was loyal to designer brands and as hard as I tried to convince her that she wasn't always getting good value for her money, she was stubborn and did not want to listen. My parents were delighted about my bargain hunting escapades and would not fail to tell all of the relatives, plus their friends, every chance they had. Soon my friends began asking me where to find certain items cheaply. I began to keep a card file and referred to it whenever necessary. Over the years, I continued to search out bargains and have thoroughly enjoyed my experiences.

In 1980, my husband was relocated to Columbus through American Electric Power and I found myself in the middle of the Midwest with he and my two children. In 1981, we opened up a women's clothing store and a gallery, Potpourri Boutique and Fantasy Designs Gallery, in the Ohio Center, now called the Columbus Convention Center. This was really a dream come true. I could use my knowledge of buying at fair prices with my fashion flair, and my familiarity with the New York Garment district to dress Columbus women in style. At the time I opened the store, there were only a few places in Columbus where you could purchase fashion forward accessories and clothing at a reasonable price. The women would "ooh" and "ahh" at the styles and were especially delighted at the colorful selection of jewelry in the showcases. They all had experienced difficulty finding jewelry to coordinate with their clothes. Would you believe that it was hard to find purple, red or even yellow earrings back then? Business was good and I was having a great time merchandising, selling and best of all, buying. It wasn't uncommon for me to spend $20,000-$30,000 in a snap over a two day buying spree in New York, I knew how and where to go to find those great wholesale bargains. My customers appreciated the exceptional values they were able to find in my store. The retail experience provided me with new insights about manufacturing, buying, selling and consumer behavior.

After my divorce in 1986, and the subsequent closing of my store, I limited my shopping experiences to personal use only. Along the way, I managed to keep mental notes and some chicken scratches of Columbus' best shopping spots. In 1990, I began to teach a class on *Bargain Hunting In Columbus,* and taught it through many adult education programs and at libraries throughout the city. At last, I had found a way in which to share all of the information I had accumulated! The course participants were literally begging for more bargain leads as a follow up to the class. Since I obviously could not fit any more information into that exciting program, I chose another option. As a result of that demand, I felt that the time was right to publish a book. The first book, Bargain Hunting In Columbus, was published in 1992. The current book, under a revised title, covers a somewhat larger geographic area than my first venture.

In July of 1990, I married my current husband, Dave, who has been a constant source of love, encouragement and support. Everyone should be so fortunate to have a spouse as wonderful as he. I am also blessed to have married a man who enjoys shopping.

HOW I RESEARCHED INFORMATION FOR THIS BOOK

In writing *Bargain Hunting In Central Ohio,* I felt that it was equally necessary to provide you with tips on how to shop, as it was to suggest places which offer excellent values.

When I visited a potential bargain business, it was done incognito. I didn't tell the staff why I was there. Instead, I tried to absorb all that I could from staff comments plus my own observations. Afterwards, I either identified myself and defined my purpose, or called back to speak with the owner/manager. In some cases, I was surprised at the difference in the information that I received as compared to what I was initially told. One store owner, who shall remain unnamed, told me that his entire inventory is discounted 40-60% as a result of making special purchases. When I tried to clarify this over the phone, I was told that he was just having a brief sale and that he wasn't discounting his merchandise. I was surprised at how many upscale businesses which were discounting their stock or selling it at a good value for one reason or another, didn't want to be associated with a book on bargain hunting. "We don't want THOSE sort of people" or "Our customers would frown on us if we were associated with your book", or "Even though I'm telling you for your own knowledge, I can't have you print that we buy overstocks from a famous New York store because our customers would think that the merchandise is not as good as it really is" were common complaints. Being the excellent sales person that I am, I convinced all but a few that it was to their benefit to be in the book (they weren't being charged to be listed anyway). Today's shopper is not hesitant to be a bargain hunter. The shopper of the

1990's is more value conscious than ever, but is also demanding quality products. And you'd be surprised how many arrive in Cadillacs and Jaguars to their favorite bargain and value priced stores!

Some store owners or managers were reluctant to share certain inside information on their business or did not want me mention brands which they carry or percentages of discounts which they offer. For this reason, you will note that some of the descriptions appear very generic and lacking in detail. This book is not intended to tell you where to purchase budget nor inferior merchandise at low prices. What kind of a deal is that? Rather, it is intended to provide you with the names and addresses of businesses where you can buy moderate to designer quality merchandise or a service, at a discount, or a good value. So, price alone, has not been the sole factor for inclusion in Bargain Hunting In Central Ohio. You should also know that in mentioning certain businesses, such as the charity operated thrift stores like the Salvation Army, that if the business offered a combination of better and low quality merchandise, that I thought it would be worth the visit.

NATIONAL BARGAIN HUNTING WEEK

The author, Debbie Keri-Brown, is the founder of National Bargain Hunting Week, which has its inaugural celebration August 5-11, 1996. It will take place the first Monday through the following Thursday in August every year and coincides with National Smile week which was developed by Heloise, from the Hints For Heloise newspaper fame. The dates for National Bargain Hunting Week were specifically chosen to coincide with the other celebration because bargain hunting is something to smile about! Listed in the book, Chase's Annual Events(which includes such formidable listings as National Stop Smoking Day, Women's History Month and others) National Bargain Hunting Week is a time when businesses and shoppers can celebrate the thrill of the hunt for those bargains and the triumph of the find through their own personal celebrations, sales and special ways of saying "I am proud to be a bargain hunter" or "this deal's for you". Write to me and let me know what you are planning or what you have done to celebrate National Bargain Hunting Week. To obtain a list of suggested activities for National Bargain Hunting Week, send a self addressed, stamped envelope to me at: Lotus Press, P.O. Box 8446, Westerville, Ohio, 43086-8446.

HOW TO USE THIS BOOK

I personally feel comfortable shopping at upscale stores, garage sales, flea markets and no frills businesses, and I'll go almost anywhere to find a bargain. If you feel uncomfortable about shopping in a certain type of environment, either turn your head the other way and head on to more comfortable territory, or practice some of the visualization techniques described in the *Keeping A Positive Attitude* section of the introduction so that you can overcome your fear or dislike of certain environments.

In conducting the research for this book, I have tried to provide a wide variety of offerings. I have not focused on those businesses which I thought might be in existence for years to come just to avoid having to revise the book in the near future. If I had, then I know you would miss learning about many bargains and values. And who could guess as to which businesses would really survive? You're probably as shocked as I am that Madison's Grand Finale, Nickleby's Bookstore Cafe, Cargo Express, Taylor Woodcraft, Seek 'N Save, Office America, DiPaolo Food Service Outlet, the Frugal Fox Wallpaper Outlet and countless other businesses have closed.

Where a business offers values in several categories, it has been cross referenced into each and is indicated at the end of each chapter under a subheading of *Also See*. All listings are in the 614 area code, unless otherwise indicated.

You may also visit our web site on the internet for updates and related information.
http://www.angelfire.com/free/BARGAINS.html

There isn't any consistency in the length of the description provided for each entry in this book. As you read you'll find some businesses which will have an enormous description, while others will have small write-ups. Please be aware that the length of the description has absolutely no reflection on how good a business is or how great a bargain you will receive there. Some businesses specialize in just one type of product and so their description can be quite concise.

If you know of any businesses/services which would be suitable for inclusion in future editions of this book, please drop me a note and provide me as much information as possible so that I can properly pursue your lead. I appreciate hearing about your experiences at the places listed in this book and welcome all comments and suggestions. I can be contacted at: Lotus Press, P.O. Box 8446, Westerville, Ohio, 43086-8446

INTRODUCTION

DETERMINING IF YOUR FIND IS TRULY A BARGAIN

The most important issue is that you need to be an informed shopper. Spend time leisurely reviewing prices, brand names, fiber contents of clothing/products, quality of construction/components, warranties, even store return policies. On certain items like appliances, televisions, cars etc., you may want to do some advance reading in the current issue of *Consumer Reports,* and maybe even check the *Better Business Bureau's* various magazines and books before committing to certain purchases.

Decide if the item you are intending to purchase is something you need now or realistically will need in the future. Will the shelf life expire before you are able to use it? Are all of the parts working or is it damaged in any way? If so, what steps are necessary and at what cost and time are needed to repair it? One year I went crazy buying pharmaceutical items on sale, only to find that I should have anticipated that I would never be able to use all of it before the expiration date. My legitimate bargains turned out to be a financial loss as I had to discard many unused items.

If you are making a purchase for someone and you are not sure if it will appeal to him or her, you will be stuck with the merchandise if the store does not accept returns. Always verify the store's return policy even if you think you will never need to return the item.

When you examine the quality of a product there are obvious things you should check for. Again, both the *Consumer Reports* book and the *Better Business Bureau's* publications can provide you with many sorts of tips on a variety of products. As with clothing, however, check the fiber content. A garment which needs frequent dry cleaning may not really be worth the bargain price in the long run.

KEEPING A POSITIVE ATTITUDE

Having a positive attitude is also very important. If you convince yourself before you leave your home that you will not find anything on your shopping excursion or that you will have a lousy time, you probably will. Expect to find what you are looking for. Expect to have a pleasant experience. Here is a very powerful mental exercise you can practice. The process is called visualization and you can say several affirmations I have developed or create your own. The affirmations, which are positive statements, should indicate the conditions which you want to achieve, but should be stated in the present tense as if they are already happening. Affirmations generally begin with the words "I have, I am, I feel or I accept". First, get comfortable: Either lay down in bed or sit upright in your favorite chair, and clear your mind of all thoughts. If soft instrumental music will relax you, by all means turn it on. Check the records, tapes, CDs section in this book for sources. You can also find some for free loan at area libraries. Here are a few affirmations to get you started: "I release the old ways of thinking and make way for the new. I am open and willing to change my negative feelings about shopping. I am able to find what I need. I am able to enjoy the shopping experience (or, I am able to tolerate the shopping experience). I am easily achieving my goals".

Next, imagine yourself entering a relaxed state, and becoming relaxed. Imagine yourself going through the process at home of preparing to go shopping. What would you be doing? Gather your belongings, put on your coat, get into the car and drive to your destination. Imagine yourself enjoying the experience. Imagine yourself going up and down the aisles and finding those bargains. If you are looking for a specific item, imagine yourself finding it, touching it, examining it and trying it on or testing it out if necessary. Continue with this mental imagery through the process of paying for the merchandise, driving home, unpacking your purchase and putting it away. Since some of you might have to release many years of negative thought patterns about shopping, don't be disheartened if you don't feel and experience an immediate change. I suggest that you spend five minutes a day for several days before embarking on a shopping excursion. For a more in-depth approach to the process of visualization, pick up a copy of *Creative Visualization* by Shakti Gawain at any of the book sources listed in *Bargain Hunting In Central Ohio*.

ASKING A BUSINESS FOR A PRICE REDUCTION

I have been equally successful with some independent stores as with the larger businesses. Certain situations are legitimate ones for you to ask for a price reduction. 1-The merchandise is being sold as first quality, but you discover a major or minor flaw. This could include, but not be limited to, scratches, mismatched components, uneven dyes, missing buttons, a pull or an open seam, a hole in a garment caused by improper price tagging, dirt, etc. 2-You've seen the same item at a competitor for less. The store may ask you for a copy of the competitor's advertisement. Many businesses will meet or beat a competitor's price. 3-The item has been in the store for a while and hasn't sold. Reductions may or may not have already been taken. Shop owners want to have a fast turnover of inventory, so bring it to their attention.

How do you actually ask for the price reduction? Here are a few tips. 1-Be prepared to show and explain why the price should be reduced. 2-Speak calmly, don't whine, don't assume you have the upper hand. Make a good impression. 3-Have your money in hand whether it is your checkbook, credit card or cash. However, you might be luckier with cash, since the store would not have to pay a fee to the credit card company and would not have to wonder of your check will bounce. 4-Ask for the price reduction. It is not sufficient to identify the reasons. You must ask for it. 5-Be sure to find out the store's return policy. Since this is a special situation, it is possible that you may not be allowed to return or exchange the item for any reason. 6-Thank the clerk and any other staff members involved in reducing the price.

After you've followed all of these steps you may or may not be successful. Here are some of the reasons for both instances. Your request might be accepted under the following circumstances. 1-The salesperson might have the authority to make a price reduction up to a certain percentage off, or only under certain circumstances. 2-It is less bothersome to reduce an item than to return it to the manufacturer. 3-The damage may increase by having the item remain on the rack or shelf. 4-The shop may feel that it is "good will" to reduce the item in anticipation of your future business. 5-The timing was right. You caught the staff in the right mood. Sales were slow that day and in order to meet sales goals, this sale could bring the store closer to its target. Days where the weather may be bad could be great times to get a better deal, because there are fewer shoppers, and less revenue for a business. 6-The merchandise has been in the store for a long time and the sales person feels it to be a good opportunity to clear it out. 7-This could just be your lucky day. Maybe the clerk is in a good mood for some personal reason and is willing and able to make the deal.

Your request for a price reduction might be denied for the following reasons. 1-You have made a bad impression with the clerk. You have offended him/her or turned him/her off to the point where they don't want to give you the pleasure of winning. 2-Your request is unsubstantiated. The problem is not severe enough nor legitimate enough to warrant a reduction in the price. Or perhaps you could not prove that you really saw the item elsewhere for less. 3-The item has already been reduced and the salesperson does not feel that a further reduction is necessary. 4-The salesperson may not have the authority to reduce the merchandise. 5-The item could be consigned and therefore does not belong to the shop. In this case, ask the clerk to call the consignor to see if she would take a lower price. 6-The clerk may tell you that word will spread in the community that they take off money for items and they may get a bad reputation. So, tell the clerk that it will be a secret just the two of you will share.

SHOULD YOU BUY YOUR ACCESSORIES FIRST OR YOUR CLOTHES?

When I owned my store, I encountered a frequent phenomenon which was very disturbing. Most people were of the mindset that you purchase your clothing before you purchase your accessories (tie, belt, hose, jewelry etc.). I don't know when or how this mindset developed, but this is one way to miss out on owning a delightful accessory and maybe even at a good price. Why can't you buy that fabulous necklace even though you may not have anything to match? Of course you can do it! I'll bet that you can find something in your closet to coordinate with it.

SHOPPING AT ANTIQUE STORES AND ANTIQUE MALLS

Even if you don't like antiques, these stores feature many items which are just used and not "that old stuff". On the other hand, antique furniture is built very solid and frequently has detailing which is difficult to find in recently made furniture. Furniture plus other collectible gift items (glassware, pottery etc) can provide exceptional values. If you don't like the look of old furniture, consider updating it with a can of spray paint, decorative designs, stenciling or even faux finishes. Central Ohio has pockets of areas where there are at least ten antique stores in a given community: High Street in Clintonville, Uptown Westerville, Powell, Sunbury, Lancaster and Lithopolis. All of these areas include antique malls, each of which has at least eight dealers, so prices will vary considerably. With few exceptions, I have not listed individual antique stores, although I have listed flea markets. Check your local yellow pages for listings.

IS IT REALLY ON SALE?

Approach the word sale with caution. Retailers have learned that consumers want to buy things on sale. Very often, they will inflate the retail price and then put the item on sale, so in essence, you are paying about the same or a little less than the real price the product should be. Very often, retailers do not expect to sell merchandise at the price they have it marked. They will take a large markup over their wholesale cost and run a big sale with supposedly great savings, expecting to make "a killing" during the special sale. Be wary of sales. Be a comparison shopper and stay alert so you can make an informed decision. In so doing, do not overlook legitimate sales.

Also, don't be discouraged from buying something which is not on sale. It could be a great value but not reduced. Remove the "on sale" mindset which you might have. Let me recount a personal experience. I was in the *Andersons General Store* and stopped by an area to admire some solid oak bathroom accessories: tissue box covers, soap dishes and the like. The items were not on sale, but were priced about 20% to 30% lower than the discounted price on more famous brands at area discount stores. The workmanship was excellent, the color was perfect and it was something which I needed. I purchased several items. When I returned home, I told my husband about my bargains. He suggested that I return them and wait until they go on sale. After carefully explaining the situation to him, he decided I was right. By the way, there are some items which, for whatever reason, never go on sale. So, forget the word sale, forget the price you are being asked to pay, and objectively determine the value you are getting for your money.

PRODUCT LABELS

Product labels do not always mean what you think they mean. In an effort to mislead consumers, some manufacturers will lead you to believe that the product is made of a material that it is not made of, or lead you to believe that it was manufactured by a company other than the true manufacturer. Let me explain.

I have seen some supposedly crystal vases and bowls which, at first glance, appeared to indicate the word "crystal" on the outside of the box or the word "cristal" (note the spelling) in a descriptive phrase on the product's outer packaging, leading me to believe that the box contained genuine crystal. In another instance, I had received a factory boxed salad bowl which, at first glance, appeared to be identified as crystal on the outside of the box. A closer look at the packaging led me to discover that there were several glass colors written on the box clearly stating, color: (x) crystal ( ) ruby. The manufacturer had used the word crystal to identify the color of the glassware and not the material from which it was created. Only by opening the box and examining its contents would you discover that it was not true crystal. This was an obvious attempt, to mislead you, the consumer. The product was also priced ridiculously lower than a true crystal bowl would have been and the quality of the packaging was less than desirable. It is not to say that you cannot find true crystal at a bargain price, but just be wary when you encounter this sort of a situation.

A friend of mine showed me a lovely necklace she had purchased for about $10 which was made of black and gold colored beads. The necklace, which was imported from India, had a hang tag which read "color: onyx". She thought that she was purchasing a necklace made out of genuine black onyx semi-precious stones and was ecstatic at her apparent "find". I really hated to burst her bubble, but when I explained to her what the manufacturer had done, she felt quite disturbed. Those little black beads were none other than coco wood heishi which were dyed black. Just as was the case with the "crystal" bowl, the word "onyx" was used to denote a color and not a material.

Oftentimes, manufacturers will give a name to a product line which is very similar to the name of a more expensive line of similar products such as the Kevin Klein jeans one of my students received as a gift from a well meaning grandmother. Again, this is usually being done to mislead you into believing that you are getting a top name, quality product. Unfortunately, in many cases, all you are getting is inferior merchandise.

TIPS WHEN PURCHASING FINE JEWELRY

I have purchased some excellent pieces of jewelry simply because the seller was not aware that he was parting with something which was actually more valuable than he had thought. If you are considering purchasing some jewelry, check the clasp and backing for the following markings which mean the type of metal used; 900 or 925 means sterling silver, S means silver, 800 means silver, 14K means 14 Karat gold, 585 means 14 Karat gold and 14K HG means 14 Karat Hamilton gold electroplate (14K HG is only a thin layer of gold on a base metal).

I purchased a thin, flat gold linked bracelet, marked 585, for twenty five cents at a flea market simply because the vendor was not aware that this Italian marking meant 14 Karat gold. You should also be aware that some gold or silver may not be marked. While it is more common that silver may not be identified as such, I own a beautiful handmade gold bracelet which does not bear any markings. Be certain to purchase any fine jewelry from a reputable dealer who is willing to stand by his products and offer you a written guarantee.

Here is a handy tip which I learned from my grandmother. She taught me that if I left my silver jewelry in aluminum foil when it was not being worn, that it would prevent it from tarnishing. Another good tip which you should be aware of is that you should not spray perfume, hairspray or deodorant on yourself while wearing costume or fine jewelry. Always let the spray dry first before putting on your jewelry. The chemicals in the sprays can damage the finish on your favorite accessory.

FLOOR MODELS, DAMAGED MERCHANDISE, AS IS AND MORE

For heaven's sake, do not turn up your nose and walk away from something which might be labelled as damaged, "as is" or irregular.

When you come across something which is supposedly damaged, assess the extent and nature of the imperfection. Certain bakery thrift stores sell some merchandise which is not suitable for regular supermarket distribution. When a retailer is purchasing first quality products, he expects, as do his customers, that the merchandise is in perfect condition and meets all standards set forth on the labels. A baked goods shipment which is a bit underweight will not pass inspection in the plant, so it is sent to a thrift store to be sold. The quality is the same as that found in the supermarkets. On food items, other irregularities may include slightly crushed boxes, or those close to or past expiration date. None of these so called irregularities should pose a problem for the consumer, with the exception of the expiration dates, unless the item is perishable. I have purchased cookies weeks past the printed "sell by" date on the package and have still found them to be fresh.

Furniture and appliances which have cosmetic scratches can generally be touched up quite easily and inexpensively using special paints and crayons found in your local hardware store. Also, depending on the location of the cosmetic damage, it may be hardly noticeable when you set up the item at home. I purchased a beautiful bedroom suite in New York from a dealer who dealt in slightly damaged merchandise at bargain prices. The suite had obvious flaws which had been touched up quite well. It also had distressed marks all over the surface which added to its charm. The store owner told me that the furniture was not originally intended to have a distressed surface, but as a way of making the scratches and nicks less noticeable, one of his staff members distressed all of the furniture to make the surface look more uniform.

When an electrical appliance, television or other item is sold "as is" there could be some minor cosmetic flaws or some possible malfunction which you will not be able to detect until you have used it for a few days. Before purchasing an "as is" item, check with the salesman and find our what is wrong with the product and what sort of a warranty would be available. It is also important to find out about the store's return policy in the event that you are not satisfied. As a personal choice, I try to stay away from purchasing floor samples on which children have been allowed free rein. I would feel more comfortable purchasing a floor model refrigerator than a boom box. However, there are big savings which are possible when purchasing floor models. Weigh the pros and cons of each.

Damaged merchandise should be clearly identified as such. Clothing manufacturers have various ways of identifying damaged merchandise. Let me state here that not all damaged merchandise is inferior. There are all degrees of damages. From a slight pull to an inconspicuous spot, to an unsightly grease stain where it counts, they all should catch your attention so that you are aware of them. I have taken the time to stitch loose seams or tears after having purchased a wearable and have even hidden tears and discolorations under appliques and fabric paints which come in tubes.

Storekeepers and manufacturers attempt to identify their damaged garments in one or more of these ways:

1. By using a piece of masking tape on top of the damage.
2. By cutting a slit through the manufacturer's label which is usually found on the neckline or by the waistline.
3. By stamping the sewn in label with a red, often undecipherable mark, "Irregular".
4. By stamping the word "Irregular" on a hang tag or a price tag.

Sometimes garments which have become damaged in the store are not identified as such. When this happens, and if you are interested in purchasing the item, ask the store manager if he can reduce the price for you. After all, it is damaged. If the price is reduced, is it to be sold "as is" with no return policy?

Also notice where the price tag has been attached to the garment. The appropriate place is through a seam or label so that it will not make an unsightly hole. If it appears as if a potential problem hole has been created by the price tag, bring this to the manager's attention and nicely suggest that the stock people be a little more cautious in the future. If you decide that you want to purchase that item, ask for some money off the price and explain why. Do not be surprised if you occasionally will not get a reduced price. I am not implying that you should nit pick and drive the store managers insane, but when the situation warrants it, there is no reason to remain tight lipped.

CONSIGNMENT, RESALE, THRIFT AND PAWN SHOPS

An abundance of these have popped up over the years selling varying qualities of clothes, toys, children's accessories, furniture, cameras, musical instruments and the like. If you're concerned about buying merchandise which is used, consider this. Most people buy a house which is used (someone else lived in it before), a used car, furniture/estate jewelry at auction and even antiques in an antique store, all of which are used.

In writing this book, I have included those which offer upscale products or which have a combination of upscale and budget. Merchandise at these sorts of stores can be gently used and sometimes you will even find some new items. Some of shops carry new salesmen's samples and buyouts/closeouts of new merchandise mixed in with the used items. The savings can vary from 30-80% off "if new" prices. Consignment items belong to the original owner until such time as they are sold by the store. If they do not sell, the owner is obligated to pick up the merchandise or it will be donated to charity. Resale shops purchase items from the owners and sell them in their business. The merchandise is immediately owned by the shop. If it does not sell, the business will generally donate it to a charity. Thrift shops sell merchandise which has been donated to them. Pawn shops loan money to people in exchange for collateral such as gold jewelry, musical instruments, cameras, watches etc. If a client chooses not to repay a loan or is unable to, the merchandise is sold. Most of it is used. You will also find antiques and collectibles as well.

MERCHANDISE DISPLAY

Inventory in most stores is set up to encourage you to make a purchase. In supermarkets especially, most shoppers circulate around the outermost aisles. As a result, the stores have their most profitable items such as produce, meat and high priced gourmet goods, in these areas. Stock clerks usually place the most expensive and profitable items at eye level. So, look high and low on those shelves for values.

Some of the bargain places mentioned in this book, have done little to make their stock appealing. Messy, disorganized shelves and racks, simplistic display stands and even basic decors can be found. Do not be discouraged! If you want to find the great bargains, be prepared to weather the storm! One such store, whose name I cannot mention, but is generically described in this book, has sold two piece Neiman-Marcus silk suits for $40 (which have not been steamed pressed and which look quite wrinkled) and haphazardly arranges some of its stock. On a recent visit, I saw a designer crystal vase on a shelf next to a budget quality household item. Be persistent and go in with your bargain hunting antennas fully extended. These places offer wonderful values.

Also keep in mind that most everything looks like junk in a store which sells low quality merchandise or which doesn't maintain its stock in an appealing fashion. So be sure to look selectively through a store's inventory so you don't bypass some wonderful bargains. Use the visualization technique to imagine yourself wearing the intended purchase or placing it in your home or office. This will help you to gain a better perspective on whether or not this item is something which you will really enjoy. Also keep in mind that some stores which sell budget quality merchandise, occasionally get moderate to designer quality goods. Read the description of Family Dollar in this book. This is a classic example of an occasion when I saw Paolo Gucci (formerly with THE GUCCI business) earrings for $5, regularly $35. That was hardly typical of the type of stock in their store. Yet, it was there.

VARIATIONS IN INVENTORY

Very often, a business which has several locations, will vary some of its inventory from store to store, based on what sells best in different parts of town. Another reason for variations in inventory, is that there may not be enough of a particular style or color to be distributed to each branch. My suggestion to you is to check out as many of the business's other locations as possible. This is especially true if you have decided that you do not like a particular store's merchandise. You might find that one of their other sites offers more to suit your taste. Sometimes, the difference between the stores' offerings is like night and day. Another important tip is to try shopping at a store several times before you make the decision that you don't like it.

TIMING YOUR SHOPPING

Don't be embarrassed to ask the staff of your favorite stores when their new merchandise will be put on the shelves or racks. Some stores have certain days and times set aside for this. On the other hand, deliveries to some stores are so sporadic, that the store may not know when their next shipment will arrive. Armed with the timing information, you will be able to select the cream of the crop.

IS THERE A PMS CONNECTION TO YOUR SHOPPING?

My internist and gynecologist laughed at me when I posed this issue to them. They probably thought I was joking, but I kid you not! In fact, at many of the bargain hunting presentations I have given, I generally mention the Debbie Keri-Brown theory on this subject. You'd be surprised at how many women have instantly agreed or agreed after hearing my thoughts. My theory developed form my own experiences with PMS. During the PMS phase of the month, which varies among women (mine lasts eight to twelve days), all of my interests, fears and dislikes become greatly intensified, and sometimes mildly obsessive.

I don't develop any which I have never experienced, it's just that the existing ones seem to become severely exaggerated. So naturally, since I enjoy shopping, this phase of the month had been a problem for me at one time, because I found myself spending wildly. Of course they were great deals, but they weren't always things that I needed. Even though, I had managed to convince myself that I needed to make these purchases. I tended to spend much more money at this time than at other times. Because I am now aware of what I experience during that dreaded PMS phase, I force myself to stop and think more objectively about my intended purchase.

The visualization exercises in the introduction can be used to assist you. If you make any purchases during this time of the month, be sure to pay very close attention, more so than usual, to the store's return policy. Purchases made during this time could be stored away until the PMS phase is over. This will allow you the chance to reconsider your purchase in a better frame of mind. By recognizing that your spending may be influenced by these hormonal changes, you'll be on your way to self monitoring and reducing your unnecessary spending. On a positive note, I have to say that PMS has also been a blessing. During this phase, I am filled with so much energy that I can literally accomplish at least twice of what I can during the rest of the month. PMS hit me during the week before we went to press with this book, and without it, we might not have made our deadline!

MONEY MAKING OPPORTUNITIES FOR BARGAIN HUNTERS

Why not put your bargain hunting skills to good use and earn some extra money? "Pickers" are people who buy items and resell them to stores or put them on consignment in the business. Antique/collectible stores have used pickers for ages. The best way to approach this is to speak with the owners of area antique stores and learn what they are looking for and about how much they are willing to pay for certain items. Check with area consignment/resale stores which sell clothes, accessories and home furnishings. Probe their needs and find out what to avoid and what to find. As you're out at garage sales, flea markets and other places looking for stuff for yourself, you can keep your eyes open for items to sell/consign to the retail stores.

There are some drawbacks. First, it might take some time to succeed in fully understanding the stores' needs. You might buy items only to be turned down at the front desk. Or, in a consignment situation, your items may be accepted but may never sell. You might end up donating them to a local charity (and getting a tax deduction) or selling them at your own garage sale. I was a successful at being a picker for antique and collectible items. In fact, the experience blossomed into leasing space at antique malls in the area. I currently have eight antique spaces.

Another money making opportunity which many shoppers would enjoy is mystery shopping. Follow the newspapers' employment section for these infrequent opportunities. A mystery shopper evaluates a retail store, restaurant or service incognito, checking on timeliness, presentation, customer service and cleanliness. You will be asked to fill out paperwork (2-15 pages) and mail it back to the company. Compensation varies from a flat rate fee to a free meal (if a restaurant).

How would you like to participate in a test market survey or a focus group? Contact market research firms in the yellow pages to be added to their permanent calling list. Initially, you'll have to fill out a form with questions about your demographics and interests. If called to participate, you're generally paid $20-$75 for one half hour to three hours of your time, on a one time basis. A focus group is where a pre-selected group of consumers meet to respond to questions about a product or service. A taste test is where you are asked to sample food or beverage products and provide your opinions. For instance, if a company, large or small, wants to better understand the public's perceptions of its operations, an initial phone screening would occur and then selected people would be asked to come in to share their opinions. You should be aware that if you or a family member work for an advertising agency, marketing firm or the media, you generally would not be able to participate in taste tests/focus groups.

OTHER STUFF

It's okay to use an item in a way other than originally intended. I purchased a lovely miniature mirror with a handpainted porcelain figure on the reverse, removed its handle and inserted a gold chain through the loop at the top. I realize that I may have played havoc on its original value, but I loved it and wanted to wear it. That $10 purchase is the most eye-catching accessory in my wardrobe. I have purchased old buttons at flea markets and randomly sewn them on sweaters, and even used an old child's potty trainer as a planter! Antique kitchen implements can be used to adorn you walls. Old jewelry can be restrung or used in wearable art collage jewelry.

Post earrings can be used as a pin on your suit or dress. Even the big, gaudy ones which would weigh down your ears can look smashing as a pin. Just push the post through your garment and attach the earring back. Keep in mind that this works best on garments which have thick weaves and may leave a permanent hole on fragile fabrics.

There is another way to add pizzazz to your ho-hum apparel purchases. A simple shirt, dress or denim jacket can be embellished with glitzy doo-dads and fabric paints, adding considerable value to the garment. Look carefully at the clothes in your favorite stores and try to copy some of the embellishment techniques. Go to your closest craft shop and pick up ideas and products which can be used to add intrigue and excitement to your garments and home furnishings, at a fraction of the cost of hand decorated store bought merchandise. Sign up for a class to learn these skills or take out a book at the library. The chapter on classes in this book offers a listing of value priced instruction.

Local team sports apparel retailers have been selling screen printed tee shirts with a little gummed paper tag on them indicating that certain missprints or poor registration (misalignment) in the design are an inherent part of the process and should not be viewed as irregularities. This is preposterous!!!!! Poor screen printing methods or lack of sufficient monitoring are to blame. Do not be misled into believing that some major misprint "makes each garment unique", as the label implies.

A recent direct mail flyer I received, advertised a cheap crystal clock for $19.95 which was "inspired by clocks selling up to $89.95". This does not mean that the clock you are being asked to buy is worth that much money. This is not a "compare to" price.

And while we're on the subject of "compare to" prices, please be aware that not all of these prices are correct as written on price tags in stores. Often what will happen is a store may receive merchandise and might have to guess at what the original price really was. When they cannot verify this information, do not have the time to do so or want to intentionally mislead you, you'll see a compare to price which is not realistic. On the other hand, I noticed that a business had grossly under identified the compare to price and when they ticketed the item, it was marked far below the price I expected to see on the price tag. Had the store realized what the real price was, it likely would have offerd it at a higher price. On a recent visit to a local store which deals in buyouts, they had some purses by Brio with an alleged retail price of $150 and their price at $39.99. Having stocked Brio bags in my store, I knew this was not the correct original price. However, the store's price was still a good deal, as I know that the bag retailed for about $85.

One of the new fashion trends is garments which have been pigment dyed and are intended to fade, creating a weathered color tone. These must be washed separately as the dyeing process used to create this look will result in a color loss with each wash. So if you don't want to put in the extra care, choose others which would pose less of a problem.

Recycle your outdated business cards by crossing out the old information, and writing in the new. Use these at the many restaurants in town which have a weekly drawing for a free meal.

There are many galleries in town which do not charge an artist a commission on the sales of his/her artwork. As a result, the artwork which is exhibited, is often priced considerably less than in other galleries. You might easily save 30-50%. These galleries are found in municipal buildings, recreation and community centers, the Columbus Cultural Arts Center, libraries and many office buildings. To obtain a listing, check the Arts Datebook section in Sunday's Arts In Ohio section of the Columbus Dispatch or other publications which have gallery listings.

Check out those clearance sections in stores. It is a prudent business decision for a store to feature an area of clearance merchandise which is overstocked, end of the season, as is or discontinued. Most stores have such an area, but it may not be that easy to find. It could be tucked away in an inconspicuous corner of a business or might be at the end of an aisle. When in doubt, ask the store's personnel.

AUTHOR'S PERSONAL FAVORITES

<u>ANGELICA DELI AND CAFE:</u> The ambiance is simple but cozy, and the food is meticulously prepared. Its setting in the heart of Old Powell, provides you with the chance to browse through the many antique shops in the village after your meal.

<u>ART STUDIO CLEARANCE SALE:</u> A noteworthy distinction for an event which experienced its first presentation in 1996. You've seen the finely executed works at Winterfair, but what happens to those items which don't meet the standards for shows or exhibitions? The sale offers the opportunity for professional artists and craftsmen to sell discontinued or slightly imperfect items.

<u>B-WEAR SPORTSWEAR OUTLET:</u> The merchandise is well made, the designs are unique and have broad appeal.

<u>BETTER CLOTHES AND BARGAINS:</u> This men's and women's wear boutique offers gently used apparel and accessories by famous designers and better manufacturers. It's an excellent source to consign your unwanted wearables and earn some extra money to purchase others.

<u>BIG FUN:</u> I dare you to leave the store without a smile on your face! This business offers an uplifting experience, the chance to reminisce amongst the kitsch and collectibles of the 1950's-1980's, and the best selection of items priced at under $10 in the universe.

<u>CAFE ON 5:</u> The coziness of this little cafe and its selection of savory buffet foods, makes this a wonderful place for a quiet interlude or to pop that special question to the one you love.

<u>CANDY COTTAGE:</u> You'll feel as if you've stepped into grandma's kitchen as you savor the aromas from the fresh roasted nuts. The store features a selection of chocolates molded in unusual designs such as babies and tool sets.

<u>COLUMBUS NEIGHBORS</u>: At last, a source to obtain recommendations for service providers who are honest and dependable.

<u>COLUMBUS RECREATION AND PARKS DEPARTMENT PROGRAMS (MUSIC IN THE AIR, COLUMBUS CULTURAL ARTS CENTER, DAVIS DISCOVERY CENTER, ARTICIPATION, GOLDEN HOBBY SHOP, AND SPECIAL EVENTS):</u> The facilities and programs are fine examples of your tax dollars at work. The Columbus Recreation And Parks Department programs should be part of your life.

<u>CREATIVE SPIRIT WORKSHOP AND GIFT OUTLET(FORMERLY BENZLE APPLIED ARTS):</u> The artist has consistently maintained a high degree of artistic excellence in the execution of his porcelain jewelry and gifts. The colors and designs of the jewelry are contemporary and easily adaptable to enhance your outfits. The gifts are decorative and appealing.

<u>DESIGNER SHOE WAREHOUSE:</u> You'll find the most diverse and unusual selection of quality men's and women's shoes in Central Ohio.

EDDIE BAUER SALVAGE SALE: Keep those bargain hunting antennas fully extended as you rummage through boxes of imperfect items, many of which can be easily repaired with some minor sewing.

ENTERTAINMENT 96/97/98 BOOKS: Excellent opportunity to dine at some of the top establishments in the city, in addition to great savings on entertainment, hotels and services. Everyone should own a copy of this book.

FAMOUS SPORTSWEAR: A great place to buy embroidered or appliqued apparel for the family.

FRANKLIN COUNTY METRO PARKS: Enjoy nature's splendor at its finest and experience many free programs for fun or personal enrichment. A special acknowledgement goes to Inniswood Metro Gardens, the crown jewel of the Metropark system.

GREATER COLUMBUS ANTIQUE MALL: This is such a fun place to shop! Look in the attic, in the closets and every nook and cranny to discover those deals. Your first experience will leave you awestruck. Don't miss an inch of the mall.

HALF PRICE BOOKS, RECORDS, MAGAZINES: The inventory changes frequently to provide one of the best selections of used and closeout books in Columbus.

MJR WEEKEND WAREHOUSE: Find great prices on fashion apparel and accessories from your favorite companies.

RED SQUARE IMPORTS: If you appreciate fine, handcrafted work, then visit this business which offers Russian jewelry and gifts.

SCHOTTENSTEIN'S: The stock changes frequently to offer an enormous selection of name brand and designer products for the whole family.

SUPER SAVER 8 CINEMAS: Aside from the fair price of only $1.50, the theaters feature a great light show and space tunnel decor!

TARGET GREATLAND: These stores were chosen primarily for the high quality, contemporary styling and fair prices of their private label brands of housewares, linens and apparel.

TUESDAY MORNING: Find better brands of unusual household gifts and accessories at substantial savings.

WESTERVILLE PUBLIC LIBRARY: My decision is based largely on the merits of the library's extensive free loan art collection. However, it also has great used book sales and special events.

APPLIANCES/
TELEVISIONS/
ELECTRONICS

AL'S VACUUM
4252 E. Main St., Columbus, 43213, 236-0707

New, first quality Hoover, Eureka, Panasonic and Royal vacuum cleaners are sold at 25-40% off regular retail prices. A small selection of used vacuum cleaners is available at 30-50% less than "if new". Repairs are also value priced. M-F 9:30-5:30, Sat 9:30-4.

AUDIO EXCHANGE
3500 N. High St., Columbus, 43214, 263-4600

This retailer sells top quality brands of used audio and video equipment such as VCRs, CD players, tape decks, receivers, televisions, stereos and other products by such brands as Pioneer, DCM, JVC, Pinnacle, Nikoh and Rotel. Savings are about 25-50% off the "if new" prices. Most of the inventory comes with a 30 day warranty. M-F 12-7, Sat 11-5.

B & B VACUUMS
3657 Sullivant Ave., Columbus, 43228, 274-2070

Only used and rebuilt vacuums are offered here starting as low as $29.95. You'll find all popular brands including Eureka, Panasonic, Kenmore, Rainbow, Hoover and others at savings of 40-60% less than "if new". M-F 11-8, Sat 10-2.

B & C VACUUM
3003 N. High Street, Columbus, 43214, 267-7511
251 E. Main St., New Albany, 43054, 855-1933
5062 Cemetery Rd., Hilliard, 43026, 777-7975

Save about 20% off the manufacturer's suggested retail price on new vacuums. The stores also have a selection of used/rebuilt models at savings of 30-60% off new prices and are featured in the $39-$79 range. You'll find such brands as Royal, Eureka, Kirby and others. M-F 10-6, Sat 10-4.

BEST BUY
5745 Chantry Dr., Reynoldsburg, 43068, 759-9779
5800 Britton Pkwy., Dublin, 43017, 793-8630
3840 Morse Rd., Columbus, 43229, 471-9510
5899 Frantz Rd.,Dublin, 43017, 792-8205

Find small and large appliances, plus consumer eletronics, videos, CDs and computers under one roof at savings of 15-30%. The stores have lots of interactive product information stations throughout the store for video games, movies and other items. Most CDs are priced at $11.99. The stores also sells videos and computer software. The stores offer a four year parts and labor warranty for $39 and under. You won't feel pressured to shop here as the staff are noncommissioned. M-Sat 10-9, Sun 11-6.

BLACK AND DECKER U.S.A., INC.
3975 E. Livingston Ave., Columbus, 43227, 237-0461

First quality, blemished, unclaimed and discontinued small appliances as well as house and garden tools by Black And Decker, are available at savings of 20-40% off regular retail prices. You can also purchase parts and accessories for Black and Decker products at this manufacturer's outlet store. M-F 8-6.

BLANCHARD VACUUM CLEANERS
1071 S. High St., Columbus, 43206, 443-9479

The most popular brands of new vacuum cleaners are available at savings of 10-30%. Used models which start at $49, are sold "as is" at 30-50% less than the manufacturers' list price for new merchandise. A selection of reconditioned vacuum cleaners is available at about 25% less than "if new". Warranties vary depending on the product. M-F 9-5:30, Sat 9-1.

CARMEN'S VACUUMS
85 S. Hamilton Rd., Columbus, 43213, 864-0190
4505 N. High St., Columbus, 43214, 262-4900

Whether you're in the market for a new or used vacuum cleaner, you'll find deals here. Brands offered include Eureka, Hoover, Kirby, Panasonic, Royal and others. Most used vacuums are in the $30-$80 range and represent a savings of about 20-60% less than new prices. New vacuums offer discounts of about 20% on certain models. M-Sat 10-6.

CLASSIC MAYTAG HOME APPLIANCE CENTER
1250 Morse Rd., Columbus, 43229, 436-4414

Offers quality rebuilt washers, dryers, ranges and refrigerators at savings of 30-50% less than "if new". The store stocks all major brands and also sells new Maytags at competitive prices. M-Th 9-8, F 9-6, Sat 10-6.

COOK'S USED APPLIANCES
2515 Summit Street, Columbus, 43202, 261-8471

Save on used appliances in all major brands. Washers and dryers are $75 and up, stoves are $95 and up, refrigerators are $150 and up. Offers free delivery. Appliances are clean and guaranteed. M-F 10:30-6, Sat 10:30-5.

DON MILMINE APPLIANCES
40 WesterviewDr, Westerville, 43081, 891-4870

Find a large selection of new scratch and dent appliances at savings of 25-40% less than "if perfect". All popular brands are offered. For instance, a side by side refrigerator regularly $1,700 is only $1,000 here, a flat top stove regularly $900 is $500 here. You'll also find a selection of first quality appliances at competitive prices. Tu/W/F/Sat 9-5:30, M/Th 9-8.

DUNKLE'S SWEEPERS
429 N. Columbus St., Lancaster, 654-4968

Although this store sells mostly new vacuum cleaners at typical prices, the best deals are on the small selection of used/rebuilt models starting at $59.99. You'll find major brands, when available, such as Hoover, Eureka, Sharp and others. M-F 9:30-5:30, Sat 9:30-3.

ENCORE RECYCLED APPLIANCES
3700 Parkway Lane, Hilliard, 43026, 777-5666
2175 Eakin Rd., Columbus, 43223, 272-8038

Reconditioned refrigerators, washers, dryers and stoves are offered at a savings of about 50-60% off new prices in this no frills warehouse environment. The store is so sure you'll be satisfied, that they offer a money back guarantee. M-F 8-5.

HI-FI TRADER
North end of Columbus, 261-6360

Save on 60's, 70's and 80's vintage electronics by popular brands such as Pioneer, Marantz and others at this no frills business. You'll find CD players, speakers, receivers, power amps and other items as available. Prices vary, but most items will cost you about 30-60% less than "if new". By appointment only.

HOLTON TV/R&R ELECTRONICS
6969 Worthington Galena Rd., Worthington, 43085, 846-4445

Super savings are to be found from this hotel, hospital and business liquidator of televisions. You will find factory rebuilt and used console and table top models at savings of 35-60% off regular retail prices "if new". Warranties are available, but vary according to the item purchased. The store also offers free estimates on repairs of televisions, camcorders, computer monitors, stereo systems, Nintendos and car audio systems. Repair prices are very reasonable. M-F 9-6, Sat 9-4.

INCREDIBLE UNIVERSE
3599 Park, Hilliard, 43026, 529-5800

More than two football fields worth of stuff can be found under one roof, and the only word to describe it is -- Incredible! This is the largest consumer electronics store in the world and you can save 10-35% here. This interactive, hi-tech superstore features car stereos, electronics, computers, cameras, appliances, cassettes and CDs plus related items. Demonstrations, entertainment and special events are frequently featured and you can even dine at the in house McDonald's. Visit the Black Hole clearance area for substantial savings on customer returns, "as is", floor models and discontinued savings. The Kidsview area provides free childcare for ages 3-9 while you shop. There's also a computer upgrade and repair center offering value prices. Earn bonus points when you shop, which can save you even more money on future purchases. M-F 11-9, Sat 10-9, Sun 11-6.

J & J's CARDINAL ELECTRONICS
399 S. State St., Westerville, 43081, 895-1975 or 895-7252

What does an electronics repair shop do when its customers fail to pick up their serviced televisions and VCRs? This business has solved the dilemma by offering these used items for sale at about 25-40% less than "if new". VCRs start at $80, televisions start at $95. M-F 9-6, Sat 9-4.

JACK'S APPLIANCES
5310 Center Street, Hilliard, 43026

You'll find appliances, stereos, televisions and VCRs by all popular brands at savings of 20-30% off suggested retail prices. The store also sells a small selection of moderate quality furniture at 25-40% savings. M/Th 9-9, Tu/W/F 9-6, Sat 9-5.

JACOB'S-THE ELECTRONIC STORE
850 King Avenue, Columbus, 43212, 421-2700

A Columbus landmark for many years, this store sells and installs satellite systems for about $2,700-$5,500, saving you about 20-40%. There is no charge for a warranty, which I am told, other businesses typically sell for $500. The store also sells Sony, JVC and Mitsubishi televisions at factory direct prices. M-F 9-7, Sat 8-1.

LINCOLN TV
1108 N. High St., Columbus, 43201, 299-0417

Save about 25-40% off new prices by buying a used television or VCR at this business. There's generally about fifty TVs and ten VCRs in stock by popular companies at most times. A 30 day parts and labor warranty is in effect for purchases. Repairs are done at a flat rate of $59.95 plus parts, regardless of the problem. M-Sat 10-6.

NEW WAY ELECTRONICS
812 Bennett Street, Marion, 382-9266

This store buys, sells and repairs used home and car stereo systems, televisions, VCRs, computers, camcorders, microwaves, CD players, tape decks and other audio/video equipment. Popular brands are offered including JVC, Honda, Techtronics, Fisher, Kenwood, Pioneer, Yamaha and others at savings of 40-60% less than "if new". TVs and VCRs start at $60, car stereos at $119. M-F 10-6, Sat 10:30-5.

NORTHLAND SEWING MACHINE CENTER
1955 E. Dublin Granville Rd., Beechcroft Center, Columbus, 43229, 888-1900

New sewing machines by Viking, Singer and White are discounted 20-40%. About 5 times per year, this business offers further savings on buyouts of new overstocks and unclaimed sewing machines at savings of up to 60%. Offers full warranties and 90 days same as cash financing to qualified buyers. M 9:30-7, Tu-Sat 9:30-5:30.

RADIO SHACK OUTLET STORE
4343 Williams Rd., Groveport, 43125, 836-3060

Demonstration, as-is, overstocks and box damaged products are available at savings of 20-70% off their regular retail prices. You'll find calculators, telephones, electronic toys and games, answering machines, radios, stereos and more. Many products are available with a warranty. The annual tent sale is held in May and features similar discounts on a much larger variety of merchandise. All of the Radio Shacks in town have a free battery club. Pick up an identification card at any branch, and you'll be entitled to one free battery of your choice per month. No purchase is required. M-Sat 10-9, Sun 10-6.

RESTAURANT EQUIPPERS
635 W. Broad St., Columbus, 43215, 464-0505

Choose from used and new restaurant equipment such as mixers, utensils, pots, cast iron skillets, tables and chairs, many of which are adaptable to home use. The best deals are on the use items, which can save you about 20-40% off new prices. M-F 8-5, Sat 8-12.

REX
Southland Mall, Marion, 389-3155
1475 Upper Valley Pike, Springfield, (513) 324-0028

Save 10-25% on top brands of televisions, VCRs, camcorders, appliances, stereos and related items . M-Sat 10-9, Sun 12-5.

SOUND EXCHANGE
1647 N. Memorial Dr., Lancaster, 653-7878

Find a large selection of new and used CDs and cassettes at this business. Save 15% on new items but the best deals are on the used items, priced between fifty cenets to ten dollars. The business buys, sells and trades. M-Sat 10-6, Sun 12-5.

SUN TV
Six Columbus stores plus the following locations
674 Hebron Rd., Newark, 822-2191
3528 Maple Ave., Zanesville, 455-2909

Save 10-25% off manufacturers' suggested retail prices on an extensive selection of brand name televisions, large and small appliances, computers as well as audio and stereo equipment. Ask about the one year replacement guarantee for small electronics. Specially designated areas at the Alum Creek Drive and Morse Road locations, serve as the clearance centers for their area stores, where savings are up to 40% off discontinued, overstocks and scratch and dent merchandise from all of their stores. Watch for intermittent sales at their far south end warehouse, where you'll save 40-50% off a large selection of scratch and dent, floor samples and serviced items. M-Th/Sat 10-9:30, F 10-12mid, Sun 11-6.

UNCLE ED'S CASH SHOP
3575 E. Livingston Avenue, Livingston Ct. Flea Mkt., Columbus, 43227, 237-7296

This business operates three locations within the flea market, each with a different inventory, and each with buy/sell/trade options. The largest has an in-depth selection of pagers by Uniden, Express, Lifestyle Plus, Bravo Classic, NEC Sport II and Advisor available in both new and used options. Compare their amenities of no processing fee, no contract requirement, 1000 free calls per month and free local calls at public pay phones. Local and extended area coverage is available. A second site offers used CDs at $5-$7 each and includes about 125 in stock. The third site features new and used car stereos by Panasonic, Sony, Pioneer and other popular brands. A salesman showed me a used Kenwood car stereo for $250, regularly about $600. F-Sun 10-7.

WARRANTY ELECTRONICS
5350 N. High St., Columbus, 43214, 848-3788

New and used home and car stereo equipment, VCRs and televisions can be found here. The best deals, and the biggest inventory, are on used equipment where savings are 40-60% less than suggested new prices. New items are discounted about 10-30%. The store carries such brands as JVC, Sherwood, Yamaha, Pioneer, Panasonic and others. Repairs on home and car stereo equipment are also reasonable. M-F 10:30-7, Sat 10-3.

WEISHEIMER'S VACUUM CLEANER SALES
235 N. 4th St., Columbus, 43215, 221-5597

Save about 20-30% off manufacturer's suggested retail prices on popular brands of vacuum cleaners such as Hoover, Bissell, Kenmore and Eureka. The store also stocks some used models at savings of 40-60% less than "if new". M-F 8:30-5:30, Sat 9-2.

ALSO SEE

Berwick Corner Outlet, Bargain House Furniture, Columbus Police Property Auction, Extravaganza, Franklin Co. Sheriff's Dept., Globe Furniture Rental, Kitchen Collection, Lazarus Final Countdown, OfficeMax, J.C. Penney Outlet, Sam's Club, Schottenstein's, Sears Outlet, Service Merchandise and Uncle Sam's Pawn Shop

ARTS AND CRAFTS/ PHOTOGRAPHY/ CAMERAS

ARTS AND CRAFTS

ART FAIRS AND FESTIVALS
see Ohio Arts Council listing in this chapter

ARTIST'S WORKSHOP
2583 1/2 N. High St., Columbus, 43202, 262-2589
44 S. Washington, Columbus, 43215, 224-1993

Utrecht brand art supplies such as gesso, acrylics, oil paints and watercolors, are sold at 40-60% less than similar products by other manufacturers. The owner indicated that many of the Utrecht supplies are better quality than the popular brands. Other brands offered include Old Holland and Talen Rembrandt. Canvas is also priced well. Hours vary by location.

BEN FRANKLIN CRAFTS
4030 W. Broad St., Columbus, 43228, 272-6004
5780 Brice Outlet Mallway, Columbus, 43232, 575-1177

Superstore environment features a full line of arts and crafts. Savings are 25% on fine art paint brushes and paints by Grumbacher, Bob Ross, Liquitex, Windsor Newton and William Alexander. You'll also save 50% off metal sectional frames, 15% off craft instructional books, and 40% off greeting cards. The other general craft items are offered at 10-15% below suggested retail prices. M-Sat 10-9, Sun 11-6.

BILL LANDIS
411 Siebert St., Columbus, 43206, 444-4104

Step into Bill's garage to purchase polished and tumbled precious and semi-precious stones in assorted shapes and sizes. If you cast your own jewelry, or would like to purchase a stone and have a jeweler set it for you, then this is an ideal source. You'll find flat backed and well as pointed backed stones, faceted gems, rough specimens, cabochons and more. As Bill does his own lapidary work, he can custom cut stones to your specifications. Bill will also remove chips from glass or crystal goblets at a cost of $3.50, but cannot guarantee that the glass will not explode during the process, so you will be taking your chances. He also can attempt a similar process on small vases and bowls up to five inches in diameter. The items for glass repair may be dropped off at the Golden Hobby Shop, 630 S. 3 Street (645-8329). The lapidary shop is only open Wednesday from 8a.m.-11a.m., but call ahead.

BYZANTIUM
245 King Ave., Columbus, 43201, 291-3130

A large selection of beads from around the world is sold here by the piece for those who are interested in making their own earrings, necklaces and bracelets or using them as embellishments on clothing and other objects. The store stocks a full line of findings and related supplies. Staff members are always available to provide assistance in creating jewelry, which can be done on the tables in the store or in the comfort of your own home. The beads start at a nickle each and go up in price, but most are under $1.00. By making the jewelry yourself, you can save 50-80% off the price of ready made jewelry in other stores. Certainly, the other advantage is being able to design and create items which are one of a kind. The Central Ohio Bead Society meets monthly at Byzantium and presents discussions, workshops and demonstrations of interest to bead lovers. The Society sponsors an annual Bead Bazaar and Jewelry Jamboree in the fall. Don't miss the bead museum in Byzantium which offers a small, but interesting selection of antique jewelry and other items incorporating beads. Stop by the adjacent King Avenue Coffee House where you'll find a large selection of teas and vegetarian foods. M-Sat 12-7, Sun 12-5.

COLUMBUS CLAY COMPANY
1049 W. Fifth Avenue, Columbus, 43212, 294-1114

Ceramic materials such as glazes and clays are available at savings of about 20% from this manufacturer. New pottery equipment such as kilns and wheels are sold at savings of 10-15%. Used equipment, when available, is sold for 30-50% less than new. As used equipment is hard to obtain, the inventory fluctuates. M-F 8-5, Sat 9-1. Accepts cash and checks only.

CRAFT CATALOGUE
6095 Mc Naughten Center, Columbus, 43232, 861-4164

Formerly called Crafts 'N Things, this business operates as a discount mail order craft supplier and also operates this retail store. In both cases, prices are 15-30% less than retail on a wide variety of general line craft items. Call to be added to their mailing list. M-F 10-9, Sat 10-6.

CREATIVE SPIRIT WORKSHOP AND GIFT OUTLET
1936 W. Henderson Rd., Columbus, 43220, 876-5340, 876-2159

Curtis Benzle is an internationally recognized porcelain artist who creates bowls, gift accessories, lights and 22K liquid gold trimmed jewelry, all of which are available in the outlet store. The outlet has seconds, discontinued styles and prototypes priced at 50-85% off the regular retail prices of $10-$175. Curtis' full priced work is found in galleries and craft shows across the country. The business also doubles as a workshop where you can create quality art or craft projects between $10-$100, with most being in the $25-$35 range. Compare this to the cost of buying a finished product from an artist at a craft show, and you'll be saving about 25-50%. While the projects are available for all skill levels, they were planned with the novice or those with no experience to be able to create a spectacular finished project such as silk painted scarf, redware ceramics, kaleidoscopes, blank books, beaded jewelry or other items. To encourage this creativity, many of the projects are either partially assembled or partially prepainted and the person simply has to add their own finishing touches. Many items can be personalized with your own trinkets if you like, and the nature of the projects also allows for choices by the person participating. Another great point to consider is that these projects can be created in about an hour of your time (although they will need additional time for Curt to fire them, steam them, or otherwise complete the process when you're not there). Projects may be finished on a walk-in, no appointment basis, so if your feel the creative urge after you've had your haircut, dropped off the kids for gymnastics practice or gone to the grocery store, you can stop by and let those creative juices start flowing. Projects are available for kids (most in the $15 range) and adults alike. Birthday parties and group projects can also be scheduled. This business was formerly called, Benzle Applied Arts. It seems as if I have had some sort of connection with Curt for the last fourteen years. It started when I purchased his jewelry for sale in my boutique down at the Convention Center in the early 1980's. I remember selecting jewelry from an unpretentious basement studio on the Eastside. I have faithfully followed his trail to new locations and to increased levels of creativity. This outlet is one of my personal favorites and I am sure it will be yours too! M-Sat 10-9.

DAME JULIANA
1261 Grandview Ave., Columbus, 43212, 488-4844

Fisherman have known about this store for years. This wholesale and retail business sells supplies for you to make your own flies to attach to your fishing lines. You'll find value prices on an assortment of beautiful feathers from canaries, turkeys, peacocks, pheasants, partridges, quails and other birds. Related fly tying supplies are available at typical retail prices. Inquire about the free fly tying lessons, generally offered once a month. The hour long program offers free supplies for use during the session. You'll leave the hands-on class with several creations. Also, if the store is not busy, you can get a free, mini instructional assistance, generally up to fifteen minutes, on fly tying. You may also want to consider the more intensive classes priced at $45 for four sessions. The shop does repairs on all types of rods and even builds bamboo ones. Craftspersons will also enjoy shopping in this business as the selection of feathers is unlike any available locally. At various times during the store's operating hours, you can watch the owner in the midst of fly tying. M-F 12-7, Sat 12-5.

DAME JULIANA OUTLET
4170 W. Broad St., Westland Flea Market, Columbus, 43228, 488-4844
(Note: the phone number is for their main location in Grandview)

The store features a selection of discontinued merchandise from its Grandview location (see description above) at savings of 25-30%. You'll also find collectible tackle, flies and related fishing items at prices similar to their Grandview site. F/Sat 10-7, Sun 12-5.

DICK BLICK ART MATERIALS
6510 Riverside Dr., Village Sq. Shpng. Ctr., Dublin, 43017, 791-1900
7203 E. Broad St., Blacklick, 43004, 866-7790

Save about 10-25% off manufacturer's suggested list prices on fine arts supplies such as watercolor paper, foamboard, paints, pastels and more by Winsor and Newton, Arches etc.

Many of their own brand of paints and related products are about 15-35% less than comparable products by other companies. M-Th. 10-7, F/Sat 10-5, Sun 12-4.

EICKHOLT GLASS STUDIO
401 W. Town St., Columbus, 43215, 463-1274

Extraordinary handcrafted glass paperweights, perfume bottles, vases and scultptural pieces are available for your home or office. You'll visit this studio of artist, Robert Eickholt, whose works have been exhibited nationally. While most the stock is first quality and sold at typical craft show prices of $35-$125, the studio occassionally has seconds or works with slight imperfections from time to time. Prices for these items are based on the nature and severity of the imperfection or other aesthetic reasons determined by the artist. By appointment only.

FRAME WAREHOUSE
7502 E. Main St., Reynoldsburg, 43068, 861-4582

Thousands of ready made frames in all shapes and sizes are in stock at this no frills store. Savings are off regular retail prices on signed and numbered limited edition prints, posters and photography by Ansel Adams, Nagel and others as well as custom and ready made frames. If you call ahead, the business can often arrange to custom frame your artwork while you wait. The inventory consists of overstocks, special purchases, and discontinued goods, all at savings of 40-60% off regular retail prices. M-F 9-5, Sat 9-4.

FRANKLIN ART GLASS
222 E. Sycamore St., Columbus, 43206, 221-2972

Scrap stained and leaded glass is available at savings of 50-75% off in the scrap bin. At only $1.50 per pound, your savings can add up as compared to their regular $3.75-$6.50 per square foot. If you can use small pieces of glass for craft projects, this is a great source. The store also sells supplies at regular retail prices. M-F 8-4:30, Sat 8-12.

JO'S CLOTHING FOR BEARS AND GEESE
4170 West Broad St., Westland Flea Market, Columbus, 43228, 272-5678

Watch Jo stitch two piece outfits for stuffed bears and cement geese right in her tiny flea market booth. The outfits are priced at $10. F-Sun 10-7.

KEEPSAKE ARTS AND CRAFTS MALL
4236 Eastland Sq. Dr., Columbus, 43232, 863-8696

The store carries a small selection of handmade crafts in various price ranges, some of which are value priced. However, the cement geese outfits are priced well at $6-$10. Tu-F 11-8, Sat 10-6, Sun 12-5.

KOVAL KNIVES
5819 Zarley St., New Albany, 43054, 855-0777

This is the only store of its kind east of the Mississippi and one of only five similar type stores in the country. The business sells component parts and kits for the hobbyist or professional, with which to make cutlery and hunting knives. The store also sells supplies for repairs. For example, a hunting knife kit which sells for $25.95 here, is sold as a finished product in stores for $75-$100. Savings amount to about 50-80% when you make the knives yourself from Koval's supplies, as compared to store bought knives. You can pick up a large mail order catalogue in the store at no cost. M-F 9-4.

LEATHER FACTORY
4683 Morse Center, Columbus, 43229, 781-1700

This full line distributor for the homecrafter and professional leather industry (and supplier to large chain and specialty craft stores) offers a large selection of products. You'll find suede lace, tools, leathers and snakeskins, leathercraft kits and other items. The more you buy, the more you'll save, but expect to save about 20-40%. The store has a free mail order catalogue. M-Sat 10-6.

MICHAEL'S CRAFTS
2766 Brice Rd., Columbus, 43232, 868-5103
2290 Morse Rd, Columbus, 43229, 471-8555
6765 Dublin Ctr. Dr., Dublin, 43017, 764-4500

This superstore of crafts sells a full line at savings of 10-25% less than other stores. You'll also find weekly sales where items are further reduced often to 40-50% off. Membership in the Kids Club is free and enables participants to create a craft project for $1-$2 every Saturday. M-Sat 9-9, Sun 12-6.

OHIO ARTS COUNCIL
727 E. Main St., Columbus, 43205, 466-2613

Call to be added to the mailing list to receive the free quarterly magazine, Artspace. It includes feature stories about the visual, literary and performing arts around the state, issues of national importance such as private funding for the arts, and a description of upcoming major arts events. The publication can be enjoyed by artists and arts supporters alike. The Ohio Arts Council distributes copies of the Art Fairs And Festivals Guide for only $1.28, payable in four 32 cent stamps only. The guide lists all of the events statewide. The book is updated annually by the Ohio Arts And Crafts Guild and is a valuable resource if you are interested in purchasing handmade fine arts or arts and crafts. In most cases, you will be able to save 20-50% off typical gallery prices by purchasing directly from the artist, as the gallery's markup is thereby eliminated. OAC maintains an artists' slide bank as a low cost service to practicing artists. For only $5, twenty slides and your resume will be maintained on file for review by gallery curators and other individuals. Many leads and sales have been generated from this slide bank. Call for an application. M-F 8:30-5.

OLD AMERICA
1824 W. Henderson Rd., Columbus, 43220, 451-1517

When you purchase dried/silk flowers and a container ($10 minimum), the designer will provide free floral arranging. There aren't any labor charges on picture framing when you purchase a ready made frame; matting and glass are optional. The framers will insert your artwork, put on a dust cover and hanger at no cost. This can generally be done while you wait. M-Sat 9-9, Sun 10-6.

P.M. GALLERY
726 N. High St., Columbus, 43215, 299-0860

This Short North gallery offers discounts on custom framing to artists who wish to frame their creations. In this case, savings will be 10% off the retail price on the frame, mat and glass if you let the gallery assemble it for you. Another option is that if you are ambitious and would like to frame the artwork yourself, you will be charged 10% above the gallery's cost which is roughly equivalent to 40% off the regular retail prices. Additional savings are available for the purchase of several custom frames of the exact size, shape and color. You may ask the gallery for details. The store also offers a unique selection of fine arts and crafts, some of which are bargain hunters' delights. Tu-Sat 11-6, Sun 12-5. During the first Saturday of each month (for the Gallery Hop), the store is open from 11-10.

PEDDLER'S VILLAGE CRAFT AND ANTIQUE MALL
1881 W. Henderson Rd., Columbus, 43220, 326-0022

The state's largest craft and antique mall features quality items in all price ranges. Since vendors rent booths and each price their own stock, costs will vary from booth to booth. At least 35% of the craft dealers offer exceptional values while others feature typical craft shop prices. You'll find geese clothing, jewelry, ceramic items, stained glass and other quality miscellaneous items. The back of the store features an antiques section where prices too, vary from dealer to dealer, but there are still good deals to be found. The uniqueness of this business not only lies in its merchandise assortment, but with its Picnic Basket Eatery. Housed in a quaint general store within the shop, Granny (Beverly) cooks and bakes homemade foods with old fashioned goodness. M-W/F/S 10-6, Th 10-8, Sun 12-5.

PHILATELIC CENTER, U.S. POSTAL SERVICE
850 Twin Rivers Dr., Columbus, 43215, 469-4223
6316 Nicholas Dr., Worthington, 43085, 793-1725

You will pay the face value for regular issue and commemorative stamps, envelopes and postcards at these stores which are operated by, and located in the post office. As independent stamp and coin dealers add a markup to their inventory above the price they pay for it, your savings can amount to 10-30% at the Philatelic Centers. The shops also sell low cost stamp gift packets with varying themes. M-F 7a.m.-8p.m., Sat 8a.m.-12N Closed from 1:30-2:30 for lunch.

PHILLIP'S YARN SHOP
4509 Cleveland Ave., Columbus, 43229, 476-3942

Red Heart, Coats and Clark and Aunt Lydia brands of yarns/string are available at savings of 20-60% off regular retail prices. About 40% of the stock consists of mill ends which offer the greatest savings. Yarns/string are sold by the ounce and most skeins are missing the manufacturers' labels. You'll find synthetics, weaving wools, cottons and cotton blends suitable for hooked rugs, macrame, crochet, weaving and knitting. Before you leave, take a peak in the back room where the yarns are in enormous hanks prior to being rolled up into smaller ones! M-Sat 10-5.

RE:ART
448 Dublin Ave., Columbus, 43215, 228-9400

Community recycling program collects discards from area businesses and allows artists, non-profits and educational facilities to choose what they would like to have. The stash includes wooden crates, mirrors, glass, decorating materials such as wallpaper and fabric, carpeting, leather and other items. The annual membership fee is $25, but you'll certainly get your money's worth.

S-T LEATHER
2135 S. James Rd., Columbus, 43232, 235-1900

Over 4,000 square feet of space, features all colors of leather, suede, snakeskin, furs, leather working supplies and instructional books. This business supplies manufacturers of clothing, belts, purses, wallets, saddles, orthopedic braces as well as artists and craftsmen. Deerskin and elk are $3.50 per square foot, embossed leathers are $1.45-$1.95 per square foot and other skins vary in price. Suede scraps are $1.75 per pound. You can also buy upholstery leathers and full fur pelts such as fox or coyote. The prices are about 20-30% less than in other businesses and the selection is enormous. The company does a brisk mail order business, or you can stop in to make your selections. Due to the nature of the business, classes and detailed instructions on the use of their products are not available. M-F 8:30-5, Sat 10-2.

STAR BEACON PRODUCTS
1104 W. Goodale Blvd., Columbus, 43215, 294-4657

Health and beauty products in addition to general variety merchandise such as light bulbs, office supplies, inexpensive gift items, toys, infant products by Evenflo such as nipples and teething rings in addition to party supplies are available at savings of 30-75% off regular retail prices. This wholesaler, who sells to flea market vendors, fundraisers as well as the general public, also offers a wide selection of arts and crafts supplies at similar savings such as construction paper, calligraphy sets, Exacto knives, drawing pads, tempera paints, origami paper and more. Although you can purchase small or large qualities, the higher discounts are for bulk sales. During the Christmas season, the store features holiday supplies and an expanded toy selection at similar savings. The merchandise consists of first quality manufacturers overstocks, discontinued items as well as liquidations. This is also a great place to purchase party favors and stocking stuffers. M-F 9-5:30, Sat 9-12.

WESTERVILLE LIBRARY
126 S. State St., Westerville, 43081, 882-7277

The library features a collection of 440 framed art prints available for a 28 day loan, simply by presenting your library card. This free service is used by people who want to test out a new decorating theme, offices, nursing home residents, stage sets for theatrical presentations and any one who just has an interest. The collection includes works by Monet, Picasso, Ansel Adams, Wyeth, O'Keefe, Campanelli, Cassatt, Matisse and local artists. Categories run the gamut from impressionism, abstract, American folk, still life, florals, portraits, Americana, photography, children's themes and posters. Pieces withdrawn from the collection for a variety of reasons, are offered for sale during the fall (usually October) and spring (usually April) used book sales. The sales feature most hardbacks for $1, paperbacks for fifty cents, magazines and collectable books at various prices. Every Monday evening, from 6:30 to 8:30 p.m. the library features a sale of used books on a cart near the A-V, priced at a dollar and under. The children's area of the library features a free loan (with library card) of wooden puzzles. The library features many special events throughout the year such as author visits, lectures, musical performances, storytimes etc. One of their major events, Tunes and Tales, is held in March every year in conjunction with the Westerville Civic Symphony. The Westerville Public Library is one of my personal favorites. It was chosen largely on the merits of its circulating artwork collection although the special events are also noteworthy.

ALSO SEE

Allen's Coin Shop, Aurora Farms Factory Outlet, Business Equipment Electronics, Ci Bon, Doll House, Educable 25, Experienced Possessions, Greater Columbus. Antique Mall, Hancock Fabrics, Jeffersonville Outlet Center, Kitchen Place, Lake Erie Factory Outlet, Majestic Paint Store, Miniatures Unlimited, Model Home Furniture and Accessories Sale, My Cousin's Closet, Odd Lots, Ohio Factory Shops, J.C. Penney Portfolio, Sofa Express Outlet, Special Events/Sale Index, Starr Beacon, Tag Sales, Village This And That, WOSU Channel 34 and Waterford Hall

PHOTOGRAPHY/CAMERAS

CHICK'S CAMERA EXCHANGE
42 E. Long Street, Columbus, 43215, 228-1991

Save 20-50% on new, used, discontinued and overstocked cameras and accessories. You'll find a large selection of all popular brands including Nikon, Fuji, Pentax and others. M-F 10-6, Sat 10-4.

COLUMBUS CAMERA GROUP
55 E. Blake Ave., Columbus, 43202, 267-0686

Used cameras, related equipment and accessories, for the novice or professional photographer, are available at savings of 20-60% off "if new" prices. The store also stocks a limited amount of new buyout merchandise at similar savings. All popular brands can be found including Pentax, Minolta, Olympus, Polaroid and Kodak. The store also stocks some cameras for kids, antique and collectible photographic equipment in addition to picture frames. Extended warranties are available. M-F 10-6, Sat 10-4.

CORD CAMERA
1132 W. Fifth Avenue, Columbus, 43212, 299-1441

This superstore location is the only site in the local chain to sell used cameras. All popular brands are available including Konica, Pentax, Minolta and others at savings of 30-50% less then "if new". The store generally has about twenty to fifty used models in stock, in addition to a large selection of new models at competitive prices. Basic photography classes are featured once a month at no cost. M-F 8a.m.-9p.m., Sat 9-6, Sun 11-6.

K MART
10 locations throughout Franklin County plus Marion, Marysville and Newark

K Mart is well known throughout the retail industry as a discounter which sells merchandise at a low markup. The stores are filled with many popular name brand products in addition to K Mart brands or "unbranded" products (such as canned foods, automotive supplies and light bulbs) at even greater savings than a branded comparable item. Read the fine print on the labels or the cartons to find the words "made for K Mart". The book section, called the Readers' Market, offers savings of 5% on magazines and 10-30% off all current and overstock books for adults and children. Each of the stores has its own permanent photography studio offering value prices on package deals. M-Sat 9:30-9:30, Sun 10-6.

MCALISTER CAMERA COMPANY
1454 W. Lane Ave., Columbus, 43221, 488-1865
594 W. Schrock Rd., Columbus, 43229, 794-1865
6610 Sawmill Rd., Columbus, 43235, 766-1865
341 W. Bridge St., Dublin, 43017, 764-9910
791 Bethel Rd., Columbus, 43214, 457-2545
529 High St., Worthington, 43085, 847-1931

About 75% of the stock is available at savings of about 10-40% off regular retail prices. You will find all of the popular brands of cameras and camcorders including Pentax and Nikon. Used cameras are available at the Lane Avenue and Schrock Road locations at about 30-60% less than "if new". A variety of services are offered including film processing and video duplication at standard retail prices. Financing is available. M-F 10-8, Sat 10-5, Sun 12-5.

MIDWEST PHOTO EXCHANGE
3313 N. High St., Columbus, 43202, 261-1264

Save 40-80% off previously owned and 20-50% off new cameras and photographic supplies, for the amateur as well as professional photographer. Film processing is competitively priced. The extensive selection consists of popular brands such as Minolta, Pentax, Nikon, Olympus, Kodak, Polaroid and others. The business allows trade-ins and will also purchase your cameras and equipment outright. Collectors will appreciate the extensive selection of hard to find antiques. A camera repair service is also available at substantial savings. Offers an unconditional 30 day warranty. M-F 10-6, Sat 10-4.

ALSO SEE

Columbus Metropolitan Library, Columbus Police Department Auction, Drug Emporium, Franklin County Metro Parks, Giant Columbus Fantastic Camera Show And Computer Swap, Incredible Universe, K Mart, Lazarus Final Countdown, Ohio Camera Collectors Society Show And Sale, OSU Department Of Photography And Cinema, J.C. Penney Outlet, Schottenstein's, Sears Outlet, Service Merchandise, Uncle Sam's Pawn Shop

AUTOMOTIVE

AUTO SOURCE
3833 W. Broad St., Columbus, 43228, 279-2886
2100 Morse Rd., Columbus, 43229, 431-3330

Save on parts, tires plus automotive maintenance and repair services. The stores also feature a Nite Source Walk-Up Parts Window which is open from store closing until midnight Monday through Saturday. Free, do-it-yourself clinics are offered throughout the year. M-F 7a.m.-9p.m., Sat 7a.m.-8p.m., Sun 9-6.

BATTERY MANUFACTURER'S OUTLET
1220 W. Broad St., Columbus, 43222, 272-1007

You'll find an enormous selection of automotive, truck, motorcycle, tractor, golf cart and aircraft batteries at savings of 10-50% off regular retail prices. A complete line of automotive accessories is also available, but at full retail price. The inventory consists of first quality overstocks, liquidations, current merchandise and reconditioned new batteries from such companies as Delco and East Penn. M-F 7:30-5.

D. JAY'S TIRE AND AUTO SERVICE CENTER
863 S. Hamilton Rd., Whitehall, 43213, 237-7631

Why pay $16-$22 when you can have a chassis lube, oil change and oil filter for only $12.95 ? M-F 8-7, Sat 8-6.

HUBCAP ANNIE
4423 E. Main St., Columbus, 43213, 237-7778

New and used hubcaps, 20,000 to be exact, are in stock, ranging from current years and makes to those dating back to the 1940's. Used OEMs (original equipment from the manufacturers) are priced at 30-50% lower than you would expect to pay for the hubcap if it were new. New replacement hubcaps are priced at about 10-30% off comparable caps in other retail stores. M-F 9a.m.-5:30p.m., Sat 10-3.

IRON PONY ACCESSORIES
5309 Westerville Rd., Columbus, 43231, 891-2461
2040 Eakin Rd., Columbus, 43223, 272-1165

First quality, liquidations and blemished stock of motorcycle parts, accessories and clothes are available at savings of 10-25% off manufacturers' list prices. M-F 10-7, Sat 10-5, Sun 12-5. From October to February, the hours are shortened.

NATIONAL TIRE WHOLESALE
5840 Scarborough Blvd., Columbus, 43232, 863-6222
6700 Schrock Ct., Columbus, 43229, 846-8001
655 N. Wilson Rd., Columbus, 43204, 274-5500

Goodyear, Michelin, Pirelli, B.F. Goodrich and other popular and private brands of first quality tires are sold at 10-50% savings off manufacturers' list prices and comparable retail prices. General automotive repairs are also available at value prices. M-F 7:30a.m.-8p.m., Sat 8-5, Sun 10-3.

TIRE AMERICA
4481 Kingsland, Columbus, 43232, 864-5000
4475 W. Broad St.,Columbus, 43228, 272-2227
4800 Sinclair Rd., Columbus, 43229, 436-1303
1327 Brandywine Blvd., Colony Sq. Mall, Zanesville, 43701, 452-0007
3575 Maple Ave., Zanesville, 43701, 452-0007

Purchase Patriot, Dunlop, Goodyear, Michelin, B.F. Goodrich, Century and Pirelli brands of tires here at savings of 35% off regular retail prices. Automotive parts such as shocks and struts are sold at similar savings. Alignments and other services are provided at savings of about 15-20% lower than at other service centers. Has 90 days same as cash financing available to qualified buyers. Tire America features a 125% price guarantee. M/Tu 8-5, W-F 8-8, Sat 8-5, Sun 10-3.

ALSO SEE

City of Columbus. Police Dept., Columbus Spring Swap, Dirty Chin's Motorwear, Extravaganza, Franklin Co. Sheriffs, K Mart, Ohio Auto Auction, Only $1, Rideshare and Sam's Club

BOOKS/MAGAZINES/ NEWSLETTERS

ACORN BOOKSHOP
1464 W. Fifth Ave., Columbus, 43212, 486-1860

This bookstore specializes in natural history, science fiction, aviation and military books, but has a general line of used hardbacks and paperbacks, out of print and rare books as well. Most paperbacks are 50% off the cover price. Hardbacks are priced according to condition, age and scarcity. This business buys, sells and trades books. Accepts checks and cash only. Tu-F 11-8, Sat 12-5.

B. DALTON BOOKSELLER
771 Bethel Rd., Olentangy Plaza, Columbus, 43214, 459-9191
2753 Eastland Mall, Columbus, 43232, 861-6860
520 S. State St., Westerville, 43081, 890-8277
193 Columbus City Ctr. Dr., Columbus, 43215, 228-4581
5091 E. Main St., Columbus, 43213, 861-5505

Membership in the Booksavers Club costs $10 annually and provides you with several benefits. You'll get a 10% discount on all regular priced and sale books and the opportunity to purchase selected super saver books at a 50% discount. The stores offer a selection of bargain priced books at 30-70% off the cover price, which are overstocked, out of print or hurt. M-Sat 10-9, Sun 12-5.

BARNES AND NOBLE
3685 W. Dublin Granville Rd., Columbus, 43235, 798-0077
3280 Tremont Rd., Columbus, 43221, 459-0920
5160 E. Main St., Columbus, 43213, 863-3050

Although these stores sell books at cover price, with minimal discounts on certain titles, you'll find great deals in the bargain book areas. These large areas feature savings of 30-80% on hurt, discontinued and overstocked books. The stores also feature frequent free programs for adults and children including author visits, entertainment and storytimes. Enjoy some pastries and sparkling water at the cafes. Daily 9a.m.-11p.m.

BOOK HARBOR
32 W. College Ave., Westerville, 43081, 895-3788

Housed within an older home in uptown Westerville, you'll find used and rare books and some collectibles. Many books are about 30-50% off the cover price, but others are priced according to age and scarcity. Although you'll find books in most subjects, the store specializes in mystery, adventure, older historical novels, Ohio, presidents and poetry. M-W/F 12-8, Sat 10-8, Sun 1-5.

BOOKHAVEN OF SPRINGFIELD
1549 Commerce Rd., Springfield, 45504, (513) 322-9021

You'll find about 20,000 used hardbacks, paperbacks and some comics in stock in this multi level older building. Prices vary with condition and scarcity, but non collectors' books are about 40-50% off the cover price. M-Th/Sat 12-6, Sat 12-8.

BOOK LOFT OF GERMAN VILLAGE
631 S. 3 St., Columbus, 43206, 464-1774

Thousands of first quality, discontinued and publishers' overstocks as well as hurt books, are sold at savings of 30-95% off the cover price. Current N.Y. Times best sellers are 30% off, other new titles as well as special orders are available at 10% off the cover price. Thirty-two rooms are brimming with books in every subject, for adults and children. Check the basement area for a large selection of hurt books at substantial savings. Many of the rooms play peaceful music which is also available for purchase. The store is so large, a city block long to be exact, that you'll appreciate the free maps to guide you through the maze. The spring and summer times are the most beautiful at this store as their courtyard is all abloom with impatiens. There's benches to sit on and browse through your new purchase, or bring a sack lunch and relax. Hours are seven days per week from 10-10.

BOOK RACK
5346 N. High St., Columbus, 43214, 846-0036

Thousands of gently used current paperbacks are available at half off the cover price. A selection of in-stock, new books, as well as special orders, are available at savings of 10-20%. You'll find non-fiction, romance, historicals, fiction, westerns, science fiction, mysteries, best sellers and seventeen other categories for adults, young adults and children. You may also choose to trade in your unwanted books for those in the store at 1/4 the cover price, which will be issued as a store credit towards future purchases. Ask about the opportunity to rent newly released hardbacks at a cost of $3 per week. Twice a year, in the spring and the fall, the store features their half off sale where you can save 50% off their already low prices. M-Sat 10-7, Sun 11-3. Accepts checks and cash only.

BOOKS ON HIGH
3030 N. High St., Columbus, 43202, 267-7774

This used and antiquarian book mall has 6,000 or so books in stock from eighteen dealers who lease space in this quaint shop. Organized by dealer, each prices their own merchandise, so the values will vary from booth to booth. Collectible/rare books are priced accordingly, but other used books are priced at 30-60% off the cover price. Tu-Sat 11-6.

BOOKWORM
30 W. Woodruff Ave., St. Stephen's Episcopal Church, Columbus, 43210, 294-3749

Step down to the church's basement to find a great selection of used books in every subject, plus young adult/kids books. Most books are in the 25 cent to $3 range with original cover prices up to to $25. Park in the lot on the west side of the building. W/Th 10-2.

BORDERS BOOKS & MUSIC
4545 Kenny Rd., Columbus, 43220, 451-2292

Most hardcover books are sold at 10% off the cover price, and New York Times hardcover best sellers are discounted 30%. Monthly staff selections in both the adult and children's areas are also discounted 30%. The hurt books section at the store's entrance, offers savings of 60-80% off the cover price. The bargain book area of closeouts and overstocks, features savings of 30-50%. The store has free adult and children's programs including storytimes, author visits, holiday parties, musical performances and other events throughout the month. The back of the store, sells CDs and tapes at fair prices. Check out the espresso bar in the store where you can indulge in croissants, pastries, lattes, espresso, Maria's authentic baklava and other goodies. M-W 9-9, Th-Sat 9-11, Sun 11-8.

CINDAMAR
218 Granville St., Newark, 345-6327

Step into this quaint older home to find used and collectible books in all genres. Although prices vary according to age and scarcity, the books are priced very reasonably. Tu-F 12-7, Sat 9-4

DISCOUNT PAPERBACK CENTER
1646 N. High St., Columbus, 43201, 291-5136

Current and back issues of comics, magazines, paperbacks, hardbacks, adult magazines and the latest releases of Comics Weekly can be found in this unpretentious store. You can save 10-20% off the cover price of new publications and 30-50% off used merchandise. Although this store specializes in science fiction and fantasy publications, you will find an assortment of subjects mainly for adults. M-F 11:30-8:30, Sat 11-8, Sun 12-5.

FAN THE FLAMES
3387 N. High St., Columbus, 43202, 447-0565

Save 50% off the cover price on a large selection of used books at this feminist bookstore. Topics include African American, gay/lesbian, feminist, recovery and children's titles. The store also sells new books, music and jewelry at typical prices. Tu-F 11-7, Sat/Sun 12-6.

FAR AWAY
6072 Busch Blvd., Columbus, 43229, 848-KLUE (5583)

Mystery, suspense and horror novels line the shelves of Ohio's premier mystery bookstore. New books are sold at regular retail prices, but the large selection of used books is available at 50% off the cover price. The store also sells board games, gifts with a mystery theme and other small items at full retail price. M-Sat 10-9, Sun 12-6.

FIRESIDE BOOK COMPANY
503 City Park Avenue, Columbus, 43215, 621-1928

This quaint bookstore, in an older brick home ion German Village, sells used books in all genres, but specializes in literature, cooking and history subjects. Many books are half off the original cover price, but collectible and antique books are priced accordingly. The store offers a free cup of gourmet coffee to visitors. And you can step into the cyberspace by accessing their inventory on the Internet's World Wide Web or you can E-Mail the store if you have specific questions. Tu-Sat 11-9, Sun 12-5.

FORECLOSURE NEWSLETTER
Bill Randall, 882-0198

This eight page newsletter is issued weekly, and features listings, pictures and financial analysis of foreclosed bank and government owned properties in Franklin county. Homes include handyman's specials as well as those in great condition. As the homes and condos are scattered throughout the city, it's just as likely that you'll find these sales in Dublin as you would on the city's southside. A sample issue is only $2. Bill, a licensed real estate broker, recommends that serious buyers should invest in the yearly subscription of $99, so as to get a feel for the market. Properties generally sell for 80-85% of their values. One secret of a good investment, according to Bill, is knowing how much money you'll need to spend to fix up the property, if it needs work.

FRIENDS OF THE LIBRARY BOOKSALES
All area libraries feature at least one large sale of donated and library discard books per year. Most libraries have ongoing mini sales on a rack or cart in the libary, which consist of the same type of items but on a much smaller scale. Prices are generally $1 and under.

FRIENDS OF THE LIBRARY BOOKSTORE
John McIntyre Library, 220 N. 5 St., Zanesville, 452-4893

This is the largest used bookstore in the country to be operated by volunteer Friends Of The Library members. The enormous selection in all genres, is housed in the former children's wing of the library. Most books are priced at ten cents to $2, with collectible books slightly higher. Tu/Sat 10-2.

HALF PRICE BOOKS, RECORDS, MAGAZINES
2660 Bethel Rd., Carriage Place Shpng. Ctr., Columbus, 43220, 457-6333
2659 Brice Rd., Reynoldsburg, 43068, 755-4110
1375 W. Lane Ave., Columbus, 43221, 486-8729

Save 50% off and more on new and used books, magazines, records, videos, CDs and tapes. The inventory consists of manufacturers overstocks, discontinued merchandise, as well as used items in all subjects for adults, teens as well as children. The inventory changes frequently, so stop in whenever possible. The store has earned the distinction of being one of my personal favorites. M-Sat 10-10, Sun 11-7.

HOFFMAN'S BOOK SHOP
211 E. Arcadia Ave., Columbus, 43202, 267-0203

Several rooms are brimming with used and rare books in all genres, although the store specializes in photography, Ohio, James Thurber and modern literature. Paperbacks are about 30-70% off the cover price and hardbacks are about 50% off the penciled in price unless marked "net". Rare and collectible books are priced according to scarcity and condition. The business also sells value priced small antiques and small artwork which are scattered throughout the store. Tu-Sat 11-5.

KAREN WICKLIFFE BOOKS
2579 N. High St., Columbus, 43202, 263-2903

Used and rare books, 40,000 titles to be exact, line the shelves of Columbus' largest used book dealer. The store features titles in all subject areas, but specializes in history, fine arts, science and technology, medicine, science fiction and children's titles. Most of the books are sold for 20-50% off the cover price, with the exception of rare books. M-Sat 11:30-5:30. Accepts checks and cash only.

LIBRARY STORE
96 S. Grant Ave., Columbus, 43215, 645-2617

Housed within the Main Library, this small store is truly a bargain hunters paradise, brimming with business, entertainment, crafts, children's, fiction and nonfiction books at rock bottom prices. The books consist of library discards as well as donations. Most of the books are priced at $1-$3 with values up to $35. Encyclopedias and other reference books are priced at $5-$15 with values up to $200. Small paperbacks are priced at 50 cents. M-Th 10-8, F/Sat 10-5.

LITTLE BOOK SHOP
58 E. Main Street, Westerville, 43081, 899-1537

Nestled among the quaint older homes in uptown Westerville, you'll find this off the beaten path shop. The store is filled with used and collectible books in many genres, but specializes in military, aviation, children's and Americana titles. Located within a home, the main structure and the adjacent garage are both dedicated to books. Although prices vary according to scarcity, you'll find many used titles at least 50% off the cover price. Tu/Th/Sat 12-5 or by appointment.

LITTLE PROFESSOR BARGAIN BOOK ANNEX
1595 W. Lane Ave., Columbus, 43221, 486-9800

Thousands of publishers' overstocks, promotional reprints, used library books, remainders and hurt books are available at this store. Savings are 30-80% off the cover price. M-Sat 10-9:30, Sun 12-5.

LITTLE PROFESSOR BOOKSTORES
155 Worthington Sq., Worthington, 43085, 846-4319
6490 Sawmill Rd., Sawmill Place Shpng. Ctr., Columbus, 43235, 766-7775
1657 W. Lane Ave., Lane Ave. Shpng. Ctr., Columbus, 43221, 486-5238

Each month, twelve books are chosen as the "staff selections" which are then sold at 20% off the cover price, as are the New York Times bestsellers. Every January and July, the stores have library buyout book sales, where hardcover books are sold for $2.59 each or ten for $18.90. The Worthington Square and the Sawmill Road sites feature a paneled library, fireplace and couches for relaxation. Special programs are held in this area as well, including regular meetings of their poets guild. The guild critiques members' works and learns about the various aspects of the writer's craft. Stay posted on the many free programs such as pre-school storytimes, author visits and booksignings, musical performances and informative discussions. M-Sat 10-9, Sun 12-5.

LONG'S BOOKSTORE
1836 N. High St., Columbus, 43210, 294-4674

Check out the perpetual sale of irregulars and seconds of OSU imprinted, hooded and crew neck sweatshirts in all sizes, priced at $20-$22, but regularly $32-$45 if perfect. The heavyweight, reverse weave Champion sweats are not misprinted, but do have small holes, open seams or other nuisances which can generally be repaired with little difficulty. The front of the store has closeouts of used textbooks in many subjects priced at $1-$2 each. The back of the store features a large selection of buyouts of new books for adults and kids. You'll find all subjects, from art to gardening, at savings of 30-75% off the cover price. These consist of overstocks, out of prints and closeouts. M-F 8-8, Sat 9-5, Sun 11-5.

MEDIA PLAY
4328 W. Broad St., Columbus, 43228, 272-8400
2261 S. Hamilton Rd., Columbus, 43232, 863-3223
7690 New Market Center Way, Columbus, 43235, 766-9499

CDs, videos, books, cassettes and some toys are found in great quantity. Save 10% on all paperbacks, audio books and magazines, 34% on NY Times Bestsellers and 15% off on regional, children's and hard cover books. CDs are generally priced under $12. Check out the many bargain bins scattered throughout the store offering savings up to 70% on overstocks, out of print and special purchase items. Videos, toys and related paraphernalia are offered at varying savings from 10-50%. The stores also feature frequent free special events for adults and kids such as storytimes, musical performances, movies and educational discussions. M-Sat 10-9, Sun 11-6.

OSU FOLKLORE DEPARTMENT
Columbus, 688-3639

The department publishes a free, quarterly folklife newsletter, Folklines, which is available to the general public. It lists community classes and workshops of interest to folklorists, upcoming folklore conferences, folk activities and feature stories on other subjects relative to folk performance, arts and crafts and folklife in general.

OUTREACH CHRISTIAN BOOKS
4352 Indianola Ave., Columbus, 43214, 268-2008

Christian oriented games, books and bibles are discounted 25%. Records, cassettes and CDs are sold at a 20% savings off regular retail prices. M-Sat 10-8, Sun 12-5.

PAGES 'N PAGES
502 S. Westgate Ave., Columbus, 43204, 351-7662

31,000 comics, paperbacks and hardback books are available in all subjects. Most books are priced from 25 cents to $3. M/Tu/Th/F 12-5, Sat 10-3.

PAPERBACK EXCHANGE
4866 W. Broad St., Columbus, 43228, 878-1307

Used paperbacks are sold at 50% off the cover price and new paperbacks at 10% off. All genres are available. There's also a small children's/young adult's section offering similar values. The store has a bargain area in the front with even greater savings. This business buys, sells and trades paperback books. M-F 10-7, Sat 10-5, Sun 12-4.

PAPERBACK EXCHANGE
120 N. Columbus Street, Lancaster, 43130, 654-5856

Save 45% off the cover price on a large selection of used paperbacks in all subjects. Accepts checks and cash only. M-F 10-5, Sat 10-4.

PAPERBACK PLACE
800 James St., Zanesville, 43701, 452-1474

Over 50,000 used books are available at great prices from 25 cents to about $7. You'll find all subjects for young and old alike. M-F 10-6, Sat 10-5.

PENGWYN BOOKS, LTD.
2500 N. High St., Columbus, 43202, 267-6711

Thousands of used, rare and curious books are offered in all subjects, although the store specializes in philosophy, history (including medieval and Renaissance) as well as scholarly works. Savings are 30-50% off the cover price on used items. Check out the clearance tables too. M-Sun 11-6.

PUBLISHER'S OUTLET
5827 Brice Outlet Mall, Columbus, 43232, 866-6235

Save 30-80% on new books in all genres. You'll find titles for adults and children which are closeouts, overstocks and out of prints. M-Sat 10-9, Sun 12-6.

READMOR BOOKSTORES
1649 Morse Rd., Northland Lazarus, Columbus, 43229, 265-1459
4141 W. Broad St., Westland Lazarus, Columbus, 43228, 278-4972
131 N. High St., Columbus, 43215, 464-3092
2677 S. Hamilton Rd., Eastland Lazarus, Columbus, 43232, 860-1594
141 S. High St., downtown Lazarus, Columbus, 43215, 463-3327
313 W. Bridge St., Dublin, 43017, 889-7468

The top ten books on the New York Times best sellers' list are discounted 25% off the cover price. Check the bargain book areas for special prices on out of print and overstocked books. Inquire about the frequent shopper card. M-Sat 10-9, Sun 12-5. North High St. hours are shorter.

TOOT'S BOOK EMPORIUM
30 N. State St., Westerville, 43081, 890-2788

Save 40-50% off the cover price on used paperbacks, in romance, western and science fiction genres. A small selection of new books is discounted about 10-15%. M-Sat 10-5.

UPPER ARLINGTON PUBLIC LIBRARY
2800 Tremont Rd., Columbus, 43221, 486-9621
1945 Lane Rd., Columbus, 43220, 459-0273

The Tremont Road location has a daily book sale near the library entrance containing about 300 books in a variety of subjects. The prices range from 50 cents to $2. I recently picked up a hard back copy of Trader Vic's Bartending Guide for $2 which would have cost about $15 if new. The Friends Of The Library also offer a used book sale in the lobby every Wednesday from 9:30-5, every Saturday from 9:30-3 and every Sunday from 1-5. The Lane Road Library has a small selection of used books and magazines, from 25 cents to $1, on a cart as you enter the library. As is the case with most area libraries, the Arlington branches offer many free and low cost lectures, seminars, book discussions, poetry readings, performances and craft workshops each month for adults and children. Some previous programs have been "Hand And Nail Care", "Life Without Guilt", "Creative Bow Making And Gift Wrapping Ideas" and more. The Tremont Road branch lends out framed art work and sculptures with your library card. The same branch features an annual musical series, Eine Kleine Nachmusik, which presents free monthly performances from September to June with local as well as regional talent. This branch also rents slide projectors for $5 per day and $1 per day to rent a screen. The equipment may be taken off site. M-F 10:30-8:30, Sat 9-6, (Sun 1-6 at the Tremont branch only).

VILLAGE BOOK SHOP
2424 W. Dublin Granville Rd., Worthington, 43085, 889-2674

Publishers' overstocks, out of print and closeout books in all subjects, are available at savings of 10-90% off the cover price in this former church. You'll find over two million books for adults, young adults and children, most of which are new, plus a small selection of used books and magazines in the upper level. The owner indicated that this is the largest remainder bookstore in the country, outside of New York City. M-Sun 10-10.

VILLAGE THIS AND THAT
32-24 S. Main St., Mt. Gilead, (419) 947-9272

Find a large selection of mostly fiction paperbacks priced at ten cents to $2, which is about 50-80% off the cover price. The store also stocks some arts and crafts supplies, but the best price in that department is on the large selection of lace, priced at 45 cents to 75 cents per yard. Several dealers lease shelves in the store and offer new handmade handicrafts and some small used bric-a-brac at fair prices. M/Tu/W/F 10-5, Sun 12-5.

VOLUNTEERS OF AMERICA BOOKSTORE
2511 Summit St., Columbus, 43202, 262-3384

The upstairs level houses all of the books, records and tapes collected citywide by this nonprofit organization. Used paperbacks and hardbacks cost about 50 cents-$2, records and tapes cost $1 or less. Wednesday is bargain day with all books 25% off. Another opportunity for savings is when you purchase twelve or more books at one time on any day, you'll save 25%. M-Sat 9-4:30.

WALDENBOOKS
3575 N. Maple Ave., Zanesville, 455-3439
1641 Northland Mallway, Columbus, 43229,262-2354
4221 Westland Mallway, Columbus, 43228, 279-2732

1445 Marion Waldo Rd., Marion, 389-5557
1635 River Valley Circle S., Lancaster, 653-6463
771 S. 30 St., Newark, 522-3638

The stores feature small sections at the front where overstocked, "as is" and closeout books are offered at savings of 25-60% . M-Sat 10-9, Sun 12-6.

WILLIS' BOOK GALLERY
3510 N. High St., Columbus, 43214, 262-6061

Thousands of used, rare and collectible books are available in all subjects, although the store specializes in science fiction, mystery, art and horror titles. The store features a large selection of art, mystery, horror, science fiction and fantasy books in addition to small antiques and collectibles. Savings on many used books are about 20-50% off the cover price. M-Sat 11-6. Accepts checks and cash only.

WORTHINGTON PUBLIC LIBRARY
805 Hartford St., Worthington, 43085, 645-2620

The library offers a self serve used book, video, magazine, cassette and compact disc area called the Bargain Place which is in the lower level. Prices are 50 cents for magazines or paperback books, $1 for hardcover books, cassettes/record albums/CDs and videos vary in cost. The merchandise consists of items no longer needed by the library as well as patron donations. The library also offers free book discussions, musical performances, storytimes and other special events (Fridays By The Fire Series, Book And Bag lunchtime series). M-Th 9-9, F/Sat 9-6, (Sun 1-5 Sept.-May).

WTTE CHANNEL 28 KIDS CLUB
6130 Sunbury Rd., Westerville, 43081, 895-2800

Sign up your child for the free monthly newsletter which provides discount coupons and freebies for entertainment, services, food and other desirables. The newsletter also includes stories and games. Your child will receive a special mailing for his/her birthday, which includes additional coupons for special surprises. Children up to age fifteen can participate. M-F 9-5.

ALSO SEE

Arts Midwest Jazzletter, Columbus Bookfair, Drowsy Dragon, Extravaganza, K Mart, Jeffersonville Outlet Center, Microcenter, Nearly New Shop, Ordinary Mysteries, OSU Friends Of The Library Book Sale, Otterbein College Book Sale, Pearls Of Wisdom, Sam's Club, Shadow Realm, Software Etc., TWIG Attic, Used Book Sale, WDLR Radio and Westerville Library Book Sale

CLASSES

CAPITAL UNIVERSITY
2199 E. Main St., Columbus,. 43209, 236-6200

Senior citizens aged 60 and over may enroll in selected university courses at no cost on a space available basis in the Senior Audit Program. Books and lab fees, if needed, must be paid by the senior. Call M-F 9-5.

COLUMBUS CULTURAL ARTS CENTER
139 W. Main St., Columbus, 43215, 645-7047

Housed in one of the earliest arsenals existent in Ohio, this multifaceted arts facility offers free and low cost programs in the visual, performing and literary arts for adults and children. 48 exhibitions are featured annually, in four galleries within the building. Adult studio classes are offered year round in eight week sessions and include weaving, drawing, painting, bronze casting, stone carving, ceramics, sculpture, metalsmithing, and copper enameling. The fee for the eight week term is $19 for classes meeting once per week and $38 for those meeting twice per week. Supply fees are extra. Each month, the Center offers a changing menu of workshops such as basketry, papermaking, Fimo jewelry, collage, handcoloring black and white photographs and more. Most are priced at $10-$30. The free, weekly Conversations And Coffee series presents practicing artists discussing their works, often accompanied by a slide presentation or a demonstration. Lectures, performances, poetry readings and many children's programs offer exciting opportunities for learning and experiencing the arts. Free special events and festivals are featured throughout the year. Admission to the building and its exhibits is free. The instructional staff are top in their fields, with several educators being nationally recognized. Comraderie is high among participants whose creativity truly flourishes in this environment. The building can be rented for private functions at a cost of $10 per hour for up to 99 people or $20 per hour for 100 or more people. This facility has earned the distinction of being one of my personal favorites. The Columbus Cultural Arts Center is operated by the City of Columbus, Recreation And Parks Department. M-F 8a.m.-5p.m., M-Th. 7p.m.-9:30p.m., Sat/Sun 1-5.

DAVIS DISCOVERY CENTER
549 Franklin Ave., Columbus, 43215, 645-7469

Quality, free and low cost programs are offered for youths aged 4-18 in music, dance and drama, stage combat, magic and theater illusion, special effects makeup for the stage and more. Housed within the old Players Theater building, the Davis Discovery Center provides excellent opportunities for kids to grow through the arts, under the direction of trained professionals. Some classes culminate in free public performances at the Center as well as at sites within the community. Sign up for their mailing list. This facility has earned the distinction of being one of my personal favorites.

DAWES ARBORETUM
7770 Jacksontown Rd., S.E., Newark, 43055, 323-2355

This botanical delight offers free and low cost (usually $5-$8) programs for the family on nature and horticulture related topics. Discussions and slide programs on Victorian graveyards, pest identification and control, gardens of Europe and plant habitats, as well as workshops on composting, bonsai, perennial landscaping and brick patios have been offered. Children's programs include films, hikes and crafts workshops. Also offers a master gardener's certificate program and a free drive through auto tour. M-F 8-5, Sat/Sun 1-5. Accepts checks and cash only.

DELAWARE COUNTY METRO PARKS
368-1805 or 363-2934

Offers a free nature lovers lecture series year round at the Perkins Observatory, 3199 Columbus Pike and the Township Hall. Past topics have included beekeeping, attracting wildlife to your yard, composting, caring for wildlife babies and trees in the urban environment. At this time, there are no metro parks in Delaware County, but this organization has been looking for some suitable land. Call M-F 9-5

EDUCABLE CHANNEL 25
36 W. Gay St., Suite 301, Columbus, 43215, 469-8825

A changing sampler of quality programming is available on this cable television station. You can take telecourses for college credit (or for personal enrichment) in subjects such as foreign language instruction, psychology, business communications, marketing and physics. Or learn how to paint in a regular class on this station. Call for their free program guide.

GRANDPARENTS LIVING THEATER
Columbus, 228-7458

Free oral history workshops are offered once a week for senior citizens. Through discussions, exercises and some homework, you'll learn the art of story telling using your own life's experiences, and will share them with other members of the group. Material from these workshops, often becomes subject matter for plays, which are performed by a theatrical group of the same name. While there is no obligation to perform in a production, many of the oral history group members enjoy having that opportunity.

HARDING HOSPITAL
785-7426

Offers low cost ($5-$10) lectures 2-3 times per year through the Harding-Evans Foundation such as with Judith Viorst, author of "Necessary Losses". Programs are held at various sites in Worthington. Contact the Foundation to sign up for the mailing list. M-F 9-5.

JITTERBUG CAFE
4801 E. Broad St., Columbus, 43213, 868-6882

Free Jitterbug lessons are offered every Wednesday evening from 8-9 p.m., instructed by members of the Sock Hop Club. The Cafe is located in the Quality Inn East.

OSU PROGRAM 60
1050 Carmack Rd., Columbus, 43210, 292-8860

Ohio residents aged 60 and over, may attend classes on a non-credit basis for free regardless of their prior educational training. There are so many classes from which to choose in all subject areas from indergraduate through Ph.D. levels. Book or lab fees are extra where needed. Some classes require pre-requisites. Registration is held in January, March, June and September. Program 60 is administered by the Office of Continuing Education. Current Ohio law requires state funded colleges and universities to open their classrooms to seniors at no charge on a space available basis. M-F 9-5.

OSU SCHOOL OF MUSIC
292-0789 or 292-6571

The division of music history offers a free public series, Lectures In Musicology in the winter, spring and fall. The series is held on Wednesdays at 4p.m. in the music library of Sullivant Hall, 1813 N. High Street. Previous topics have included, A Clash Of Two Cultural Paradigms In Russian Music Of The 17th Century, Liszt's Les Preludes Who Told The Truth? Draft Of Inspiration: Perspectives On The Nature Of Musical Composition From Lully To Stravinsky. The department also offers the William Poland Lectures In Music Theory during the year, at no cost. Call to sign up for their mailing list. M-F 9-4:30.

SENIOR FREE AUDIT PROGRAM
Otterbein College, N. Grove and W. College Ave., Westerville, 43081, 898-1356

Seniors aged 65 and over may enroll in college courses at no cost, except for book and lab fees where applicable. Participation is on a space available basis for the non credit classes. M-F 8-5.

SHADOW REALM
21 W. Brighton Rd., Columbus, 43202, 262-1175

This small store features books, incense, herbs and crafts with a magical/esoteric theme, at typical retail prices. There's a small selection of used and hurt books at savings of 40-60%. This shop also features free magical classes, presented by experienced practitioners, on a regular basis. (Note: The author does not endorse this belief system. The business is listed in this book, because it provides free classes for those with this particular interest). M-Th 11-6:30, F/Sat 11-7:30.

<u>**WOSU CHANNEL 34**</u>
2400 Olentangy River Rd., Columbus, 43210, 292-9678

This public television station offers several weekly instructional classes on cooking, painting and sewing. Auction 34, the station's annual fundraising event, is held from late April through early May. Viewers have the opportunity to bid on a variety of items and services such as artwork, trips, jewelry, meals at restaurants, household items etc., often saving 20-40% off the regular retail price. M-F 9-5.

ALSO SEE

Byzantium, Builders Square, Columbus Metropolitan Libraries, Columbus Museum Of Art, Columbus Swim Center, Dame Juliana, Delaware County Cultural Arts Center, Educable Channel 25, Fabric Farms, Franklin Co. Cooperative Extension Service, Franklin Co. Metro Parks, Golden Hobby Shop, Hancock Fabrics, Home Quarters, Lowe's, Majestic Paint Stores, Martin Luther King Center, Michael's Crafts, Microcenter, Nancy's Fabrics, ODNR-Division Of Watercraft, OSU Department of Architecture, Ohio Tuition Trust Authority, Panel Town And More, Pearls Of Wisdom, Sun TV, Universal Light Exposition, Upper Arlington Public Library, Wallpaper 4-U, Wallpapers To Go, Wines Inc.

CLOTHING

Invest a few dollars in a D-Fuzzer. It's a plastic object with a metal, finely serrated blade that removes lint and fuzz from clothes when you brush it across your garments. Area sewing shops and the gadgets section of grocery stores usually have them for $3-$4. This will keep your garments looking fresh and like new. It can also help you to make excellent purchases on clothes which have been reduced because they've become too fuzzy on the store's racks.

Each manufacturer cuts their clothes and shoes differently. So don't be stubborn about trying on something which is several sizes larger or smaller than you usually wear. Another reason to check the racks in other sizes is that some people will misplace clothes they have tried on into the wrong size on the rack. Another tip is to search the racks for clothing in the opposite sex's department. Many fashions are made nowadays so that men and women could be equally flattered in certain styles. I have found that on the clearance racks in the men's department, there always seems to be an abundance of colored garments, possibly considered to be feminine, in addition to patterns which are unpopular with men.

ALAN RAY AND COMPANY BRIDAL HOUSE
2700 Billingsley Rd., Worthington, 43235, 761-1023

Alan Ray has been in the custom design business in Columbus for over fifteen years. A graduate of the prestigious Clariss Design School, he also provides freelance design services to posh New York bridal boutiques. The custom gowns include such special touches as hand looped buttons, lined and boned handbeading (no glue is used) and other couture quality amenities. Custom wedding gowns are priced at $850 and up, custom bridesmaids gowns are $225 and up. This talented man can create likenesses of designer gowns such as Priscilla etc. and save you about 30% off the cost to buy the original designer's garment. Keep in mind that I am referring to couture quality, not a knockoff of a J.C. Penney special. This business also stocks a selection of unique wedding gowns in the $300-3000 range as well as long and short formals in the $105-260 range. These are discounted 15-20% as are special orders. A selection of discontinued styles is available at a a savings of 50%. The store sells Watters and Watters, Alfred Angelo, Jane Phoenix and other brands. Alterations are extra, but will still save you about 20-30% compared to some other businesses. Other formalwear, not purchased here, can be altered at a similar savings. Tu-Th 12-8, F 12-6, Sat 9:30-4:30.

ALTERNATIVE SHOP
1806 W. 5 Ave., Columbus, 43212, 486-0225 or 486-8088

Consignment men's, women's and children's clothing as well as bridal wear, can be found at this store at savings of about 30-75% off "if new" prices. You'll also find a limited amount of accessories. M 10-5, Tu-Sat 9-6.

ANOTHER GLANCE/ANOTHER GLANCE ACCENTS
2390 E. Main St., Bexley, 43209, 237-0636
1232 N. 21 St., Newark, 43055, 366-6716

Upscale gently used women's evening wear, silk, satin and beaded garments in sizes 3-42, are sold here at savings of 30-50% less than if they were purchased new. Never worn salesman's samples and remainders from area boutiques and specialty shops are also available at savings of 40-60% off regular retail prices. Accessories such as jewelry, purses and belts can be found at similar savings. Moderate to designer quality brands you will find here include J.H. Collectibles, Liz Claiborne, Forenza, Dawn Joy, Anne Klein, Louis Vuitton, Gucci and others. The store also stocks a small amount of maternity wear and men's shirts and sweaters. Sign up for a free membership in their Clothes-A-Holics Unanimous Club, which is a frequent purchaser plan. The Newark location features a large selection of bridal gowns and veils in addition to the other merchandise described above, and is well worth the trip. The Bexley location also features a home decor and furniture section, Another Glance Accents, which is filled with consigned furniture at similar savings. Sign up for their mailing list to stay posted on their sales and fun special promotions. M-Sat 10-6.

AURORA FARMS FACTORY OUTLETS
549 S. Chillicothe Rd., Aurora, 44202, (330) 562-2000 or 1-(800) 837-2001

You can enjoy a delightful atmosphere at Ohio's first factory outlet center where 30 stores offer savings of up to 70% off name brand merchandise. All of the stores are factory owned and operated and include such merchandise as craft items, clothing for the family, cosmetics, paper products, gift items and furniture. Some of the stores you'll find include Aileen, Crazy Horse, Gitano, Champion Hanes Activewear, Harve Benard, Izod, Jonathan Logan, Ann Taylor Loft, Jones New York, Big Dog Sportswear, Boston Traders, Brooks Brothers, B.U.M. Equipment, Casual Corner, Van Heusen, Bass Shoes, L'eggs And Hanes, Carter's, Toy Liquidators, Fila, Gant, Geoffrey Beene, Haggar, Liz Claiborne, Manhattan, Off Fifth-Saks Fifth Avenue, Dansk, Mikasa, Oneida, Royal Doulton, What On Earth, Levi's By Design, Corning/Revere, American Tourister, Wallet Works, Ribbon Outlet, Book Warehouse and others. Aurora Farms features many special events throughout the year including sidewalk sales (which offer greater savings), arts and crafts festivals and classic car shows. Aurora Farms is close to Sea World and the Geauga Lake Theme Park, four miles north of Ohio Turnpike exit 13. It is about 2 1/2 hours from Columbus. M-W 10-6, Th-Sat 10-9, Sun 10-5.

AVALON
1434 N. High St., Columbus, 43201, 294-9722

This vintage clothing store seasonally features beaded sweaters from the 1950's, in addition to cocktail dresses, shoes, hats, sweaters and other wearables. It specializes in used denims at about $18, regularly $45 if new. The vintage sportcoats from the 1960's are an exceptionally good buy at $20. The inventory is a combination of military surplus, used and vintage items as well as sportswear and accessories. This fun, energizing atmosphere is sure to please men and women alike. A large portion of the merchandise is unused, although vintage, as a result of being warehoused for many years. You'll find fairly priced, unique wearables in top shape. M-F 10-8, Sat 11-7, Sun 12-5.

B-WEAR SPORTSWEAR OUTLETS
5891 Brice Outlet Mallway, Columbus, 43232, 864-6677
200 Sunrise Center, Zanesville, 454-8453
711 S. 30 St., P.O. Box 9047, Indian Mound Mall, Heath, 522-3572
1635 River Valley Circle S., P.O. Box 5073, River Valley Mall, Lancaster, 654-0069
3575 Maple Avenue, Colony Sq. Mall, Zanesville, 454-7770

Manufacturer and embroiderer of fleecewear and cotton/polyester wearables such as sweatshirts, tee shirts, sweaters, pants, skirts and infant apparel can save you at least 50% off their better quality products. The stock consists of mostly first quality discontinued and overstocked garments from their B-Wear stores with some seconds also available. The company produces items for major league sport teams, colleges, Disney, the Limited, Nutmeg, Coca Cola, Velva Sheen, Champion, Bike Athletic, Galt Sand, Rough Hewn and others. You'll find beautifully embroidered garments with sayings for various professions, heartwarming statements, floral designs, seasonal motifs, sport designs and other patterns for men, women and children. The Zanesville site also offers free factory tours and a larger selection of seconds. The businesses are among my personal favorites. Mall location hours are M-Sat 10-9, Sun 12-5. Zanesville hours vary.

BABE DISCOVERY SHOP
1198 Kenny Center, Columbus, 43220, 457-4227

This resale shop is operated by volunteers of the American Cancer Society and features upscale and designer women's apparel, accessories, bric-a-brac and furniture. You'll find casual, business, sport and dressy items, all of which have been donated to the society. There's a full range of sizes up to 18 and occasionally larger sizes too. You'll see such brands as Liz Claiborne, Jones New York, Escada, Saks Fifth Avenue, Castleberry and others. This shop does not accept consignments. All profits benefit the Cancer Society. Tu-Sat 10-5.

BABY SUPERSTORE
2744 Brice Rd., Reynoldsburg, 43068, 577-1950
3610 W. Dublin Granville Rd., Columbus, 43235, 799-2229
Morse Rd. location to open in 1997

Nursery furniture, toys, clothes and related children's accessories are found in these enormous stores. The first quality merchandise consists of moderate to better quality stock at savings of 10-25%, but the best deals are on the children's furniture. M-Sat 10-9, Sun 12-6.

BARGAIN BOUTIQUE
107 N. Columbus Street, Lancaster, 43130, No phone

Current season and style apparel for men, women and children, can be found at this consignment shop. Careful searching can unearth some treasures. Merchandise is gently used and everything must be pressed before it is accepted. The stock includes budget to designer goods. Some brands offered include Oshkosh, Guess, Abe Schrader, Liz

Claiborne, Chaus and others. Dresses are priced at $3-$21, wool suits at $18-$35, blouses at $1.50-$9. You'll also find some household items, lamps, accessories and bric-a-brac. Proceeds from the store support the Lancaster-Fairfield Hospital emergency room. The store will be closed from about December 13-January 5. Accepts cash only. Hours are W-Sat 10-1.

BEAR-A-FAIR
914 Adair Ave., Zanesville, 43701, 455-2741

You'll find quality resale children's clothing in sizes infant to 16, most of which is gently used. The stock is fairly priced, with two piece sets selling for about $6, sweaters in the $3-$5 range and pants for about $4-$6. Tu/W/F/Sat 12-5, Th 12-7.

BEARLY WORN CLOTHES
557 Hill Rd. N., Pickerington 43147, 833-0909

Quality resale clothing for children in sizes newborn to 14, plus toys and related accessories such as car seats, are offered at savings of 50-75% less than if you were to purchase these new. The savings depend on whether the merchandise is slightly used or never worn. Some of the brands the store carries include Martha Miniatures, Brian Dresses, Health-Tex and Oshkosh. This shop also sells better women's and maternity apparel. Grandmothers can obtain a free "grandmother's discount card" which entitles them to a 10% discount off all purchases. M-Sat 10-5, Sun 1-5.

BETTER CLOTHES AND BARGAINS
9226 Dublin Rd., Powell, 43065, 889-1520

Men's and women's upscale and designer clothing, jewelry and related accessories are available in this boutique. You'll find current season, new merchandise at 30% off manufacturers' suggested retail prices and gently used consigned items at least 50% below "if new" prices. The new stock consists of salesmen's samples and special purchases. Brands carried include Evan Picone, Char, Phoebe, Datiani, Semplice and Anne Klein in the women's area; Polo, Ashworth, Hilfiger, Dockers, Segna and Armani in the men's department. The store, Again for Men, moved into this store and dropped its name. This business is one of my personal favorites. Tu-Sat 10-6, Sun 12-4. Accepts checks and cash only.

BEXLEY CANCER THRIFT SHOP
911 S. James Road, Columbus, 43227, 237-5353

Profits from the sale of merchandise from this shop, benefit the local chapter of the American Cancer Society. The stock consists of gently used men's, women's, and children's apparel, accessories, small gifts and household items. While the stock is a mixture of contemporary, traditional and outdated styles, the careful shopper will instantly recognize those better and designer goods by Liz, Tony Lambert, Talbotts etc. The shop accepts donations and consignments. Prices are lower than the trendy resale shops in other parts of town. Tu-F 12:30-4, Sat 10-4.

BLACKHAWK GOLF PRO SHOP
8830 Dustin Rd., Galena, 43081, 965-1042

Save 20% on men's and women's golf clothes, shoes, clubs and accessories. You'll find all popular brands such as Wilson, Cobra, Lynx, Ashworth, Izod Club, Titleist and Ping. The store is open daily during the season from 7a.m. to dusk, but may close early due to inclement weather. The store participates in a large sale in November with several other similar shops. The clearance sale is called The Ultimate Garage Sale. See the special sales and events chapter in this book for a description. It's best to call ahead. Closed January and February.

BLOOMERDALE'S
7191 E. Broad St., Reynoldsburg, 43068, 575-1983

The shop sells gently used, upscale children's, women's and maternity apparel at savings of 40-70% off "if new" prices. Toys and related accessories are available at similar savings. You'll find such brands as Popsickle, Her Majesty, Calvin Klein, Liz Kids, The Limited, Liz Claiborne and others. M-Th 10-6, F 10-5, Sat 11-5.

BOBBI GEE
1733 N. Memorial Dr., Lancaster, 43130, 653-3727
2984 Derr Rd., Springfield, 45503, (513) 390-6188

First quality overstocks in men's and women's contemporary apparel, are available at savings of 20-40% off manufacturers' suggested retail prices. You'll find moderate to better quality casual and career wear by such brands as L'eau Vive, Gitano, L.A. Gear and Palmettos. Men's wear is priced at $26.97 and under and women's wear is priced at $24.97 and under. The stores also offer a small selection of women's accessories. M-Sat 10-9, Sun 12-5.

BON WORTH OUTLET
5810Brice Oulet Mallway, Columbus, 43232, 575-1032

Sizes from 6-46 can be found at this outlet whose factory is in Hendersonville, North Carolina. Mix and match separates in traditional and basic styles are available at savings of 30-40% lower than comparable quality merchandise from other manufacturers. You'll also find children's clothing at comparable savings. The store is owned and operated by the manufacturer. The inventory bears the Bon Worth label and is not sold at unaffiliated businesses. M-Sat 10-9, Sun 12-5.

BRICE OUTLET MALL
5891 Scarborough Blvd., Columbus, 43232, 863-0884

Find thirty stores, most of which featuring value prices on a wide range of products. Some of the businesses include Bonworth, Ten Below, B-Wear, Ninth Street Wedding and Formal Outlet, Shoe Sensation, Video Trader, Famous Footwear, Publisher's Outlet, Sears Outlet, Ben Franklin Crafts and others. M-Sat 10-9, Sun 12-6.

BRIDAL EXPRESS (WEDDING PLANTATION ANNEX)
5055 E. Main St., Columbus, 43213, 868-5817

This is a clearance center for the Wedding plantation (see listing in this chapter). Save about 30-50% off wedding gowns which are purchased off the rack, as this store does not provide special order options. You'll find such brands as Jasmine, Alfred Angelo and others, which are largely discontinued styles. You'll also find traditional and contemporary styles of long and short formal wear at comparable savings. M-W 2-8, F/Sat 11-5.

BURLINGTON COAT FACTORY WAREHOUSE
270 Graceland Blvd., Columbus 43214, 885-2628
6426 Tussing Rd., Consumer Sq. E., Reynoldsburg, 43068, 863-3791

Find current, first quality casual, sport and career wear for men, women and children at savings of 20-40% off regular retail prices. Petite, regular and large sizes are available by nationally recognized moderate to designer quality brands such as Carole Little, J.H. Collectibles, Pierre Cardin and Ocean Pacific. Purses, hosiery, lingerie, fashion jewelry and shoes are also available. The shoe department is operated by Capezio and is only found at the Graceland site. The linen department sells towels, comforters, sheets, bathroom accessories and pillows at savings of 20-70% off suggested retail prices. Nationally recognized brands are featured. The Graceland location has a baby room which stocks quality furniture, clothes, accessories and carriages by all popular brands such as Fisher-Price, Graco, Gerry Century and others. Savings are 10-40% off regular retail prices. M-Sat 10-9:30, Sun 11-6.

CASUAL MALE BIG AND TALL
7617 New Market Centerway, Columbus, 43235, 764-9165
3659 W. Broad St., Columbus, 43228, 272-1881
2579 S. Hamilton Rd., Columbus, 43222, 861-9484

Save 20-40% off casual slacks, shirts and shorts for large and tall men. The contemporary clothes are found in sizes 1x-4x, 17 1/2-22 and 40-60. M-Sat 10-9, Sun 12-5.

CATHERINE'S
1055 N. Bechtel Ave., Springfield, 45504, (513) 323-4676

This business is a cousin to P.S. Fashions mentioned elsewhere in this book. See the description as the merchandise is the same. M-F 10-9, Sat 10-6, Sun 12-5.

CLOTHING WAREHOUSE
2609 E. Main St., Springfield, 45502, (513) 323-2943

First quality, moderate to designer quality women's apparel by Skyr, Gordon of Philadelphia, Act I, Breckinridge, Albert Nippon, Maggy Boutique, Joanie Char, David Warren and others is available in sizes 6-44. You'll find casual and formal wear as samples, overstocks and special purchases from salesmen, manufacturers and boutiques. Men's wear by Austin Reed, London Fog etc. are also available. Occasionally, children's clothing can be found as well. Savings are 20-60% off regular retail prices. The inventory is priced at $15-$80 with most being under $50. You will find simple polyester garments to high fashion exclusive boutique items. Look throughout the whole store as this business initially gives the appearance of offering only traditional styles. This store used to have a branch on Hoover Road in Grove City. M-F 10-6, Sat 10-5.

CUPID'S BRIDAL GALLERY
360 Morrison Rd., Gahanna, 43230, 866-4389

Check out the extensive selection of quality bridal, formalwear and prom dresses at savings of 10-30% off manufacturer's list prices. The front room contains samples and overstocks at about $39.99 with values to $175. An area in the back room also has a selection of 50% off dresses and 30% off veils. The store carries sizes 2-44 plus a few flower girl dresses. Brands carried include Alyssa, Alfred Angelo and Moonlight. Invitations are available at a 20% savings. M/W 1-8, F 1-7, Sat 11-5.

DAN HOWARD'S MATERNITY FACTORY OUTLET
6622 Sawmill Rd., Columbus, 43235, 766-1255

Quality contemporary maternity wear is available at savings of 20-50% off manufacturer's suggested retail prices and comparable prices for similar merchandise in other stores. This factory direct business operates 90 stores throughout the country and sells 80% of their stock as merchandise which was made in their factories, and 20% of their stock as private label goods made by other manufacturers for these stores. All of the inventory bears the Dan Howard Maternity label. The stock is available in sizes 4-20 and includes casual and career wear, lingerie and bathingsuits. M/Tu/F/Sat 10-6, W/Th 10-9, Sun 12-5.

DAVID'S BRIDAL FOR BETTER AND FOR LESS
6666 Sawmill Rd., Columbus, 43235, 798-8906

America's largest discount bridal superstore can save you 30-50% and more on wedding gowns, formals, bridesmaid and mother of the bride gowns. Merchandise is sold off the racks, with no special orders available. The price tags don't show a "compare to" or manufacturer's suggested retail price, so it may be confusing to consumers on how much you're really saving. The store sells such brands as Gloria Vanderbilt, Oleg Cassini and Ted Lapidus. Carries sizes 4-26. Save 20% off headpieces, jewelry, shoes, gloves, hose and foundations. Check out the special January and July events in which a large selection of gowns are priced at $99 each. M-Sat 10-9, Sun 11-5.

DEJA VU AND KING SHOES
11 N. State St., Westerville, 43081, 890-1150

Quality branded women's clothing up to size 22 is offered here at savings of 30-70% below "if new" prices. This consignment shop offers fashions from Dawn Joy, JH Collectibles, Halston, Mariea Kim, Liz Claiborne, Calvin Klein and others. Introduce yourself to owner, Erlene. She's a gracious and friendly soul. The store also stocks new shoes. M-F 10-6, Sat 10-5.

DIRTY CHIN'S MOTORWEAR
14 N. State St.(rear), Westerville, 43081, 882-0740

New, used and consigned leather goods, apparel, motorcycle parts and related items (luggage racks, tourpaks) are sold at 25-60% less than "if new". You'll also find some motorcycle related artwork and gifts at fair prices. The owner, Dirty Chin, is a cat, from whom the store derived its name and concept. M-F 11-7, Sat 10-5.

DOTS
1733 N. Memorial, Lancaster, 43130, 653-3727
613 Hebron Rd., South Gate Shpng. Ctr., Heath, 43056, 522-4488

Junior, missy and plus sized women's apparel is sold at $10 and under. The stock consists of first quality overstocks of budget to moderate quality casual and dressy wear in addition to lingerie and accessories. M-Sat 10-9, Sun 12-5.

DRESS BARN/DRESS BARN WOMAN
7624 New Market Center Way, Columbus, 43235, 764-0557
5610 Cleveland Ave., Columbus, 43231, 882-5533
6464 Tussing Ave., Reynoldsburg, 43068, 863-0041
759 Bethel Rd., Columbus, 43214, 538-0538
17 S. High St., Columbus, 43215, 228-1690

Save 20-50% off current, first quality fashion merchandise by such popular manufacturers as Jonathan Martin, Dawn Joy, Carole Little, Liz Claiborne, Jennifer Reed and others. The fashion conscious larger woman, who wears size 14-24, will be pleased with the similar selection of fashion conscious items. You will find moderate to better quality career and casual attire in addition to accessories. Ask about the free in store wardrobe seminars. M-Sat 10-9, Sun 12-5.

ECLECTIC FASHION ALTERNATIVES
3139 N. High St., Columbus, 43202, 267-2900
47 W. Fifth Avenue, Columbus, 43201, 421-9990

Upscale men's consignment shop sells Hickey Freeman, Joseph Abboud, Perry Ellis, Ralph Lauren, Donna Karan, Tino Cosma, Cole-Hahn, Barry Bricken, Armani, Boss, Ferre, Corneliani and other quality brands of contemporary suits, slacks, sportswear, shirts, shoes, sweaters and silk ties. There is also a large selection of European Designer merchandise. The regular price on the merchandise would be about $50-$1,000, but here, the prices are about $13-$300, saving you about 30-60%. The Fifth Avenue site shares space with a tailor, formerly from Jacobson's. The store also stocks new salesmen's samples and off price goods at similar savings. The merchandise is in top shape and the decor is simplistic chic. M-Sat 11-6 (Fifth Avenue is not open Monday).

EDDIE BAUER SALVAGE SALES
4545 Fisher Rd., Columbus, 43228, 278-9281

Get those bargain hunting antennas cleaned and fully extended to embark on a thrill that only the adventurous can appreciate. The Salvage Sales are held six to eight times per year, generally at the Fisher Road site, which is adjacent to the warehouse outlet, and feature seconds, customer returns, previously worn merchandise (which might not have measured up to the customers' expectations), those which are slightly soiled or in need of repair (holes, rips, unraveling fabric, missing buttons). By checking the pockets or looking for a sticker on the items, you'll generally be able to determine the nature of the damage or problem. Stuff your finds into the large bag you'll be given as you enter and drag it around with you or fling it over your shoulder like a hobo if it's not too heavy. Merchandise is not arranged by style nor size, so you'll have to rummage through boxes of stuff to locate what you want. Prices are 70% and more off their regular prices and include: purses $2, leather boots $15, unlined coats $8, sweaters $4, dresses $8, umbrellas $1, leather briefcases $10, beach towels $2, sheets $4 etc. As if this weren't cheap enough, on the third or fourth day of these four day sales, prices are generally dropped to $1 per item! The sales include men's and women's clothing to size XXL. The Eddie Bauer Salvage Sale is one of my personal favorites. Th-Sun 11-6 during scheduled sales.

EDDIE BAUER WAREHOUSE OUTLET
4545 Fisher Rd., Columbus, 43228, 278-9281

Save 50% off the ticket price on first quality men's and women's clothing, shoes, accessories, gifts and linens. The better merchandise consists of overstocks and discontinued items from the catalogue and retail stores. Frequent sales drop the prices even lower so you save up to 70%. The merchandise is well organized on racks and shelves. The company also features salvage sales (see listing above), occasional sales of larger home furnishings (sometimes at a different site) and at least one large winter sale at Veteran's Memorial Auditorium (see listing at the back of the book under the special sales chapter). M-F 10-7, Sat 10-6, Sun 12-5.

FABULOUS FINDS
206 Graceland Blvd., Columbus, 43214, 436-1870

This upscale consignment/donated items store operates in cooperation with the Alzheimer's Association and gives 50% of the proceeds of donated merchandise to the association. You'll find designer as well as moderate and better quality merchandise including small bric-a-brac, furniture and jewelry. Wedding and special occasion dresses are available for rental from the inventory at a cost of about $25. M-Sat 11-6.

FAMOUS SPORTSWEAR
2060 Hardy Pkwy., Grove City, 43123, 875-8180
Great Western Shopping Center, Wilson Rd., Columbus, 43228, 275-0211

Overstocks, misprints and erroneously colored designs are sold by this factory outlet which is in the custom screen printing business. You'll find college, fraternity and business logos, as well as decorative designs emblazened on windbreakers, tee shirts, sweatshirts, caps and anything which is printable. There are items for men, women and children. Savings are 30-60% off the price of comparable products. In mid September, the business features a gigantic, two day tent sale at the Grove City location. You should note that some of these items are not generally offered for sale through typical retail operations. The stores are among my personal favorites. Grove City is open M-F 9-5. Wilson Road is open Tu-F 11-7, Sat 10-6, Sun 11-5.

FEZZ
1488 Grandview Avenue, Columbus, 43212, 488-5640

By 20% over wholesale costs on a unique line of hand loomed, free spirited gauze separates and classic silk and wool garments. You'll remember their merchandise from a former location in the Continent called Tangos. This business sells its merchandise to upscale boutiques across the country. M-Th 11-5, F 11-6, Sat 10-2.

FREE STORE
S. United Methodist Church, 181 E. Morrill Ave., Columbus, 43207, 443-3458

Free clothing is available to low income families (no qualifying data is needed). Although you may not visit more than once a week, you can select those items you would like to take home. Items are in various stages of wear and include dated and contemporary styles as well as budget to better quality. Look carefully to unearth some treasures. M 6p.m.-8p.m., W 1-3, Sat 10-12.

G.I. DEPOT
1377 Logan Lancaster Rd., Lancaster, 43130, 654-9563

New, used and surplus military merchandise is available including 100% wool blankets for $19, military soap for fifteen cents, adult/children's camouflage and military designed clothing plus related items. Most of the stock is very value priced and there are also some very unusual items which would make great conversation pieces. M-Sat 10-8, Sun 12-5.

GENERAL MERCHANDISE SALES
13690 E. Broad St., Pataskala, 43062, 927-7073

6,000 square feet of surplus military type goods includes coveralls, heavy duty socks, sleeping bags, mess kits, books and what-not. The new and used quality merchandise is available at savings of about 10-40% off comparable retail prices. M-Sat 10-7, Sun 12-5.

GENTRY SHOPS
1000 Morse Rd., Gentry Plaza, Columbus 43229, 436-2288

Gentlemen in all shapes and sizes can save 30-50% off dress and sport attire and accessories in popular and designer brands. Suits, ties, belts, socks, sweaters, shirts and jackets are offered in sizes up to 52 and include regular, short, long, extra long, big man and athletic cuts. Tailors are on premises who offer prompt alterations at a nominal cost. This off-priced retailer buys tail end inventory from manufacturers, which is a small amount of merchandise considered to be remaining stock that hasn't been sold to other stores. M-Sat 10-9:30, Sun 12-6.

GOODWILL THRIFT STORE
291 E. Leffel Lane, Springfield, (513) 324-8638
340 W. Fairgrounds, Marion, 387-7023
1609 Marion Mt. Gilead Rd., Marion, 389-3396
55 S. 5th St., Newark, 349-3887

Find clothing for the family, bric-a-brac and some furniture at rock bottom prices. Most items are pruced at under $5. While quality varies from budget to better, and styles run the range of vintage to updated, the careful shopper can always find a good deal on brand name items. Check your purchase carefully. Hours vary by store.

GRANDMA'S ODDS AND ENDS
409 S. Maple St., Lancaster, no phone

This shop features bric-a-brac, toys and some children's clothes by Health-tex and other brands at garage sale prices. While the quality varies from budget to some better goods, the careful shopper will enjoy rummaging in this no-frills shop where most items are priced at $3 and under. Tu-Sat 10-5.

GROVE CITY THRIFT SHOP
3684 Garden Ct., Grove City, 43123, 871-1126

Check out the spacious new location for this shop which benefits the American Cancer Society. The store accepts consignments and donations of family clothing, gifts, housewares, toys, collectibles and small furniture. Quality varies from budget to better, so check the racks and shelves carefully for some great deals to benefit a great cause. Tu-F 12-4, Sat 10-3.

GUYS AND DOLLS
2610 Hilliard-Rome Rd., Hilliard, 43026, 529-1169

Kids' resale shop offers clothes, toys, dancewear and related accessories in sizes infant to 14. The upscale merchandise is gently used and offers savings of 40-60% off "if new" prices. You'll find all popular brands including Oshkosh, Guess, Health-Tex, Fisher-Price and others. M-Sat 10-6.

HIT OR MISS
2025 Henderson Rd., Columbus, 43220, 451-0628
7648 New Market Center Way, Columbus, 43235, 766-0981
2707 Northland Plaza Dr., Columbus, 43229, 523-1786
3872 E. Broad St., Town and Country Shpg,. Ctr., Columbus, 43213, 237-8090

Moderate to better quality missy, junior and petite fashions are available at savings of 20-50% off regular retail prices. You'll find such brands as Dawn Joy, Kasper, Jonathan Martin, Leau Vive, Nilani and others. Accessories are similarly discounted. The store stocks casual and career wear. M-Sat 10-9, Sun 12-5.

HUNTINGTON CLOTHIERS / REAR DOOR CLEARANCE STORE
1285 Alum Creek Dr., Columbus, 43209, 252-4422

Traditional styling in quality men's apparel, is available at this retail store and mail order outlet. Dress shirts, suits, ties, trousers, sweaters, belts, outerwear as well as formal wear and related items, are available in such sought after fabrics as Oxford cloth and Pinpoint Oxford in 100% cotton and 60/40 blends, Egyptian cotton broadcloth, worsted wool blends, wool gabardine, silk, camel hair, alpaca, shetlands, Belgian linen and silk/wool blends. The store carries such brands as Ruff Hewn, Boston Traders and Huntington Clothiers. Savings are about 15-45% on first quality goods. The Rear Door Clearance Store is in an adjacent warehouse where savings are up to 90%. The merchandise there consists of overstocks, overruns, irregular and second quality goods. Call to be added to their mailing list. Store hours are only Sat 10-2.

IN REVIEW THRIFT STORE
4768 N. High Street, Columbus, 43214, 261-7377

This store operates on behalf of Birthright, an organization which offers free pregnancy tests and counseling. The store sells apparel for the family, accessories, toys and some housewares,. The stock is an eclectic mixture of out of date merchandise, vintage and upscale contemporary fashions. Prices are rock bottom with sweaters in the $2-$6 range, two piece pant sets in the $8-$12 range and other stock in similar price ranges. Accepts consignments and donated merchandise. Tu-F 10-4, Sat 12-3.

IT'S MY TURN
4610 N. High St., Columbus, 43214, 267-2810

This upscale men's and women's consignment shop offers gently used clothing, outerwear, shoes, costume jewelry and purses at savings of 40-70% off "if new" prices. Ralph Lauren, Lillie Rubin, Nippon, Evan Picone, Hart Schaffner and Marx, Structure, Liz Claiborne and other brands grace the racks. The store stocks sizes 4-18 in women's wear (including petites), men's sizes are medium and up. You'll find casual, business and formal wear. Tu-Sat 10-5.

J.C. PENNEY OUTLET
2361 Park Crescent Dr., E., Columbus, 43232, 868-0250

Customer returns, overstocks and past season merchandise from the stores and catalogues are available at savings of 20-80%. You will find furniture, shoes, clothes for the family (including chubby, husky, petite, tall and large sizes in additional to bridal and formal wear), linens, sporting goods, lingerie and gift items. The back corner of the store features an area of customer returns which offer the greatest savings. The J.C. Penney Outlet is the top tourist attraction in Ohio! M-Sat 9-9, Sun 10-6.

JEFFERSONVILLE OUTLET CENTER
1100 McArthur Rd., Jeffersonville, 426-6991

On my recent visit, I saw over seventy stores such as Spiegel, The Clearinghouse-Saks Fifth Avenue, Evan Picone, J.H. Collectibles, Oshkosh B'gosh, Carters, Harve Benard, Liz Claiborne (also sells Villager), John Henry and Friends, Mikasa, Lenox, Fragile Outlet, Van Heusen, Nine West, Pepperidge Farm, Maidenform, Adolfo II, Bass Shoes, Cape Isle Knitters, Leather Loft, Jones New York, Chaus, Champion Hanes, Carter's, Colors and Scents, Corning/Revere, Crazy Horse, Perfumania, Creme De La Creme, Hoover, Dan River, National Book Warehouse, Sara Lee Bakery, Geoffrey Beene and others. M-Sat 10-9, Sun 12-6.

JILLIAN'S BRIDAL AND TUXEDO
24 S. Main St., London, 43140, 852-5086

New wedding gowns are discounted 20% and include a free headpiece. You can save 30-40% on a purchase of previously rented formal wear for proms and pageants, priced in the $75-$130 range. The store carries moderate to better quality items such as Zum Zum, Jessica McClintock and 1001 Nights. M-Th 10:30-7, F 10:30-4:30, Sat 9-3:30.

KATHRYN'S
1247 N. High St., Columbus, 43201, 299-7923

Sells mostly vintage wedding gowns from the 1800's to the 1960's, vintage formalwear and other used more contemporary wedding gowns. Prices range from $175 to about $400, with values up to $2,000. Consignments are welcome. Sat 12-5 or by appointment.

KIDS AND MOMS AGAIN
1207 Delaware Ave., Marion, 382-4930

Find gently used children's and maternity clothes plus toys and related items at savings of 40-70% off "if new" prices. Quality varies from moderate to better, but the careful shopper can find some good deals on popular brands such as Oshkosh, Health-Tex, Guess, Mothercare, Fisher Price and others. M-F 10-8, Sat 10-6.

KID'S CHOICE AND ALTERATIONS BY GOSIA
7410 E. Main St., Reynoldsburg, 43068, 866-7416

Gently used children's clothes (newborn to size 5), toys and some furniture are available at this resale shop. Savings are 35-60% less than "if new". The store also operates an alterations business for men's and women's apparel. M/Tu/Th/F 10-5, Sat 10-6.

KIDS KASTLE
5480 Roberts Rd., Hilliard, 43026, 529-1170

Children's and maternity resale shop features gently used, quality clothes, toys and accessories at savings of 30-60% off "if new" prices. The store has recently begun to stock used men's and women's apparel at similar savings. M-F 10-6, Sat 12-6.

KIDS R US
4360 W. Broad St., Columbus, 43228, 274-7766
1700 Morse Rd., Columbus 43229, 841-1600
2560 S. Hamilton Rd., Columbus, 43232, 759-9422
6525 Sawmill Rd., Dublin, 43017, 793-0405

The world's largest clothing store for kids features sizes newborn to 20 in regular, chubby and husky sizes. First quality, name brands such as Hanes, Levi's, Bugle Boy, Health-Tex, Oshkosh, Ocean Pacific, French Toast, Le Tigre, Justin Charles and others are offered at savings of 20-50% off suggested retail prices. Don't overlook their socks, hairclips, backpacks and other necessities at similar savings. M-Sat 10-9, Sun 10:30-5.

KINDERDUDS
843 1/2 E. Fifth Ave., Marysville, 43040, (513) 644-3264

Gently used maternity, women's and children's apparel, plus toys, furniture, video games and related accessories are available at savings of 30-80% off "if new" prices. The stock consists of moderate to better quality items and includes such brands as Polly Flinders, OshKosh, Guess, Buster Brown and others. Tu-Sat 10-6.

KOENIG SPORTS
50 Westerville Sq., Westerville, 43081, 523-3700

The Westerville location of this chain has a very large clearance area offering past season, "as is" and discontinued apparel, sneakers and related sports items. The stock is mostly fromthe Westerville site, but other Koenig stores also ship merchandise to the clearance center here too. Popular brands are offered at savings of 25-60%. M-Sat 10-9, Sun 12-6.

KUPPENHEIMER
2886 S. Hamilton Rd., Columbus, 43232, 864-4122
2203 Morse Rd., Columbus, 43229, 471-7677
6238 Sawmill Rd., Dublin, 43017, 793-9901

You can find quality men's suits, slacks and sport coats here in all fabrics ranging from wools, wool blends, poplin, silk blends and more. Savings are about 20% less than what you would expect to pay for a comparable product elsewhere. The Kuppenheimer label only appears in retail stores bearing its name. However, the company has designed and manufactured career apparel for Delta Airlines, the Shriners and Realtors. Offers rock bottom prices on alterations of garments purchased in their stores. Or, you can bring in your clothes from another store and let them alter it for you. If you choose this latter option, you will pay double the alteration price, which is still about 20% lower than having the alteration done elsewhere (Hemming men's pants costs $7.50, $15 to shorten a pair of jacket sleves). M-F 10-9, Sat 9-9, Sun 12-5.

LABEL CONNECTION
988 N. High St., Columbus, 43201, 294-8890

This women's upscale/designer consignment shop sells such brands as Liz Claiborne, Carole Little, Nicole Miller, Donna Karan, Lillie Rubin, Escada, Ann Klein, Spitalnik and others. You'll find casual, sport, dressy and business apparel and accessories for discriminating tastes. This store also sells new merchandise which was purchased as overstocks and closeouts. M-F 11-6, Sat 11-5.

LAUREN'S 2X NICE
3538 Broadway, Grove City, 43123, 875-9543

Upscale consignment shop for children's clothes in sizes newborn to 14, plus toys and accessories. You'll find Brian, Polly Flinders, Oshkosh, Health Tex and other brands at savings of 40-60% off "if new" prices. M-Sat 9-7.

LAZY J WESTERN WEAR
5055 State Rt. 29, West Jefferson, 879-7079

This wholesale/retail business has a full line of western square dance and two step apparel at savings of 30-60% off manufacturer's suggested retail prices. The stock consists of first quality buyouts and salesmen's samples for men, women and children, with sizes up to 4X. You'll find bolos, hats, jewelry, pants, blazers, western shirts, blouses, skirts and more. There is even a clearance room where savings are a bit higher. Even if you're not into square dancing there might be a few funky looking items which might interest you. M/Tu/W/Sat 10-6, Th/F 10-8.

LIL RASCALS RESALE
46 E. Main St., West Jefferson, 879-5437

Gently used children's clothing, toys and accessories are available at this upscale resale shop. You'll find such brands as Polly Flinders, Oshkosh, Weathertamer, Polo, The Gap Too and others at very reasonable prices. Tee shirts and pants are in the $2-$6 range, dresses are about $4-$10, overcoats are about $5-$20. W/F/Sat 9-3, Th 12-7.

LITTLE PEOPLE-WEAR IT AGAIN
2400 Thompson St., Columbus, 43235, 764-2500

This small shop offers big savings for small people. You'll find gently used clothing, toys and accessories at savings of 35-60% off "if new" prices. M-F 8:30-5:30.

M & H SCREENPRINTING
1486 Hebron Rd., Heath, 43056, 522-1957

Save on overstocks of first quality imprinted sweatshirts and tee shirts, many with university logos, from across form the country. Kid's sweats are $8 and adults are $10 with values up to $35. Blank tee shirts are also available and can be imprinted. All sizes are available from toddler to adult XXL. M-F 10-6, Sat 10-4.

MJR WEEKEND WAREHOUSE
2350 International St., Columbus, 43228, 529-9075

Sales are generally held once per month, but may be more often as inventory levels dictate. The stock consists of mostly upscale merchandise by such brands as the Limited, Victoria's Secret etc. Prices vary from sale to sale, but are generally $15 for dresses with values up to $140, sweaters are $5-$10 with values up to $75, leather jackets $75 with values up to $399, blazers are $25 with values up to $170. Accessories such as jewelry, shoes, lingerie and belts are available for $2-$10. Some children's wear is also available. The stock consists mostly of first quality goods, with some irregulars and seconds mixed in. Check your intended purchases carefully. The sale is one of my personal favorites. F 8-8, Sat 8:30-5 during sale periods only.

MARSHALLS
805 Bethel Rd, Columbus, 43214, 451-5486
2300 S. Hamilton Rd., Columbus, 43232, 863-0189
2681 Northland Plaza, Columbus, 43231, 794-1017

The inventory consists largely of manufacturer's overruns and special purchases of men's, women's and children's apparel and accessories, shoes for the family, linens, designer fragrances for men and women, giftware, framed art work, lingerie and leather goods at savings of 20-60% off regular retail prices. You'll find missy, junior, petite, large and pre-teen sizes. Moderate to designer quality can be found in such brands as Chaus, Diane Von Furstenburg, John Henry, Liz Claiborne, Adolfo, Polo, Jasmine, 9 West, Bass, Stacy Adams, Bugle Boy and others. While most of the inventory is first quality, the irregulars are clearly marked. M-Sat 9:30-9:30, Sun 11-6.

MEN'S WEARHOUSE
3862 Morse Rd., Columbus, 43229, 475-5580

Better men's discounter features suits, tuxedos and business casual wear. You'll also find related accessories including shoes, belts and tires. The first quality, in season merchandise consists of private label and better popular brands at savings of 20-30%. There's a full range of sizes in big and tall men's offerings. The store offers free pressing of your garments at any time after purchase and free alterations if you outgrow your purchase or lose weight. M-Sat 10-9, Sun 12-6.

MONA LISA
55 S. High St., Dublin, 43017, 764-0509

Gently used women's apparel and accessories are available at savings of 50-80% off "if new" prices. This consignment shop sells upscale and designer merchandise in sizes 4-18, by such popular brands as Liz Claiborne and Nilani. You will also find a small selection of bric-a-brac at similar savings. Tu 10:30-7, M/W-Sat 10:30-5. Accepts checks and cash only.

MY SISTER'S CLOSET
526 Market St., Zanesville, 450-2011

Find men's, women's and children's gently used clothes plus toys, accessories and bric-a-brac. Prices are about 40-60% less than "if new". The store stocks popular brands of casual and dressy items including Liz Claiborne, Oshkosh and Dockers. M-Sat 10-5.

NEARLY NEW
923 W. Main St., Springfield, (513) 323-9345

This shop accepts donations and consignments of used items, with proceeds benefiting the Springview Hospital, Planned Parenthood and the Red Cross. You'll find clothes for the entire family, bric-a-brac and miscellaneous items. The quality ranges from budget to better and consists of gently used and some comfortably worn merchandise. Look closely and you'll discover famous brands at a fraction of their new cost. Tu-F 10-2, Sat 11-1.

NEARLY NEW SHOP
3894 E. Broad St., Columbus, 43213, 231-7861

Visit their new, larger location at the Town and Country Shopping Center. This nonprofit resale shop offers clothing, books, toys and housewares at savings of 60-80% off "if new" prices. While the inventory is a mixture of quality, the careful shopper will not overlook an inch of this store. On a recent visit, I spotted a curly lamb jacket for $40, a genuine Gucci cosmetic bag and a Polo shirt for $5 each. Tu-Sat 10-5.

$9.99 STOCKROOM
4393 Westland Mall, Columbus, 43228, 351-9449

The majority of the missy and junior clothes are priced at $9.99 with values to $32, a savings of about 20-60% off regular retail prices. The merchandise is first quality, contemporary casualwear and related separates. M-Sat 10-9, Sun 12-5.

NINTH STREET WEDDING AND FORMAL OUTLET
5843 Scarborough Mallway, Columbus, 43232, 863-1010

Moderate to better quality bridal gowns, prom dresses, veils, formal and special occasion wear are offered at savings of 40-60% off regular retail prices. The inventory consists of manufacturers' closeouts, showroom samples and store buyouts in sizes 6-22 1/2. Some petite garments are also available. Brands offered include Priscilla, Alfred Angelo, Milady and Piccione. M-Sat 10-9, Sun 12-6.

NORTH AMERICAN KNITTING COMPANY
490 Dewey Ave., Mansfield, 44901, (419) 524-1112

Upscale and designer knitted women's clothing are available at this manufacturer's outlet. The company creates merchandise for Castleberry, Pendleton, Andrea Jovine and other quality brands. The stock consists of first quality, samples, prior season, irregular and seconds in sizes 4-20. Some petite sizes are also offered. Savings are 50% and more off regular retail prices. Professional alterations are also available. While men are not permitted in the store, they may wait at the cafeteria in the building. Free factory tours are offered at 12:30 on Tuesdays and Thursdays. U.P.S. delivery and phone orders are also available. The outlet is open Tuesdays and Thursdays from 12-5, and one Saturday per month from 10-2, April, May, September and October. Special clearance sales, offering even greater savings, are held in June and November at which time, hours will vary. Write or call the company to be added to their mailing list as the sales are by invitation. Accepts cash and checks only.

NU LOOK FACTORY OUTLET
5080 Sinclair Rd., Columbus, 43229, 885-4936

This manufacturer owned and operated store sells first quality men's suits, sportcoats, slacks and shoes at savings of about 30-50% less than the same products in other stores. Nu Look makes suits for Lazarus, J.C. Penney's and other department and specialty stores across the country with that store's own labels sewn into the garments. At Nu Look, these same garments, 200,000 in 142 different styles, have the Gino Capelli, Barryton and Elmhurst labels. You'll find wool, wool blends, silk and polyester fabrics in traditional and contemporary styles. Sizes 36-52, short to extra long, are available. The alteration department offers value prices on repairs of clothes purchased in the store as well as those men's and women's garments which were purchased elsewhere. The prices include $6.50 to cuff pants, $5-$7 for hems, $8 to take in the waist and the seat. Other types of alterations are also available. The tailor is open Monday-Friday from 11-6 and can be reached at 436-2135. Store hours are M-F 10-7, Sat 10-6.

OHIO FACTORY SHOPS
State Rt. 35 off I-71, Jeffersonville, 948-9090

Seventy-five outlet and value priced shops include Esprit, Van Heusen, Galt Sand, Casual Corner, Westport Woman, Brooks Brothers, Levi's, Laura Ashley, Petite Sophisticates, Ann Taylor, Coach, Donna Karan New York, Aileen, Evan Picone, Bass Shoes, Guess, Alexander Julian, Danskin, Rack Room Shoes, Russell Athletic, Applause, Allen Edmonds, Barbizon, Perfumania, Toy Liquidators, Farberware, Reed and Barton, Villeroy and Boch, Eddie Bauer, Leather Loft, Royal Doulton, Mark Cross, American Eagle, Nature Company, Lenox, Totes and other businesses. Savings are 15-60%. Purchase a Come Back Pack coupon book for only $3 which offers discounts and freebies at most of the businesses plus 20% off a hotel room at the Amerihost Inn. Watch for the third phase of the outlet center to be completed by the fall of '96, with many new businesses to save you money. M-Sat 10-9, Sun 12-6.

OLDFIELD'S ODDS AND ENDS
1632 Harrisburg Pike, Columbus, 43223, 276-0398

Used and new infant and toddler clothes, toys, strollers, carseats and related items are available in this business which operates out of a large garage adjacent to a residence. You'll find items in various stages of wear including some gently used, plus a range of quality from budget to better. Brands represented included Health-Tex, Fischer Price, Cosco and others. Look thoroughly and undoubtedly you'll unearth some treasures. Park at the rear of the house. The sign on the lawn says "used clothes" or "garage sale". M-Sat 10-6, Sun 12-6.

OLD NAVY CLOTHING COMPANY
2736 Brice Rd., Reynoldsburg, 43068, 759-0419

The Gap's value priced division features clothes for men, women and children. You'll find similar styling to that found in the Gap stores, but at a slightly lesser quality. For example, men's flannel boxers were priced at two for $12, corduroy shits at $26, jeans at $22, toddler's dresses at $12, a corduroy backpack at $ 12 and other similar values. M-Sat 9:30-9:30, Sun 11-6.

ONCE UPON A CHILD
5760 Frantz Rd., Dublin, 43017, 761-8488
399 S. State St., Westerville, 43081, 899-6654
1901 Northwest Blvd., Columbus, 43212, 488-8806
2964 E. Broad St., Bexley, 43209, 236-5550
644 High St., Worthington, 43085, 885-0885
385 Stone Ridge Lane,Gahanna, 43230, 337-0200
2199 Stringtown Rd., Grove City, 43123, 875-9000
1540 River Valley Circle S., Lancaster, 653-8338
7420 Sawmill Rd., Columbus, 43235, 791-3900
6026 E. Main St., Reynoldsburg, 43068, 863-9777
1052 Upper Valley Pike, Springfield, (513) 322-8697

Quality used children's toys, accessories and clothes are available here at savings of 30-70% below "if new" prices. Brands such as Oshkosh, Ocean Pacific, Health-Tex, Youthland, Rothschild and more, in sizes newborn to 14, fill these stores. The stores also feature buyouts and salesmen samples of new merchandise at similar savings. M-F 10-8, Sat 10-6, Sun 11-5.

ONCE UPON A MOM
55 S. High St., Dublin, 43017, 761-8588

Quality resale maternity wear and related accessories (lingerie, nursing items, maternity support pillows) are available for the mom to be at savings of 50-75% less than new. Most dresses and jumpsuits are in the $10-$20 range and include such brands as JCKU, Laura Ashley and Mothercare. The store also stocks separates, career wear, swimwear, and buyouts of new merchandise at similar savings. M-F 10-8, Sat 10-6, Sun 12-4.

ONE MORE TIME
1521 W. 5 Ave., Columbus 43212, 486-0031 or 486-2229

Gently used quality clothes are sold at savings of 40-70% off department store prices "if new". Some new garments and accessories are also available at similar savings. It's not unusual to find designer garments by such brands as Nippon, Tahari, Lillie Rubin and Liz Claiborne. This store sells mostly high fashion apparel although you'll find quite a few classic styles as well. Sizes carried are 4-46. A limited amount of maternity and men's clothes are also available at similar savings. This upscale women's consignment shop also sells accessories such as jewelry, belts and purses and a small selection of gift items. The store features its annual sidewalk sale in early August, where savings are 75% and more. Sign up for their mailing list and you'll receive a coupon valid for $5 off your purchase during the month of your birthday. Tu-F 12-6, Sat 10-6.

ONE PRICE $7

6452 Tussing Rd., Consumer Square, Reynoldsburg, 43068, 868-1818
3445 Cleveland Ave., Northern Lights Shpng. Ctr., Columbus, 43224, 267-3200
3892 E. Broad St., Town & Country Shpng. Ctr., Columbus, 43213, 236-5200
4101 W. Broad St., West Broad Plaza, Columbus, 43228, 351-9992
959 Hebron Rd., Crosscreek Shpng. Ctr., Heath, 522-2927
1735 N. Memorial Dr., Lancaster, 654-4112
3259 Maple Ave., Zanesville, 455-6410

Everything in this store is priced at $7 each or several items for $7. You'll find moderate and some better quality junior, missy and large size women's apparel, as well as hair accessories, socks 5/$7, fashion jewelry 3/$7, sunglasses 3/$7, by such brands as Gitano, Cherokee, Prima Class and Carmel. A limited selection of children's apparel, in sizes 4-14, is also available. The inventory is first quality and includes mostly casual wear. Prices are about 30-60% less than manufacturer's suggested retail prices. M-Sat 10-9, Sun 12-6.

OTTERBEIN WOMEN'S THRIFT SHOP

177 Park Street, Westerville, 43081, no phone available

Located within an older home by Otterbein College, this shop is brimming with used clothing for the entire family. You'll also find books, jewelry, small appliances, bric-a-brac and curiosities. The merchandise is an eclectic mixture of gently used, current and dated items as well as some great vintage wearables, all at fair prices. The quality ranges from budget to better. W 10-5, Sat 10-2 from mid September through early June (closed in the summer).

P.S. FASHIONS

2100 Morse Rd., Columbus, 43229, 431-2133
2561 S. Hamilton Rd., Eastland Plaza, 43232, 868-5022
4210 W. Broad St., Columbus, 43228, 272-0016

"Plus sizes, plus savings" is the motto here. You'll find moderate to better brands of contemporary, large sized women's dressy, sport, business, casual and outerwear. There's also lingerie and accessories. The stores carry sizes 16-32 in such brands as Maggy McNaughton, Robert Too, David Rose, Alfred Dunner, Youngstuff, Special Thyme and Notations at 10-40% off regular retail prices. However, the stores' price tags rarely indicate a "compare to" price, which can leave you baffled as to how much you're really saving. This chain also operates similar stores in other cities under the name, Catherine's. M-Sat 10-9, Sun 12-5.

Q'S SPORTSWEAR

2238 W. Dublin Granville Rd., Worthington, 43085, 888-3400

Women's better tennis and golf clothing plus accessories are discounted about 20-50%. You'll find first quality stock by Le Coq, E.P. Pro, Quantum, Sport Haley, Head, Ixspa and Jean Bell. Check out the hall rack with reduced items. Sells sizes 4-16. Tu-Sat 10-5.

RECYCLED BRIDAL, FORMAL TOO

52 N. State Street, Westerville, 43081, 890-7622

Gently used bridal, long and short formals and mother of the bride apparel is available at savings of 40-60% off "if new" prices. The store also stocks a small selection of tuxedos, flower girl dresses, costume jewelry and miscellaneous items. There's a generous selection of veils at similar savings. Wedding gowns range from $35-$600, formalwear from $25-$150, veils from $15-$115 and tuxedos from $75-$125. The upscale merchandise, which also includes some new items, features such brands as Bianchi, Mon Cheri, Jeanne Phoenix, Angelo, Bridal Originals, Marianna, Nippon, Victor Csta, Ann Taylor and A.J. Bari. Sizes range from 2-24. Tu-Sat 11-6.

REYNOLDSBURG CANCER THRIFT SHOP
7125 E. Main St., Reynoldsburg, 43068, no phone

This well stocked shop is small, but brimming with merchandise in various states of wear. You'll find stuffed animals, toys, curtains, clothing for the family, shoes, bric-a-brac and costume jewelry. The stock is well organized and consists of vintage, dated and contemporary styles in budget to better quality. Most items were priced at $5 and under. Check the clearance areas for further reductions. The annual half price sale is held in July. The store accepts consigned as well as donated items. Accepts cash only. Tu/W/F/ 12-4, Sat 10-4. Summer hours are F 12-4 and Sat 10:30-4.

S & K FAMOUS BRANDS
2643 Northland Plaza Dr., Columbus, 43231, 794-2407
7655 New Market Center Way, Columbus, 43235, 764-7435

Moderate to better quality menswear is sold at about 30-50% off comparable retail prices. Much of the inventory has the Deansgate and Granby Club labels, which are the store's own brands. S & K is able to sell their quality products so low because they are made by nationally recognized manufacturers who do not sew in the exclusive labels, but instead have S&K's private labels sewn in. These clothes are sold in upscale department and specialty stores throughout the United States. Membership in the Premier Club is free and guarantees free alterations for the life of your suit. You just need to pay your initial alteration fee when the suit is purchased. By the way, alterations are budget priced. The store will also alter your clothes which were purchased elsewhere for an additional $2, which still makes their fees lower than in many other businesses. Prices are $5 to hem pants, $6 to adjust the seat of the pants and $12 to lengthen a pair of sleeves. I noticed some Botany 500 and Adolfo suits in the store on my last visit, which were about 30% less than the suggested retail price. You'll find suits, sportcoats, slacks as well as casual wear for gentlemen with discriminating tastes. This chain also operates stores in Milan and Toledo. M-Sat 10-9, Sun 12-6.

SALESMEN'S SAMPLE SALES

Look through the classified ads section at the back of the Columbus Dispatch and the community newspapers to find these great sales. Salespeople who represent different lines of adult and children's clothes, giftware, and purses in budget to designer quality, need to find a way to dispose of these products after their selling season is over, as they have already paid for all of their samples. Sometimes the samples are placed in area consignment shops (see other listings for these stores in this chapter), or sold at these salesmen's sales. Savings are generally 40-75% off regular retail prices. Don't expect to find nickel and dime prices typical of other types of garage/home sales. You should be aware that a salesperson's selling season typically ends about two months before the merchandise is shipped to the stores which placed the orders. So the merchandise at these sample sales is always suitable for the current or upcoming season. Often, there is a limited size range in garments. When you go to these sales, ask the salesperson if he/she maintains a mailing list, as many do. Scan the newspapers regularly as these sales are held year round.

SALVATION ARMY
Six Columbus locations plus the follow sites
317 W. Church, Marion, 382-2156
1101 Mt. Vernon Ave., Marion, 389-3397
34 S. 5th St., Newark, 345-8120
123 E. Hubert Ave., Lancaster, 687-1921
554 W. Central Ave., Delaware, 369-2093

The stock consists of clothing, shoes and accessories for the whole family, plus bric-a-brac, toys, linens and furniture which have been donated to the stores. You'll find a wide range of quality from budget to designer, and clothes will be in well worn to never worn states. Styles range from outdated to contemporary with most items priced at $1-$5. The careful shopper can unearth some great deals on quality merchandise. Hours vary by store.

SAUNDRA'S CONSIGNMENT AND SPECIALTY STORE
2242 W. Dublin Granville Rd., Columbus, 43085, 888-8818

Find men's, women's and children's gently used clothing and accessories, plus small bric-a-brac at savings of 40-70% less than "if new". The stock consists of moderate to better quality items in traditional and contemporary styles. You'll also find new arts and crafts items. Tu/W/F 10-6, Th 10-8, Sat 10-5.

SCHOTTENSTEIN'S
3251 Westerville Rd., Columbus, 43224, 471-4711
6055 E. Main St., Columbus, 43213, 755-9200
34 North Boulevard, Columbus, 43204, 278-6000
1887 Parsons Ave., Columbus, 43207, 443-0171
Sawmill Rd. site is in the planning stages

This mini department store offers moderate to couture merchandise at savings of 20-90% off regular retail prices. Brands such as Adrienne Vittadini, Stanley Blacker and Anne Klein run rampant in the designer section. You can purchase a cordless phone for $39.99 regularly $90, luggage for $19.99-$39.99 regularly $60-$130, wallpaper for $1.99 regularly $12.95-$24.95, children's Health-Tex separates at $2.99-$4.99 regularly $6-$21. Other merchandise includes clothes for the family (including large and maternity sizes), furs, lingerie, small appliances, bicycles, fishing/golf and other sporting goods, toys, gardening supplies, lamps, patio furniture, watches, health and beauty aids, fine jewelry, cameras, housewares and giftware. The Westerville Road and Main Street locations have gourmet food departments where you'll find pastas, jellies and snacks at similar savings. All widths of shoes are offered for the family in dressy and casual styles by such brands as Giorgio Brutini, Reebok, Bally, Evan Picone and Joan And David. The linen department offers savings of 20-90% off suggested retail prices on first quality and irregular merchandise by Utica, Stevens and other popular brands. The pharmacy department offers similar savings on brand name cosmetics, snacks, personal grooming items and seasonal merchandise. The fine jewelry department sells watches plus gold and silver jewelry at similar savings. The inventory consists of first quality, irregulars, seconds, buyouts and liquidations. This store has earned the distinction of being one of my personal favorites. M-Th. 10-9, F 10-7, Sun 10-8. Closed Saturday.

SCHOTTENSTEIN'S SALVAGE CENTER
1887 Parsons Ave., Columbus, 43206, 443-0171

Here's an adventure for the most daring. Dust off those bargain hunting antennas and get ready. The basement of the Parsons Avenue store operates as a salvage center for all their local and Value City locations. You'll find all types of merchandise that are typically available in the stores, but everything is either soiled, damaged, "as is", customer returns which did not wear/wash well, or otherwise not perfect (missing a button, broken zipper etc). While many of the problems can be fixed with a little time and creativity, others are way beyond logic to invest your time to repair. I purchased a leather attache for my son for $5, which was missing a grommet. Schottenstein's had sold it originally for $39.99, but it was valued at $89.99. I brought it to a shoe repair store and had the handles removed and restitched for only $9. Voila! My son's attache (Jason is going to be a doctor, you should know) looked great. Prices are rock bottom, with most items in the 50 cent to $5 range. M-Th 10-9, F 10-7, Sun 10-8. Closed Saturday.

SECOND ACT
800 James St., Zanesville, 455-3990

Find gently used clothing and accessories for men, women and children at savings of 30-60% less than "if new". You'll find popular brands such as Liz Claiborne, Chaus, Oshkosh and Dockers. M-Sat 10-5.

SECOND CHANCE CONSIGNMENTS
1790 W. Fifth Ave., Columbus, 43212, 488-3006

Gently used upscale casual, sport, dressy and business women's apparel is available at savings of 40-75% off "if new" prices. The store also sells a small amount of men's wear. The stock consists of current season, contemporary and traditional styles by such companies as Liz Claiborne, Carole Little, Peter Popovich, Structure and others. Tu-F 11-6, Sat 10-6, Sun 12-5.

SECOND IMPRESSIONS
5381 N. High St., Columbus, 43214, 781-1572

Upscale consignment store offering mostly women's apparel and accessories. The store also features some men's and children's wear as well as small gift items. Operated in cooperation with the Ohio Chapter of the American Diabetes Association, it also accepts donations on behalf of the ADA, with 50% of the proceeds of the sale being donated to that organization. The merchandise is reasonably priced. I saw an Eddie Bauer leather jacket for $35 and Liz Claiborne blazer for only $10. Other brands include Karen Kane, SML Sport, L.L. Bean etc. You'll also find some vintage apparel as well. Tu-F 10-5, Sat 10-4.

SELECT RESALE BOUTIQUE
2007 E. Dublin Granville Rd., Village Ctr., Columbus, 43229, 888-3121

Gently used women's clothing and accessories are available at savings of 40-70% off new prices. The upscale stock includes sizes 2-24, plus maternity wear, in casual, business and formal styles. The owner's intriguing accent and salesmanship, make you feel as if you're shopping in a fine European boutique. M-F 10-6, Sat/Sun 12-5.

SEQUIN! SEQUIN!
Northland Mall, Columbus, 43229, 888-8810 or 888-8825

Save 40-60% on sequined and beaded evening and special occasion wear at this wholesale and retail outlet. Most items are made from silk. You'll also find blouses, caps, vests and collars at affordable prices. Sequined dresses start at $59, sequined/beaded bustiers are about $45. Custom orders are available. The store carries sizes to 3x. (This store is planning to move from Morse Road to the mall in late April 96.) M-Sat 10-9, Sun 12-6.

SHOP WITH SUZY
1987 W. Henderson Rd., Columbus, 43220, 457-7606

Save about 20-60% on high quality women's apparel and accessories by such brands as Jessica Howard, Jones New York, SML Sport, Virgo and other brands. Owner, Suzy, is a former buyer for Madison's and she brings that store's merchandise appeal to her own venture. Sizes are 4-24, including petites. Ask about the frequent shoppers' club and after hour private shopping parties for groups of six or more (includes cheese and wine). M-W/F 10-7, Th 10-8, Sat 10-5:30, Sun 12-5:30.

16 PLUS
3752 E. Broad St., Columbus, 43213, 231-2080

This store is under the same ownership as Sizes Unlimited (see the description in this chapter) and sells the same merchandise. M-Sat 10-8, Sun 12-5.

SIZES UNLIMITED
222 Graceland Blvd., Columbus, 43214, 436-2150
3499 Cleveland Ave., Northern Lights Shpng. Ctr., Columbus, 43224, 262-8581
3827 S. High St., Great Southern Shpng. Ctr., Columbus, 43207, 497-1039
4125 W. Broad St., Columbus, 43228, 274-0885

Large size women's clothing is available at savings of 20-50% off regular retail prices. You'll find first quality casual and career wear by Sasson, Gloria Vanderbilt, Signature A, Chaus and other companies in sizes up to 52. Good values are also available on the stores' private label merchandise sold under the brands Adrian Jordan, Forelli and Signature A. The 16 Plus store, mentioned elswhere in this chapter, is under the same ownership and carries ismilar merchandise. M-Sat 10-9, Sun 12-5.

SOMETHING OLD, SOMETHING NEW
283 Cedar Hill Rd., Lancaster, 653-9955

Your one stop family resale shop features clothing, toys, small furniture, accessories and some bric-a-brac at savings of 30-70% less than "if new". Quality varies from moderate to better, and styles are a mixture of current and some dated items. The careful shopper will be able to find many great deals on brand name goods such as Oshkosh, Fisher Price and others. This shop will buy your gently used items on the spot. W/Th/Sat 12-5, F 12-7.

STEINMART
1765 Kingsdale Center, Columbus, 43221, 459-9600

Upscale specialty, store offers savings of 25-60% off first quality men's, women's and children's apparel (including plus sizes), accessories and home furnishings. The stock is a mixture of contemporary and somewhat traditional styles, including a couture department. You'll instantly recognize all of the famous labels. I am particularly fond of the costume jewelry. M-Sat 10-9, Sun 12-6.

STILL TICKING
320 S. State St., Westerville, 43081, 899-9398

A portion of the proceeds from this business is donated to the Homeless Families Foundation. This store is authorized to accept you tax deductible donations of merchandise for the Foundation, although it is privately owned. This resale shop features clothing for the entire family, bric-a-brac, shoes, toys and accessories. You'll find current and some dated items in moderate to better quality. I even found a Polo and Tommy Hilfiger shirt here. Most items are priced at $6 and under. M-Th 11:30-7, F/Sat 11:30-6.

SURPLUS WORLD
2590 Morse Rd., Columbus, 43229, 475-1111
4200 W. Broad St., Columbus, 43228, 351-1211

Find a large selection of new and used military clothes, backpacks, camping gear, a kid's commando headquarters and the midwest's largest selection of patches and medals at value prices. M/Th/F 9-9, Tu/W/Sat 9-7, Sun 12-6 .

T.J. MAXX
4117 W. Broad St., Columbus 43228, 272-1141 ·
1871 W. Henderson Rd., Columbus, 43220, 451-9924
5929 E. Main St., Columbus, 43213, 864-7005
2210 Morse Rd., Columbus, 43229, 476, 1964

Moderate to designer quality fashions for men, women and children, in addition to giftware, linens, lingerie, shoes, luggage, designer fragrances, leather goods and purses, accessories as well as fine gold and silver jewelry are sold at 20-60% off regular retail prices. The inventory consists of first quality manufacturers' overstocks and some past season merchandise. A small quantity of irregular goods is clearly marked. M-Sat 1:30-9:30, Sun 12-6.

TARGET GREATLAND
6000 Sawmill Rd., Dublin, 43017, 798-8160
5855 Chantry Dr., Columbus, 43232, 575-2840
3720 Soldano Blvd., Columbus, 43228, 279-4224
270 Airport Pkwy., Newark, 788-8600

This general merchandise store offers moderate to better quality family clothing (including plus sizes), linens, housewares, toys, gifts and related items at value prices. In particular, the store's private label clothing (Surrey, Greatland, Trend Basics, Honors, Sostanza, Merona, Circo, Lullabye Club) and private label linens/home accessories (Furio) lines are exceptional values for the top quality and contemporary styling they offer for the price. You'll be amazed! Target oversees the design and production of these items, with most being made to their exclusive design specifications. The stores also feature an in house portrait studio which offers value prices on services. The best deal is when you join the Portrait Club for $24.99 for two years. As a member, sitting fees will be waived during this period (these are generally $4 per person), you'll get two free 8x10s (a $30 value) and you'll receive 10% off all portrait packages. The membership is valid for the entire family.

Target is one of my personal favorites particularly because of the value and quality associated with their private label merchandise mentioned above. M-Sat 9-9:30, Sun 10-16.

TEN BELOW
Ten Columbus locations, plus the following
771 S 30 St., Indian Mound Mall, Heath, 522-5667
1139 Columbus Pike, Rt. 23, Delaware, 363-0969
1635 River Valley Circle S, Lancaster, 653-2911
3575 Maple Ave. #520, Colony Sq. Mall, Zanesville, 452-7648
U.S. Rt. 23, Circleville, 474-2390
1475-Marion-Waldo Rd., Marion, 389-4099

This chain of women's apparel and accessories stores sells most of the inventory at $10 and under. Manufacturers' overstocks and cancelled orders comprise the budget, moderate and better quality items in such brands as The Limited, Victoria's Secret, Gitano, Miss Lizz, Erika, Bonjour, Counterparts and others. The store carries missy, junior and large sizes, in addition to accessories such as earrings, socks, scarves and purses. M-Sat 10-9, Sun 12-5.

THRIFT STORES OF OHIO
3900 Sullivant Avenue, Columbus, 43228, 351-2900
1580 Alum Creek Drive, Columbus, 43207, 351-2900
647 Harrisburg Pike, Columbus, 43223, 272-6281
67 Great Southern Blvd., Columbus, 43207, 491-5305

Operated by the Kidney Foundation, these enormous stores claim to be the largest thrift stores in Ohio. They offer used apparel for the entire family including, used books at 25 cents each and miscellaneous toys, housewares and some furniture. The stock is generally neat and well organized. However, within each category (men's sweaters, women's blouses etc.) the stock is organized by color which makes it time consuming to locate your size. The inventory consists of current and dated styles in various states of wear. Styles tended to lean more towards the simple and traditional overall, with some funky items mixed in. Vintage items are occasionally seen here. Some new merchandise is always mixed in among the stock which includes donations from area stores. Check out the better/designer section for special items. Most clothes were in the $3-$6 range. If you feel adventurous, this is a great place to start. So get your bargain hunting antennas ready. On a recent visit, I purchased a purple embroidered Adrian Pappel dress for $7 in "like new" condition, and a real black patent leather evening bag by Morris Moskowitz for only a dollar and a half!!!!! Keep in mind, that this is the exception, rather than the rule. These stores are a step up in quality from Salvation Army stores, but not quite up to par with the city's upscale resale shops. Unfortunately, there are no dressing rooms. The stores are open most holidays and generally feature half off sales or other special deals on those days. M-Sat 9-9, Sun 11-6.

TOUJOURS
8 N. Sandusky St., Delaware, 43015, 363-2193

Gently used men's, women's and children's clothing and accessories are available at savings off 30-60% less than "if new". The stock consists of moderate to better quality items by such brands as Liz Claiborne, the Limited and others. You'll find traditional and contemporary items. M-Sat 10-6.

TRADER TOTS
1828 W. Fifth Ave., Columbus, 43212, 488-8687 or 488-6520

Resale children's clothes, toys and equipment as well as maternity clothes can be found here at prices 50-80% lower than new.   Toys are priced 40-60% lower than new prices. Accessories such as cribs, strollers and car seats are about 50% less than new items.   The quality, upscale merchandise includes such popular brands as Fisher-Price, Health-Tex, Oshkosh, Polly Flinders, Carters, Brian dresses, Recreations, Harvey Seller, Ninth Moon and Lady In Waiting.   Offers formal maternity wear rentals for $45 for two nights, including dry cleaning costs. M-F10-8, Sat 10-6, Sun 10-4.

TREASURE TRUNK
1183 W. Church St., Newark, 43055, 344-7232

Upscale consignment shop sells quality children's clothes in size newborn to pre-teen size 16. You'll find Gunne Sax, Oshkosh, Buster Brown, Health Tex, Polly Flinders, Brian and other brands.   A small selection of toys, shoes and maternity wear is also available. Savings are about 50-60% less than "if new".   M-F 10-5, Sat 10-4.   Accepts checks and cash only.

TRI-VILLAGE TRADING POST
1944 W. First Ave., Columbus, 43212, 488-6564

This moderate and upscale quality shop has been in operation for forty years.   Family apparel, accessories and bric-a-brac are consigned or donated, and priced very reasonably. The stock consists of gently used items in a combination of contemporary, dated and vintage styles.   The careful shopper will unearth some treasures including clothes by Jones New York, Hart Schaffner and Marx, Polo and Oshkosh. Check the bargain room at the back of the store which offers a perpetual reduction of items which have overstayed their welcome. M-Sat 10-4.

TRUDY'S CLOSET
618 Locust Ave., Zanesville, 43701, 454-6500

Upscale consignment shop for quality, gently used men's, women's and children's clothes also includes accessories, lingerie, uniforms and maternity wear.   Located in an older home, it has five rooms brimming with goodies. While some clothes were a little outdated, there were many current style and season items by Abe Schrader, Villager, Polo, Liz Claiborne and other designer brands. Tu-Sat 10-4:30

TWICE'S NICE
3866 Sullivant Ave., Columbus, 43228, 278-9164

Don't miss this Westside treasure. Better women's clothing, plus outerwear, is available in sizes up to 22. You'll find casual, business and even formalwear in gently used condition, and priced very reasonably. I picked up a red wool Pendleton skirt for $8. You'll find all the popular brands you love include Chaus, Liz Claiborne, Evan Picone, Abe Schrader and others. While most of the stock is current style and season, there are a few outdated and some vintage items mixed in. The store also stocks some accessories. Tu-F 10-6, Sat 10-4.

UPTOWN KIDS
9246 Dublin Rd, Powell, 43065, 766-6722
3806 Fishinger Blvd, Market At Mill Run, Hilliard, 43026, 777-1754

These resale operations will purchase in-season, current styles of children's clothing and accessories (plus toys). There's also some new salesmen's samples as well. Brands offered include Oshkosh, Polly Flinders, London Fog, Bugle Boy, Esprit and others. You'll be delighted at the quality of the merchandise. Most dresses were in the $5-$10 range, jeans were in the $5-$7 range. Sizes carried are infant to 14. Kids can enjoy watching videos while mom shops. The stores will provide a free helium filled balloon to your child simply by asking. M-Sat 10-6.

VALUE CITY DEPARTMENT STORES
725 Hebron Rd., Heath, 522-8125
721 N. Memorial Dr., Lancaster, 653-5280
969 N. Bechtel Ave., Springfield, (513) 328-7400
725 Hebron Rd., Heath, 522-8125

Outside of the Columbus area, Schottenstein's operates mini department stores. These businesses offer a larger selection of seconds and irregular merchandise than the Columbus Schottenstein's site, and don't generally have as much better/designer items. The stock includes budget to moderate quality goods. A few designer items are also available. Keep your bargain hunting antennas fully extended here as you might bypass the great bargains which are mixed in with some undesirables. The stores sell housewares, shoes, apparel for the family, luggage, leather goods, fine jewelry, linens and toys. M-Th 10-9, F/Sat 10-9:30, Sun 11-7.

VAN DYNE-CROTTY COMPANY
3877 S. High St., Columbus, 43207, 491-7777

Used men's uniforms including overalls, jackets, lab coats, shirts and pants are available at savings of about 50-70% less than "if new". Pants are priced at $2.95, shirts are $1.95 and jackets/coveralls are $5.50. M-F 8-5, Sat 8-4.

VILLAGE DISCOUNT OUTLET
1880 Parsons Ave., Columbus, 43207 , no phone
3480 Cleveland Ave., Columbus, 43224, no phone

You'll find trash to treasure at these enormous shops. In these stores, you'll need to have those bargain hunting antennas fully extended. All merchandise has been donated to the Amvets, which receive some of the proceeds here. You'll find clothes for the entire family, accessories, bric-a-brac, toys and books. There are gently worn, never worn and worn to death items; current, dated and even vintage styles. Quality varies from budget to better and there's even a special designer department. Men's sportcoats average $2-$10, men's suites average $10-$35, sweaters $1-$6. Merchandise in the better departments may be priced slightly higher. You can find Polo, Liz, Jones N.Y., Structure, Tommy Hilfiger and other brands if your look over the merchandise with a fine tooth comb. Often, local retail stores will donate merchandise and you may see some with the original price tags. You won't find any dressing rooms and everything is sold "as is". The stores are open most holidays and generally feature great sales those days. M-Sat 9-9, Sun 11-5.

VINTAGE VOGUE
22 S. High St., Dublin, 43017, 766-6548

This tiny shop is packed with vintage apparel, accessories and home decor, all meticulously maintained. While some items tend to be somewhat pricier than other shops selling vintage items, the careful shopper should be able to find those special niceties at good values. Of course, when comparing the items to newer ones of comparable quality and styling, you know you've made a good purchase. W-Sat 11-4

VOLUNTEERS OF AMERICA
Ten Columbus locations

Find new, used and vintage apparel, accessories, furniture and bric-a-brac at rock bottom prices. Most items are priced at fifty cents to $4. The careful shopper can unearth some great deals which may have been donated by your own neighbors, consignment shops or other area businesses! Obviously there is a mix of budget to designer quality and items are in various states of wear. I have purchased many designer items for myself and family, but I have had to weed through many items in order to find the cream of the crop. The site at 5640 West Broad Street is their largest location. Hours vary by site.

VOSZI DESIGNS
3575 E. Livinsgston Ave., Columbus, 43227, 231-7726, 291-4681 or 231-7726

Fashion designer, Voszi, will design and sew a unique fashion garment for you using her fabric or yours. Most of her jackets, dresses, tops etc., have tie or Velcro closures or slip over the head, making them additionally suitable for the elderly or people with disabilities. Her fabrics range from simple to ornate, cotton to linen, and styles are funky to casual chic. The quality is excellent and the prices are very low. She'll design a "wear me anywhere" overcoat or a dress for your favorite occasion. Hard to find sizes are welcome. Dresses range from about $35-$70, tops range from $20-$40. Although prices vary according to style and fabric used, you can expect to save 30-60% off the price of comparable store bought goods. She also maintains an inventory of garments to buy off the rack, most of which is designed for the African American customer, including some clearance merchandise. Visit her at the Livingston Court Flea Market. Accepts checks and cash only. F/Sat 10-6, Sun 12-5.

WEDDING EXPRESSIONS
7676 Sawmill Rd., Columbus, 43235, 792-9710

Full service wedding planning store can save you about 20% on in-stock wedding gowns and about 15% on special orders. Check the clearance racks for savings of 40% and more on discontinued wedding gowns. Mother of the bride, bridesmaids and specialty dresses are not discounted unless found on the clearance rack. M-Th 10-8, F/Sat 10-6, Sun 1-5.

WEDDING PLANTATION
3900 Noe Bixby Rd., Columbus 43232, 837-5817

Step into this business which looks like a home on a Southern plantation. You'll save about 20% on wedding gowns, mother of the bride apparel and formalwear. The store also offers tuxedo rentals, invitations and related necessities at comparable savings. The store also rents bridesmaids dresses. Their outlet store, Bridal Express (see listing in this chapter), offers savings which are even greater. M/Tu/Th/F 11-7, Sat 10-5, Sun 12-5.

WENDY'S BRIDAL
4182 Westland Mall, Columbus, 43228, 274-0167

Save 20-30% on first qiuality wedding, bridesmaid and mother of the bride gowns and formal wear. Many popular upscale brands are offered including Alfred Angelo, Bari Jay, Carmi Couture, Demetrios, Galina, Ilissa and Jessica McClintock. M-Sat 10-9, Sun 12-6.

WE'RE 4 KIDS
324 S. Hamilton Rd., Hunters Ridge Mall, Gahanna, 43230, 476-1794
7208 New Market Ctr. Way, Columbus, 43235, 792-2715

Salesmen's samples comprise a large portion of the inventory at these stores and are marked at 20-40% off regular retail prices. The stores specialize in pageant and party dresses, but also sell casual clothes at similar savings. The boutique type garments are certainly eyecatchers. You can find infant through size 16 for boys and girls. Some of the brands offered include Martha Miniatures, Weather Tamer, Pazaaz, Ruth Of California, Miss Nannette and Donmoor. The merchandise is all first quality. M-F 10-9, Sat 10-7.

WE THREE
74 Mill St., Gahanna, 43230, 471-1567

Gently used children's clothing and toys, as well as women's clothes are sold at savings up to 75% off "if new" prices. You'll find popular brands such as Polly Flinders, Oshkosh and Brian dresses as well as Fisher-Price and Little Tykes toys. On a recent visit, I saw a wool Harve Benard suit for only $25 and other wearables by Evan Picone, Liz Claiborne and other sought after brands. Check the back room for additional merchandise. M-Sat 10-6. Accepts checks and cash only.

WOOLEN SQUARE
3900 Groves Rd., Columbus, 43232, 861-8006

Ohio's largest collection of Pendleton apparel is sold here at regular retail prices. However, the store has a clearance area in the back where men's and women's clothes are reduced 30-50%. The area also includes wool and wool blend fabrics at similar savings. M-Sat 9:30-5:30.

WORTHINGTON THRIFT SHOP
5600 N. High Street, Worthington, 43085, 848-8408

Operated by the American Cancer Society, this consignment/donation shop sells current, dated and vintage clothes for men, women and children in various states of wear. The front of the store sells bric-a-brac, books and miscellaneous household items. Styles range from contemporary to dated, with a few vintage mixed in. A thorough hunt through the racks, with your bargain hunting antennas fully extended, will likely unearth a few treasures. Prices are very reasonable and generally less than the more trendy consignment shops. This is a shopping trip for the adventurous. All proceeds, after expenses, are earmarked for cancer research and education. Accepts cash and check only. Fall, winter and spring hours are W, Th 1-4, F/Sat 10:30-4. Summer hours will change.

WORTH REPEATING
1281 Grandview Ave, Columbus, 43212, 488-1992

Upscale women's apparel, accessories, table/bath linens and small gift items are available at this consignment shop. You'll find all popular brands including Liz Claiborne, Tahari, Nilani, Carole Little and others at savings of 30-60% off "if new" prices. Inquire about the in-home closet organizing service. Tu-F 11-6, Sat 11-5.

ALSO SEE

Acorn Warehouse Sale, Baby Bargain Boutique, Bellepointe, Berwick Corner Outlet, Colorado Ski And Sport, D.E. Jones, Department Of Defense, Dublin Music Boosters Giant Garage Sale, Early Childhood Sale, Eddie Bauer Warehouse Sale, Extravaganza, Golden Hobby Shop, Greater Columbus Antique Mall, J. Crew Warehouse Sale, Just For Feet, Lake Erie Factory Outlet, Liquidations Now, Long's Bookstore, Odd Lots, Only $1, Paul's Marine, Sam's Club, Sanctuary Re-Run Sale, Springfield Antique Show And Flea Market, Sunbury Flea Market, Tag Sales, Talbott's Semi-Annual Sale, Tuesday Morning, Urban Concern Garage Sale, Value City Department Stores, WDLR Radio

COMPUTERS
&
SOFTWARE

BLOCKBUSTER VIDEO
Twenty locations in Franklin County
1209 Hill Rd., Pickerington, 43147, 759-7878
3191 Maple Ave., Zanesville, 453-4114
616 Hebron Rd., Heath, 522-2233

Has a series of free loan, community service videos for adults and children on such topics as back pain, say no to drugs, the facts of life, arthritis, how to plan a fire escape from your home, divorce and other topics. There are about 30 different videos and the selection varies from store to store. It is necessary to have a Blockbuster Video membership card in order to borrow these videos. The stores also sell previously rented Nintendo tapes, some of which are missing the instructions, for only $9.99-$14.99 each. These are usually $20-$40 "if new". A selection of previously rented videos is also available for $9.99-$19.99. When these movies first came out, the videos were selling for $25-$80. Open seven days per week from 10a.m.-midnight.

COMPUQUICK
3758 Town and Country Shopping Center, Columbus, 43213, 235-1180

Located in the rear of the shopping center, you'll find this store filled with new and used Amigas, Commodores, 386/486, Pentium based systems and other computers plus software. Used components offer savings of about 40-60% off new prices. M-F 11-7:30, Sat 11-7.

COMP USA
7588 New Market Center Way, Columbus, 43235, 766-4045

All popular brands of computer hardware and software can be found here including Apple, Compaq, Epson, IBM, Toshiba, Compudyne, Packard Bell and others. Savings are 10-30%. The business also features expert technical advice by phone, even if you didn't buy your computer there. The advice hotline can be contacted at (800) 896-9393, Monday through Friday 8a.m.-9p.m., Saturday 9-6 and Sun 12-6. The first minute is free, then you'll be charged $2.49 for each extra minute. The store is open M-Sat 10-9, Sun 12-6.

COMPUSAVE
3293 N. High St., Columbus, 43214, 261-4600
Note: Moving to Bethel Rd. in Spring '96

One of the area's largest selections of used computers will offer you deals on such brands as IBM, Panasonic, Compaq, Packard Bell, Epson, Toshiba and others. Savings are 50-75% less than new prices, but some new closeout models are also available at competitive prices. Special orders and custom designed systems are also available. Ask about their 90 day trade in/trade up policy. For do-it-your-selfers, the store offers a large selection of parts. The move to the Bethel Road site will allow the company to concentrate more on the new computers, including closeouts, at substantial savings. Repairs are available at reasonable rates. M-F 10-7, Sat 10-6.

COMPUSED
5992 A Westerville Rd., Westerville, 43081, 898-1088

Computer consignment store for used Apples and IBM compatibles can save you 30-50% off new prices. The inventory also consists of liquidations and buyouts. Laptop computers, monitors, software with business and entertainment applications, as well as accessories are available. M-F 10-9, Sat 10-5, Sun 12-5.

COMPUTER GAME EXCHANGE
(614) 341-7283 or 873-3785

Owner, Dan McKean, became frustrated paying big bucks for the computer games he loves to play. So he began this business as a way to help himself and others to trade games. When you call, you'll hear a recording which lists the games currently available for trade. The list is updated every few days. Simply leave your name and phone number on the answering machine, indicating the name of the game you want and what you are willing to trade in. Dan will call you back to let you know how much of an additional fee, in the $5-$15 range, you'll have to pay for the trade. The exchange takes place via mail, with each party responsible for their own postage costs. Dan checks the disks to ensure that they are virus free.

COMPUTER SUCCESS
5025 Olentangy River Rd., Bethel Ctr. Shpng. Ctr., Columbus, 43214, 457-2983

Save 20-80% on new and used computers, accessories and software by IBM, Panasonic, and others. The software is available in both business, personal and entertainment applications. You'll find a large selection of merchandise that changes almost daily. Trade-ins are accepted or the business can buy your items outright. M-Sat 10-8, Sun 12-5.

COMPUTER WAREHOUSE
31 Arcade Pl., Newark, 345-3682

This business buys, sells and trades new, used and refurbished systems and parts. You'll find such brands as Toshiba, Hewlett Packard and others. Competitively priced repairs are also offered. M-F 11-5.

COMPUTRADE CIT SYSTEMS
150 Graceland Blvd., Columbus, 43214, 841-1212

About forty or fifty used computer systems are in stock at all times and include all major brands. Savings are 30-40% less than if purchased new. The systems start at $299. The store offers a thirty day guarantee on its used systems. M-F 10-7, Sat 10-6.

CUSTOM COMPUTER WAREHOUSE
7444 Sawmill Rd., Columbus, 43235, 761-4100

Krazy Kenny chops down the prices on custom computers and upgrades to save you money. You'll find hardware, computer accessories and related items. Value priced repairs are also available. M-F 11-9, Sat 11-7, Sun 12-5.

HACKERS HEAVEN
862 W. 3 Ave., Columbus, 43212, 421-1517

New, used and refurbished computer systems, parts, electronics and surplus items are available with the area's largest selection. Save about 30-65% on used items compared to new, and very competitive prices on new merchandise. Repairs are also value priced. M-F 11-7, Sat/Sun 11-4

MICRO CENTER
85 Westerville Plaza, Westerville, 43081, 794-4400
747 Bethel Rd., Coumbus, 43214, 326-8530

Find new IBM, Macintosh, Apple, Epsom and Laser brands of computers, in addition to software, floppy disks, books, paper and related items, at savings of 10-40% off manufacturers' suggested retail prices. Bargain tables can be found throughout the stores, which offer savings of 20-90% off used, demonstrator and reconditioned merchandise as well as selected books. The Bethel Road location is a superstore concept offering an even larger selection than the other two sites. Bethel Road also has a free walk-in support desk which can provide technical advice, offers an extensive selection of computer classes, over 20,000 book titles and repairs at competitive prices. Sign up for their mailing list. M-F 10-9, Sat 10-6, Sun 12-5.

SOFTWARE ETC.
Columbus City Center #199D, Columbus, 43215, 224-8731

Educational, business and entertaining software for adults and children, to be used on the Macintosh and IBM computers, is discounted 10-30% off regular retail prices. Don't miss the large selection of software which is priced at $10 and under and includes discontinued, overstock and closeout merchandise. M-Th 10-8, F/Sat 10-6, Sun 12-5.

VIDEO GAMES EXPRESS
5480 Westerville Rd., Westerville, 43081, 794-1888
5861 Sawmill Rd., Dublin, 43017, 798-1808
6012 E. Main St., Columbus, 43213, 866-2685
10 E. 13th Ave., Columbus, 43201, 291-0108
2149 Rome-Hilliard Rd., Hilliard, 43026, 777-1288
3953 Hoover Rd., Grove City, 43123, 539-5555
1736 Memorial Dr., Lancaster, 653-1888

Purchase used computer and gaming magazines for 25-50% off the cover price. Used Super Nintendo, Sega, Gameboy, Neogeo, Turbo Graft and Genesis electronic game cartridges and systems are available at 30-50% off the original new selling price. New games and systems are discounted 10-15%. The store buys, sells and trades used items. M-Sat 11-8, Sun 12-5.

VIDEO TRADER'S TRADING ZONE
6072 Busch Blvd., Columbus, 43229, 785-0070
5811 Brice Outlet Mallway, Columbus, 43232, 575-0402
3660 S. High St, Southland Expo Ctr., Columbus, 43207, 491-2211
2544 Bethel Rd., Columbus, 43220, 459-4401
315 N. Hamilton Rd., Columbus, 43213, 475-7443
2215 Stringtown Rd., Grove City, 43123, 539-1670
1404 River Valley Blvd., Lancaster, 681-1944

These stores buy, sell and trade mostly used, and some new videos, lazer disks, video games and comic books. Some of the sites also offer new and used CDs and cassettes in the $3-$8 range. Prices are very reasonable and savings are 40-75% off "if new" prices. You'll find such sought after brands as Turbo Grafix, Nintendo, Super Nintendo, Genesis, Lynx, Gameboy and Game Gear. A 30 day warranty is offered. M-Th 10-9, F/Sat 10-10, Sun 11-7.

VIDEO UNIVERSE
1460 Morse Rd., Columbus, 43229, 888-8944

This store rents and sells new videos and computer games at typical retail prices. Offers free movie rental on your birthday to members in good standing. Sells used movies and computer games at good values with most in the $9.99-$15.99 range. The stock varies but there's generally about 100-150 on hand. Sun-Th 10-12mid, F/Sat 10-1a.m. Open 365 days a year.

ALSO SEE

Columbus Microsystems Warehouse Sale, Extravaganza, Greater Columbus Fantastic Camera Show And Computer Swap, Grandview Heights Public Library, Incredible Universe, Meijer, Phar Mor, Radio Shack Outlet Store, Sam's Club, Service Merchandise, Sun TV, Tag Sales, Toronto Business Equipment, Toys 'R Us, Uncle Sam's Pawn Shop

ENTERTAINMENT

AARDVARK VIDEO
612 N. High St., Columbus, 43215, 461-6302

International cinema, art videos, experimental works, avant garde and collector items are available at this business which buys and sells new and used videos and rents new ones. The inventory of used videos also consists of those which have been previously viewed from the store's collection and can be purchased at $3.99-$6.99 a savings of about 50-70% off the "if new" prices. Used collector videos are priced according to market value and new videos are at full retail price. Aardvark is well known for its unusual selection not found elsewhere in the city. You can join their video club at a cost of $20 annually or $50 for a lifetime membership. This entitles you to discounts off the usual rental rate of $3.75 per video. Lifetime member can also rent one free movie per month for life. Regular club members receive a one time, two free video rental. M-Sat 10-9, Sun 12-6.

ACTOR'S SUMMER THEATER
444-6888

Watch free outdoor theatrical productions of Shakespearean plays in German Village's Schiller Park. Performances are held Thursday-Sunday at 8p.m. from June-August. Bring a lawn chair or a blanket to sit on.

ANHEUSER-BUSCH BREWERY
700 Schrock Rd., Columbus, 43229, 847-6270

Free self guided factory tours provide an inside look into the processes used to create these fine beers. At the end of the tour, everyone will receive a free sample of Eagle Snack pretzels. Adults will also receive two free glasses of beer. If you have a passion for souvenirs, the gift shop offers many items emblazoned with the Anheuser-Busch name at regular retail prices. M-Sat 9-4.

ARTICIPATION
139 W. Main St., Columbus, 43215, 645-8517 or 645-7446

The City of Columbus, Recreation and Parks Department, offers an exciting eight week series for adults on Saturdays from 6-9p.m., and for kids on Fridays, from 4-6p.m. The cost is $20 for the entire eight week term and features a changing sampler of art programs including hands on workshops and excursions to visual and performing arts events and facilities throughout the city. The children's price includes transportation to events from a central site. The adults must carpool or provide their own transportation. Adult programs have included Ballet Met's Nutcracker at the Ohio Theater, CATCO's Thurber Carnival, a performance of the Columbus Symphony Orchestra, a calligraphy workshop and a trip to the Short North Gallery Hop. Children's programs have included a performance by a ventriloquist, a sketching trip to the North Market and the opportunity to see a theatrical performance. Articipation is operated out of five recreation centers: Barnett, Schiller, Marion-Franklin, Westgate and Whetstone. Call to be put on their mailing list. This program has earned the distinction of being one of my personal favorites.

BALLETMET
Ohio and Palace Theaters, Columbus, 43215, 229-4848

Students of all ages are eligible for half price tickets to performances if purchased on the day of the show. The discount is valid for all performances except the Nutcracker. Full price seating generally costs $14-$35.

BARBER MUSEUM
Canal Winchester, 43110, 833-9931

Free tours of probably the only museum of its kind in the United States, are available by appointment only. The attraction displays six barbershops from different decades and memorabilia dating back to 1790. You will find 600 razors in the collection, including an eight foot one which was used as a promotional piece, 285 shaving mugs and the world's largest library on hair.

BLUE JACKET
P.O. Box 312, Xenia, 45385, (513) 376-4318

This epic outdoor drama about a white man adopted by Shawnee Indians, portrays how he became their chief 200 years ago. Performances are held Tuesday-Thursday at a cost of $12, Saturday prices are $14. Children under twelve are admitted for $6 any night. The best value, however, is on Sundays when adult tickets are only $8. This is one of three similar outdoor dramas in Central Ohio, but is the only one to offer reduced price tickets for any of their performances. This family oriented production is held at 8p.m. from early June through Labor Day. The First Frontier sponsors these productions, and is located on Stringtown Road near Xenia.

BROADWAY SERIES
Ohio/Palace Theaters, box office is at 10 W. Broad St., Columbus, 43215, 224-7654 or (800) 294-1892

See the nation's best theatrical performances with top name entertainers appearing in such plays as Buskers with Tommy Tune, Damn Yankees with Jerry Lewis, Cats, Grease and more. Although season subscriptions can offer substantial savings off individual ticket prices, if you're willing to sit way up in the back of the theater, you can see seven shows for only $85 per person, a savings of $150-$230 off the regular subscription rate. Granted, if you are afraid of heights, this is not for you. But if you can handle the altitude, you can even bring binoculars if needed, it is a great way to save money by joining this Cloud Club. Club participants can choose from most of the shows with the exception of Friday and Saturday at 8p.m. Students have a similar opportunity. The last five rows of the balcony are also set aside to provide substantial savings off ticket purchases to individual shows (rather than the series) at a cost of only $12.50-$13.50 per ticket, when a valid student I.D. is presented. This is a savings of 40-50%. By purchasing tickets at the box office, Monday to Friday 9-6, you'll save the service fee tagged on at Ticketmaster and other outlets.

CAPITAL UNIVERSITY
2199 E. Main St., Bexley, 43209, 236-6411 (music dept.), 236-6497 (theater dept)

Free faculty vocal and instrumental recitals are held frequently throughout the year. The NOW Music Festival is held annually in February and celebrates contemporary music with concerts by the composer-in-residence, students, faculty, prominent local musicians and other guest artists. Admission is $2 for adults and $1 for seniors and children. Four quality theatrical productions, some of which are family oriented, are held from October-April at a cost of $4 for general admission and $3 for seniors. Past productions have included "Once Upon A Mattress", "Monsters In My Spumoni" and "A Shayna Maidel", and have been aimed at adult and/or family audiences.

CINEMARK MOVIES 12
2570 Bethel Rd., Carriage Place Shpng. Ctr., Columbus, 43220, 538-0403

One of Ohio's largest discount movie theaters features a $1 general admission fee at all times. You'll see second run movies, which are those that have been out about four to six weeks.

CLAREMONT SHOWGOERS CLUB
684 S. High St., Columbus, 43215, 443-1125

Enjoy the convenience of a single phone call to arrange a dinner/performance package as a member of the club. Your $25 annual fee entitles you to reserved seating at your choice of Columbus Symphony Orchestra, Opera Columbus, Ballet Met, CAPA or Broadway Series performances, parking and a gift certificate for $25 per person (based on a party of two) to dine at the Claremont Steak House. The typical price for the evening would normally be about $116, but you'll pay about $94, which amounts to a $22 savings. The more you use the club, the more you'll save.

COLUMBUS ASTRONOMICAL SOCIETY
P.O. Box 16209, Columbus, 43216, 459-7742

The Perkins Observatory in Delaware is the site of free monthly programs which include a film, discussion on astronomy and the opportunity to view the night sky through a powerful telescope (weather permitting). The two hour weeknight programs are sponsored by the Columbus Astronomical Society, OSU and Ohio Wesleyan University. You may request up to six tickets by mail. Be sure to include a self addressed stamped envelope. The presentation is suitable for adults and children.

COLUMBUS METROPOLITAN LIBRARY
96 S. Grant Ave., Columbus, 43215, 645-2000

The library is more than just books. The media production center offers free use of office/hobby equipment such as the Elleson letter cutter, light table, heavy duty stapler, paper cutter and comb binder. The library also provides free on site rentals of their IBM PC computers and their extensive selection of business and educational software including typing and computer tutorials. Reservations are necessary in order to use the equipment in this area. An enormous selection of videos on every subject from cooking, sports, crafts, performing arts, car repair, gardening, physical fitness, sign language, tutorial as well as entertaining videos for adults and kids, are also available for free loan. The second floor maintains 20,000 pieces of sheet music for free loan upon presentation of your library card.

A large selection of CDs and audio cassettes for enjoyment and personal growth, including business and managerial subjects, are also available for free loan. The Grantsmanship Center houses a large collection of books addressing how and where to obtain grants for individuals, businesses and nonprofit organizations. The Center For Discovery, the children's section, features interactive computers and CD-ROM software as part of their Reading Readiness Center. The Center For Discovery maintains its own mailing list of kids programs. Call to be added. The library has free slide programs, story times, book discussions, puppet shows, craft sessions, musical performances and other diversions for all ages. Call to be added to the mailing list for Novel Events which provides information on programs at each of the branches. Plan to attend their large used book sale in September which also has a pre-sale party. See the Special Sales section for details. The library has an extensive collection of two and three dimensional artwork gracing the building. Free audio tape tours of the building are available. The library has a used bookstore offering fantastic bargains. Refer to the write-up in the chapter on books. The Debit Card is a way in which you can save a nickel off each photocopy made at the main library or any of its branches. "Add Value" stations are located at various locations in the libraries where you put money into the machine and your card is credited with that amount. If you just put coins in the copy machine, in lieu of the card, you'll be charged fifteen cents. I think very highly of the library. Some of the research for this book was completed there. M-Th 9-9, F/Sat 9-6 (Sun 12-5 Sept.-May only).

COLUMBUS MUSEUM OF ART
480 E. Broad St., Columbus, 43215, 221-6801 or 221-4848 (24-hour hotline)

An annual membership at the museum costs $50 for a family and ernitles you to reciprocal membership benefits at the Dayton Art Institute, the Cleveland Museum of Art, the Cincinnati Museum of Art, the Contemporary Arts Center (Cincinnati) and the Akron Art Museum. Parent/child workshops are offered for children aged 3-5 with an adult companion and include gallery tours and creative hands-on activities. The fees are generally $4-$7 per class. A variety of workshops for youths of other ages is available at similar prices. Every Friday at 7p.m., you can watch a film or several shorts for $1. Each month, the museum has a different theme for the movies which includes experimental, science fiction and non-traditional flicks. Admission to the museum is free on Thurday evenings from 5:30 to 8:30p.m. The popular, Tuesdays At 1 program, presents free lectures on art history and other topics on a weekly basis. In the summer, the Meet Me In The Garden series presents quality weekly jazz performances. The cost is only $4 per concert or $20 for the series. The First Thurdays program is a monthly party and open house which features live music, hors d'ouevres and a cash bar. It is held from 5 to 9p.m., the first Thursday of each month year round. Admission to the party and the gallery exhibits is free, as is the parking. Closed Monday. Tu/W/F 11-5, Th 11-8:30, Sat 10-5, Sun 11-5.

COLUMBUS SWIM CENTER
1160 Hunter Ave., Columbus, 43201, 645-3129 or 645-6122

This indoor pool offers year round fun and exercise for a mere fifty cents admission. Swimming lessons are offered for pre-schoolers through adults in all skill levels, at a cost of $5 per session. An adult water aerobics class is available for 50 cents per class. Advanced classes are available at higher rates. Outside groups and individuals may rent the pool during non-recreational hours simply by submitting a request to the pool manager at least two weeks in advance. The cost is $15 per hour, plus $10.00 per hour for each lifeguard needed. This is a fun and low cost way to have a private party. Ample free parking is available on premises. The pool is operated by the City of Columbus, Recreation and Parks Department which also operates fifteen outdoor pools around the area, from May-September, at a similar admission fee. To find out about the other pools, call 645-3300. Sat/Sun 2:30-5:30, Tu 8p.m.-9:30p.m., W 1-3:45, Th 11a.m.-2p.m., F 1-3:45 & 7-9:30p.m.

COLUMBUS SYMPHONY ORCHESTRA
55 E. State St., Columbus, 43215, 224-5281 or 224-3291

Half price student Rush tickets are available an hour before the performance. Students must present a valid I.D. to buy the tickets which are regularly priced at $15-$36. This special pricing is only available for performances which are a part of the regular subscription series and not for any special performances.

COMMUNITY THEATER GROUPS
Curtain Players, Westerville 885-7000
Worthington Community Theater, 447-8168 or 841-5925
Little Theater Off Broadway, Grove City, 875-3915
Millersport Community Theater, 467-2474
Zanesville Community Theater, 455-6487
Roundtown Players, Circleville, 474-5856
Licking County Players, Newark, 366-6793

Community theater productions provide a low cost, opportunity to view performances featuring mostly local talent. Guys and Dolls, One Flew Over The Cookoo's Nest, Personals and other productions command ticket prices of only $5-$10 per person. If you take out a subscription to a series, your prices drop by about 25-30% per ticket. Many well known Hollywood actors and actresses had humble beginnings in community theaters. So who knows, maybe you'll see the Burt Reynolds or Elizabeth Taylor of the future!

CONTEMPORARY AMERICAN THEATER COMPANY (CATCO)
512 N. Park St., Columbus, 43215, 461-0010

This unpretentious theater, with its faux finished exterior, reminds me of the off-Broadway theaters in New York. You can attend their preview night performances on the Wednesday prior to the official opening night, for half the regular ticket price. On this night, the director has the opportunity to make any last minute changes before the official opening. Changes, if needed, are made after the performance, never during. This is not a dress rehearsal. Another savings opportunity is to purchase a subscription, which amounts to a savings of up to 40% off the individual ticket price. Yet another great value is the opportunity for you to purchase Rush Tickets one hour before curtain time, and you'll only pay half price for any unsold ticket. There is a limit of two tickets per person. Free monthly play readings are held featuring the works of African Americans. M-F 10-5.

COVER TO COVER BOOKSTORE
3337 N. High St., Columbus 43202, 263-1624

An enormous selection of books for parents and children can be found here at regular retail prices. Sign up for their mailing list to learn about their many free events for kids including meet the author book readings, story times with seasonal and fun themes, performances and craft sessions. A small selection of hurt books is available at 50% off the cover price. M-F 10-8, Sat 10-6, Sun 1-5.

DELAWARE COUNTY CULTURAL ARTS CENTER
190 W. Winter St., Delaware, 43015, 1-369-2787

Housed in an older building resembling a small castle, and perched high on a hill, it is a delight to visit as well as participate in their programs. In a brief period of time, this facility has managed to develop and implement a large and varied selection of programs and exhibitions. The arts center offers an extensive selection of visual, literary, performing and culinary art workshops, lectures and performances for the entire family in day, evening and weekend times.   Programs are fairly priced and are consistent with others in the community.   However, they also offer many free concerts, literary readings, book discussions and other special events. Don't miss browsing through their gift shop which features handmade arts and crafts, jewelry and gift items from artists across the state. While the prices reflect those typical of a gallery, the selection is unique. Proceeds from the gift shop are used to support the programs at the Delaware County Cultural Arts Center. The gift shop is open Monday through Saturday from 11-4.

DELAWARE COUNTY METRO PARKS
40 N. Sandusky St., suite 201, Delaware, 43015, 368-1805

The free, Nature Lovers Lecture Series is held year round and features a monthly presentation on such topics as bird watching, wildlife photography, geology and environmental toxicology. The programs are generally held at the Perkins Observatory on Thursday evenings, but occasionally include daytime hikes to see impressive natural formations. Oddly enough, there aren't any Delaware County metro parks, but this organization is the driving force behind obtaining land for this purpose.

DENISON UNIVERSITY
Granville

The music department, at 587-6220 or 587-6539, offers free and low cost performances featuring faculty, students as well as regionally and nationally recognized artists. A variety of musical performances are featured including the Denison Jazz Ensemble, directed by Rick Brunetto. The theater department at 587-6231, features quality adult productions such as Poor Murderer, Miss Firecracker Contest and Antigone and Joe Egg. The fee is $5 for adults and $2 for students or seniors. The dance department at 587-6712, features four productions during the school year which feature students, faculty and the visiting artist. Ticket prices are $5 for adults and $2 for seniors and students. All programs are held from October-April. Call each department to be added to their mailing list. Plan to spend some time in the quaint and peaceful city of Granville which features antique and gift shops. M-F 9-4. Accepts checks and cash only.

DOVE FAMILY FILM FESTIVAL
1-800-218-DOVE or (616)554-9993
Or you may visit thier website at http://www.dove.org

This semi-annual film festival is featured twice a year at area first run movie theaters. It shows in eight week sessions in those weeks before Easter and Thanksgiving and features quality family movies approved by the Dove Foundation. The spring 1996 series was held at the AMC Dublin 18 and AMC Eastland 8 theaters and featured such films as Thumbelina, Babe, The Indian In The Cupboard and Free Willy 2. Children aged twelve and under are admitted for free, while adults are charged only $1 admission.

DOWNTOWN DANCE CLUB
YWCA, 65 S. 4 St., Columbus, 43215, 231-3760

This club has been in existence for twenty years offering instruction and dancing opportunities. You can learn the foxtrot, waltz or other ballroom dancing from 6:30-7:20p.m. every Sunday. It is followed by ballroom dancing and a little square dancing, from 7:30-10:30p.m. The fee is $2 for the lessons (observers do not have to pay!) and an additional $2 to attend the dance. Refreshments are included with your admission fee. While the dances attract single adults aged 40-60, they are open to the general public, so couples are welcome. Approximately 100-150 people attend the dances and about 25 attend the lessons. Accepts cash only.

DREXEL THEATERS' PREMIER MOVIE CLUB
2254 E. Main St., Columbus, 43209, 231-9512

For an annual fee of $40, you can become a member of this club which offers you a pair of tickets to a minimum of ten movie previews and private screenings of major new releases at the Drexel and other area theaters. Your membership also entitles you to $1 off the general admission price of $5.75, or $3.75 before 6p.m., everytime you visit each of the two theaters, and a free month's trial membership at Aardvark Video, which will save you 50% off the price of rentals. Depending on how often you use all of the benefits, you're savings can range from $40 to $110. M-F 9-5.

ENTERTAINMENT 96/97/98 BOOK
4465 Professional Pkwy., Columbus, 43125, 836-7283

This annual publication contains discounts on hundreds of restaurants, theaters, sports, travel opportunities, hotels and services usually as "buy one, get one free" or a percentage off arrangement. There are also a few coupons which entitle you to 50% off a meal when dining alone. Some use restrictions may apply. Also keep in mind that your 50% off coupon for a hotel stay reflects the savings off the usual "rack rate" that is the highest priceat which the room is offered. Depending on the timing of your visit, there could be a special rate available to the general public which may be less than the rate you would pay using your coupon. You can purchase the book for $39.95 at various sites (call for locations), or you can save $5 by purchasing it through local nonprofit organizations. This coupon book has earned the distinction of being one of my personal favorites. M-F 8-5.

FAMILY CONCERTS ON THE GREEN
c/o Worthington Parks and Recreation Dept., 43085, 436-2743

Every Sunday evening from mid-May through mid-August, the free, outdoor music series offers a variety of family, musical concerts. The programs are held at 7p.m. on the Village Green, High Street and West Dublin-Granville Road. Bring a lawn chair or a blanket to sit on. In case of inclement weather, the concert will be cancelled. Performers have included local and regionally recognized groups such as Arnett Howard's Creole Funk Band, the Worthington Civic Band, the Sounds Of Swing, the Sweet Adelines and Rainbow Canyon. The concerts are open to the general public. Call between 9-5, Monday-Friday if you have any questions.

FIRST CONGREGATIONAL CHURCH
444 E. Broad St., Columbus, 43215, 228-1741

Throughout the Lenten season, from mid February through late March, the church offers a free series of lunchtime organ recitals on Tuesdays from 12:15-12:45p.m. Guest performers have included such virtuosos as Stanley Osborn of Kenyon College and G. Dene Barnard. You may bring your lunch. Reservations are not needed. Other free organ concerts are held September through May intermittently on Sunday evenings. M-F 9-5.

FLICKERS CINEMA PUB/GRACELAND CINEMA
5227 Bethel Center Mallway, Columbus, 43220, 457-0492
230 Graceland Blvd., Columbus, 43214, 888-8946

Purchase an annual pass for only $10 and you will be entitled to unlimited free admission to second run movies at either location. Although the restriction is that it's only valid Sunday through Thursday, if you plan your schedule accordingly, you can save money. Tickets are generally $1 a piece for these showings. The theaters will admit you for free on your birthday if you bring proof.

FRANKLIN COUNTY METRO PARKS
Battelle-Darby Creek, 1775 Darby Creek Dr., 43119, 891-0700
Blacklick Woods, 6975 E. Livingston Ave., Reynoldsburg, 43068, 891-0700
Blendon Woods, 4265 E. Dublin-Granville Rd., Westerville, 43081. 891-0700
Chestnut Ridge, Lancaster-Winchester Rd., 891-0700
Highbanks, 9466 N. High St., Worthington, 43235, 891-0700
Inniswood, 940 Hempstead Rd., Westerville 43081, 891-0700
Pickerington Ponds, Bowen and Wright Rd., Pickerington, 43147, 891-0700
Sharon Woods, 6911 Cleveland Ave., Columbus, 43231,891-0700
Slate Run Living Historical Farm, 9130 Marcy Rd., 43110, 833-1880
Spring Hollow, 1069 W. Main St., Westerville, 43081, 891-0700

Eleven area metro parks offer the opportunity to experience nature at its finest. Bicycling, hiking and jogging trails take you through scenic areas filled with animal observation sites, wildflowers and natural formations. Each park has its own personality and I recommend that you visit each one. The Metro Parks offer an extensive selection of year round programs for preschoolers through seniors including hikes, bird and animal watches, campfires, canoe trips, junior naturalist programs, salamander hunts, wildlife exhibitions, lectures and craft programs, most of which are free. The parks also feature major special events throughout the year such as the Herb Fair at Inniswood. Inniswood, by the way, is my favorite Metro Park. Its herb garden features many varieties including the nation's largest collection of thyme. Inniswood's woodland rock garden is breathtaking at the height of the season. Two of Inniswood's major trails are boardwalks, which makes them ideal for wheelchair users. Many Metro Parks have picnic areas and reservable shelters for family gatherings and special events. The Lens And Leaves Camera Club meets on the second Thursday of each month at the Blacklick Woods site, and presents a discussion on photography techniques relating to the outdoors or to nature. The meetings are free and open to the public. The beauty and diversity of the Metro Parks makes them among my personal favorites listed in this book. Call to be added to their mailing list, or stop by any public library to pick up one of their flyers. Parks are open 6:30am-dusk year round.

FRANK W. HALE JR. BLACK CULTURAL CENTER
153 W. 12 Ave., Columbus, 43210, 253-4620

Offers many free and low cost programs relating to the African American experience including movies, discussions/lectures, concerts, bus trips and more. Call to be added to the mailing list.

FREE MOVIE PREVIEWS

Follow Columbus Alive, the Guardian and the Other newspapers, all found in Columbus, to learn about these opportunities which occur about two to four times a month. Look for the large movie advertisements which say "Preview Screening", "Sneak Preview" or "Advance Screening" and the location where you can pick up your free passes. The pickup sites change each time and you'll need to arrive there as soon as you can, otherwise the passes will be gone. Each pass admits two people for free. Keep in mind that more passes are offered than there are available seats, since not everyone shows up. You'll need to arrive at least an hour before the movie begins to ensure that you'll be able to get a seat, otherwise once the theater is filled, you'll be turned away at the door. Movie distributors like to offer these opportunities for the new, first run movies, to gauge initial audience response.

GALLERY HOP
Columbus, 299-0860

On the first Saturday of every month from 6-9p.m., you can attend one of the most exciting events, the Gallery Hop. The businesses and galleries in the area bounded by North High Street from Goodale to Third and the adjoining streets, feature a giant opening reception for the new exhibitions. Entertainment is often found in the galleries and on the streets. Free munchies are also available in some of the galleries. Gallery Hop admission is always free. This is an exciting way to enjoy an evening as you walk through boutiques, exhibition spaces and galleries to find handwoven clothing, jewelry, antique furniture, pottery and a variety of other two and three dimensional media. The Short North has been likened to a mini Soho. The monthly Taste The Arts event, is generally less crowded than the Gallery Hop. It is featured on the last Thursday of each month, from 5-9p.m., except in January, and offers the opportunity to browse and shop in the stores and galleries which offer free, delicious edibles from Rigsby's and other area eateries. Tu-Sat 11-5 . The stores are also open the first Saturday of the month from 6-9p.m. during the Gallery Hop.

GALYAN'S TRADING COMPANY
6111 Sawmill Rd., Dublin, 43017, 798-1111

Test your mountain climbing skills on the 42 foot high climbing wall. While there are no age restrictions, you'll be able to select from three different skill levels. The store provides climbing shoes and verbal instructions for your free experience. Store personnel are there to ensure your safety. Open limited times during regular business hours.

GRANDVIEW HEIGHTS PUBLIC LIBRARY
1685 W. 1 Ave., Columbus, 43212, 486-2954

As is the case with many community libraries, the one in Grandview Heights offers a multitude of mostly free lectures, performances, book readings, kids' programs, crafts workshops for all ages, films, storytimes and special events. In the past, they have had lectures on rare books, consumer law for the layman and managing your financial future.

Workshops have included CPR and tee shirt painting. Their annual Music In The Atrium series is held from November-April and features free instrumental performances once a month, on Tuesday evenings. Use your library card to check out a framed art print from the 200 or so pieces in their collection. Their semi-annual book sale, usually held in October and February, provides you with the chance to purchase magazines for 50 cents and under as well as books for 25 cents to about $1. The free, Music On The Lawn program, is held on the second and fourth Tuesday at 7p.m., from June-August at the nearby Edison Kindergarten Annex. The rainsite is at the Grandview Heights High School. Prominent local groups such as Trilogy and Arnett Howard's Creole Funk Band, perform hour long concerts. Some programs require advance registration or tickets, even though they are free. M-F 9-9, Sat 9-5.

GRANVILLE RECREATION COMMISSION
Box 483, Granville, 43023, 587-1976

A free, summer outdoor concert series is held every other Sunday at 5:30p.m. on the lawn of Monomoy House, the residence of Denison University's president. The rainsite is Burke Recital Hall at Denison University. Concerts are held from May-August and feature a wide range of styles. Local as well as regionally known performers have included the OSU Alumni Band, the Hotfoot Quartet, the Windrich Quintessence Woodwinds, Seona McDowell and others. You'll enjoy visiting the quaint town of Granville, which is only 30 minutes from the east side of Columbus, so save time to browse through the downtown area and drive through the surrounding neighborhoods.

HYATT ON CAPITOL SQUARE
75 E. State St., Columbus, 43215, 228-1234

The former Rally In The Alley, has taken up a new home at the Hyatt on Capitol Square, where, on one Friday per month, the Affair On The Square (as it is now called) features free outdoor concerts. The events are held from early June through late August at Darby's Cafe. Local and regionally known performing groups such as Beauty And The Beats as well as Arnett Howard's Creole Funk Band will perform from 5-8p.m. The Affair is co-sponsored by WTVN Radio. Food and beverages will be available for purchase. On all other Fridays, during these months, the Hyatt features a similar after work gathering, but with a little less hoop-de-lah. Admission is free at all times.

KIDS DISCOVER COLUMBUS
645-3300

Registration opens in early April for this highly recognized travelling day camp program for kids aged 6-11. Campers can board a special COTA bus at designated Columbus recreation centers and take off for a fun filled adventure. They will explore various sites and attractions around Columbus such as the Park Of Roses, factory tours, COSI and other interesting attractions. The fee is $25 per week and includes all site admission costs, bus fares, a tee shirt and a daily beverage. Children can attend one or more weeks. The program is sponsored by the Columbus Recreation and Parks Department. The camp is held from mid-June to mid-August. M-F 9-5.

KROGER
30 area stores, see telephone book for listings

This supermarket chain serves as the site to purchase discount tickets to a variety of major entertainment and special events in the Columbus area such as the Ice Capades, Sesame Street Live, the Parade of Homes, the New Car Auto Show and Wyandotte Lake. Savings are usually $1-$3 off the ticket price. All Kroger bakery departments offer a free sugar, chocolate chip or peanut butter cookie to children ages twelve and under at any time, when accompanied by a parent. Pick up a free Fruit Of The Month Club card for your child which entitles him/her to a free fruit each month. Each Kroger store will sharpen your knives for free in their butcher department. The stores also feature a fax service where incoming or outgoing faxes are only $1 per page anywhere in the U.S. The savings will obviously be on the long distance faxes, since area office supply stores generally charge $2 a page for this service.

LITHOPOLIS AREA FINE ARTS ASSN.
Wagnalls Memorial, 150 E. Columbus St. Lithopolis, 837-4709 or 837-4765

Here's your chance to enjoy quality theatrical and musical performances with local, regional and nationally known artists utilizing a wide variety of styles. Individual tickets are usually $10 and are several dollars less expensive than the same performances in Columbus. Purchase a series subscription and save 20-30% over the single ticket price. Programs are held in the Wagnalls Memorial Auditorium, an extraordinary Tudor-Gothic building which also features libraries, artifacts and special collections. Lithopolis is about half an hour from downtown Columbus and is just south of Canal Winchester. M-F 8-5 (box office).

MAGIC MOUNTAIN FAMILY FUN CENTER
5890 Scarborough Blvd., Columbus, 43232, 863-6400

Buy your child a kid's meal for $3 then he/she can play in the kids' gym for free Monday through Thursday from 11-3. Another ongoing special is on Tuesdays where kids aged 1-4 can use the kids' gym for only $1. Prices are generally $2.95-$4.95 for use of the kid's gym.

MARTIN LUTHER KING CENTER FOR PERFORMING AND CULTURAL ARTS
867 Mt. Vernon Ave., Columbus, 43203, 252-5464

Performances, lectures, demonstrations and hands-on workshops, most dealing with topics relating to the African-American experience or featuring black artists, are offered year round. The center is the only historical building in Columbus which was designed by a black architect, Samuel Plato. Big name entertainers performed there during the 1930's and 40's. While programs vary in price, but there are several free and low cost diversions which are offered throughout the year. The adjacent Garfield School, also affiliated with the MLK Center, features the Elijah Pierce Gallery which offers changing exhibits with a similar focus. Gallery admission is free. M-F 9-5.

MARYSVILLE CINEMA
121 S. Main St., Marysville, (513)644-8896

Central Ohio's best price for first run movies can be found at this theater. All shows before 6p.m. are $2.50 admission and all shows after 6p.m. are $3.50. Prices are the same for all ages and regardless of whether the show is on a weekday or weekend.

MUSIC IN THE AIR
645-3800 (24 hour taped hotline May-September),
645-7995 at other times of the year

This free, annual showcase of local, regional and nationally recognized performing artists features poetry readings, children's programs, special events and concerts several times per week from Memorial Day weekend through Labor Day. Programs are held at area parks throughout the city including Bicentennial Park, the Riverfront Amphitheater, Schiller Park, Westgate, Griggs Reservoir, the Statehouse Lawn and Sensenbrenner Park. The latter two are held during a weekday lunchtime, and the balance are held on weekends. The Magical, Musical, Mornings In The Park are held on Wednesdays at 11:30a.m. at Westgate Recreation Center and at the same time on Thursdays at both the Park of Roses Gazebo and the Livingston Park. Performances have included Kirk's Puppets, African storytelling, theatrical productions and more. Annual special events, which are held downtown along the riverfront include the Big Bear Rhythm And Foo Festival, the two day Mcdonald's Gospelfest in mid June, Choices Country On The River Festival is in late June with nationally recognized singers, musical entertainment on July 3 at the Red, White and Boom Celebration, the Jazz and Ribfest in late July and a three day Labor Day Blues weekend. Music In The Air is a program of the City of Columbus, Recreation and Parks Department, but it also has many corporate sponsors. It has earned the distinction of being one of my personal favorites.

OHIO STATE UNIVERSITY ARTS HOTLINE
292-ARTS (2787)

This taped hotline operates 24 hours a day, seven days a week. It provides information on all of the events taking place at OSU which are open to the public including those at Mershon Auditorium, Weigel Hall, the Wexner Center and those offered through the dance, theater, photography, architecture and other departments. In December 1995, the dance department was ranked the top in the country by Dance Teacher Today magazine. Many of the programs are free or low cost. You can also request to be on the mailing list of the College Of The Arts by writing them in care of the Office of Communications, 1871 N. High Street, Columbus, 43210.

OHIO STATE UNIVERSITY-COLLEGE OF HUMANITIES
186 University Hall, 230 N. Oval Mall, Columbus, 43210, 292-1882

Sponsors many free programs for the general public. Previous programs have included literary readings, lectures on Aristotle On Artifacts, Judaism And Law, Medieval Disputation, Race, Class And Gender In U.S. Society and a play on AIDS. From 9:30-10:30a.m. on Saturdays during the fall and winter seasons, the Saturday Scholar Series presents free lectures such as Excavation Of Greek Ruins Yields Link To Olympic Games, Feminist Looks At Hollywood Actresses, Politics Of Style and Renaissance Exotica And Erotica. A continental breakfast is served at no charge. The programs are held at the Fawcett Center. Phone 292-1882 for information on the Saturday Scholar Series. The

Humanities department publishes a free calendar of events which you can obtain by calling this same phone number. Other departments within the College of Humanities which you might want to contact directly about free programs include the English Department (292-6065), the College of Law (292-0967), the Department of Philosophy (292-7914), the Black Studies Department (292-4459) and the Center For Women's Studies (292-1021). Most programs on held on campus and all are open to the general public. M-F 9-4.

OHIO STATE UNIVERSITY-DEPT. OF ARCHITECTURE
189 Brown Hall, 190 W. 17 Ave., Columbus, 43210, 292-5567

Offers a free lecture series in the autumn, winter and spring on such topics as geological architecture, European castles etc. There are eighteen two hour programs offered each year at various campus sites, generally on Wednesday evenings. The programs are open to the public. Call to be added to their mailing list. M-F 9-5.

OHIO STATE UNIVERSITY-THEATER DEPARTMENT
292-2295

Presents a variety of quality programs from October through May at several campus theaters. Prices range from free to about $10 and have included such productions as an MFA Actors' Showcase, musicals, dramas, comedies and mysteries.

OHIO WESLEYAN UNIVERSITY
Delaware

Features free lectures in the fall, on world affairs and political issues as part of the OWU National Colloquium Speakers Series. Topics such as The Promise Of Democracy , are discussed by local, regional and nationally recognized individuals. Phone 368-3335 for details. The University also offers frequent free student/faculty vocal and instrumental performances from October-April each year. Phone 368-3700 for information. A performing arts /lecture series is held on Friday evenings from September through April and features theatrical productions, discussions and musical performances by local, regional, national and internationally known artists. Single seat general admission is $6-$9 for adults. A season series subscription will save you about 50% off the single ticket price. Occassionally, performances which are featured here are also featured in Columbus for several dollars more. A recent progduction of Mahalia was priced at $9 here, but $14 when sponsored by the Worthington Arts Council! For information, phone 368-3185. The Chapelaar Drama Center is the site of quality dance as well as theatrical performances from September through May at a cost of $4-$7 for general admission. Phone 368-3845 for information. Programs are open to the general public.

ORDINARY MYSTERIES
245 W. 5 Ave., Columbus, 43201, 294-2000

On the second Thursday of each month, this curiosity shop features an open mike for area poets who are given fifteen minutes in which to read their uncensored works. Some acoustic presentations are also included. Herbal tea and admission are free. The store also features musical and dance performances, workshops and discussions on new age/alternative topics which are free or low cost. This interesting shop sells rocks, jewelry, new and used books. Unusual gift items are value priced. Tu-Sat 5-9, Sun 2-6.

OTHER SIDE COFFEE HOUSE
First Unitarian Universalist Church, 93 W. Weisheimer Rd., Columbus, 43214, 267-4128 or 851-1437

Enjoy a coffee house with a variety of folk musicians in concert, sponsored by the Columbus Folk Music Society. Held the last Saturday of the month at 8p.m. The informal atmosphere is warm and inviting. Admission is $4 plus a can of food.

OTTERBEIN COLLEGE
North Grove and College Ave., Westerville, 43081, 898-1508 or 898-1600, 823-1316 (astronomy programs only)

Presents quality theatrical productions year round at a cost of $7-$14 such as A Streetcar Named Desire. Free faculty and student vocal and instrumental performances are held from October through April on a frequent basis. A performing artist series is held monthly and features local and regionally known musicians in concert at reasonable prices. Free public astronomy nights are held the first Saturday of every month at 7:30p.m. They include a lecture, planetarium program and observation session (weather permitting).

PEARLS OF WISDOM BOOKSTORE
3224 N. High St., Columbus, 43202, 262-0146

This book store is a favorite of the New Age community. New books are sold at cover price, but used books are about 30-70% of the cover price. Sign up for their monthly newsletter which will describe new books, gifts, tapes, sales as well as their free, low cost and moderately priced classes, workshops, seminars and performances on ancient religions, tarot, psychic phenomenon, wellness and similar topics. Some recent free programs included a discussion on the biology of happiness by Steve Wilson and a Tibetan tea ceremony/discussion with Philip Sugden. The bookstore also has a video rental club which allows you to choose from over 300 titles not readily available elsewhere. The one time membership fee is $10. Videos rent for $1 per day. M-Sat 10-8, Sun 12-6.

SAMPLE THE ARTS
Greater Columbus Arts Council, 55 E. State St., Columbus, 43215, 253-9777

The arts sampler package enables you to try music, dance, theater and visual arts at savings up to 50% off regular ticket prices. About eighteen participating organizations include the OSU College of the Arts, Opera Columbus, BalletMet, ProMusica Chamber Orchestra, Columbus Symphony and others. For a $45 fee, you'll receive eight vouchers, a newsletter three times per year offering other community discounts and a calendar describing the upcoming arts events. Each event requires a certain number of vouchers, but you can choose which performances to attend.

SNEAK PREVIEWS AT AREA FIRST RUN MOVIE THEATERS
see addresses below

All first run movie theaters feature a bargain matinee price before 6p.m. which can save you about $2 off the regular admission fee of about $5-$5.50. Another opportunity for savings exists in viewing preview movies which are screened at the theater before being officially released to the general public. Usually the movie theater will charge you their regular rate to see a first run movie and will allow you stay to "preview" another movie not yet released. It is like a two for one price. You need to follow the newspapers (read the fine print in the advertisements as the previews are not well publicized) or call the movie theaters and speak directly with someone in the box office. As this is usually a last minute decision, the theaters will generally know three to six days in advance. Also, area radio stations occasionally offer free movie passes at special community promotions such as new store openings and special events. Sometimes you can find out by calling your favorite station. Sneak previews are a way in which film distributors can determine audience demographics which will assist in marketing efforts for the movies. Some theaters offering these special sneak previews include:

AMC Theaters: Eastland Plaza 6 (861-8585), Dublin Village 10 (889-0563), Westerville 6 (890-3344), Eastland Center 8(863-1539). Offers about fifteen sneak previews per year at each theater. These are generally featured on Saturday evenings. Admission is $5.50 for adults, $4.50 for students and $3.50 for seniors. The theaters have begun a Movie Watcher Club which entitles you to free snacks during your first four visits to the theater. On the fifth visit, you will receive a pass valid for one free admission. Thereafter, you'll automatically be a lifetime member of the club, and will receive free posters, passes to sneak previews and other special opportunities. There is no charge to become a member of the club.

Loew's Continent 9: (846-6202). Usually one sneak preview per month is offered on a week night. Adult admission is $6, children under twelve and seniors admitted for $3.50

General Cinemas: Northland 8 (447-0066) and University City (263-5435). Sneak previews are offered about six times per year on varying days and times.

Cinemark Movies 12: (777-1010). Located in Hilliard and Gahanna, these theaters offer about four to six sneak previews annually, often on a Thursday through Sunday evening. An unexpected surprise is that the theaters will allow you a free pass to view a movie on your birthday, just bring proof.

SOUNDS OF SUMMER
Groveport Parks And Recreation Dept., 605 Cherry St., Groveport, 43125, 836-5301

This department offers a free summer concert series from June through September. The programs are typically held on the first Sunday of the month at 7p.m., on the stage behind the Log House, near Wirt and College Roads. The type of music varies, but has included the Red Mud Ridge Band, the Sounds Of Swing and the Columbus Pops Concert Band. Bring a lawn chair or a blanket to sit on. Concerts are open to the public. M-F 9-5.

SOUNDS OF SUMMER/COMMUNITY BAND NIGHTS
c/o Westerville Parks And Recreation Dept., 43081, 890-8544

The Alum Creek Park Amphitheater on West Main Street in Westerville, is the site of a weekly series of free concerts from June through late August. The annual Sounds of Summer series is held on Sundays at 7p.m. and includes a wide range of styles by local and regionally known performers. Groups which have performed in the past have included the Greater Columbus Concert Band, the Delaware County Sweet Adelines, the Bluegrass Hoppers, the DeVry State Band and the Columbus Pops. Community band nights are Mondays at 7p.m. at the same site and feature various groups as well. Concerts are suitable for families. Bring a lawn chair or a blanket to sit on. In case of rain, the concerts will be held in the Battelle Fine Arts Center of Otterbein College. To obtain more information, call M-F 9-5.

SPRINGFIELD ARTS FESTIVAL
Springfield Arts Council, 8 N. Limestone, Springfield, 45501, (513) 324-2712

This annual performing arts festival celebrates its 30th year of quality, free programs. Annually, about 28 afternoons and evenings of performances from early June through mid July, include such groups as the Springfield Symphony Orchestra, the Springfield Concert Band, the Springfield Civic Theater, the Ohio Lyric Theater, the Ian Polster Orchestra, Phil Dirt And The Dozers, Johnny Lytle, the Letterman, the Platters, the Glen Miller Orchestra, the Irish Brigade and the National Shakespeare Company. Theatrical performances have included Sweet Charity, Oliver and the Man Of La Mancha. Each year, the schedule changes to include the brightest stars on the local, regional and national scene and features entertainment for the entire family. Events are held in the Veteran's Park Amphitheater off Cliff Park and Fountain Roads. Parking is also free. Call to be added to their mailing list.

STUDIO 35
3055 Indianola Ave., Columbus, 43202, 261-1581 or 262-7505

Admission is $2 at all times and provides you with the opportunity to see two second run movies. Pizza, beer and subs are available for purchase at typical take-out store prices.

SUNDAYS AT FIVE CONCERTS
Graves Recital Hall, 5798 Karl Rd., Columbus, 43229, 847-4322

Local and nationally recognized performing artists present some of the world's finest music on the third Sunday of every month from September through June. The free concerts are held at 5p.m. and showcase a wide variety of styles. Guest performers have included Andre LaPlante (pianist), and Barbara Conrad (mezzo soprano of the N.Y. Metropolitan Opera). Call to be added to mailing list. M-Sat 10-9, Sun 12-5.

SUPER SAVER 8
5996 Westerville Rd., Westerville, 43081, 890-2624
5899 Scarborough Mallway, Columbus, 43232, 864-1064

If you like high tech decors, you'll love the fantastic star wars type tunnel with digital sound, and the magic light show which greet you prior to entering the movie. The ceilings in the lobbies are also filled with an unusual grouping of colorful lights, Astro Spiders (imported from Italy), which spin and shimmy as they create wild patterns on the walls. Young and old alike will enjoy the ambience. These movie theaters charge a $1.50 admission fee at all times, and feature second run movies. These theaters have earned the distinction of being among my personal favorites.

TRIUNE CONCERT SERIES
St. John's Evangelical Protestant Church, 59 E. Mound St., Columbus, 43215, 224-8634

Columbus' oldest church concert series was founded in 1966. It is featured annually on a Friday or Saturday evening in January, February and March. In the past, performances have included the Brass Band of Columbus, Tom Battenberg's High Street Stompers, the Oberlin Baroque Ensemble, the Early Interval, Dennis James and the Columbus Symphony String Quartet. Admission is free. Call to be added to the mailing list.

UPPER ARLINGTON CULTURAL ARTS COMMISSION
c/o Municipal Services Ctr., 3600 Tremont Rd., Columbus, 43221, 457-8050

Free Music In The Park outdoor concerts are held at 7:30p.m. every Thursday at the above address, from early June through late August. The top local and regionally known talent is presented with all musical styles featured. Bring a lawn chair or a blanket to sit on at these family concerts. The rain site is indoors. The Hausmusik Chamber Music Series features 5 performances from June through December at a cost of $4 per concert or $16 for the series. The commission also sponsors changing exhibitions in its lobby at which admission is free. Free and low cost movies, lectures, workshops and other performances are offered year round. All programs are open to the public so call to be added to their mailing list. Their annual Labor Day Arts Festival presents some of the finest crafts and fine arts for sale by local, regional and nationally known artists.

VETERAN'S MEMORIAL AUDITORIUM
300 W. Broad St., Columbus, 43215, 258-9411

As an usher, you'll assist show patrons to their seats and have the opportunity to obtain a free pass to the show, plus a stipend. The intermittent hours are 6-10 p.m. with occasional morning and afternoon matinees on weekends. This is a great way to enjoy concerts featuring local and nationally recognized performers. Why not plan to participate with your significant other and you'll both get free passes!

VOLUNTEER VACATIONS

Volunteer vacations can cost anywhere from thousands of dollars to those which cost nothing more than your time and energy. Opportunites include everything such as those dealing with earth sciences, business, education, archeology and ecology. Try these books for sources: New World Of Travel by Arthur Frommer, Environmental Vacations: Volunteer Projects by Stephanie Ocko, Volunteer Vacations by Bill McMillon or the Directory of Alternative Travel Resources by Diane Brause.

WEXNER CENTER FOR THE ARTS
30 W. 15 Ave., Columbus, 43210, 292-2787

This highly recognized facility on the OSU campus, features regional, national and internationally acclaimed performances by the Paul Taylor Dance Company, the Juillard String Quartet, Eiko and Koma and others. Visiting artist book readings; restored, long unseen and controversial movies and videos; lectures and other special events are priced from $3 to about $20. Several other free programs are offered quarterly including guided tours of the exhibits, faculty recitals and more. The Young Arts programs are held about twice per month at a cost of $2.50-$3.50 per person, and include a variety of fun, hands-on activities that relate to the current exhibits. Family Day activities are free and are held three times a year. They feature several hours filled with art activities, performances, movies and other events that also relate to current exhibits. The Occasional Sundays Series of various types of performances costs about $5. Wednesdays from 5-9p.m., admission is free to the gallery exhibits. Become a volunteer usher and you can watch performances for free. You must be able to volunteer at five events. Training is provided. To learn about volunteer usher opportunities, call 292-6310, 688-3890 or 292-6311. Sign up to be added to their mailing list. M-F 9-5.

WYANDOTTE LAKE
10101 Riverside Dr., Powell, 43065, 889-9283

Over sixty water rides, land amusement rides and entertainment make this a fun experience for the whole family at this theme park.   Kroger's sells discounted daily passes to Wyandotte Lake. Or you can enter the park any time after 4p.m. and pay a reduced rate of $6.95 per single admission ticket at the gate. Wyandotte Lake also features special events throughout the season such as concerts and outdoor movies which are included in your admission fee.   During the last week of August, their annual "Banana Bunch" discount promotion entitles you and nine of your friends to admission for only $29 for the group. M-Th 10-7, F-Sun 10-9. Accepts checks and cash only.

ALSO SEE

Aardvark Video, American Youth Hostels, Barnes And Noble, Columbus Clippers, Columbus Cultural Arts Center, Dawes Arboretum, Delaware County Metro Parks, First Community Village Oktoberfest, Gold C Savings Spree, Incredible Universe, Jewish Bookfair, Just For Feet, Little Professor Bookstore, Media Play, ODNR Division of Watercraft, ODNR Rent-A-Camp Program, Ordinary Mysteries, OSU Office of Women's Services, Senior Salute, Southwest Community Center Indoor Pool, Special Sales And Events Index, U.A. High School Natatorium, U.A. Library, Westerville Library and Women's Health Day

FABRICS/LINENS/ WALL & WINDOW COVERINGS

FABRICS

BEXLEY FABRICS
2476 E. Main St., Columbus, 43209, 231-7272

Over 100 different lines of drapery and upholstery fabrics are available at savings of 20-60% off suggested retail prices. The first quality decorator goods are largely current stock from Waverly, Schumacher, Covington, Robert Allen, Spectrum, Kauffman and others. A shop at home service is available. M-F 10-5, Sat 11-4.

BOONE FABRICS
6100 Huntley Rd., Columbus, 43229, 785-0121,

Save 25-70% off moderate to designer quality home decorating fabrics by Waverly, Robert Allan, P. Kauffman, Mastercraft and other popular brands. Over 1500 bolts of upholstery and drapery fabric are in stock at all times. Their extensive selection is certain to please even the most finicky tastes. M-Sat 9:30-6.

EXQUISITE FABRICS
3740 Town and Country Shopping Center, Columbus, 43213, 236-0725

Designer fabrics in cashmere, mohair, silk, wool crepe, gabardine and other materials are available at substantial savings which can amount to 15-40%. The owner purchases end bolts and remnants after designers such as Calvin Klein, Liz Claiborne and others are finished with them. The store also stocks bridal fabrics and laces as well as evening wear fabrics. M 11-5, Tu-F 11-6, Sat 11-4.

FABRIC AND DRAPERY MART-THE FABRIC STORE
6112 Boardwalk St., Columbus, 43229, 888-5640
169 W. Main St., Lancaster, 654-1880
961 Hebron Rd., Heath, 522-2582

Over 50,000 yards of top quality, mill direct drapery, upholstery and multi-purpose fabric is in stock at all times. Savings are 25-50% off suggested retail prices. Buy seven yards of fabric and your eighth yard is free. The store maintains an in-house workroom with qualified seamstresses, which enables even custom orders to be priced at similar savings. Over 40 window treatments are on display. You can save 40-58% on custom vertical blinds, fabricated in their own showroom, which includes a top of the line headrail system. The store offers a free shop at home service. M-Th 10-7, F/Sat 10-6.

FABRIC FARMS
3590 Riverside Dr., Columbus, 43221, 451-9300

Sells Waverly, P. Kaufman, Covington and other decorator quality lines of garment, home decorating and upholstery fabrics at savings of 20-50% off manufacturer's suggested retail prices. The merchandise consists of past season, overstocks and some irregular goods. Frequent craft and home decorating classes are offered. Call to be added to their mailing list. M-F 10-9, Sat 10-6, Sun 1-5.

HANCOCK FABRICS
Six Columbus locations plus the following
2138 N. Limestone St., Springfield, 45501, (513) 390-2703

Offers first quality sewing, upholstery, home decorating and bridal fabrics at savings of about 20-40% off regular retail prices. The stores have a special section where irregulars and misdyed fabrics are sold at $1.44 per yard, a savings of about 50-75% less than the "if perfect" price. Another section features other specials at $1.88 a yard with values to about $12.99 per yard. This full service business also features a "notion of the week" sale item which is reduced 30-50% off their regular price. Offers free and low cost sewing seminars several times during the year. M-Sat 10-9, Sun 12-5.

JERRY'S FABRICS
37 S. 3 St., Newark, 349-7195

If you like to sew, or need fabrics and notions for clothing, crafts and home decorating, this is a great place to shop. You'll find two levels with mostly first quality fabrics obtained as mill ends or special purchases with such brands as Brunswig and Fils, Kauffman and others. There's a small selection of irregulars or seconds which are clearly marked. You'll find everything from calicos, lames, wool's, wool blends, upholstery and drapery fabrics plus everything in between. I have always been impressed with the variety found here, which includes many unique designs and textures at abut 20-75% off regular retail prices. You'll also find large cones of sewing thread, foam, imported lace, sequined appliques and other items. Even if you don't do much sewing, why not pick up some items to use as embellishments on apparel? I purchased a one pound bag of Ultrasuede scraps for $10 and I am still trying to figure out how I will use it. M-Sat 10-6.

JO-ANN FABRICS
10 Franklin County locations
21 Troy Rd., Delaware, 363-3464
1311 Delaware Ave., Marion, 389-2141
633 Southgate Shpng. Ctr., Newark, 522-4700

Save about 20-30% off comparable fabrics, lace, ribbons and other sewing notions and related needs at this national chain. A large selection of fabrics for home decorating, bridal wear and fashion apparel can be found. Their private label, Beechwood, includes craft and sewing products such as glues, fabric paints and other items at savings of 30-50% less than popular brands of similar quality. The stores also sell sewing machines and gifts at similar savings. Sign up for their mailing list to be notified of their frequent sales. M-Sat 10-9, Sun 12-5.

JOYCE IRON AND METAL COMPANY
1283 Joyce Ave., Columbus, 43219, 299-4175

Although this business deals primarily in salvaged metal products, it also has a large area of vinyl coated wallpaper in assorted patterns, and vinyl Naugahide material sold at $1/pound. Remnants, mill ends and scraps, available in various sizes, can be used to reupholster boat seats, kitchen chairs and other home and craft uses. M-F 7:30-5, Sat 7:30-12.

MCGRAW'S SOUTHERN MILL OUTLET
1 E. Main St., S. Vienna, (513) 568-4257
4601 E. Broad St., Columbus, 43213, 759-7549

Upholstery fabrics, carpeting, tools and supplies are priced at 20-60% less than suggested retail. The large inventory consists of remnants, mill ends, bolt ends and discontinued fabrics, all of which are first quality. Some of the brands include La France, American Textiles and Robert Allen in nylon, Herculon, prints, tweeds, plaids, brocades and Naugahydes. Also, do-it-your-selfers can find all the upholstery needs such as threads, webbing, gimp, tacks and related items at a 25% savings. Although the store offers upholstery services at typical prices, your savings will obviously be on the fabrics. The South Vienna business custom builds furniture frames which can be upholstered, and are value priced. They also offer savings of 20-50% on their showroom samples at that site. Tu/W/F 9:30-5, Th 9:30-6, Sat 9:30-4.

NANCY'S FABRICS
140 W. Olentangy St., Powell, 43065, 766-5660

Designer drapery, slipcover and upholstery fabrics are sold at savings of about 30-60% off regular retail prices. The inventory consists of first quality, short bolts, mill overstocks and inspected seconds. Custom made draperies and other window treatments, slipcovers and upholstered work can be done by the staff. However, you might want to consider taking one of the store's "how to" classes" which will teach you the methods of creating jabots, swags and shades, or even ways to design and paint a faux finish on your walls! The classes are actually demonstration sessions and cost about $15-$25. Major fabric sales are held in March, and September when savings are even greater. M-Sat 10-5, Sun 1-5.

THREADWORKS
2025 W. Henderson Rd., Columbus, 43220, 538-9300

Save on an exquisite collection of designer silks, linens, ramies, wools, rayons and blends from popular mills and well known designers, all suitable for apparel. Overstocks and discontinued fabrics designed for Ralph Lauren, Liz Claiborne, Jones New York, Ann Taylor and others can be found here at value prices. Jacquard silks start at $10.99 per yard, woven cottons at $6.99 per yard, a fabric imitating Victorian crazy quilts was $18.99 per yard, colorful plaid mohair was $49.99 per yard, Ralph Lauren linen was $16.99 per yard etc. The business has a frequent purchaser club which offers a $10 gift certificate for each $100 you spend. You'll find Burda patterns at $6.95-$9.95, an assortment of decorative buttons at 25 cents to $5 and a small boutique where you can display and sell items which you have made. M/Tu/W/F/Sat 10-5:30, Th 10-9.

ALSO SEE

Camp And Williams, Experienced Possessions, Liberty Street Interiors, Northland Sewing Machine Center, Nu Look Factory Outlet and Woolen Square

LINENS

COTTON MILL OUTLET
1061 N. Bechtel Ave., Springfield, 45504, (513) 323-8829

Operated by the Leshner Corporation, this business sells first quality and some imperfect linens and domestics, at savings of 20-50% off and more. There's comforters starting at $12.99, dishtowels, placemats, oven mitts, waterbed sheet sets, bed linens and other items. The stock consists of those which Leshner's manufacturers for chain and department stores, plus those by other manufacturers such as Springmaid. M-F 9:30-8, Sat 9:30-6, Sun 12-5.

LINENS 'N THINGS
6035 Sawmill Rd., Dublin, 43017, 792-0090

Save 20-70% off the regular retail prices on towels, linens, tablecloths, placemats, area rugs, bedspreads, shower curtains, bath accessories, dinnerware and draperies. This superstore carries such popular brands as Wamsutta, Cannon, Beacon Hill, Royal, Springmaid, Laura Ashley, Burlington, Waverly, Eileen West, Krups, Calphalon, Braun, Mikasa and others. The inventory consists of first quality and irregulars. On a recent visit, I saw a 100% wool blanket for $39.99 regularly $80, a Burlington bedspread for $79.99 regularly $120 and other items. M-Sat 10-9, Sun 12-6.

LINEN SUPERMARKET
3690 Soldano Blvd., Consumer Sq. W., 43228, 275-0100
3776 E. Broad St., Town and Country Shp. Ctr., 43213, 237-1800
2600 E. Dublin Granville Rd., Columbus Sq. Shp. Ctr., Columbus, 43231, 523-2929
6599 Dublin Center Dr., Dublin Vill. Ctr., Dublin, 43017, 761-7699
1855 W. Henderson Rd., Arlington Sq., Columbus, 43220, 459-4811

These stores offer quality linens, bathroom accessories, kitchen gadgets, table accessories, curtains and other home items at savings of 10-65%. The stock consists of special purchases, closeouts and discontinued items. You'll find such brands as Cannon, West Point Stevens, Dan River, Fieldcrest, Wamsutta, Martex, Utica and others. For example, 200 thread count king or queen sheet sets regularly $75-$100 are here for $29.99, designer balloon valances regularly $10-$20 are $4.99, twenty piece dinnerware set for four people, which is regularly $60-$80, is $19.99. M-Sat 10-9, Sun 12-6.

TODAY'S QUILTS
24 Westerville Sq., Westerville, 43081, 898-0002

Find first quality quilts from mail order catalogs such as L.L. Bean and Spiegel plus other sources. The merchandise consists of liquidations, closeouts and discontinued items at savings of 30-50%. Quilts start at $49 and go up to about $300. You'll also find quilted pillows and lap throws at comparable savings. The business features at least one warehouse sale per year, in Westerville, where savings are even greater. M/Tu/W/F 10-5, Th 10-8.

TOWELS AND THINGS
70 S. Main St., London, 43140, 852-4415

You'll find a small selection of moderate quality linens, comforters, beach towels, waterbed sheets, pillowcases and regular sheets at savings of about 20-30%. Brands such as J.P. Stevens, Cannon, Royal and Briggs are available. M-F 9:30-6, Sat 9:30-5:30.

ALSO SEE

Burlington Coat Factory, Eddie Bauer Salvage Sale, Eddie Bauer Warehouse Sale At Veteran's Memorial, Eddie Bauer Warehouse Outlet, Homeplace, J.C. Penney Department Store, J.C. Penney Outlet, J.C. Penney Portfolio, Jeffersonville Outlet, Lazarus Final Countdown, Marshalls, Odd Lots, Ohio Factory Shops, Schottenstein's, Sears Outlet, T.J. Maxx, Target Greatland and Tuesday Morning

WALL & WINDOW COVERINGS

ACCENT DRAPERIES
1180 W. Goodale Blvd., Columbus, 43215, 488-0741

Save on custom tailored draperies, vertical blinds, mini blinds and other alternative window treatments. Draperies are made on premises. M-F 9-5.

AMERICA'S WALL AND WINDOW
3395 Dahlgreen Dr., Westerville, 43081, 442-0800

Mini blinds and verticals, in a variety of patterns and materials, are available here at savings of 55-65% off regular retail prices. The business carries Graber, American and Hunter Douglas brands, and has also begun to manufacture its own verticals at similar savings. Custom made valences, draperies and other fabric window treatments are about 25-50% less than those of comparable quality in other stores. This is a shop at home service. M-Sat 10-10.

BLIND FACTORY OUTLET
3670 B Parkway Lane, Hilliard, 43026, 771-6549
471 E. Morrison Rd., Gahanna, 43230, 337-9635
1727 Brice Rd., Reynoldsburg, 43068, 860-1110
6375 Sawmill Rd., Dublin, 43017, 799-9444

This manufacturer of vinyl, fabric and channel verticals has 2,0000 patterns, colors and textures and can save you about 40-70% on your next decorating project. The company also makes pleated fabric shades in 300 colors and patterns as well as fifty colors of metal mini blinds. This business sells to upscale department stores and other retailers. Measure your windows and install the products on your own and you'll avoid the installation fee. Hours vary for each store.

BLIND OUTLET
614 W. Schrock Rd., Westerville, 43081, 895-2002

Shop at home or in the store to save on custom made mini, pleated and cellular blinds. You'll find a large selection at savings of about 50%. M-Sat 10-5 and by appointment.

BLINDS N SHADES U.S.A.
431 Lazelle Rd., Westerville, 43081, 781-1040
Dublin, 43017, 792-2872

Save about 40% on custom blinds and shades in a large selection of patterns, colors and textures. M-Sat 10-6.

CAMP AND WILLIAMS
33 N. State St., Westerville, 43081, 898-7092

Upscale fabrics, blinds, wallcoverings, furniture and accessories are available at this interior design studio. Cowtan and Stout, Lebis, Brunswig And Fils and other better fabrics are discounted 15% if you buy five or more yards. Simply wonderful trims are available at 15% off five or more yards. The store features custom upholstering, curtains and draperies and custom pillows at about 15-30% less than in full price stores. A small selection of furniture is discounted by 30% and includes such brands as Beacon Hill, Michael Thomas, Sherrill, Hickory and others. Special orders are similarly discounted. Decorator pillows are part of their former wholesale division which had created these unique home decor accents for department and specialty stores throughout the United States. Save 15% on five or more rolls of decorator wallpapers by Ralph Lauren, Blonder, Thibony, Kenny, Payne, Schumacher and other brands. Tu-Th 10-5, Sat 10-3 and by appointment.

DECORUM WINDOW AND WALL COVERINGS
5776 Frantz Rd., Dublin, 43017, 889-8895

Save 25-70% off wallcoverings from all popular brands including Waverly, Schumacher, Imperial, Blonder and others. The first quality merchandise is available in stock and by special order from over 800 books. Coordinating fabric is also available at similar savings. In home design services can be arranged. M 10-8, Tu-F 10-6, Sat 10-4.

HOUSE OF BLINDS AND MORE
3663 Fishinger Blvd., Hilliard, 43026, 771-6224

Save 50-80% on custom mini, vertical, fabric, wood and cellular blinds and shades. The store also offers 30% savings on popular brands of upscale wallcoverings. M-F 10-8, Sat 10-5, Sun 12-4.

J & L BLIND CO.
4703 N. High St., Columbus, 43214, 267-6464

Save about 20-40% on mini and vertical blinds, pleated shades and custom draperies at this business. M-Th 10-7, F/Sat 10-3.

KATHY NYE-WINDOW TREATMENTS
Columbus, 476-4597

Kathy features custom window treatments such as drapes, valences, swags and balloons at very competitive prices as she and her staff make them in their workroom. Kathy has developed quite a following and can dress your windows in style. She also features savings on new blinds and verticals. By appointment only in your home.

MAJESTIC PAINT CENTERS
35 stores in Central Ohio. Check the phone book for listings.

The businesses discount custom blinds, verticals and pleated shades by about 30-40%. You can also save 10-30% off the regular retail price on art supplies such as lap easels, brush sets, watercolor paper postcards and more. Carries Blonder, Schumacher, Waverly, Imperial, Eisenhart and other brands of quality wallpaper which are discounted 30-50%. The stores offer a free rental of a video on how to hang wallpaper. The "Goof Proof Guarantee" allows you to exchange the wallpaper you purchased if it does not suit your taste once hung, or if you "goofed" in the hanging process. In the Spring and Fall, the stores feature a series of free how-to clinics on such topics as faux finishes, sponge painting, easy decorating ideas, beginners' refinishing tips and wallpapering. M-F 8a.m.-9p.m., Sat 8-6, Sun 11-5.

MAJESTIC PAINT OUTLET STORES
1665 Parsons Ave., Columbus, 43207, 444-4847
2000 Leonard Ave., Columbus, 43219, 253-4494

The Parsons Avenue Back Room Warehouse section offers quality wallpaper and borders by Mayfair, Vymura, Blonders and other brands at prices of $1.99-$21.99 per single roll. Window shades, blinds, painting tools, paints, stains, driveway sealants as well as varnishes are all discounted 50-75% off regular retail prices. The inventory consists of discontinued, closeouts as well as scratch and dent merchandise. The Leonard Avenue site has similar merchandise, but does not sell wallpaper. The annual warehouse clearance sale is held for five days in mid April. Savings are up to 80% off during this sale. Hours vary per store.

PANEL TOWN AND MORE
1063 Dublin Rd., Columbus, 43215, 488-0334
1050 N. Belmont, Springfield, 45503, (513) 323-0611

Save 25% on special order wallpapers and borders by Imperial. You'll love the large selection of contemporary and traditional patterns. Hardwood floors, bathroom vanities, kitchen cabinets and countertops are discounted up to 20%. Save up to 65% on sheet vinyl flooring. Paneling starts at $2.99 per sheet. Full layout and design services are available. The stock consists of manufacturers' closeouts and discontinued goods. Brands offered include Armstrong Mannington, Domco, Congoleum, Bruce and Hartco. M-F 8-8, Sat 8-6.

72 HOUR BLIND FACTORY
511 Main St., Groveport, 43125, 836-1802

Save up to 60% on all types of custom made blinds including mini, vertical and micro blinds. Similar savings are available on duette shades, pleated shades and toppers. The business offers free installation, free in-home consultation and free valences. Choose from Graber, Hunter Douglas, Kirsch, Silhoutte and other brands. M-F 9-5, Sat by appointment.

T C WALL FASHIONS
4087 Broadway, Grove City, 43123, 871-9040

Save 20-50% off manufacturer's suggested retail prices on first quality carpeting, special order wallcoverings from over 100 books, micro and mini blinds as well as verticals in this homebased business. There's also a small selection of in-stock wallpapers, with most at 99cents to $3.99 per single roll. In-stock silks are priced at $7.99 per roll. All wallpapers are sold in double rolls. In stock borders are priced at $4.50 per bolt, which is about fifteen feet. Brands offered include Essex, Vymura, Millbrook, Lindenstreet, Sandpiper Studios, Jenny Wren, Royal Scott, Stainmaster, Hunter Douglas, Joanna and others. Accepts checks and cash only. Sat 9-3 and other times by appointment.

VAUGHN PAINT AND WALLCOVERINGS
1392 S. High St., Columbus, 43207, 443-0002

Save 20-50% off manufacturer's suggested prices on popular brands of paints, varnishes, stains and wallcoverings. The inventory is first quality, overstocks and discontinued merchandise. M-F 9-5:30, Sat 9-3:30.

WALLPAPER BOUTIQUE
1230 Morse Rd., Columbus, 43229, 888-1115

Wallpapers and borders are available at 25-75% off manufacturers' suggested retail prices for first quality styles. There are thousands of rolls in stock, with tons of books from which special orders can be placed at similar savings. Brands offered include Waverly, Seabrooke, Kinney, Patton, Blonder, Warner and others. Also offers discounts on coordinating fabrics. The kids' play room is well equipped so your child can be occupied while you shop. M-Th 9:30-8:30, F/Sat 9:30-6, Sun 1-5.

WALLPAPER EXPRESS
479 Zanesville Rd., Roseville, 453-7999

Choose from thousands of rolls of wallpapers and borders at savings of about 30%. Wallpapers start at about $5 for a double roll and go as high as about $24. Most borders are in the $5-$10 range. M-F 10-6, Sat 10-4 and by appointment.

WALLPAPER FACTORY CLOSEOUTS
3968 Broadway, Grove City, 43123, 871-4343

Over 15,000 rolls of wallpaper and borders are in stock. The first quality merchandise is available by such brands as Borden and Walltex, and includes basic as well as novelty styles. Prices range from $2-$19 for a double roll. Savings are about 50-80% off manufacturers' suggested retail prices. The store also stocks a small, but interesting selection of framed prints and lampshades at small savings. M-F 10-5:30, Sat 10-4. Accepts checks and cash only.

WALLPAPER 4-U
334 S. Hamilton Rd.(Hunters Ridge Mall), Gahanna, 43230, 475-2808

Save 30-50% off regular retail prices on first quality in stock and custom order wallpaper in such brands as Sanitas, York, Pfaltzgraff Collection, Eisenhart, York, Mayfair, Waverly, Schumacher and Essex. There are hundreds of patterns to choose from starting at $1 for a single roll and $2 for borders. Free "how-to" wallpaper classes are offered four to five times per year. Occasionally you will find seconds here, but these are clearly marked. M/Th 9:30-8, Tu/W/F, Sat 9:30-6.

WALLPAPER MADNESS
5470 Westerville Rd., Westerville, 43081, 890-1722
6351 Sawmill Rd., Dublin, 43017, 761-2446

Over 50,000 rolls of first quality wallpapers and borders are in stock at savings of 30-65% off suggested retail prices. Special orders are also available at similar savings. The stock consists of first quality, seconds, closeouts and discontinued goods. The store features merchandise from Waverly, Imperial, Color Tree, Laura Ashley, Eisenhart, Louis Nicole, Color House, Milbrook and others. Coordinating fabrics are available at savings of 20-30% off manufacturers suggested retail prices. Children will love to play in the toy filled room while mom and dad shop. M-F 9:30-8:30, Sat 9:30-6, Sun 1:30-4.

WALLPAPER OUTLET
1024 Mt. Vernon Rd., Newark, 43055, 345-4235
3818 Columbus Lancaster Rd., Carroll, 43112, 756-7225
632 Main St., Zanesville, 452-6280

Odd lots, overruns and discontinued wallcoverings are sold as first quality and seconds at a cost of $5.50-$20.99 per double roll. Borders are available at a cost of $1.99-$5. On a recent visit, the wallpapers were simple patterns and florals in muted colors. M/W/F 10-5:30, Tu/Th 10-8, Sat 10-5.

WALLPAPERS TO GO
4560 Morse Center Dr., Columbus, 43229, 431-0500

Save 20-50% on first quality decorator wallpapers by Kingfisher, Mayfair, Cherry Hill, Legend and other popular brands. Offers coordinating paint, fabrics and window fashions at similar savings. The stores maintain a large selection of these upscale products. Free clinics are offered intermittently which provide instruction on how to hang wallpaper. M-F 10-8, Sat 10-6, Sun 12-5.

WINDOW SHOP
4720 Kenny Rd., Columbus, 43220, 457-0718

This company has been in business for about 28 years and features a large selection of designer fabrics by Brunswig and Fils, Coraggio, Cowtan and Tout, Pierre Frey and Osborne and Little. Custom window treatments are made on premises. Blinds, cushions and wallpaper are also available. Everything is value priced. M-F 8-5, Sat 11-3 and by appointment.

ALSO SEE

Andersons General Store, Berwick Corner Outlet, Fabric And Drapery Mart, Greystone Design, Harts, Nancy's Fabrics, J.C. Penney Outlet, Schottenstein's,

FINE JEWELRY/LUGGAGE & PURSES/COSTUME JEWELRY & OTHER ACCESSORIES

FINE JEWELRY

ALLEN'S COIN SHOP
399 S. State St., Westerville, 43081, 882-3937

The coin shop offers savings of 50% on a large selection of pre-packaged stamps. Antique and pre-owned jewelry are displayed in cases in the coin store and include sterling silver charms, and an interesting selection of old stickpins for $4-$10. Allen's closed their baseball card shop and moved everything into this location. This wholesale and retail vendor sells all types of sports cards, sport memorabilia, comic books, albums, storage boxes and related items at savings of 25-40%. The store offers savings of 40% Hummels, 25% on Precious Moments Collectibles, 20-40% off Royal Doulton gift items and similar savings on such brands as Bing and Grondahl, Rockwell, Bareuther and others. Estate jewelry is value priced. The shop also has an extensive selection of stamps, coins and other collectibles worth investigating. M-F 10-6, Sat 9-5.

INTERNATIONAL DIAMOND AND GOLD COMPANY JEWELERS
1704 Morse Rd., Columbus, 43229, 431-2500
830 Bethel Rd., Columbus 43214, 459-4500
2597 Hamilton Rd., Columbus, 43232, 861-7777
4180 W. Broad St., Columbus, 43228, 276-9910

Save big bucks off suggested retail prices on an extensive and unique selection of gold and diamond jewelry. These stores offer the best prices in town on gold jewelry. It pays to have a goldsmith on premises as the store is able to eliminate the middleman needed for jewelry repairs. The prices on repairs are one of the best in town and include: prong repair

$10, ladies'/men's ring sizing $10-$12 and chain repair $8. Savings on repairs are about 40-60% off the price at other jewelers. M-S 10-8, Sun 12-5.

KIMBERLY'S
12 W. Olentangy St., Powell, 43065, 436-4653

This small store has s a full range of fine jewelry including chains, rings, earrings and bracelets. She specializes in unique items and wedding sets and offers investment quality gemstones. Kimberly takes a lower markup than many jeweler, and her prices reflect about 20-30% less than most other businesses. Tu/W/F 10-6, Th 11-7, Sat 11-5.

MOSES JEWELERS
189 S. High St., Columbus, 43215, 224-0061

This wholesale and retail gold manufacturer offers a broad selection of gold jewelry at value prices. Contemporary and traditional styles are sold in. mostly 10K gold. The merchandising reminds me of the stores on the street in Chinatown or 47th Street in New York, so you bet I felt like being back home when I walked in. The prices will be further discounted from those appearing on the tags. M-F 10-6, Sat 12-6.

SPENCER'S GIFTS
1740 Northland Mallway, Columbus, 43229, 267-0201

Your favorite styles of 14K gold or silver neck chains and earrings are available here at savings of 35-50% off regular retail prices. The gold consists largely of Italian imports, most of which are marked, "585", on the clasp. The store also features a unique selection of gifts at regular retail prices. M-Sat 10-9, Sun 12-5.

ALSO SEE

Baggerie, Berwick Corner Outlet, Central Ohio Gem-Mineral And Jewelry Show, Columbus Police Property Auction, Drug Emporium, Extravaganza, Franklin County Sheriff's Department, Greater Columbus Antique Mall, International Gem And Jewelry Show, K Mart, Phar Mor, Revco, Right House Interiors/E And E Exclusives, Schottenstein's, Service Merchandise, Springfield Show And Flea Market, T.J. Maxx, Uncle Sam's Pawn Shop and Value City Department Store

LUGGAGE & PURSES/COSTUME JEWELRY & OTHER ACCESSORIES

BAGGERIE
90 Worthington Sq. Mall, Worthington, 43085, 888-8511
4810 Sawmill Rd., Columbus, 43235, 442-7767 (store called Excess Baggage)
3135 Tremont Rd., Columbus, 43221, 326-2244

Upscale and designer quality attaches, luggage, purses, pen sets and small gift items such as watches, unique calculators etc., are available at savings of 10-30% off suggested retail prices. Some merchandise is discounted up to 70%. The stock consists of mostly first quality goods including closeouts, discontinued merchandise, special purchases and some items especially made for this store. The owner is constantly searching for unique items for his businesses and you may be delightfully surprised at what he finds. Some popular brands that the stores carry include Samsonite, Travellers Club, Scully, Briggs and Reilly, Koltov, Kenneth Cole, Jack Georges, Infinity and others. M-Sat 10-9, Sun 12-5.

GALLERIA LEATHER AND LUGGAGE
7640 New Market Center Way, Columbus, 43235, 761-9555

Antigua, Buxton, Samsonite, Boyt, American Tourister, Hartmann, Delsey, Travel Pro, Le Sportsac, Atlantic, Halliburton, Lark, Travel Well, London Fog and High Sierra brands of luggage and small leather goods are discounted 20-70% off suggested retail prices. You'll also find briefcases, some purses, desk accessories and related items at similar savings. The store also does repairs. M-Sat 10-9, Sun 12-6.

LEATHER DIRECT
1219 W. First St., Springfield, 45504, (513) 323-8979

Save 40% on slightly imperfect and first quality small leather goods for men and women including wallets, checkbook covers, French wallets, billfolds, calendars, address books and desktop accessories. Save 85% on a small selection of seconds. You'll find impeccable quality goods, many of which are hand stained, normally selling for $20-$200. Traditional and novelty leathers, some with snake trim, are available. They can be found at major upscale department stores throughout the country such as Nordstrom's, Macy's Bloomingdales and Marshall Fields. The goods are marketed under the name Hugo Bosca and each item sold bears this insignia. From late November through Christmas, the store features their annual holiday sale where all merchandise is 60% off. M-Sat 9-5:30. Sunday hours are added from late November through Christmas.

SUZANNE'S SUEDE AND LEATHER
400 N. High St., Columbus Convention Ctr., Columbus, 43215, 221-1958

Luggage and purses are available here at savings of 20-30% off regular retail prices. Through the efforts of the knowledgeable buyer, he is able to select value wise items which are lower priced than those of other manufacturers, but still provide the quality you are seeking. There is also a large selection of clearance merchandise at 50% off their already low prices. The stock is all first quality upscale goods. The sales staff is friendly and eager to please. M-Sat 10-8, Sun 10-5.

ALSO SEE

Amos Indoor Flea Market, Babe Discovery Shop, Burlington Coat Factory, Creative Spirit Workshop And Gift Outlet, Byzantium, Deja Vu, Designer Shoe Warehouse, Dress Barn, Dress Barn Woman, Drug Emporium, Extravaganza, Golden Hobby Shop, Greater Columbus Antique Mall, It's My Turn, Jeffersonville Outlet Center, Kids 'R Us, Label Connection, Lake Erie Factory Outlet Center, Liquidations Now, MJR Weekend Warehouse, Marshalls, Ohio Factory Shops, One More Time, Red Square Imports, Sally Beauty Supply, Schottenstein's, Second Chance Consignments, Select Resale, Steinmart, T.J. Maxx, Ten Below, Tri-Village Trading Post, Tuesday Morning, Uncle Sam's Pawn Shop and Worth Repeating

FLEA
MARKETS/AUCTIONS

FLEA MARKETS

Here's a few quick tips to help you through this experience: arrive early, bring a shopping bag or several, have plenty of singles and small change, look quickly and move on, wear comfortable shoes, bring a small magnifying glass to locate inscriptions, hallmarks and gold/silver markings. At the outdoor markets, plan on arriving at least an hour before the scheduled opening times, so you can be there when the dealers set up. Bring your flashlight and you'll be among the first to snag those deals. Buyer beware, many flea markets are offering bogus Tommy Hilfiger, Louis Viutton and other brand name items. A good place to find out about flea markets and even church bazaars, which can also offer rock bottom prices, is in the classified section of the local and community newspapers. This section lists those flea markets which are open during typical business hours during the week and/or weekends throughout the month and those featured regularly once a month for at least six months out of the year. Other flea markets which may be held only once or a few times during the year are listed under the special events section.

AMOS INDOOR FLEA MARKET
3454 Cleveland Ave., Columbus, 43224, 262-0044

Be prepared to rummage through aisles of junk and hidden treasures: hair accessories, perfume samples, gold and silver jewelry, incense, antiques, seasonal fruits and vegetables, leather purses, bridal wear and more. Some merchandise is new while other items are used. However, most vendors cater to an African American clientele. Check your intended purchases carefully as most vendors will not accept returns. The food concession against the far right wall, sells hot dogs for only 25 cents. Vendors frequently change, and not all booths are open during regular posted hours. However, there are about 100 dealers under one roof. Admission is free and there is plenty of free parking. F-Sun 10-7.

CEASER'S CREEK FLEA MARKET
Wilmington, Ohio at the junction of I71 and S.R. 73,(513) 382-1669

Large, open air and indoor flea market features new and used crafts, clothes, housewares, jewelry, toys, tools, coins, produce, antiques and collectibles. About 300-400 vendors are set up selling their wares. The flea market is located about one hour and fifteen minutes from Columbus. Open every Saturday and Sunday 9-5. Admission is 35 cents per person.

DELAWARE ANTIQUE SHOW AND FLEA MARKET
236 Pennsylvania Ave., Delaware Co. Fairgrounds, Delaware, 43015, 363-3353

Held one weekend a month from April through October, this flea market features about thirty indoor vendors selling moderate to better quality antiques and collectibles. There are also about 15-30 flea market vendors outdoors selling new, used, collectible and what not stuff. Free admission. Sat/Sun 9-5.

DUMONTVILLE FLEA MARKET
Rt. 158 at Ginder Rd., Dumontville, 756-4457

This small, no frills flea market features trash to treasure, who-zits and what-nots. About ten to twelve vendors sell some used clothes, housewares, antiques , crafts, collectibles and tools. Prices vary among dealers, but the careful shopper can unearth some real treasures. Th 1-6, F-Sun 10-6, and holidays which fall on Mondays 12-6.

HILLIARD ANTIQUE SHOW AND FLEA MARKET
Franklin County Fairgrounds, Hilliard, 43026, 852-2229, 852-6495 or 882-0660

Held one weekend per month from April through December, these shows feature antiques, collectibles, furniture, new and used items and flea market finds. Since each dealer marks their own merchandise, prices will vary from booth to booth. The careful shopper can unearth some treasures among the 75 or so dealers. Admission is $1. Sat 8-5, Sun 9-4.

KINGMAN DRIVE-IN THEATER FLEA MARKET
Cheshire Rd., Delaware, 43015, 548-4202 or 548-4227

Bargains abound at this seasonal, outdoor flea market. From trash to treasure, you will find an assortment of new and used merchandise including antiques, collectibles, furniture, clothes, housewares, gifts, tools and who knows what. Admission is 50 cents per carload and parking is free. The number of vendors varies each week, but ranges from 50-150. Many vendors leave early, so don't arrive too close to the scheduled closing time. Open Sundays from the first week of April to the last week of October, 7a.m.-2p.m.

LITHOPOLIS ANTIQUE MALL AND FLEA MARKET
9 E. Columbus St., Lithopolis, 837-9683

Multi-level mall features antiques, collectibles, furniture, new and used items as well as what knots. The business leases space to dealers so prices and stock vary from booth to booth. You'll find some items priced at fair market value while others are great deals. The flea market portion is on the two lower levels. Stop by the Stratford Tea Room across the street and the beautiful, Tudor style, Wagnalls Memorial Auditorium down the block. The building was once the home of Wagnalls from Funk and Wagnalls fame. The building is partially a library and partially an auditorium for concerts (see listing elsewhere in this book for Lithopolis Performing Arts Association). M-Sat 10-5, Sun 1-5.

LIVINGSTON COURT INDOOR FLEA MARKET
3575 E. Livingston Ave., Columbus, 43227, 231-7726

Porcelain dolls, antiques, office supplies, Amish baked goods, books as well as miscellaneous new and used items, are available in this no frills atmosphere. Vendors frequently change and not all booths are open during the posted hours of operation. Hot dogs are available at the concession stand for only 25 cents apiece. You'll find over 100 vendors. Admission is free and there's plenty of free parking. F-Sun 10-7.

MANSFIELD ANTIQUE SHOW AND FLEA MARKET
Richland Co. Fairgrounds, 237-2485 or 237-3689

Mostly antiques and collectibles are sold on the last weekend of every month, except December, from 9-5. About 200-250 vendors are on hand to sell their wares. Take the Trimble Road exit off U.S. Route 30 to find the flea market.

MARION FLEA MARKET
1238 Linn Hipsher Rd., Marion, 383-9027

About fifteen to twenty indoor vendors sell antiques, collectibles, crafts, used books and miscellaneous new and used items of varying qualities. During the warmer months about ten vendors set up outside with similar merchandise. Admission is free. F-Sun 9-6.

MID AMERICA ANTIQUE SHOW AND FLEA MARKET
Fairfield County Fairgrounds, Fair Ave., Lancaster, 756-9393 or 756-4411

About 75-125 antique, collectible and flea market vendors hawk their wares at these popular shows. While prices vary among dealers, you're sure to find some great deals. Sat 9-5, Sun 10-5. Free admission after 3p.m.

RED BARN FLEA MARKET
10501 Columbus Expressway Park SW, Pataskala, 43062, 927-2276 or 927-1234

Open year round, this flea market features about 30 inside dealers and weather permitting, up to forty outside dealers. You'll find all sorts of new and used items including gifts, furniture, collectibles, antiques, food, tools and what nots. Quality and price vary from booth to booth, but there's always some good deals to find. F-Sun 9-6.

SOMEWHERE IN THYME IN OLD GAHANNA
161 Granville St., Gahanna, 43230, 471-1877

This upscale flea market features antiques, furniture, collectibles, crafts, new and used items as well as what-nots in a meticulously maintained setting. It operates as a mall where dealers lease space, so prices and stock vary from booth to booth. You'll find some items priced at fair market value, while others are great deals. Seven days a week 11-6.

SOUTH DRIVE-IN THEATER FLEA MARKET
3050 S. High St., Columbus, 43207, 491-6771 or 491-2583

This seasonal, outdoor flea market features mostly used and some new merchandise from 125-200 vendors. You will find everything including toys, antiques, collectibles and what not. As with all flea markets, you have to dig through piles of merchandise to discover real "finds". Admission is 50 cents per carload and parking is free. W/Sat/Sun 6a.m.-2p.m. Arrive early as many vendors close before 2. Open from the first week of April through the end of October.

SOUTHLAND EXPO CENTER
3660 S. High St., Columbus 43207, 497-0200

Indoor flea market features new and used general merchandise, garage sale items, videos, CDs, gifts, crafts and cement geese clothes. You'll also find several booths selling antiques and collectibles plus a large antique consignment area in the North end of the building. While prices and quality vary from vendor to vendor, the careful shopper will find some deals. Don't miss The World's Largest Garage Sale (listed in another chapter), which is located with this expo center. F 12-8, Sat 10-8, Sun 10-6.

SPRINGFIELD ANTIQUE SHOW AND FLEA MARKET
P.O. Box 2429, Springfield, 45501, (513) 325-0053

On the third weekend of every month, the Clark County Fairgrounds buzzes with excitement as 600-3,000 vendors sell new and used merchandise including antiques and collectibles, tools, toys, furniture, food, jewelry and miscellaneous items. There's about 150,000 square feet of indoor space plus the outdoor spots, which allow this to be a year round bargain hunters' delight. The shows are held on Saturday and Sunday except for the extravaganza shows, where 2,000-3,000 vendors exhibit, which are held from Friday through Sunday. Admission is $3 per person to the extravaganzas (4% for early shoppers arriving before noon on Fridays) and $2 to all other shows. Friday 5-8p.m., Sat 8-5, Sun 9-4 for regular shows. (Extravganza shows' Friday hours are 12N-6.)

SUNBURY FLEA MARKET
Town Square, Sunbury, 43074, 965-2684

You can find an eclectic offering of new and used merchandise from 150-250 vendors, such as clothing, jewelry, antiques and collectibles, furniture and more. Admission varies from 50 cents to $1 depending on the flea market. Three major events are held on Memorial Day, the Fourth Of July and Labor Day each year. 9-5.

36/37 FLEA MARKET
4059 State Rt. 36/37 East, Delaware, 43015, 363-4101 or 363-6446

This indoor flea market features the stash of about twenty dealers. You'll find trifles and treasures, kitsch, what-nots and oh-no's including housewares, gifts, crafts plus some antiques and collectibles. Prices vary with each vendor, but there's always a deal to find. M-Sat 10-5, Sun 12-5.

3-C FLEA MARKET
6930 Chandler Dr., Westerville, 43081, 882-5076

This no-frills business leases space to about thirty dealers who sell new, used, antique and collectible items. Housewares, gifts, books, small furniture, toys, tools and miscellaneous stuff are offered in various price ranges. You'll find trash to treasure, what-nots and who-zits so look high and low as you wander the aisles. The business is open all holidays, except Christmas, which fall during their normal hours of W-Sun 10:30-5.

URBANA FLEA MARKET
Champaign Co. Fairgrounds, (513) 653-6013, (513) 788-2058 or (513) 653-6945

Usually held the first Saturday and Sunday of each month year round. You'll find antiques, collectibles and new and used items. There's about 200-600 vendors depending on the show. Admission is fifty cents. The fairgrounds is at Park Avenue, off U.S. Rt. 68.

WASHINGTON COURTHOUSE FLEA MARKET
Fayette Co. Fairgrounds, 278-2721, 335-5856 or 335-5345

This show is open year round and features a sale once per month on a different weekend. The three day show features antiques, collectibles plus new and used merchandise. The June extravaganza show features about 500 vendors and other shows feature about 200 vendors. Admission is free. F/Sat 9-5, Sun 9-3.

WESTLAND FLEA MARKET
4170 W. Broad, Columbus, 43228, 272-5678

Indoor and outdoor flea market (weather permitting) has up to 300 dealers. While quality varies from dealer to dealer, you'll be able to find some treasures if you look. The booths sell everything from crafts, cement geese clothing, costume jewelry, socks, antiques, collectibles and "what the heck is it" items. F-Sun 10-7.

YELLOW BARN FLEA MARKET
142 Union St., Newark, 522-5487, 522-0087 or 927-8269

About 25 dealers sell antiques, collectibles, primitives and what nots of varying qualities. This indoor flea market is held year round, and recently moved to this new location. Th-Sun 10-6.

AUCTIONS

Overbidding is the most frequent mistake people make at auctions. The fleeting obsession of being able to beat the competition -to win- overpowers the buyer so he bids more than he anticipated. A real success at an auction is a purchase which was made carefully and at the right price. Be sure to inspect the merchandise before the sale, set a bidding limit and stick to it. Drop out of the bidding if you are feeling uncomfortable. It is equally important to understand whether you are bidding on an individual item or a set of items called a "lot". Why not test the waters by initially going as a spectator to several auctions before actually participating? Check the back of the "help wanted" section of Sunday's Columbus Dispatch for a listing and description of area auctions. Many auctions do not maintain mailing lists and so you may only be able to find out about them by reading their ads in the newspapers or by calling them directly.

CITY OF COLUMBUS, POLICE DEPARTMENT
Impounding lot, 400 W. Whittier St., Columbus, 43215, 645-6400

Auto auctions are held intermittently, usually every six to eight weeks. The cars which are auctioned are those unclaimed cars which were recovered from thefts, as evidence in a crime or those impounded due to parking or traffic violations. The police department does not maintain a mailing list so call them to find out the date of the next auction or check the Sunday Columbus Dispatch's auction, listings. Payment must be made in cash only. M-F 9-4:30.

COLUMBUS POLICE PROPERTY AUCTION
1250 Fairwood Avenue, Columbus, 43206, 645-4736

Over 36,000 items are warehoused in this 50,000 square foot property room which were evidence in homicide cases, stolen or lost property. Five annual auctions feature new and used guns, bicycles, electronic equipment and more. They do not maintain a mailing list, so you will need to call periodically or follow the auction listings in the Sunday Columbus Dispatch at the back of the "help wanted" section. Merchandise is sold "as is". M-F 9-5.

FRANKLIN COUNTY SHERIFF'S DEPARTMENT
370 S. Front St., property room, Columbus, 43215, 462-3316

Auction sales of confiscated new and used items are held about once a year whenever sufficient inventory has been accumulated. The date always changes. The stock varies widely and has included stereos, jewelry, hardware, automobiles and other items. A mailing list is not maintained so it is suggested that you call periodically, or check the auction listings at the back of the Sunday Columbus Dispatch's "help wanted" section. All merchandise is sold "as is". M-F 8:30-4.

OHIO AUTO AUCTION
3905 Jackson Pike, Grove City, 43123, 871-2771

All makes and models of repossessed cars, boats and motorcycles are offered for sale every Wednesday at 9:30 a.m. Vehicles are sold "as is" to the highest bidder, without expressed or implied warranties. I suggest that you bring along a copy of the current Consumer Reports or similar publication, to assist you in making an informed decision. You can inspect the offerings two to three days prior to the auction, at which time, you may sit in the car, turn on the ignition and look under the hood. The vehicles may not be driven. If you are handy or know enough about cars, this is a great way to save about 20-30% off the price at a used car dealer. I purchased my Toyota Camry here. At the time of the sale, the purchaser pays a $200 non-refundable deposit by cash, and the balance within 48 hours by the same method. M-F 9-5.

R&S AUCTION CENTER
810 S. Sunbury Rd., Westerville, 43081, 523-1810 or 431-0246

You can purchase gently and greatly used furniture, jewelry, collectibles and antiques at the Tuesday evening auctions which are held at 6:30p.m. Payment is by cash or check with proper identification.

SMITTY'S AUCTION
1263 Parsons Ave., Columbus, 43206. 444-5001

Thursday evening auctions of antiques, collectibles, furniture and contents of homes are held at 6p.m. Save about 20-40% less than you would pay in an antique or second hand furniture store. All merchandise is sold "as is".

STATE OF OHIO DEPT. OF ADMINISTRATIVE SERVICES
4200 Surface Rd., State and Federal Surplus Property Division,Columbus, 43228, 466-5052

State surplus merchandise such as vehicles, office furniture and equipment, computers, typewriters and miscellaneous items are sold about every three months at a Saturday auction. Occasionally, similar merchandise from the federal government is included in these sales. Payment is by cash on the day of purchase for all items except vehicles, which require 1/3 payment by cash on the day of sale and the balance by money order or bank check three days later. All merchandise is sold "as is". Call to be added to the mailing list. M-F 8-5.

WDLR RADIO
P.O. Box 448, Delaware, 43015, 363-1700, 548-5811, 363-1107

Delaware residents and those in the most northern sections of Franklin county, can tune in to 1550 a.m. every Saturday from 10a.m.-12 noon, to hear the Radio Discount Auction Merchandise such as clothing, furniture, dried flowers, meals at restaurants and gift certificates are donated to the station by businesses in exchange for free on-air publicity. Listeners can't see the merchandise, but can place live bids on the air. Savings can amount to 30-75% off regular retail prices. TRADE-EO is another opportunity which features want ads on the air Monday through Friday from 12:30-1p.m. You can buy, sell or trade anything including appliances, bicycles, animals, crafts and anything else. Dealers or businesses are not eligible to offer items for sale on the air in this TRADE-EO. However, a small homebased hobbyist may offer their goods or services. There is no charge to participate or offer your wares. WDLR also sponsors a television auction on the last Wednesday of the month at 7:30p.m., which airs on TV 56 Delaware, a UHF station, to those within a 30 mile radius. Merchandise must be picked up at the donor's business which is in the Delaware area. Accepts checks and cash only.

FOOD

In this section, you'll find listings for supermarkets, general merchandise stores which carry food products, specialty food stores and bars which feature sizeable happy hour food buffets. There's also restaurants offering good values on certain days or at certain times during early bird or sunset specials.

Did you know that supermarkets and stores which sell health and beauty aids generally place their most costly items at eye level? This method is used because they know that consumers are likely to purchase these items on impulse. I suggest that you compare the various brands before you make a decision by looking high and low on those shelves .

ABBOTT FOOD SERVICE OUTLET
358 S. Hamilton Rd., Gahanna 43230, 337-2900

About 2,000 different products are offered including sauces, frozen food, seafood, poultry, meats, hors d'ouvres, pies, spices, party/paper goods as well as serving platters. The store also features international and domestic specialty foods such as chocolate dessert shells, French wine vinegars, sun dried tomatoes, Caribbean hot sauces and other items. This business serves the food service industry as well as the general public. While many items are packaged in bulk, you'll find others in smaller quantities. The best way to know which items are offering the best values, would be to compare them on a cost per ounce/pound basis that you typically pay in a grocery store. Just because you are buying a larger size, doesn't always mean you are saving money. However, with the right selections, you can save 20-60% over comparable grocery store items. M-F 8-8, Sat 8-5.

ALDI
3831 E. Main St., Columbus, 43213
635 Harrisburg Pike, Central Pt. Shpng. Ctr., Columbus, 43223
3350 Cleveland Ave., Columbus, 43224
5990 Westerville Rd., Westerville, 43081
5487 W. Broad St., Columbus, 43228
4041 Gantz Rd., Grove City, 43123
629 N. Memorial Dr., Lancaster
775 S. 30 St., Indian Mound Mall, Heath
3500 N., Maple Ave., Zanesville
1911 S. Limestone St., Springfield
1916 Marion-Mt. Gilead Rd., Marion
15740 U.S. Rt. 36 E., Marysville

Every day low prices at this full service grocery store, are about 30-70% lower than those found at other supermarkets. Their regular prices on Tyson chicken legs are 49 cents per pound, a twenty ounce package of Oven Fresh white bread is 25 cents, a two liter bottle of soda is 49 cents, a package of eight burger or hot dog buns is 29 cents, canned tuna is 49 cents. The merchandise consists largely of products which have been made by nationally recognized companies, but do not bear their labels. Before you stock up on any one type of product, I suggest that you purchase one or two, test them out to see if you like them, then return to the store to make a larger purchase. The Aldi stores do not accept incoming phone calls. M-Th 9-7, F 9-8, Sat 9-6. The West Broad Street location is also open Sunday 10-5. Accepts cash and food stamps only.

ANGELICA DELI AND CAFE
5 S. Liberty St., Powell, 43065, 431-2444

Enjoy hearty deli sandwiches, fresh baked goods, salads, homemade soups, espresso and gourmet coffees plus imported cheeses and meats in this quaint cafe. Breakfast, lunch and dinner are available at value prices. Try an Angelica's grilled cheese sandwich for $3.25, grilled bologna sandwich for $3.95, barbecue chicken breast sandwich for $3.50, grilled Keilbasa for $4.25 or other sandwiches between $2.75 and $5.95. Freshly made salads include broccoli salad at $4.50 per pound, chicken salad at $5.99 per pound and others in a similar price range. Be sure to visit the antique and collectible shops in Powell after your meal. The cafe is one of my personal favorites.

ANGELO'S ITALIAN BAKERY
2085 Cedar Hill Rd., Lancaster, 653-1415

Home made breads and rolls, plus Italian specialties such as meat balls, noodles, spaghetti and pizzas are available at this cozy take out business. Wholesale accounts such as the Stratford Tea Room in Lithopolis and many others, purchase the delicious baked goods that are not to be missed! The stock is priced very reasonably. My favorites are the onion filled foccaccia at $3.25 per loaf and the bread pretzels at three for $1. The business is in an historic wooden structure next to the residence and is decorated with primitives and antiques. Only pure natural ingredients are used. M-Sat 10-7.

ANTHONY THOMAS CANDY SHOPPES
Thirteen Columbus locations

Each of their stores has a selection of "sweet slips" which are factory goofs, at 50% off regular retail prices. The imperfection is usually a slightly underweight or misshapen piece of chocolate, which is just as fresh and tasty as their other products. The "sweet slips" are priced at $5.50 a pound, regularly $9-$12 a pound. M-Sat 9-9, Sun 11-5.

AUDDINO BAKERY
1490 Clara St., Columbus, 43211, 294-2577

Fresh baked Italian bread, rolls, donuts, pies, cookies, croissants and sub buns are available at savings of 20-30% off retail. You'll pay $1 for a loaf of bread, $1.20 for a dozen rolls, etc. This wholesale bakery is passing the savings to you as a retail customer. M-Sat 6a.m.-5p.m. Accepts cash only.

AUTHENTIC SPECIALITIES
Maria Velalis, North Columbus, 895-5608

Maria prepares authentic Greek pastries with all natural ingredients, no artificial colors or flavors are added. You can buy Baklava (48 piece tray for $30, 24 pieces in a box $18 or a 30 piece platter for $25), Kourambiedes which are powdered sugar cookies (50 pieces for $30, 25 pieces in a box for $18 or a 32 piece platter for $25), Finikia which are honey dipped cookies topped with walnuts and spices (50 pieces for $30, 25 pieces in a box for $18 or a 32 piece platter for $25) or Karidopita which is a walnut spice cake (tray of 34 pieces for $22, 24 pieces in a box for $18 or a 30 piece platter for $25). A box assortment of 24 pieces is $18 or a platter assortment of 30 pieces is $25. Maria skillfully creates her pastries with tender loving care. Her baklava utilizes honey syrup as opposed to the sugar water found at area grocery store bakeries, and she uses more walnuts and less phyllo than those businesses. Her culinary skills have been much in demand and she has sold her pastries to Borders Book Store, Christopher's, Cafe Angelica, Umberto's, the Coffee Beanery, Savories, Insomnia Espresso Bar, Sorrento's, Moonspinners and area caterers. Buy some Greek pastries for your family or your next party.

BASKIN ROBBINS
Five Columbus Locations plus Lancaster

Stop in to any of their stores and register your child for the Birthday Club. Kids aged twelve and under will receive a yearly coupon good for a free, deluxe junior scoop ice cream cone on their birthday. With 38 flavors to choose from, there's bound to be many to please your little one. M-Th 11-9, F/Sat 11-10, Sun 11-9.

BEXLEY NATURAL FOODS CO-OP
508 N. Cassady, Columbus, 43209, 252-3951

This nonprofit business is the oldest natural foods storefront in Central Ohio. It features organic and natural foods such as whole grain cereals, herbs and spices and organically grown vegetables. Most of the stock is sugar, additive and dye free. A $25 annual fee, plus a refundable buyer's, enables you to become a member and to save about 20% off regular retail prices (15% above the wholesale cost price. Nonmembers pay 25% over the posted store prices, which amounts to a savings of about 17% off regular retail prices. The co-op is operated by paid staff as well as volunteers. M-F 9-8, Sat 9-5. Accepts cash and checks only.

BILL KNAPP'S
2199 Riverside Dr., Columbus, 43221, 488-1139
6851 N. High St., Worthington, 43085, 846-4030
2100 Bethel Rd., Columbus, 43220, 538-9064

On your birthday, you will be entitled to a percent off your meal equivalent to your age. So if you are 50 years old, your meal will be 50% off. A complimentary chocolate birthday cake is also provided on your birthday. If you can't visit the restaurant on your birthday, but show up within a week, you'll just get the free cake. This special birthday promotion is available for adults as well as children. Sun/Sat 11-10.

BLUE BIRD PIE THRIFT STORE
2777 Johnstown Rd., Columbus, 43219, 478-9003

Day old and surplus Stouffer and Blue Bird Pies, cakes and lunchbox snacks, and baked bread from a local grocery chain, are sold at savings of 40-60% off the regular retail price. Tu-F 10-6, Sat 10-4. Accepts cash and food stamps.

BROWNBERRY BAKERY OUTLET
1855 Northwest Blvd., Columbus 43212, 488-3189

This is the only Columbus thrift outlet for Entenmann's Bakery products and are offered for sale at $1.89 per box, regularly $2.29-$4.79. All natural Brownberry breads and rolls are 50% off retail. You will also find croutons and snack items, ideal for lunchboxes, at savings of 20-40% off retail. The merchandise consists largely of first quality overstocks. M-F 9-6, Sat 9-5. Accepts checks and cash only.

CAFE ON 5
Lazarus, 141 S. High St., Columbus, 43215, 463-2661

A mouthwatering selection of hot and cold items is served on the all-you-can-eat lunch buffet such as shrimp salad lemonnaise, marinated mushrooms, tarragon chicken salad, zucchini pasta salad, raisin slaw, crabmeat salad, marinated artichokes, assorted fresh fruits, green salad with toppings, chicken and walnut salad in addition to beef tetrazzini. The menu changes daily. Soup and assorted desserts are also included for one low price of $8.50 for adults and $4.25 for children aged twelve and under. Try the Sunday brunch buffet, which includes the types of food mentioned, in addition to some breakfast foods. The cafe is one of my personal favorites. M-Sat 11-2:30, Sun 12-3.

CANDY COTTAGE
745 E. Main St., Lancaster, 43130, 653-6842

The aromas from this unpretentious little wooden house, will make you feel as if you've died and gone to heaven. Home made candies, fresh roasted nuts, fancy mints and specialty items are available at prices which are about 30-50% less than comparable quality items in other stores. Jumbo blanched and Spanish peanuts are roasted on premises. You'll find peanut brittles, butter creams and peanut butter cups. My favorites are the decoratively molded specialty chocolates which include a six inch long pink/white infant for only $3, a five inch diameter chocolate record which says "I Love You" for only $2.50, a chocolate tool set for $2.50. The molded chocolates are even great to give out as party favors. The store also sells candy making supplies and has a large selection of molds. Take a peak in the kitchen before you leave, as you're likely to see the workers preparing the goodies. This business is one of my personal favorites. M-F 10-5, Sat 10-2.

CHERYL AND COMPANY
Seven Columbus locations

During the last hour of business each day, you can purchase ten cookies for $4.95, which is half the usual price. These delicious, homemade edibles include chocolate chip, macadamia nut, peanut butter chip and other melt-in-your-mouth goodies. M-Sat 10-9, Sun 12-5.

CRACKER BARREL OLD COUNTRY STORE
4210 Marlane Dr., Grove City, 43123, 871-1444
1860 Winderly Lane, Pickerington, 43147, 759-7799
1313 Hilliard-Rome Rd., Hilliard, 43026, 878-2027

This national chain of restaurants has a large gift shop in each of their locations which sells country gifts and glassware at typical retail prices. However, the business's own brands of jellies, microwavable popping corn on the cob and other edibles, offer savings of 20-50% off comparable items found in gourmet shops. Some of the smaller gift items are also value priced such as the pen which is made out of a tree branch and priced at $1.49. I saw this at a fancy shop downtown and in nature specialty shops for more than twice the price. The restaurant offers a unique dining experience in a country store atmosphere. The home cooked meals are value priced. Sun-Th 6a.m.-10p.m., F/Sat 6a.m.-11p.m.

CUB FOODS
5727 Emporium Square, Columbus, 43231, 899-0050
6500 Tussing Rd., Reynoldsburg, 43068, 863-0600
2757 Festival Lane, Dublin, 43017, 793-1495
3600 Soldano Blvd., Consumer Sq. W., Columbus, 43228, 279-8989
3621 E. Livingston Ave., Columbus, 43227, 239-8001

You can shop 24 hours a day, seven days per week at this full service grocery store. Savings are 15-30% below regular grocery store prices. Kids aged twelve and under, can obtain a free, "Kiddie Kookie Credit Card" which is good for one free cookie each time they visit the store. This same age group can also join the Fruit of the month club. The free membership card entitles the child to a free pre-determined fruit each month such as a tangelo, kiwi, mango, apple etc. The stores offer 40% off all brands of greeting cards, gift wrap and bows. Leave your unwanted coupons and take those you need from the coupon exchange located at the main entrance at all locations except Dublin. On Saturdays, Cub Foods is filled with at least twelve product marketers offering free samples of food, providing you with the opportunity to sample new products. Look for the T.P.R.'s (temporary price reductions) in their special aisle. You will need to bag your own groceries at all of their stores except the one in Dublin. Open 24 hours a day.

DENNY'S
2454 E. Dublin Granville Rd., Columbus, 43229, 891-0664
2550 S. Hamilton Rd., Columbus, 43232, 868-0323
23 Huber Village Blvd., Westerville, 43081, 882-5559
5979 E. Main St., Columbus, 43213, 864-8585
2209 S. Limestone, Springfield, (513) 324-3320

Adults or children can get any menu item for free on their birthday. Open 24 hours per day, seven days per week.

DER DUTCHMAN AND DUTCH KITCHEN
445 S. Jefferson Ave., US Rt. 42 S., Plain City, 873-3414 (Der Dutchman)
8690 US Rt. 42 S., Plain City, 873-4518 (Dutch Kitchen)

You can enjoy the delectable home cooked meals of the Amish/Mennonite people in either of these restaurants. Sandwiches are $2.40 to $.90. Dinners are $6.35 to $8.10 and include rolls, a salad bar and a side dish. All-you-can-eat family style meals, which are also offered, include two main dishes such as ham, turkey, roast beef and chicken, plus a salad bar, corn, mashed potatoes, bread, pie and a beverage. The all-you-can-eat meal ranges from $9-$10.25 per adult and is served for lunch or dinner during regular operating hours. Children's portions are $4.05-$5.35. For a special treat, you can enjoy your meal at Der Dutchman in the authentic atmosphere of the Amish buggy inside the restaurant. The buggy seats five people and is available on a first come, first serve basis. M-Th 6a.m.-8p.m., F/Sat 6a.m.-9p.m.

DISCOUNT GROCERY OUTLET
900 S. Pickaway St., Circleville, 474-6501

Popular brands of canned, bottled and boxed foods by Delmonte, Kelloggs, Chun King; dog food, cleaning supplies and health and beauty salvage items can bee found at this business. Some items are close to or past the sell by date, some are dented or partially crushed or may have torn or missing labels. Savings are 25-70%. M-Sat 10-6.

DOLLY MADISON BAKERY THRIFT SHOP
3654 Cleveland Ave, Columbus, 43224, 475-9640
2757 S. High St., Columbus, 43207, 491-2925

Sells surplus Butternut and Dolly Madison brands of bread, lunchbox snacks, rolls and donuts at savings up to 60% off grocery store prices. The merchandise consists of overstocks, first quality and some damaged cartons. M-Sat 9-6, Sun 11-4. Accepts checks and cash only.

ELEPHANT BAR
995 E. Dublin-Granville Rd., Columbus, 43229, 846-4592

The complimentary happy hour buffet is offered Monday through Friday 4-7p.m. The buffet always includes tortillas and salsa, a tray of vegetables and some snacks such as pretzels. Each day one or two different specials are added such as: hot dogs and wings on Mondays, pizza on Tuesdays, tacos and tostitos on Wednesdays, subs and rigatoni on Thursdays and Fajitas on Fridays. Anytime on Sunday and Monday, two children aged twelve and under, can eat for free when accompanied by an adult. They will be given a choice of several items from the kids' menu (regularly priced at $3.25) or may eat from the enormous Sunday brunch buffet. The buffet includes a large selection of breakfast and lunch foods such as freshly made waffles, pasta, prime rib, stir fry chicken, lasagne, made to order omelets, fresh fruits, sausage, croissants and a sundae bar. Soft drinks or fruit juices are also included. The cost is $11.95 for adults. You'll enjoy the tastefully appointed jungle/safari decor. M-Sat 11a.m.-2a.m., Sun 10a.m.-10p.m.

ENGINE HOUSE NO. 5
121 Thurman Ave., Columbus, 43206, 443-4877

Seafood and American dinners are available at this 100 year old restaurant. You will be in for a special treat for your birthday. A complimentary oversized cupcake will be delivered to your table at the end of your meal, by a server who slides down a glistening brass fire pole. Reservations are recommended. M-Th 4-10, F/Sat 4-11, Sun 4-9.

FIFTY FIVE RESTAURANTS DINERS' CLUB
Columbus, 799-9551 or 228-5555

Buy a membership in this club for $60 and you will save money off your next twelve visits to any of their restaurants. These include Nickle's Grill, Gottleib's, 55 Grille, Gottleib's East, Gottleib's Grove City, Fifty Five On The Boulevard, Wilhelms and Fifty Five At Crosswoods. Your savings will vary based on the number of people dining, but it features: 50% savings for two people, 33% savings for three people or a 25% savings for four people. The restaurants issue a limited number of membership each year which are valid from September 1 to August 31 (a full year). Depending on what you order, your savings can be about $50-$150 when all twelve visits are completed. The card is not valid with other discounts or special offers. It may not be used on Easter, Mother's Day or New Year's Eve. There are no other use restrictions.

FRISCH'S BIG BOY
Eight Columbus locations
764 Hebron Rd., Heath, 522-3085
2201 E. Main St., Springfield, (513) 325-5571
1701 River Valley Cir., Lancaster, 43130, 681-1177
255 Lafayette St., London, 43140, 852-4515

The all-you-can-eat breakfast buffet is offered Monday-Friday from 7-11a.m. at a cost of $3.59 for adults, and Saturday and Sunday from 7a.m.-1p.m. at a cost of $4.55. Children aged 6-12, are charged $2.09 at all times and those aged five and under can eat for free. The buffet includes pancakes, French toast, scrambled eggs, hash browns and an assortment of fresh fruits and melons. Twice a year, at Halloween and Valentine's Day, the restaurants feature a children's promotion. For only $1, you can buy a book of five coupons good for a free kid's meal. The meals offer a choice of burger, chili, spaghetti, pancakes or chicken fingers and are regularly priced at $1.60-$2.25 each. The coupon books go on sale three to four weeks before the holidays and are valid for five to six weeks from the date of the holiday. No other purchase is necessary.

GFS MARKETPLACE
5400 Cleveland Ave., Columbus, 43231, 891-8686
6375 Tussing Rd., Reynoldsburg, 43068, 861-0916

Choose from an enormous selection of restaurant quality fresh and frozen foods, paper and party goods and related items. If you can't find what you need from the 3,000 products in stock, the store can make another 8,000 available to you through a special order form their warehouse. This wholesale distributor of products, has been selling to schools, hospitals and restaurants since the turn of the century. You'll find items packaged in large and smaller quantities, party hors d'ouvres, cheeses, spices, vegetables, meats, seafood and other items. While the store offers many products under their own label, you'll also find such well known brands as Tyson, Pillsbury, Quaker, Keebler and others. Savings vary from 10-60% off grocery store prices. Inquire about special savings for businesses and organizations. My favorite purchases here have been the frozen sugar snap peas and the dried and crushed basil. M-Sat 8-8, Sun 12-5.

GOLD C SAVINGS SPREE
4465 Professional Pkwy., Groveport, 43125, 836-7325

This coupon book offers savings on entertainment and recreational activities, meals at fast food restaurants and savings at other retail businesses in the area. It contains cents off discounts and two for one coupons at about 300 establishments including movie theaters, roller skating rinks, video rental sites, Wyandotte Lake and more. The book, which will remind you of a mini "Entertainment 96", is sold through area schools as a fundraiser or available from the publisher by mail. Even if you already own the "Entertainment 96" book, this is a worthwhile investment for only $10. Many of the businesses in the Gold C book are not found in the Entertainment book. Accepts cash and checks only. M-F 9-5.

GROUND ROUND
12 S. James Rd., Columbus, 43213, 231-6219
5090 N. High St., Columbus, 43214, 885-4305
120 Phillipi Rd., Columbus, 43228, 279-0160
2690 E. Dublin Granville Rd., Columbus, 43231, 882-5850

On Thursdays, children aged twelve and under can pay what they weigh for a child's meal or can pay what the day's temperature is outside, at the rate of one penny per degree or per pound. On your birthday, call ahead and the business will give you a free birthday cake with your meal in the dining room. There is no minimum number of people required in your dining group. The offer is valid for adults as well as kids. M-Sat 11-10, Sun 11-12.

JAMES TAVERN
160 W. Wilson Bridge Rd., Worthington, 43085, 885-5050

Celebrate your birthday with freebies and special offers. The birthday person will get a percent off their meal equal to their age, plus a free celebration Polaroid picture and a free chocolate mousse. There are no age restrictions, so young and old alike can participate. Call in advance to make your reservation. M-Sat 11-11, Sun 10-10.

KLOSTERMAN'S BAKING COMPANY
619 W. Fair Ave., Lancaster, 43130, 654-0963
501 E. Columbia, Springfield, 45506, (513) 322-7658
2655 Courtright Rd., Columbus, 43232, 338-8111

Day old, surplus, package damaged and discontinued Klosterman's products are sold here at savings of 25-60% off regular retail prices. You'll find buns, rolls, snacks Italian bread, croissants, mini hamburger buns, and lunchbox treats. M-Sat 8-5. Accepts cash and foodstamps.

LAZARUS RESTAURANTS-CLUB 61
All Central Ohio locations

All restaurants in the Lazarus department stores, including the buffets, offer a special birthday freebie. Seniors aged 61 and over can register for a free membership in Club 61 which entitles them to a free meal on their birthday, plus 10% off their meal any other time.

LITTLE CAESER'S
21 Central Ohio locations

Great prices and delicious pizza are what you will find here. At all times, you will get two pizzas for the price of one. For instance, for $13.49, two large single topping pizzas can be yours, or for $10.29, two medium single topping pizzas are available. Don't miss their crazy bread for $1.29 which includes a bag of freshly baked bread sticks topped with butter and Parmesan cheese. Little Caeser's is a frequent advertiser, so carefully watch the newspapers and the advertisements you receive in the mail. The stores also offer many in store specials at additional savings. In a recent national survey conducted by Restaurants And Institutions Magazine, Little Caeser's was voted to be the best pizza value in America as compared to all other restaurant and pizza chains. Sun-Th. 11-11, F/Sat 11a.m.-1a.m.

MCL CAFETERIAS
3160 Kingsdale Ctr., Columbus, 43221, 457-5786
2491 E. Dublin Granville Rd., Columbus, 43229, 882-4691
5240 E. Main St., Columbus, 43213, 861-6259
4500 Eastland Dr., Columbus, 43232, 866-7635

This family owned and operated Midwest chain prepares all of their foods from scratch-even the salad dressings. There is a large selection of tasty items on their Heartwise menu (a program sponsored in conjunction with Riverside Hospital's Heart Institute of Ohio) which is aimed at those having high blood pressure, elevated blood cholesterol level, obesity, diabetes or even health conscious persons. The balance of their menu is so extensive and delectable that there is something to please everyone's palate. There's carrot and raisin salad, fresh baked breads and muffins, carved prime rib of beef, stuffed flounder, baked cod and stuffed chicken breast. The desserts include pumpkin pie, coconut cream pie, cheesecake, strawberry pie, hot desserts and other delectables. Entrees are a la carte and range in price from $3.50-$5.50. The Jack Benny Value Plate offers a reduced size portion, ideal for seniors or anyone else. It includes an entree, two vegetables and bread and costs $3.50-$3.83. Kids' specials are $2.75. The Eastland Drive location has the nicest decor, both inside and out. This stately brick building features several carpeted rooms with mock fireplaces, faux fieldstone walls and decorator wallpaper. It is hard to believe that this is just a cafeteria. The staff is always friendly and courteous. M-Sun 11-8:30.

MARK PI'S FEAST OF THE DRAGON
3663 Soldano Blvd., Columbus, 43228, 272-0210

This perpetual Chinese buffet has an enormous selection. There's four appetizers (such as crab Rangoon, egg rolls), salad with eighteen different toppings, eighteen entrees and side dishes such as (lo mein, General Tso's Chicken, Singapore Noodles, garlic chicken) and twelve desserts (such as fresh fruits, puddings etc.). All meals come with your choice of a beverage. The cost is $5.25 for lunch Monday through Saturday, $6.95 for dinner daily and all day Saturday and Sunday. Or if you want to have your meal to go, make your selection for only $3.50 per pound. M-Th. 11-9, F/Sat 11-10, Sun 12-9.

MEAT PACKERS OUTLET
317 S. 5 St., Columbus, 43215, 228-9074

If you don't mind purchasing cold cuts, bread, meat, cheese and other edibles close to their expiration date, then this is the place for you. A short shelf life plus volume buying and low markups, add up to savings of 10-50% off regular grocery store prices. You will find such popular brands as Oscar Meyer and others. You can also save about 20% on bottled cajun seasoning. Check the expiration date before paying. M-Sat 8-6.

MISSY'S CANDY COMPANY
1459 E. Livingston Ave., Columbus 43205, 252-2104

Find gumballs, Good 'N Plenty and other candies at savings of about 25-40% less than you would pay through a vending machine. If you can use bulk packed (no individual wrapped products), large quantities of sweets, this wholesaler can supply your needs. The candies can be used for parties, school groups or individuals. M-F 8:30-5:30. Accepts cash only.

MR. BULKY'S
2713 Northland Plaza Drive, Columbus, 43231, 882-5839
7602 New Market Center Way, Columbus, 43235, 764-9677

Candies, cookies, nuts, spices, pasta, rice and baking mixes are available here in bulk food bins and sold by weight. Decorative tins and containers, which can be filled with goodies, offer a unique gift giving opportunity. About half of the inventory is priced at about 10-30% lower than in a supermarket. However, the wide selection of hard to find items and sugar free candies, certainly makes this a store you won't want to miss. M-Sat 10-9:30, Sun 12-6.

NICKLE'S BAKERY SURPLUS STORE
1255 Alum Creek Dr., Columbus, 43209, 253-6075
590 N. Hague, Columbus, 43204, 276-5477
3477 E. Main St., Columbus, 43213, 239-6687
725 E. Weber Rd., Columbus, 43211, 262-9611
5185 N. High St., Columbus, 43214, 436-0227
787 N. Main St., Marion, 383-1450

Surplus baked goods such as breads, cakes, rolls, buns and lunch box snacks are sold at 30-50% off grocery store prices. Large decorated birthday cakes are $7.12. Wednesdays are bargain days with an additional 10% off all purchases. M-F 6:30a.m.-7p.m., Sat 7a.m.-6p.m., Sun 10a.m.-4:30p.m. Accepts cash only.

94TH AERO SQUADRON
5030 Sawyer Rd., Columbus, 43219, 237-8887

Monday through Friday from 4:30-7p.m., you can enjoy the complimentary happy hour buffet which includes several items such as chicken wings, meatballs, fruits, vegetables and cheese. The Sunday brunch buffet offers a large selection of breakfast and lunch items for $12.95, but you'll save $5 per person if you arrive between 9a.m.-10a.m. during their Beat The Clock special. You'll enjoy the view of the Port Columbus runway and the delightful French World War.

NORTH MARKET
29 W. Spruce St., Columbus, 43215, 463-9664

You'll find vendors selling an extensive selection of produce, meats, cheeses, spices, gourmet foods, poultry, flowers, freshly baked pastries and ethnic foods. One business sells baskets, beads, silver jewelry and ethnic arts and crafts. The prices at the North

Market are often lower than you would find at area groceries and the food is very fresh. There's a few tables scattered throughout the market for those of you who would like to enjoy a light meal. The North Market features cooking demonstrations, entertainment and other special events intermittently throughout the year. Accepts checks and cash, with credit card acceptance varying among vendors. M-Sat 7a.m.-5:30p.m.

NORTHWEST NATURAL AND SPECIALTY FOODS
1636 Northwest Blvd., Columbus, 43212, 488-0607

Columbus' largest natural food store sells most of their stock at 15-20% less than you'll find elsewhere due to low markups. Solgar, Twin Lab, Nature's Plus and other brands are available. Greenhouse Ware (biodegradable products), cruelty free cosmetics (which were not tested on animals), body care lotions and conditioners, wheat and yeast free bread as well as salt and/or sugar free products can be found here. The store has also established quite a reputation as a gourmet food business selling such necessities as cooking vinegars and oils. There is a 5% additional discount on case purchases, and 10% off books and cassettes. M-Sat 9-8.

OHIO STEAK AND BARBECUE COMPANY
895 B Parsons Ave., Columbus 43206, 445-7863

Most of the food in this wholesaler's stock is sold at about 20-30% below grocery store prices. You'll find Swift hams, Weber sausage, ribeye steaks, mozzarella cheese sticks, battered vegetable sticks, bacon, chicken and hot dogs. Bulk spices, usually in one pound tins, are priced about 50-70% less than the smaller quantities in supermarkets. The store's stock may be purchased in bulk or by the bag. M-F 9-6. Also open the first two Saturdays of every month from 9 to 1.

ORLEY'S HERBS AND STUFF
21861 Winsted Rd., Circleville, 477-2866

Over 100 types of dried herbs are available here by the ounce, pound or small package. Savings can be 20-60% less than grocery store products. For instance, an ounce of crushed basil is $1 or four ounces for $3, ground cloves are $1.90 for two ounces or $3.50 for four ounces. The more you buy, the greater your savings. In the warmer months, the shop also sells fresh herbs at competitive prices. M-F 10-6, Sat 12-6.

PEPPERIDGE FARM OUTLET
1174 Kenny Center, Columbus, 43220, 457-4800

Save 10-50% off those delicious Pepperidge Farm cookies, breads, frozen foods, croutons and desserts. Most of the bread and rolls is 50% off the regular retail price. The merchandise in this factory outlet store consists of discontinued, overstocks, dented cans and low weight products. Some of the cookies are individually packaged for institutional use and are great to take on trips or to pack in your child's lunchbox. The store also sells a small selection of soups, cookies and other changing items from assorted companies. M-Sat 9:30-6.

PLANTING TREES IN AMERICA COUPON BOOK
771-2308 or (800) 591-7720

Your $5 purchase will entitle you to a coupon book which offers savings from more than $200 at area businesses and restaurants in fifteen central Ohio counties. The books are sold from August 15 through March 1, and are valid through September 30. This fundraiser for area schools, churches and scouting groups, also has an ecological benefit. For every twenty books sold, a tree will be planted. Call to find out the group nearest you which is selling the books.

PRESTIGE DINING CLUB
1616 E. Dublin Granville Rd., Columbus, 43229, 895-3113

Membership allows you to be able to buy one dinner and get one for free at over 100 participating Columbus restaurants. Your $29.95 annual fee entitles you to receive a directory of restaurants and a membership card. M-F 9-6.

RAY JOHNSON'S
111 E. Main St., Columbus, 43215, 221-4203

Fish lovers line up to purchase the delicious, made to order fish specialties which are value priced. A large perch sandwich is $2.65, pickerel sandwich is $3.20. Other choices are in the $2.15-$3.75 range. Fish dinners, which include fries, cole slaw and bread, range from $5.45-$7.55. The seafood salad is $3.90 and comes with lettuce and a variety of cold fish such as shrimp and crab. The spring rolls, which cost $1.90, are egg rolls filled with vegetables and lots of fresh seafood. While most of the fish is fried, it is surprisingly not greasy. The food portions are very generous. The owner, Ray Johnson, learned many of his culinary skills from Al Capone's former chef. You may call ahead to place your order if you wish. This business offers take out only, and has earned the distinction of being one of my personal favorites. M-F 9-6, Sat 9-4. Accepts cash and food stamps only.

ROTHSCHILD BERRY FARM
3143 E. Rt. 36, Urbana, (800) 356-8933

The secret is out, I love those raspberry products! This gourmet food purveyor sells raspberry preserves, chocolates and other specialty items in their store year round at typical retail prices. But check the clearance area where items are reduced 20-85%. Twice a year, the weekend before Thanksgiving and one weekend in March or April, the business features a large warehouse clearance sale with similar savings on a broader selection of products. Pick your own raspberries at the farm in August and September for $1.69 per pound. The annual Raspberry Festival is held on a Sunday in mid September and features entertainment, demonstrations, optional cooking classes for $3-$5 and other surprises. Festival admission is free. You'll enjoy wandering the grounds of the berry farm which offers a peaceful respite from city life. Hours vary so call ahead.

SAM'S CLUB
3950 Morse Rd., Columbus, 43219, 476-4224
5252 Westpointe Plaza Dr., Hilliard, 43026, 527-1580
6300 Tussing Rd., Consumer Sq. E., Reynoldsburg, 43068, 864-2582
1663 E. Main St., Newark, 349-9345

Businesses as well as consumers will find products of interest in this no frills environment. Quality name brand stereos, toys, housewares, computers, office supplies, power tools, food, adult and children's clothing, books, hardware, health and beauty aids, furniture, fine jewelry, watches, appliances and sporting goods are available at savings of 10-40% off manufacturer's suggested retail prices. Tires and other automotive supplies are available at similar savings. Offers moderate to better quality merchandise by nationally recognized brands. All card holders can participate in the Sam's Travel Club and save money on hotels, entertainment and car rentals. Inquire in the stores for details. Members may also participate in the Sam's/MCI long distance phone service at a special rate. Sam's Club is a members only operation, but you can get a free, one day pass to try the store before you commit to a membership. Large employers, AARP, AAA, health care providers and many other businesses have arranged for their employees to have memberships. Members pay 5% above posted prices unless you purchase a special membership card for $25 annually, which will allow you to buy items at posted prices. M-F 12-8:30, Sat 9:30-6, Sun 12-6.

SCHWEBEL'S BREAD OUTLET
4485 Reynolds Drive, Hilliard, 43026, 777-1556

Purchase Schwebel's products such as bread, buns, and rolls at savings of up to 50% off regular retail prices. Other brands of edibles are offered such as Buckeye Biscuits, Hamburger Helper, Moon Pies and additional lunchbox snacks, Dolly Madison pastries and Grandma Shearer's potato chips at savings of 20-50% off regular retail prices. The merchandise consists of surplus stock as well as day old products. Schwebel's products are certified Kosher. M-F 9-6, Sat 9-5. Accepts cash and food stamps only.

SHONEY'S
Seven Columbus locations
1337 River Valley Blvd., Lancaster, 43130, 687-0262

These restaurants feature an all-you-can-eat breakfast and fruit bar for $4.99 for adults on Saturdays, Sundays and holidays ($4.49 for seniors), and $3.89 Monday-Friday ($3.49 for seniors). Kids aged twelve and under can eat for $1.99 at all times. Kids aged five and under can eat for free with each adult breakfast and fruit bar purchased. The food is delicious and includes bacon, sausage, potatoes, muffins, buttermilk biscuits, Southern style grits, cold cereal, fruits, French toast sticks and more. Children aged twelve and under, can join the Cub Club which entitles them to a free kid's meal, plus dessert, on their birthday. Wednesday is family night with children aged twelve and under eating for free with each adult meal purchased, from 4p.m. to closing. The children can choose from several items on the kids' menu such as chicken, shrimp, spaghetti, fish and chips. The kids' menu items cost 99 cents-$1.99 and includes a drink and dessert. Adult menu items are reasonably priced from $4.29 to about $7.29 and include charbroiled chicken, Hawaiian chicken, steak and shrimp, lasagne and more. The restaurants feature a seafood bar on Fridays and Saturdays from 5p.m.-10p.m. at a cost of $8.99 for adults and $4.99 for children aged twelve and under. The offerings include baked fish, fried clams, shrimp scampi, corn on the cob, catfish, fried shrimp and vegetables.

SMOKE 'N SAVE
2139 Eakin Rd., Columbus, 43223, 275-1750

Competitive prices are offered on over 100 kinds of cigarettes. Changing promotions have included a gift with purchase, freebies with purchase and other enticements. M-F 10-7, Sat 9-7.

STAUF'S COFFEE ROASTERS
5793 Frantz Rd., Karric Sq. Shpng. Ctr., Dublin, 43017, 766-2000
1277 Grandview Ave., Columbus, 43212, 486-4861

Coffee is one of the world's oldest beverages. If you are a coffee aficionado, you'll love this store. It's brimming with coffee, espresso, cappuccino, cafe latte and other tastebud pleasers. The stores sell 60 different types and blends of high grade coffee beans which are freshly roasted on premises. The high yield beans are priced at about $6.50-$20 per pound and are about the lowest price in Columbus for this quality. M-Sat 9-9.

SUNFLOWER HERBS
2591 N. High St., Columbus, 43202, 263-9391

Take a whiff of those herbs! Over 150 varieties are sold by the ounce or by the pound. Vanilla beans sell for $1.25 each and add a special flavor to sugar when you leave the whole bean in your sugar bowl. Bay leaves sell for $4.69 per pound, garlic powder is .43 cents per ounce, sweet basil is .74 per ounce. You'll save about 20-60% over bottled spices purchased in your local grocery store. You may bring in your own spice bottles and the clerk will fill them for you. M-Sat 10-6:30, Sun 1-5.

SUPER THRIFT
3621 E. Livingston Ave., Columbus, 43227, 237-7100
350 S. Hamilton Rd., Gahanna, 43230, 337-2070

Most items in this grocery store are priced at 10-20% off regular supermarket prices. Some items are priced at higher savings. For example, a family pack of chicken is 39 cents per pound for drumsticks or thighs, boxed macaroni and cheese is five for $1. This is a full service grocery store. Money orders are only 59 cents each as compared to a $2 fee charged by most banks. Open 24 hours, 7 days per week. Accepts checks and cash only.

TAT-RISTORANTE DI FAMIGLIA
1210 S. James Rd., Columbus, 43227, 236-1392

Early bird specials are Tuesday-Saturday from 3:30-6p.m. and include a choice of several main dishes: spaghetti, eggplant parmigiana, veal parmigiana, tortellini, baked or fried fish or even fettucini alfredo for only $6.50. These come with a free appetizer and dessert. Prices are regularly $6.95-$10. 95. Children under ten can enjoy the kid's menu items for $2.95 which include chicken, spaghetti, perch or other items accompanied by a choice of two side dishes. Tu/Th 11a.m.-1a.m., F/Sat 11a.m.-12mid, Sun 11a.m.-9p.m.

TEDESCHI'S ITALIAN BAKERY
1210 W. 3 Ave., Columbus, 43212, 294-3278

Fresh Italian bread, submarine buns, pizza crust and rolls are available to you at savings of 25% off retail. This wholesaler's products are typically sold in grocery stores and pizza shops. You can purchase large or small quantities. M-F 8-5, Sat 8-12N. Accepts checks and cash only.

TERRACE RESTAURANT
1739 N. High St., OSU Ohio Union , 3rd floor, Columbus, 43210, 292-6396

The delicious all-you-can-eat lunch buffet is served from 11-1:15 Monday through Friday at a cost of $5.75. The bountiful display includes hot and cold foods, soups, salads plus themed menu selections on different days such as Indian or Cajun. The restaurant is open to the general public year round, even when classes are not in session, with the exception of legal holidays.

TOBACCO DISCOUNTERS
5691 Emporium Sq., Columbus, 43231, 794-3994
208 Graceland Blvd., Columbus, 43214, 781-0050
5425 Roberts Rd., Hilliard, 43026, 527-0505
103 Great Southern Blvd., Columbus, 43207, 497-0757

Find cigars, cigarettes, snuff, chewing and pipe tobacco in all popular brands. Cigarettes are available by individual packages at a savings of 8-25%, but the best deal is on the cartons where savings are 10-30%. The store offers many specials where you can buy one item and get one free. Some examples of their pricing include a carton of Winstons was priced at $15.99, Dorals $9.06 or Marlboros $15.99. M-Sat 10-7. Accepts cash only.

TROPICAL FRUIT AND NUT FACTORY OUTLET
6580 Huntley Rd., Columbus, 43229, 431-7233

Save 10-60% off regular retail prices on an extensive line of dried fruits, bulk spices, candy making supplies, nuts, tea, coffee, noodles and even popcorn at this factory outlet. The best savings are on large purchases, so consider sharing yours with a friend. Although, if you use a lot of a particular item, you can keep it for yourself as I do. Request a free copy of their catalogue, as not everything can be found on the outlet's shelves. M-F 9-5:30, Sat 10-4. Accepts checks and cash only.

VILLAGE CUPBOARD
666 High St., Worthington, 43085, 885-1370

Reasonable prices, generous portions and true home style American cooking, have endeared this restaurant to thousands of people. Even if you just want to indulge in dessert and a cup of coffee, you will adore the marvelous selection such as tapioca pudding, pumpkin strudel or carrot cake. Take a seat by the front window and compare the High Street ambience with that depicted on the handpainted wall mural which provides a glimpse of that area as it looked 100 years ago. M-F 7:30a.m.-2p.m., Sat 8a.m.-2p.m., Sun 8:30a.m.-1:30p.m.

VISION VALUE CLUB
Big Bear supermarket customers can accumulate points whenever they make a purchase at these selected stores. Points can be redeemed for valuable merchandise such as gold jewelry, small appliances, toys, bicycles, cameras, pet supplies and camcorders. Points are maintained on computer, so there is no need to save receipts. You will be awarded points based on the total amount of your purchase, in addition to bonus points each time you buy certain brands or products. M-F 24 hours per day, Sat/Sun 7a.m.-12mid.

WINES, INC.
913 E. Dublin Granville Rd., Columbus, 43229, 486-9922

You will find an enormous selection of fine wines, beers and gourmet coffees, in addition to amateur wine, liqueur making and home brewing supplies. You can save 40-70% off the price of store bought products as compared to the make it yourself cost. Maturing time varies from several weeks to a couple of years depending on the type of beer or wine you produce. The shelf life also varies from one to three years. You can make the wines/liqueurs entirely from scratch using store bought or garden obtained fruits, or purchase concentrated juice as an option. It can cost you about $20-$30 to make a batch of beer which is equivalent to about 54 bottles. They also sell kits from $50-$80 which make great gifts. M-Th 10-10, F/Sat 10-12mid.

WONDER HOSTESS THRIFT SHOP
609 Oakland Park Ave., Columbus, 43214, 263-8846
350 Johnstown Rd., Gahanna, 43230, 471-8586
1751 Brice Rd., Reynoldsburg, 43068, 861-1136
1866 Hard Rd., Worthington, 43235, 766-0447
5440 Westerville Rd., Westerville, 43081, 895-1069
1317 Hebron Rd., Heath, 43056, 522-3205

Surplus baked goods from Wonder bread and Hostess are available at savings up to 60% off regular retail prices. You'll find bread at fourloaves for $1, donuts and other delicious edibles. Lunchbox snacks are available at similar savings and are priced at five for 99 cents at this factory outlet. Offers a frequent purchaser plan. M-Sat 9-6. Sunday hours vary per store.

WORTHINGTON FOODS OUTLET
900 Proprietors Rd., Worthington, 43085, 785-1849

Vegetarian and health food products are available in dried, canned and frozen forms, at savings of 10-25%. You'll find egg substitutes, low fat burger substitutes and other products made from soy beans sold under the name, Morningstar Farms. The store also stocks vitamins, dried fruits and nuts, Little Debbie and Archway Cookies plus Celestial Seasonings at similar savings. Case prices will save you the most money. M-Th 9:30-5:30, F 9:30-4:30, Sun 11-4.

ALSO SEE

All For One, Andersons General Store, Contemporary American Theater Company, Entertainment 96 Book, Flickers, It's Really $1.00, Itzadeal, Kaybee Toys And Hobby Shops, Liquidations Now, Odd Lots, Only $1, Schottenstein's, Springfield Antique Show And Flea Market, WDLR Radio and WOSU Channel 34

FURNITURE &
BEDDING/GARDEN

FURNITURE & BEDDING

AARON SELLS FURNITURE
2975 Morse Rd., Columbus, 43231, 475-7180

This division of Aaron Rents Inc., the nation's largest furniture rental and sales company, sells previously rented home and office furniture at about 30-50% off the original price "if new". The business has depreciated the furniture so it can sell the traditional styled merchandise at rock bottom prices. All used furniture is guaranteed for one full year against structural defects. The stock consists of moderate and some better quality items. Night stands start at $29, lamps at $9, sofa and love seat sets at $199, televisions at $99, etc. M-F 9-6, Sat 9-5.

AMISH ORIGINALS
8 N. State Street, Westerville, 43081, 891-6257

Located within the former Clothes Show clothing store, this business sells Amish handcrafted oak, maple and cherry furniture, plus baskets, pottery, collectible Amish dolls, quilts and throws. Most of the stock was very value priced, taking into account, of course, the fact that it is all handcrafted and made to impeccable specifications. The store does not feature sales as the prices have been set very low. Expanding tables have easy gears which enable you to open them and insert leaves with ease. A solid cherry table with Queen Anne legs, which expands to twelve feet, was value priced at $1,295. You'll find chairs, hutches, bookcases, bedroom furniture as well as porch swings and gliders. Special orders will take about 4-12 weeks

ANEW-CONSIGNMENT FURNISHINGS
14 E. Russel St., Columbus, 43215, 294-0294
664 N. High St., Columbus, 43215, 294-0294

Upscale, consigned home furnishings such as sofas, tables, and accessory items are meticulously displayed. The stores also sell some antiques and collectibles. Savings are about 15-60% less than "if new", and some items even appear to be at typical antique shop prices. A great deal I recently spotted, was a Henredon chair and ottoman for $400 for the set, regularly about $1,000. Tu 2-6, W-Sat 11-6.

APPLE FURNITURE
5696 Westbourne Ave., Columbus, 43213, 861-6634

Save 30-50% on quality, solid wood furniture including bedroom suites, dining room sets, curios and entertainment centers at this warehouse style business. While the selection is small, the business does special orders at comparable savings. W-Sun 11-6.

BARGAIN HOUSE FURNITURE
879 N. High St., Columbus, 43215, 297-0305

This offers reconditioned major appliances such as refrigerators, washers, dryers and ranges at about 30-50% less than "if new". The front of the store offers budget quality furniture at typical prices, but the place to look is in the back where you'll find a small and overstuffed room with good deals on used and antique furniture. M-Sat 9-6, Sun 1-6

BELAIR'S FURNITURE OUTLET
2600 Morse Rd., Columbus, 43231, 471-5682

Save 25-40% off popular brands of first quality furniture including some closeouts. You'll find Lane, Flexsteele, Koehler, Stanley, Lexington, Pulaski and others. Special orders are available at comparable savings, as are Howard Miller clocks. The business has recently revamped its pricing so it can offer your the best prices every day. M-F 10-9, Sat 10-6, Sun 1-5.

BLOOMINGDEALS
42 W. High St., Springfield, (513) 324-8568

Save 40-80% on better, gently used furniture, small appliances, gifts and related home accessories as compared to new prices. The store also has some new furniture at 25% savings. New carpets are available by special order at savings of 20-35% and some remnants are in stock at even better prices. Although brands change frequently, the store has sold Broyhill, Thomasville, Kroehler, Pulaski and others. M-F 10-5, Sat 12-4.

BRADLEY COMPANY
5164 Sinclair Rd., Columbus, 43229, 847-6020

This business sells quality new and used office furniture, but the best deals are on the used items. On these, you can expect to save 30-60% less than "if new". You'll find computer workstations, bookcases, chairs, filing cabinets, desks and other items. M-F 8-5.

BROWN-ROYAL FURNITURE COMPANY
80 E. Home St., Westerville, 43081, 882-2356

This family owned store has been in business for over ten years and sells first quality furniture and bedding at savings of 25-40% below manufacturers' suggested retail prices. The furniture is available in a variety of styles to suit all tastes. Special orders are also available at similar savings. Delivery is free. M/W/Th 10-9, Tu/F/Sat 10-5.

BUCHANAN'S FURNITURE
501 E. Main Street,Lancaster, 43130, 653-4652

Save 20-40% on popular brands of better furniture by Fitz Reed, Henredon, Sherrill, Lexington and others. You'll be impressed with this shop which offers a large selection and can special order items not in stock. The store also sells accessories at regular retail prices and offers various discounts on wallpaper. M/F 9:30-9, Tu/W/Th/Sat 9:30-5:30.

BURKE SALES
1458 Bethel Rd., Columbus, 43220, 442-6655

Save 25-40% on first quality, name brand furniture including leather sofas, window treatments, lighting and home accessories by such companies as Frederick Cooper, N. Hickory, Barcolounger, Stanley, Baldwin and others. A limited amount of stock is available on the floor for purchase, but most business is done by special order, which takes four to twelve weeks. Save 35% off in-stock Hummels and 25 % off special order. M-F 10-5, Sat 10-2.

BUSINESS, EQUIPMENT, ELECTRONICS
288 E. Long St., Columbus, 43215, 224-0144

40,000 square feet of new and used office furniture, accessories, desktop supplies and office machines are housed on three large floors of this building. Used items are sold at 50-75% off the "if new" price. New items which were purchased as manufacturers closeouts and overstocks, are similarly discounted. Current models of new office furniture and special orders are discounted 30-35%. There's chairs, desks, filing cabinets, bookcases, coat racks, end tables and a wide variety of other items, some of which could even be suited for your home. You'll also find a small selection of framed artwork such as photography, lithographs, etchings, prints, watercolors, oils as well as pen and ink works at about 75% off the "if new" prices. The artwork is found in varying quality levels. This business also sells new office supplies, which can be ordered from their catalogue, at a savings of 20-40% off regular retail prices. M-F 8:30-5, Sat 9-12.

CI BON INTERIORS
526 N. Cassingham Rd., Bexley, 43209, 253-6555

According to the owner, "This is the only high end design studio in the United States featuring low to medium furniture store prices. The values are so incredible, it allows you to move into a higher level of living. The store offers meaningful reductions from retail". Don't pass up the opportunity to visit Ci Bon. The 29 fully decorated rooms are brimming with tastefully appointed furniture, lamps, artwork and related accessories. There is also a large catalog room where you can custom order from hundreds of manufacturers. In order to maintain their low prices, Ci Bon does not offer layaways, financing nor delivery, but will provide you with names of movers upon request. The design studio also features a clearance room at the back of the business which offers greater savings on a small selection of discontinued merchandise. Tu-Th 12-9, F 12-7, Sat 10-6.

CORT FURNITURE RENTAL CLEARANCE CENTER
4870 Evanswood Dr., Columbus, 43229, 436-6440

New, discontinued and previously rented home and office furniture are available here at savings of 25-60% off "if new" prices. The store also stocks some new discontinued and closeout merchandise. Lamps and accessories can be found at similar savings. Oak cocktail and end tables begin at $69, decorative lamps from $19 and sofas from $199. The quality is moderate to better and includes such brands as Lane, Selig, Bassett and others. M-F 9-6, Sat 10-5.

CROSS ROADS HOME FURNISHINGS
Rt. 54 & 40, S. Vienna, 45369, (513) 568-5440

Save 20-50% off top quality, brand name furniture buy Pulaski, Riverside, Clayton Marcus and other brands. The store has a selection of unusual furniture and lovely oak reproductions. The business makes deliveries to Columbus. Tu/F 10-8, W/Th/Sat 10-6.

DEFENSE CONSTRUCTION SUPPLY CENTER
Bldg. 14, Section 1, 3990 E. Broad St., Columbus, 43213, 692-3468(retail store), 800)867-2431 (auction sales)

This government surplus store sells everything from plumbing, hardware, heating supplies, military clothing, furniture, televisions, mess kits, auto parts, office supplies and equipment as well as odd items. The stock consists of new and used merchandise in this 20,000 square foot warehouse. Auction sales are still held regularly and feature these and other items. Call to be added to their mailing list. Savings are about 30-70% and more. All merchandise is sold "as is". The retail store is open Monday to Saturday 10-3.

DINETTE GALLERY
2538 Morse Rd., Columbus, 43231, 476-5858

Volume buying enables this business to offer 30-50% off suggested retail prices on a large selection of in-stock and special order buffets, hutches, tables, chairs and barstools. This amounts to a savings of about $200-$600. The merchandise is sold as open stock, which means that you have the flexibility to mix and match pieces. The upscale inventory is by such brands as Douglas, Daystrom, Beechbrook and U.S. Furniture. It can be found in solid oak, laminates, veneers and glass, and includes first quality, first run merchandise. 90 days same as cash financing is available to qualified buyers. M-Sat 10-9, Sun 12-5.

ELEGANT ENCORE
471 Morrison Rd., Gahanna, 43230, 476-6960
195 Thurman Ave., Columbus, 43206, 449-1551

Traditional and contemporary styled furniture and home accessories are available at these upscale consignment shops. Savings are 30-65% less than "if new". Many items were originally custom ordered through interior decorators. If you're searching for top of the line merchandise, these stores are great places to look. The German Village location has more antiques than the Gahanna site. Hours vary by store.

EUROPEAN DESIGNS
Northwest Columbus, 221-2344 or 470-1389

Impeccable quality European designed furniture is available from this direct importer at savings of 35-50%. You'll find oak, cherry and walnut solid woods and some veneers utilizing decorative treatments such as inlaid work, intricate carvings and brass trims. Purchase individual items such as an oak CD rack for $99, an inlaid end table for $200 or a nine piece dining room set for about $8,000. The business is looking for a permanent storefront in the Northwest area, but in the meantime, you can see samples and browse through books at the temporary showroom site. By appointment only.

EXPERIENCED POSSESSIONS
9226 Dublin Rd., Powell, 43065, 889-0454

Used consignment and new samples of home furnishings such as lamps, accessories, furniture, art, antiques, table and bed linens, china, crystal, rugs and silver are available at savings of 50% and more off "if new" or manufacturers' suggested retail prices. The inventory is all better to designer quality and includes such brands as Drexel, Thomasville, Gorham, Kittinger, Wedgewood and others. M-F 10-6, Sat 10-5.

FAMOUS BRAND MATTRESS OUTLET
4741 E. Main St., Columbus, 43213, 575-0001

This sole Columbus distributor of the Chiro brand of premium quality bedding, offers a 50% discount off the manufacturer's suggested retail price on a variety of firmness and support options. Other brands such as Sealey are offered at minimal savings of about 10-15% off the manufacturer's suggested retail price. All mattresses come with full warranties through the manufacturers. Chiro brand merchandise is endorsed by the U.S. Chiropractic Association of America. M-Sat 11-8, Sun 12-5.

FLYING EAGLE FURNITURE
5270 Cleveland Ave., Columbus, 43231, 891-9478

Quality oak desks, chairs, hutches, curio cabinets, dinettes and bookcases are available at savings of about 20-30% off comparable quality products in other stores. The entire inventory of contemporary and antique reproductions is well made and fairly priced. The business is able to save you money by factory direct purchasing and by using its own trucks to transport the furniture. M-Th/Sat 10-6, F 10-8, Sun 12-5.

FURNITURE LIQUIDATION CENTER
1810 N. Memorial Dr., Lancaster, 43130, 1-687-0031

Moderate to better quality lamps, bedding and furniture are sold at savings of 20-50%. "Our prices are low, our volume is great. That's how we operate" is the store's motto. This discounter sells Pioneer, People Lounger, Horizon, Basset, Standard Bedding, Medallion and other brands in traditional, early American and contemporary styles. Layaway, warranties and delivery are available at this family operation. M-Sat 10-6.

GARTIN'S FURNITURE
379 E. Barthman Ave., Columbus, 43207, 444-6117

This small shop is in an older structure that once was used as a recreation center. You'll find used, vintage and antique furniture and accessories. While many items reflected current market values, the careful shopper can unearth some good deals. Tu-Sat 11-5.

GLICK'S WAREHOUSE OUTLET
1800 E. 5 Ave., Columbus, 43219, 251-1408

Save up to 70% off furniture, carpet, bedding, lamps, dinette sets, living room and bedroom furniture and more. The inventory consists of special purchases, overstocks, discontinued and some new merchandise purchased exclusively for the store. Check out the Rock Bottom Room where items are marked down in a final reduction of 50-70% off "if new" prices. You will find odds 'n ends, reconditioned returns, "as is", floor samples, mismatched bedding and special order cancellations. Tu-F 10-9, Sat 10-6, Sun 12-6.

GLOBE FURNITURE RENTALS
3659 E. Broad St., Columbus, 43213, 338-8666
Bethel Rd., Columbus, 43214 (will open in June '96)

Save 20-60% on previously rented furniture for your entire home. The moderate to better quality stock is in excellent condition, having been used in model homes and short term rentals. You'll find such brands as Lane, Brookwood, Douglas, National Office Furniture, Serta and others. There's cribs, beds in all sizes, living room, dining room, kitchen, bedroom and office furniture. Televisions, stereos and small appliances are also available. A new superstore will open on Bethel Road in the Olentangy Plaza Shopping Center and will include a broader selection overall, with special emphasis on the office furniture market. If you sign up for their mailing list, you'll get invitations to their tent sales which are usually held four times per year, at which prices are even lower. And, if you wear a tent to their tent sale (we're not kidding!), you'll get an extra 10% off your purchase. M-F 10-6, Sat 10-5.

GREATER COLUMBUS ANTIQUE MALL
1045 S. High St., Columbus, 43206, 443-7858

Columbus' first antique mall features five floors with over 75 dealers. 11,000 square feet of space offers antiques and collectibles including furniture, art, frames, gift items, lamps, costume and fine jewelry, architectural hardware as well as vintage clothing. Keep in mind that prices will vary from vendor to vendor, but there are many great deals to be found. The fun part about shopping in this mall, is that every inch of space has been utilized. You'll go in the attic, in closets and in rooms to search for unusual things. While the merchandise varies from kitsch to quality items, the smart shopper will take the time to look high and low to find the treasures. Don't be afraid to purchase a painting which needs to be rematted, or a chair which needs to be reupholstered. The extra expense can still amount to an excellent value for the piece. I have purchased many original paintings and etchings here in addition to fine and funky jewelry. Shop often as the inventory changes frequently. This store has earned the distinction of being one of my personal favorites. M-Sun 11-8.

GROLL'S FINE FURNITURE
149 N. Marion St., Waldo, 548-5700, 800-282-6745

A full line of furniture and bedding for the home at prices 25-40% below regular retail makes this store well worth the trip. It is only 35 minutes north of Worthington. In fact, about 60% of their business is from the Columbus area. You'll find quality brands such as Richardson Brothers, Bradington, Lane, Harden-Henkel-Harris, Century Designs, Jamestown Sterling, Hancock and Moore Leathers for every room of your home. Gifts, lamps, plaques as well as special orders, are similarly discounted. Thirteen buildings contain moderate to better quality traditional and colonial furniture. Their annual tent sale, a ten day event held in mid June, features greater savings on selected stock. Groll's operates a small warehouse outlet, a block away from their main store behind the church, which houses their cherry furniture. Savings at the outlet are 40% and more on discontinued and scratch 'n dent merchandise. M/W/F 9-5:30, Tu/Th/Sat 9-9, Sun 12-5.

HAAS FURNITURE
4094 E. Main St., Columbus, 43213, 235-6336

You'll find 100 rooms with over an acre of top quality furniture by Pulaski, Lane, Richardson, Jasper, Chromecraft, Flexsteele and others at savings of up to 60% off manufacturer's suggested retail prices. Savings of about 20-35% are available on lamps, framed prints, Howard Miller clocks and other home accessories. Special orders are similarly discounted. M-F 9-9, Sat 9-6, Sun 1-5.

HILLIARD'S FURNITURE
P.O. Box 96, Rt. 33 at Avery Rd., Dublin 43017, 889-8055

This no frills business sells early American, contemporary and traditional furniture by Tell City, Nathan Hale, American Drew, Fashion House, Flex Steel, Smith Brothers, Jasper, Lane, Hooker and Bassett at savings of 20-30%. You'll also find grandfather and tabletop clocks. Gifts, jewelry, watches, leather attaches, portfolios and wallets, crystal and small appliances at savings of 20-50%, since the store is liquidating these items with the exception of furniture and lamps. Special orders are available at similar savings. M/W/F/Sat 9-5, Tu/Th 9-8.

HOUSE OF FURNITURE
29 S. High St., Box 149, New Albany, 43054, 855-7545

Save about 30% off manufacturers' suggested retail prices on an extensive and unusual selection of quality dinettes, livingroom and bedroom furniture (for adults and kids) at both locations. The inventory features contemporary pieces, antique reproductions and some traditional furniture in addition to a limited selection of lamps and accessories. You'll find such brands as American Of Martinsville, Schweiger and Vaughan. The annual tent sale, held in late May through early June, offers hundreds of items at savings of up to 75% off suggested retail prices. This is well worth the trip especially if you have discriminating tastes as the stock is all top quality. M-F 12-8, Sat 10-6, Sun 12-6.

HOWARD BROOKS INTERIORS
7790 Olentangy River Rd., Worthington, 43235, 888-5353

Visit the newly expanded showroom of this upscale furniture and home accessories store which offers savings of 40% on leather furniture, 30% off wood and upholstered furniture and 20% off accessories and lamps. Similar discounts are available on special orders. The discounts represent savings from the manufacturers' suggested retail prices. You'll find such highly sought after brands as Hancock, Moore, Henredon, Tomlinson, and others. If you are seeking impeccable quality then this is the place to shop. M-F 10-6, Sat 10-5.

INTERIOR CONCEPTS
6693 Sawmill Rd., Dublin, 43017, 798-9795

Subdued, contemporary furniture is available at savings of 20-40% off. Accessories such as artwork and lamps are also available but are not discounted. You'll see such upscale brands as Harberry, Johnston Casuals, Bernhardt, Louis Phillip and others. The store also offers special orders at no additional cost if you stay within the same fabric grade. M-F 10-9, Sat 10-6, Sun 12-5.

INTERIOR CONCEPTS OUTLET
6500 Shier Rings Rd., Dublin, 43017, 766-2337

This upscale outlet is scheduled to open in March 1996, offering savings of 40-60% off manufacturers' suggested retail prices. The stock consists of "as is", discontinued and overstock furniture and household decor from their Sawmill Road location. Although plans were not finalized by the time we went to press for this book, the owner indicated that she anticipates having several sales per year or the outlet may be open just a few days per week. Hours to be determined.

J.C. PENNEY PORTFOLIO
3776 E. Broad St., Columbus, 43213, 236-5333
Graceland Blvd., Columbus 43214

"Is this really a J.C. Penney store, or have I accidentally stumbled into a White's or Glick's?" That is what you will ask yourself upon entering these tastefully stocked businesses. Popular furniture brands are discounted 15-30% off suggested manufacturer's list every day. Pictures, lamps and home decorating gift items are fairly priced, but not discounted. M-F 10-9, Sat 10-6, Sun 12-5.

LAZARUS FINAL COUNTDOWN
141 S. High St., Columbus, 43215, 463-2121

Final Countdown merchandise chainwide has been consolidated into 35,000 square feet of space on the Front Street level. The stock consists of carpet remnants as well as full and short rolls at savings of 45-80% off regular retail. There is a good variety of colors and textures from such brands as Karastan, Lees and Galaxy. The area also features end of season and past season clothing for the entire family. Giftware, linens and seasonal merchandise are offered at similar savings. A large selection of furniture includes plush leather sofas, dining room tables, end tables, hutches, entertainment centers and bedding which are floor samples, discontinued, customer cancellations and "as is" merchandise. You will find moderate to designer quality merchandise. Electronics can be found on the fourth floor in 8,000 square feet of selling space. The audio, video and electronics offerings include video recorders, cameras, typewriters and VCRs, some of which are overstocks, and others are floor samples and reconditioned models. Savings are 30-60% off popular brands such as Mitsubishi and Sony. The area also features some major appliances at similar savings. The clothing and giftware at the Final Countdown is initially priced at least 50% off regular retail. The furniture, audio, video and electronics merchandise is initially priced at about 20-30% off. On the last Friday of each month, the inventory is reduced by 25% of the lowest price on the ticket. The longer the merchandise stays unsold, the more reductions will be made. M-Th 10-9 F/Sat 10-6, Sun 12-5. (Furniture sales are only F/Sat 10-9, Sun 12-6.)

LEATHER EXPRESS
2400 S. Hamilton Rd., Columbus, 43232, 836-4821
845 N. High St., Columbus, 43215, 836-4800

Save 15-30% on quality leather sofas, recliners and easy chairs in over twenty different colors. A small selection of wood as well as glass/metal cocktail tables is available at value prices. The stores run special promotions continuously which can save you even more money off their every day low prices. Special orders take about 45 days. M-Sat 10-9, Sun 12-6.

LIBERTY STREET INTERIORS
15 N. Liberty St., Powell, 43065, 433-7000

Quality furniture, art prints, accessories, lamps and fabrics are discounted 25% off regular retail prices for in stock and custom orders. Lines carried include Brunswig and Fils and Laura Ashley. Financing is available. M-F 10-4:30, Sun 1-5. Closed Saturday. Accepts checks and cash only.

MACK MATTRESS OUTLET
2582 Cleveland Ave., Columbus, 43211, 262-2088
7370 Sawmill Rd., Columbus, 43235, 793-1048
15 S. 3 St., Newark, 43055, 345-5923
2691 Independence Village Center, Columbus, 43068, 866-2817

Overstocks and factory seconds of Simmons, Sealy and Beautyrest mattresses and boxsprings are available at savings of 50% off the "if perfect" price. Minor cosmetic flaws or mismatched sets will not affect the wear. Hard to find sizes are also available. This Christ centered business also sells reconditioned, used mattresses which have been sterilized and bagged. These will cost you 60-90% less than the price of a comparable new mattress. M-Sat 10-8, Sun 12-5.

MINERVA PARK FURNITURE GALLERY
5200 Cleveland Ave., Columbus, 43231, 890-5235

Factory direct, first quality furniture, in addition to antiques and used merchandise, are available at savings of 25-35%. This one man business can afford to offer low prices because of low overhead and by directly purchasing and often moving the furniture himself from som of the factories and workrooms. The stock is displayed in about fifteen different rooms and includes solid wood Amish made items and factory purchases. Special orders are available. M/Tu/F/Sat 12-7, Sun 12-5.

MODEL HOME FURNITURE AND ACCESSORIES SALES

Check the classified ads section at the back of the Columbus Dispatch and the community newspapers to find out about these excellent opportunities. Builders typically furnish their model homes with rented or purchased furniture, accessories and window coverings. If it cannot be used in another model, the merchandise will be disposed of once the model home has been sold. You'll find moderate to designer quality furniture, lamps, gift items, pictures and related accessories which are virtually in new condition. Savings are 25-60% off regular retail prices. Scan the newspapers regularly as these sales are held intermittently throughout the year by a variety of different builders and interior decorators.

MODEL INTERIORS
777 Dearborn Park Dr., Columbus, 43229, 885-8515

This no frills warehouse had more humble beginnings in a Clintonville garage. Buy first quality furniture by Lexington, Universal, American Drew, Hampton House Division of Norwalk, Singer, Bassett, Stanley, Kincaid, Pulaski and other companies. You can buy right off the floor or special order merchandise which takes about six to eight weeks. Savings are 60% off manufacturer's suggested retail prices and about 30% less than Glick's or White's sale prices, according to the owner. Weekday hours vary so call first, Sat 11-4, Sun 12-4.

OAK EXPRESS
2821 Morse Rd., Columbus, 43229, 471-0600
4410 Refugee Rd., Columbus, 43232, 759-6061

These no frills businesses can save you 20-40% on oak furniture because their showrooms also double as their warehouse. Entertainment centers are about $388 regularly $545, chairs start at $36 and similar deals. The store stocks such brands as Sheffield, Oakland, Mojave and Roanoke. There's solid wood and and veneer computer workstations, dinettes, china cabinets, bedroom suites, microwave carts and other items. M-Sat 11-9, Sun 12-6.

OAK FURNITURE SHOWROOM
8701 Columbus Pike, Lewis Center, 43085, 548-6757

Solid oak furniture consisting of antique reproductions, traditional and contemporary styles are offered at a savings of about 25-40% on comparable products at other stores. You'll also find the Cornerstone by Kincaid collection of solid ash furniture. Choose from tables, chairs, china cabinets, bedroom furniture, entertainment centers and even custom made furniture. M-F 10-9, Sat 9-6, Sun 12-5.

OHIO STORE FIXTURES
2545 Creekway Dr., Columbus, 43207, 491-0680

The largest used store fixture business in Ohio is not only for retail business needs but for consumers as well. You'll find metal racks for ties, belts, hats and clothes in every shape and size. There's Lucite display pieces for jewelry, free standing multi-shelf units for sweaters, toys or whatever. While the inventory is aimed at the retail store, you can find some unusual and functional items for your home or office which are not generally available to consumers. Most of the inventory is obtained form buyouts of stores which are closing or remodeling. Prices are about 30-75% less than "if new". This is a no frills warehouse type operation. M-F 8-5, Sat 8-12.

ORIGINAL MATTRESS FACTORY
851 W. Fifth Ave., Columbus, 43212, 291-8844
1736 Memorial Dr., Lancaster, 681-1401
2492 Morse Rd., Columbus, 43229, 475-3900
925 Hebron Rd., Heath, 522-1123
Wal-mart Center, Springfield, (513) 324-6434

Come to the factory and watch mattresses being made at the Fifth Avenue location. Two former Sealy executives have combined their talents to manufacture top of the line mattresses in a variety of sizes and firmnesses, with much of the construction done by hand. Custom sizes are also available. The mattresses feature many upgrades which are not featured by other popular brands. The fold in the mattress is thicker, the top fabric is felt backed and quilted, the coils are better made and the mattress handles are applied better to allow for ease in picking up the bedding. Prices are about 30-60% less than similar, but not the same, mattresses by other manufacturers. The best buys are on the better, top of the line mattresses, although the store offers some for those on restricted budgets. Headboards and day beds from other manufacturers are available at a savings of about 30%, but this business will provide the mattress. The Fifth Avenue site is the actual factory location. M-F 9-8, Sat 10-5, Sun 12-5.

PROVINCIAL HOUSE PATIO
6591 Sawmill Rd., Dublin, 43017, 766-2013

Save 15-30% off patio furniture. Buy merchandise as a grouping or as individual pieces by such brands as Brown Jordan, Woodard, Homecrest, Halcyon, Allibert, Telescope, Samsonite, Meadowcraft and others. M-F 10-8, Sat 10-6, Sun 12-5.

RESALE FURNITURE
1224 Hill Rd. N., Pickerington, 43147, 759-9275

Save 35-60% on gently used upscale furniture, gifts and home accessories. You'll find such brands as Ethan Allen, Drexel, Thomasville, Henredon, Sherrill and others. M-Sat 10-8.

RESIDENCE
1200 Williams Road, Columbus, 43207, no phone

Perpetual lawn sale of furniture and small bric a brac. Everything is sold "as is". The owners cover up the merchandise in the rain. You'll find trash to treasure including used, antique and someone else's discards. On a recent visit, I saw lovely ivory colored high back upholstered chairs for $15 each. F-Sun 10-5 as weather permits.

SCORZIELL MATTRESS COMPANY
3283 W. Broad St., Great Western Shpng. Ctr., Columbus, 43204, 278-2359
897 S. Hamilton Rd., Columbus, 43219, 338-0338
737 E. Hudson St., Columbus, 43211,262-1190

First quality electric beds, brass beds, waterbeds and mattresses are available at savings of 25-50% off manufacturer's suggested retail prices at this factory showroom. Odd size bedding can be made to order for campers. M-F 10-9, Sat 10-6, Sun 12-5.

SEARS FURNITURE AND APPLIANCE OUTLET
588 Brice Outlet Mallway, Columbus, 43232, 759-9030

Customer returns, overstocks, past season, floor samples, first quality, "as is" and reconditioned items from Sears stores at savings of 20-60% off regular retail prices. The stock consists of appliances, furniture, bedding and televisions. M-Sat 10-9, Sun 12-6.

SHARP'S GROVE CITY AUCTION GALLERY
4014 Broadway, Grove City, 43123, 875-0637 or 875-3584

This store features regular auctions of new, used and antique furniture, accessories and bric-a-brac, but has recently begun to operate a daily walk-in retail business on site. You'll find budget to better merchandise at savings of 40-70%. The company has recently begun to sell seconds of Simmons bedding (no plastic cover, some have snags or are discolored or mismatched sets) at similar savings. For example, full sized mattress sets sell for $189 regularly $589 if perfect. M-F 9:30-5:30, Sat 9:30-3:30, Sun 12-5.

SOFA EXPRESS
50 Morse Rd., Columbus, 43229, 836-4800
50 S. Hamilton Rd., Columbus, 43232, 836-4800
? W. Broad St., Consumer Sq. W., Columbus, 43228, 836-4800
Nebron Rd., Indian Mound Mall, Heath, 522-6633

Thousands of fabrics and styles of living room and family room upholstered furniture are available as custom orders within 35 days. The prices are about 20% less than those for comparable quality merchandise at other stores. Frequent sales provide additional opportunities for savings. Special financing plans also available. (Also see the Sofa Express Outlet in this chapter which is the clearance center for these stores). M-F 12-9, Sat 10-9, Sun 12-6.

SOFA EXPRESS OUTLET
4485 S. Hamilton Rd., Groveport, 43125, 836-4800
5640 Columbus Square, Columbus, 43221, 895-7741

Sofas, loveseats, tables, recliners, leather and upholstered furniture, sleep sofas and more are sold at 10-40% off the low prices found in their other stores. The inventory consists of discontinued, overstocked, special purchase, customer cancellations, factory buyouts and "as is" merchandise. You'll find such brands as, Coja Leather, Comfort Craft and People Lounger. There's a one year limited warranty on all merchandise, except "as is". Hours vary by store.

SUGARMAN LIQUIDATORS
971 W. Broad St., Columbus, 43222, 469-3444

Quality used office furniture, store fixtures, showcases, shelving, racks and more are sold at about 30-40% off "if new" or regular retail prices. The inventory consists of scratch and dents, special purchases and liquidations. M-F 8-5, Sat 8-12.

SUSAN BUDDE
Northwest Columbus, 761-8478

Save 50% off list price on upscale quality furniture and 30-40% off wallpaper and home accessories. Susan has many books and catalogues from which you can choose, but names can't be mentioned in print. Or you can call her with the manufacturer's name and model number and in most xases, she can get it for you at the same discount. Susan has samples of many items cattered throughout her home so you can see the quality of workmanship which she offers. And if you like, you can make a purcjase right off the floor wihout having to wait several weeks for your order to arrive! Furniture and accessories are available for every room of your home including the patiom and there are many iunique items from which to choose. She also deals with a local workroom and can get custom window treatments (drapes and cutrains) at about 40% less than through a decorator. All orders placed through Susan are fully guaranteed by the manufacturer. Tax and shipping are nominal and are added to your bill. Susan is a congenial person who won't give you a "hard sell" pitch

TAG SALES

These sales are conducted by professional sellers, who contract with a family or someone's estate, to sell all or part of the contents of their home. You'll walk through various rooms of a house or condominium to purchase artwork, furniture, computers, gifts, toys, clothes, antiques, housewares and more. These sales generally feature better quality merchandise than you would find at a garage sale, and often you can find decorator items. Arrive early as there are usually long lines to get into these tag sales. To locate tag sales, look in the classified ads section at the back of the newspapers. Also see "garage sales" in the housewares section of this book.

TRANSFORMATIONS
986 N. High St., Columbus, 43201, 298-9382

Small furniture, mirrors and other home decor are whimsically painted in geometrical, abstract and other designs. The owner searches garage sales, thrift stores and junk shops in search of items needing a facelift. She then decoratively transforms them into functional works of art, all at affordable prices. Small tables start at $25, mirrors at $15 and custom orders are available. Tu-F 12-6, Sat 11-6, Sun 12-5.

VALUE CITY FURNITURE
1789 Morse Rd., Columbus, 43229, 431-1400
6067 E. Main St., Columbus, 43213, 866-8888
3385 S. Boulevard, Great Western Shpng. Ctr., Columbus, 43204, 276-5157

Casual and formal furniture by Lane, Roanoke and other brands is offered at savings of 20-50% off regular retail prices. While most of the furniture is budget quality, the store surprisingly stocks some moderate to better quality goods such as leather sofas. Due to the enormous buying power of this chain, the stores are able to purchase goods at substantial savings and pass the values on to you. The stock also consists of discontinued goods and closeouts. M-Sat 10-9, Sun 12-6.

VILLAGE SWAP SHOP
353 W. Whittier St., Columbus, 43206, no phone

This unpretentious little store offers an eclectic mixture of antiques, collectibles, small used furniture and bric a brac. The prices are very reasonable. Expect to find a mixture of quality from budget to better. Tu-Sat 10-5. Accepts cash only.

WATERBEDS 'N STUFF WAREHOUSE OUTLET
3933 Brookham Dr., Grove City, 43123, 871-1171

About half of the inventory consists of scratch 'n dent waterbeds from their area stores at savings of about 20-40%. The balance of the stock is bedding and first quality waterbeds at their standard prices. M-F 10-5, Sat 10-3.

WHITE'S FINE FURNITURE
1395 Morse Rd., Columbus, 43229, 261-1000

This furniture store sells first quality Bassett furniture at 50% off the manufacturer's suggested retail price (plus factory direct freight charges). You'll find sofas, bedroom suites, recliners, dining room sets, home entertainment centers and small pieces as well. J.G. Hook has created a collection of pieces for Bassett and these are similarly discounted. This Bassett pricing is made possible through special factory participation which reduces many of White's operating costs. You will also find Thomasville and Stanley furniture to be discounted at least 40% compared to similar merchandise being soled in other stores. The store features the largest Thomasville gallery in the United States. M-Sat 10-9, Sun 12-5:30.

WHITE'S FINE FURNITURE WAREHOUSE STORE
5057 Freeway Drive E., Columbus, 43229, 436-3300

Floor samples, cancelled special orders, discontinued items, factory buyouts, first quality and some slightly damaged furniture and returns from model homes are available at savings of 30-60% off regular retail prices. Most of the merchandise is consolidated from their area stores which sell top of the line merchandise by Pennsylvania House, Thomasville, Broyhill and others. You'll find dining room sets, couches, chairs, bedroom furniture for the family, odd pieces and kitchen furniture. The store also has overstocks, discontinued, mismatched sets and one of a kind bedding from a local Simmons mattress factory. They call this section the Mattress Outlet. M-W/F/Sat 10-9, Th 12-9, Sun 12-5:30.

ALSO SEE

Andersons General Store, Aurora Farms Factory Outlet, Babe Discovery Shop, Baby Superstore, Builders Square, Burlington Coat Factory, Ceaser Creek Flea Market, Charles Headlee, Direct Imports, Gahanna Flea Market, Garage Sales, Golden Hobby Shop, Haggler's Day, Isabel's Design Mart, J.C. Penney Outlet, Lazarus Final Countdown, Lithopolis Antique Mall And Flea Market, Mansfield Flea Market, Me Too, Mid America Antique Show and Flea Market, Mostly Kids Stuff, My Cousins Closet, National Office Warehouse, Peddler's Village, Red Trailer, Sam's Club, Scioto Valley Hot Tubs And Spas, Service Merchandise, Sharp's Grove City Auction, Smitty's Auction, Springfield Antique Show And Flea Market, Stoneman Gallery, 3 C Flea Market, Toys 'R Us, Urbana Flea Market, Volunteers Of America, WDLR Radio, Warehouse Club, Washington C.H. Flea Market, Waterford Hall and Westland Flea Market

GARDEN

ANDERSONS GENERAL STORE
5800 Aleshire Rd., Columbus, 43232, 864-8800
7000 Bent Tree Blvd., Columbus, 43235, 766-9500

The bakery offers oversized, freshly baked goodies at value prices. You'll find pecan rolls, muffins and other specialties. The store offers excellent values in their seasonal garden center where the selection of perennials, annuals and shrubs is quite extensive. The savings on these garden items is about 20-30% less than in many other garden stores. Save 50% and more off the thousands of in stock wallpaper patterns and 30% off special orders. The businesses also feature an extensive selection of quality unfinished oak and other types of wooden furniture such as bookcases, desks, chairs, entertainment centers and microwave carts which are about 20-30% less than comparable quality products at other stores. The Brice Road location has and Outlet Alley in the middle aisle which features buyouts of manufacturers' discontinued and overstock products in all categories. Bring in your dog for a free flea dip. The event is held twice in the summer in July and August and would cost you $20-$25 if it were done at an area veterinarian clinic. Be sure to bring an old towel so you can dry off your dog. Dogs must be on a leash and collar, be handled by an adult and must be at least three months old. Area nonprofits will be on hand to assist with your optional donation benefiting these groups. The Andersons is a general store which offers a full line of regular priced hardware, housewares, fishing supplies, home improvement supplies, fruits and vegetables as well as a small gourmet food and wine department. M-Sat 8-9, Sun 10-6.

BACKSTROM
3332 Possum Run Rd., Mansfield 44903, (419) 756-3051

Nursery stock of shade trees, evergreens, flowering trees, flowering shrubs as well as ground covers are available at about 40-50% less than at other garden stores. Over 150,000 specimens are in stock for purchase at wholesale prices. Five foot tall pink flowering dogwoods are $36.95, 15" blue girl holly is $8.95, 24" Juniper is $14.95, six foot flowering cherry is $49.95, 15" rhododendrons are $5.95. If you bring a sketch and measurements of your yard, Backstrom's will provide a free landscape design service while you wait. The nursery, which grows all of its own stock, does not currently sell gardening tools or related supplies, but is planning to offer these in 1992 when it builds a garden center on the property. Adult gardening and landscaping workshops will be available at that time as well. All purchases are guaranteed for one year. M-Sat 8-8. Closed November through early March.

CASHMAN
1748 U.S. Rt. 42 N., Delaware, 43015, 363-6073

Mulch, dog food, bird seed, rock salt, fertilizer and other lawn and garden products are offered at savings of 20-75% off regular retail prices. You will find such brands as Morton Salt, Buckeye Feeds and Dad's. This full service drive through business, sells individual bags at truckload prices. The store also has two large greenhouses, where plants and flowers are sold at similar savings. Cashman's holds the record of being the largest one store retailer of cyprus mulch in the nation. At Christmas time, you can purchase five to eight foot white and scotch pine trees for only $16.95, regularly $29-$50 elsewhere. M-F 8-8, Sat/Sun 9-6.

COLUMBUS STONE CENTER
1736 McKinley Ave., Columbus, 43222, 276-3585

Shop where the professionals shop! You can purchase over fifty types of stone including patio brick pavers, landscaping wallstones, colored pebbles, marble chips and landscaping boulders at about 20-30% less than through a professional landscaping company. You'll be amazed at the varied selection. M-F 8-5, Sat 8-2.

COM-TIL
Columbus Compost Facility, 7000 State Rt. 104, Grove City, 43123, 645-3152

Com-Til is a rich compost and an excellent mulch, providing a constant organic feed for plants. It is available at the city's compost facility in a 40 pound bag for $3 including tax. Area gardening stores sell it for $3.99 plus tax. Or, if you're real ambitious and want to buy it in bulk, you can load it into your truck unbagged. Another option is to bring bags or containers and fill them yourself. For these latter two options, you'll pay only two cents per pound or fifteen dollars per cubic yard. The compost facility staff will assist you in loading the Com-Til into your vehicle. M-F 7-3 year round. Accepts checks and cash only.

DELAWARE SOIL AND WATER CONSERVATION DISTRICT
29 Grandview Ave., Delaware, 43015, 362-4011 ext 1921

Order low cost quality seedlings which are suitable for windbreaks, reforestation, CRP planting and wildlife food habitats. Tree packets cost $5-$18 and contain about 10-75 evergreens, hardwoods, blue spruce, wildlife fruit, wildlife flowers and/or black walnut seedlings. You may also purchase a ground cover packet consisting of wildflower seeds and native grasses for ornamental planting. Orders are accepted in March with pre-payment, and are available for pickup in April. M-F 9-5. Accepts checks and cash only.

HILLIARD LAWN AND GARDEN
5300 Cemetery Rd., Hilliard, 43026, 876-4054

This business sells new and used lawn and garden equipment. You'll find such brands as Mitsubishi, Deutz-Allis, Craftsmen, Toro, Cub Cadet, Snapper and Lawn Boy. Used lawn mowers sell for about $40-150. Weed eaters, snow blowers and other items offer comparable savings and reflect about 30-60% off "if new" prices. M-F 8-6, Sat 8-4.

LANGSTONE
707 Short St., Columbus, 43206, 228-5489

Landscapers, contractors and the general public can shop at this 130 year old company and svae money. You'll find cut stone for fireplaces and mantels, masonry products, marble and granite for walls/flooring/vanities, boulders and smaller rocks for gardens, decorative gravel such as lava and marble chips, cut stone for veneers and trim, plus lots more. M-F 7:30-5, Sat 8-12.

LIVINGSTON SEED COMPANY COUTLET STORE
880 Kinnear Rd., P.O. Box 299, Columbus, 43216, 488-1163

This 142 year old wholesaler, ships to accounts across the country. Vegetable, perennial and annual seed packets are priced at 49 cents each, regularly $1 and up, and are for the current year. Several types of bird seed are available in 1, 25 and 50 pound bags. Savings can average 20-30%, with the best value being in the larger quantity. The store also sells various types of grass seeds at comparable savings. Bulk beans, peas and corn are 50 cents per scoop and bulk wildflower seeds are also value priced. M-F 8:30-5, Sat 9-1.

MILLCREEK GARDENS
15088 Smart Cole Rd., Ostrander, 43061, 666-7125

This wholesaler and grower of herbs and perennials, opens its doors to retail sales on Saturdays from 8a.m.-noon, from early April through late August. You'll find about 400-500 different varieties priced at about 20-50% below plant store prices. Call before you go. Ostrander is just north of Dublin.

OHIO POTTERY
8540 E. Pike, Zanesville, 43701, 872-3137

Factory direct stoneware for your garden is available at savings of about 20-30% off regular retail prices. You'll find a large selection of fountains, religious figures, red clay flower pots, bird baths, large concrete baskets, animals and more. Take exit 152 off I-70. This business if about one hour from downtown Columbus. M-Sun 9-6:30 year round.

PICQUA GROWERS
30454 Orr Rd., Circleville, 474-6330

This grower of shrubs, hanging baskets, herbs, perrenials and other items offers value prices on their garden greenery. The business is open seasonally form mid April to mid June. Tu-Sat 9:30-7, Sun 12-5:30.

SCIOTO VALLEY HOT TUBS AND SPAS
4344 Lyman Dr., Hilliard, 43026, 876-7755

Save 20-50% off manufacturer's suggested retail prices on hot tubs, spas and outdoor furniture by such companies as Leisure Bay, U.S. Forming, Coleman Spas and Hotspring Spas. Special financing terms include 90 days same as cash or six months same as cash to qualified buyers. M-Sat 10-9, Sun 11-5

SOUTHWESTERN DESIGN
401 S. Hamilton Rd., Columbus, 43213, 236-2289

Wholesale distributor of cement statuary for the garden offers value pricing on bird baths, decorative statues and related items. A cement two foot diameter garden table with a fish motif was priced at $45 and an art nouveau style lady bird bath was priced at $59 on a recent visit. You'll find cement gargoyles, animals and other designs to decorate your landscape. The ever popular cement geese (but please don't buy me one) are priced at $7.95 and $16.95, with apparel priced at $8.95 or $14.95 respectively. All geese outfits come fully equipped with a hat. Winter hours are 10-6 seven days a week. Hours during the rest of the year are 10-8 seven days a week.

SPA AND HOT TUB OUTLET
4382 Indianola Ave., Columbus, 43229, 268-5761
6111 E. Main St., Columbus, 43213, 866-4666

Decks, gazebos, portable spas, pools, steam units and other similar items are available at savings of 10-50% off suggested retail prices. The inventory consists of first quality, liquidations and discontinued goods. Trade-ins are sold at 50-70% less than the new price. The manager said that he has customers coming from six states to purchase his products because the prices are so low. M-F 8:30-9, Sat 10-6, Sun 12-6.

SUN HOLIDAY POOLS
12981 E. Main St., Pataskala, 43062, 927-9686
2804 Johnstown Rd., Columbus, 43219, 471-1746

The strongest above ground pools in the United States are manufactured by this local company which also makes in-ground pools. A 30 year warranty is included. Savings are about 15-20% as compared to comparable (inground) and almost comparable (technically, there is no comparison because of their distinction) products. Installation costs are included in the price. April through September hours are M-Sat 8-8, Sun 11-5. October through March hours are M-Sat 10-6.

ALSO SEE

Black And Decker, Dawes Arboretum, Educable Channel 25, Fortin Welding and Manufacturing, Franklin County Cooperative Extension Service, Franklin County Soil And Water Conservation District, Grandview Cycle Shop, Herb Fair, Jo's Clothing For Bears and Geese, Orley's Herbs And Stuff, Robinson-Ransbottom Pottery, Schottenstein's, Scioto Valley Hot Tubs And Spas, Service Merchandise, Spa and Hot Tub Outlet Wines Inc.

GIFTS & HOUSEWARES/ DRIED FLOWERS

ALL THINGS CONSIGNED
5937 E. Main St., Columbus, 43213, 866-1967

Upscale home accessories, gifts, sporting goods, collectibles, antiques and furniture are available in this consignment shop. Savings are 30-70% off "if new" prices. I recently purchased a handmade oak hanging cabinet for a mere $50 which was meticulously assembled. M/Tu/F/S 10-6, W/Th 10-8.

BEAUMONT BROTHERS POTTERY
315 E. Main St., Crooksville, 43731, 982-0055

This pottery specializes in early American, traditional stoneware and hand turned salt glazed pottery. The pieces are recognizable by the rich gray of the fired clay and the vibrant cobalt blues of each hand decorated piece. Visit the seconds room where savings are 50-80% off, with most items priced at $6 and under. Prices in the first quality room are in the $12-$30 range. M-F 8:30-5, Sat 10-4, Sun 12-5.

BERWICK CORNER OUTLET
2700 Winchester Pike, Columbus, 43232, 235-6222

Nationally recognized moderate to designer quality brands of cologne, shoes, small appliances, watches, crystal, computer games, office equipment, sporting goods, giftware, toys and apparel are offered at savings of 25-75% off manufacturers' suggested retail prices. The inventory comes from a variety of sources including nationally recognized upscale department stores and consists of some freight damaged as well as first quality goods. Insome cases, the box or packing may be damaged, but the merchandise is not. This no frills business is the site of some of the most chic and sought after merchandise. However, the stock changes so radically from shipment to shipment, that you'll never know what you will find. It is not unusual to see designer clothes strewn in boxes on the floor or hung with creases, on racks. You'll find a crystal vase, valued at $200, on a shelf next to a $2 candle. This is definitely the place to have your bargain hunting antennas fully extended. Don't be alarmed if you arrive and the store looks like it's going out of business, because the shelves and racks are literally emptied by customers routinely! Shop often as new shipments arrive daily. This store has earned the distinction of being one of my personal favorites. W-F 10-4, Sat10-2.

BIG FUN
1782 N. High St., Columbus, 43201, 294-4386

Pop culture kitsch of the 50's-80's is available in this fun store on campus. You'll find gag gifts (hand buzzers, fart spray), wind up banks (a skeleton in a coffin which grabs your coin), corny what-nots (a boxing nun, a lobster harmonica) and other fun stuff (magic eight ball key chain, etch a sketch watch, crime scene tape just ;like the police use). There's also corn candles, swaying hip Elvis clocks, a pen syringe, oak drawers filled with nickle and dime items and more. Many items are reproductions from the original, but you'll also find authentic items too. Some items have been stored untouched for years in warehouses until the owner gets wind of them. You'll also find Star Wars and other memorabilia which the owner is always looking to buy. Not just for its nostalgic quality, but for its great values (most items are priced under $8), this store is a fun place to shop. It has earned the distinction of being one of my personal favorites. M-Th 11-7, F/Sat 11-8, Sun 12-6.

BLOOMS DIRECT
1266 W. Goodale Blvd., Columbus, 43212, 487-5700

Fresh flowers arrive daily and combine with the silk florals, to make this an unusual marriage. Imagine choosing from 54 different types of roses! The best deals are when you buy flowers by the bunch instead of by the single item. Offers custom design services. M-Sat 10-6.

BOHEMIAN GLASS AND CRYSTAL (CRYSTAL CLASSICS)
Bexley, 43209, 338-8877

Save 20-40% on first quality crystal vases, bowls, tableware and decorative items from this wholesaler/importer. The impeccable quality merchandise is sold at the finest stores. Some of the wares include Strossmayer Crystal (which has made part of a line for Waterford Crystal), Orrefors and other brands. The business once operated a storefront, but has moved the inventory to a house nearby which takes customers by appointment only.

BURLEY CLAY POTTERY OUTLET
26 N. Shawnee Ave., S. Zanesville, 43701, (800) 828-7539 or 452-3633

The outlet, which is open from mid March through mid October, sells mostly seconds at 50% off the retail price. You'll find bird baths, decorative flower pots, garden statuary and related items. Prices at the outlet are in the $4.50-$25 range, with most under $10. Free factory tours are offered Monday through Friday from 7a.m.-3p.m. Outlet hours are M-Sat 7a.m.-8p.m., Sun 1-6.

CLAY CITY OUTLET CENTER
222 Scenic Crest Dr., Zanesville, 450-2529

Housed in one of the world's largest log structures, this center features about thirty businesses under one roof. While many offer typical retail prices, several feature great deals that make this worth the trip. The Zanesville Stoneware Company features 50% off first quality, decorative planters and serving pieces. The Hartstone Pottery features 30-50% off a grouping of seconds. The Robinson Ransbottom pottery features their typical value priced planters, serving pieces and home accessories in sponge decorated and other designs. The Burley Clay Company features savings of 20-40% and the Kitchen Collection offers 15-40% savings. Other vendors offer crafts, housewares and miscellaneous gifts. M-Sat 10-9, Sun 10-6.

CLOCK 8 CLOCK CENTER
1263 Hebron Rd., Heath, 522-5888

Save 35-50% on over 300 Howard Miller, Sligh, Loricron and New England Clock Company grandfather, wall, mantel, gift and cuckoo clocks. You'll also find Black Forest cuckoo clocks. Special orders are also available at comparable savings. The business repairs clocks at typical rates. Free delivery is offered within a 75 mile radius. Tu-F 10-5, Sat 10-12.

COLUMBUS' LARGEST GARAGE SALE
Southland Expo Ctr., 3660 S. High St., Columbus, 43207, 497-8781

Auction purchases, liquidations and closeouts account for the source of merchandise you'll find here at savings of 20-60%. There's new, used, antique and collectible items ranging from budget to better quality in this no-frills, perpetual garage sale. You will find paper party goods, toys, gifts, stationery, household and other items. On a recent visit, the owner was unpacking musical gift items purchased from a recently closed Hallmark store. They were 50% off the regular retail price. F 12-8, Sat 10-8, Sun 12-6.

D.E. JONES
3531 Cleveland Ave.,Northern Lights Shpng. Ctr., Columbus, 43224, 261-9500
932 S. Hamilton Rd., Great Eastern Shpng. Ctr., Columbus, 43213, 861-9417
117 Graceland Blvd., Graceland Shpng. Ctr., Columbus, 43214, 888-9141
3781 S. High St., Great Southern Shpng. Ctr., Columbus, 43207, 497-9080
3287 Maple Ave., Zanesville, 454-9242

Among the budget quality housewares, comforters and children's clothing, you will find some moderate quality treasures such as Burlington hosiery, funky children's hair accessories, yarns and general merchandise. Savings throughout the store are 30-50% off regular retail prices. The inventory changes frequently. M-Sat 9:30-9, Sun 11-6. Accepts checks and cash only.

D & R NOVELTIES
4020 Old Columbus Rd., Carroll, 43112, 756-9121

Trinkets, flea market items, tools, glassware, ceramic figurines (some kitsch like ceramic pigs), crafts, candies, inexpensive toys, seasonal and holiday gifts and some clothing are available at savings of 20-50% on most items. Quantity purchases earn larger discounts. While most of the stock is budget quality, the careful shopper could unearth some real treasures. This store specializes in sales to flea market vendors, but sells to the general public too. W/F 9-5, Tu/Th 9-8, Sat 10-4.

DIRECT IMPORTS
2586 S. Hamilton Rd., Columbus, 43232, 338-8566
3575 E. Livingston Avenue, Livingston Ct. Flea Market, Columbus, 43227, 866-3398

Furniture, giftware and leather purses are available at savings of 20-50% off comparable retail prices. This direct importer of merchandise from China and Taiwan features a wide variety of styles in budget to moderate quality. M-Sat 11:30-8:30, closed W, Sun 1-6 (Hamilton Rd location). F-Sun 12-6 at Livingston Ave.

DOLL HOUSE
109 N. High St., Gahanna, 43230, 471-8484

This shop specializes in a large selection of Victorian, Country French and country dolls, crafts, gifts and collectibles at prices which are about 10-20% less than comparable retail prices or manufacturer's suggested retail prices. Dressed bears can be found as little girls, country boys, sophisticated ladies in fur stoles as well as outrageous gals in feathers and jewels. The most outstanding feature of this business, is its selection of collectible porcelain dolls which include Delton, Seymour Mann, Dynasty and Dolls By Pauline brands. These are priced at $32-$110. Handmade modern collectible dolls can be special ordered as well. The store also offers custom wedding flowers and accessories in addition to window swags at similar savings. Since many of the craft items are handmade by the owner and a few select local craftspersons, the middle man is eliminated and prices are kept to a minimum. Inventory changes frequently, with many unique one-of-a-kind gifts and collectibles available. The shopping experience takes place in the relaxed and friendly atmosphere of an older home converted to a doll's house. Tu-Sat 11-6.

FAMILY DOLLAR
Seven Columbus locations plus the following
180 Sunrise Ctr. Rd., Zanesville, 43701, 454-4111

Budget quality housewares, toys and clothes fill these stores. The knowledgeable and persistent shopper should return often as these businesses also feature buyouts of first quality overstocks and irregulars of moderate to better quality apparel and accessories. On my recent visit, the menswear department featured current season Hobie, Ocean Pacific, Graffiti and Surfstreet clothes for adults and children at savings of 50-70% off regular retail prices. Many of the manufacturers' garment labels had been removed. However, a careful examination of the merchandise could often disclose a manufacturer's name on a paper hang tag, a label which was not entirely removed or a logo imprinted on the front of the garment. During another visit, I stumbled upon a fantastic buyout of exclusive fashion earrings by Paolo Gucci (formerly with THE Gucci Company in New York). The earrings originally sold for $20-$35 in upscale department stores and boutiques, but were priced at only $5! At the back of the display cards for the Paolo Gucci earrings, there was this comment: "Paolo Gucci is no longer associated with Gucci America". Here is another fine example of a store which you should not bypass just because the quality of its stock may not usually be up to your standards. M-Sat 10-9, Sun 12-5. Accepts checks and cash only.

FORT STEUBEN COMPANY
2250 Westbelt Drive, Columbus, 43228, 876-7177

Buy cloisonne, stone carvings, lamps, oriental rugs, bronze statues, small furniture and jewelry at wholesale prices. There's an exceptional selection of handpainted objects (boxes, screens etc.), cinnabar bracelets for $4, reverse painted snuff bottles for $7, necklaces on cords with reverse painted beads for $2.50 and more. A sizeable collection of antique statues and pottery, some thousands of years old, have been tested through thermoluminescense and are authenticated. This collection is the largest of Chinese excavated artifacts in the midwest. F/Sat 10-5.

FOUNTAIN PENS
c/o Heart's Content, 9 N. State St., Westerville, 43081, 891-7627 or 891-6050

This business buys, sells, trades and repairs all brands of fountain pens. You'll find Parker, Waterman's, Conklin, Schaeffer, Wahl-Eversharp and other brands in stock plus desk sets at very competitive prices. The repair prices are also very reasonable. The business is located within the Heart's Content Antique Mall, a quaint shop featuring new, used, antique and collectible gifts from several dealers. M-Sat 10-5, Sun 12-4.

GARAGE SALES

You'll find listings for these in the back of the community newspapers and in the back of the "help wanted" section of Sunday's Columbus Dispatch. Neighborhood sales provide you with the opportunity to shop at many sales in a limited area, thereby saving you time and gas. As many garage sales are not listed in the newspapers, sellers rely on drive-by traffic to see signs which they have posted by the roadside. Don't overlook the non-advertised sales! An advantage of early arrival at any garage sale is that you will have the first pick at the merchandise. On the other hand, arrival towards the end of the sale often places you in a position to pay much less than the asking price because the seller is often more motivated to sell the remaining items than she would have been at the beginning of the sale. You'll find new and used merchandise including clothes, toys, hardware, housewares, furniture, arts and crafts and who knows what. Savings are 30-95%. Also refer to "Tag Sales" in the furniture section and "Salesmen's Sample Sales" in the clothing section.

GLOBAL GALLERY
682 N. High St., Columbus, 43215, 621-1744

This shop is operated by local churches and benefits artisans in developing countries by helping them to become self sustaining. You'll find a wide variety of handmade items such as jewelry, wooden carvings, ceramics, baskets, fiber arts and handmade paper from Peru, Pakistan, Bangladesh, India and the Phillipines. What you'll notice at the gallery is not discount prices, but rather many items which are exceptional values, considering of course, that they are hand crafted. Tu-Sat 11-5.

GOLDEN HOBBY SHOP
630 S. 3 St., Columbus, 43206, 645-8329

The art and handicrafts of seniors are showcased in this store which is housed in an old school. Many rooms are filled with paintings, darling doll clothes, toys, lawn accessories, gift items, dollhouses, birdfeeders, afghans, quilts and wearable art. While a large portion is bazaar type crafts, the knowledgeable shopper will spot the true quality items. The shop is operated by the City of Columbus, Recreation And Parks Department which only takes a 10% commission on the sales to cover administrative costs. As a result, the prices are kept to a minimum and savings are 20-70% less than comparable quality items in art galleries and other retail stores. The shop also features free quilting classes for adults of all ages and craft demonstrations every weekend. M-Sat 10-5, Sun 1-5. Accepts checks and cash only.

HARTSTONE POTTERY
1719 Dearborn Rd., Zanesville, 43701, 453-7200 ext 7350 or 452-9000
222 Scenic Crest Dr., Clay City Outlet Mall, Zanesville, 450-2529

Save about 30-50% on discontinued and seconds of nationally recognized pottery at this factory outlet.   You'll find hand decorated stoneware, dinnerware, serving pieces, microwave cook and bakeware, lamps as well as cookie and shortbread molds. Most of the flaws are hardly noticeable. The pottery is sold at major department stores throughout the country. Special sales are held twice a year from April to late May and mid-November to early December, at which time savings are even greater. Call to be added to the mailing list. Zanesville is known as the pottery capital of the world. Hours vary by location.

HOMEPLACE
3616 W. Dublin Granville Rd., Columbus, 43235, 799-1950
111 Huber Village Blvd., Westerville, 43081, 882-0816

Popular upscale brands of housewares, linens, small furniture and gift items are priced at 15-40% off manufacturer's suggested retail prices. Meticulously arranged, you'll find such brands as Revere, Farberware, Burlington, T-Fal, Corningware, Pfaltzgraff, Martex and others. The stores also feature a value priced monogramming service at $4-$6 which can be done on the premises while you shop. This is certainly a rarity among discount operations. Special cooking demonstrations and events are held throughout the year. The store's motto is " everyday prices at or below department store sale prices". One thing you won't find here is "compare to" prices which sometimes makes it a little difficult to determine how much you are saving. M-Sat 9:30-9, Sun 11-6.

INFINITY 99 CENT STORE
1776 Parsons Save., Columbus, 43206, 449-0021
5466 Westerville Rd., Westerville, 43081, 891-9809

Unlike its predecessors which sold items for a buck, this store seems to have a preponderance of generic and otherwise unfamiliar brands of products. You'll find housewares, costume jewelry, infant rattles, tin foil, boxed magnets, toys, cleaning supplies and toiletries. Although the stock is priced at 99 cents per item, only a small amount of the stock is worth more than that. However, it's interesting to see what 99 cents will buy. Open 9-9 seven days per week.

ISABEL'S DESIGN MART
1041 Mediterranean Avenue, Columbus, 43229, 848-5555

Save 30-50% on better quality gifts from Gumps, Horchow's, Bloomingdales and buyouts from manufacturers. You'll find crystal, majolica reproductions, small furniture, Limoge and other specialty items. The business can also order upholstered furniture from the manufacturers, shipped to your door, at savings of about 30%. W/F/Sat 10-6, Th 10-8.

IT'S REALLY $1.00
3659 Soldano Blvd., Columbus, 43228, 276-0534

This store is under the same ownership as All For One and Itzadeal . See their listings elsewhere in this book for description as the store has the same merchandise. M-Sat 9-9, Sun 10-6.

ITZADEAL
2703 Eastland Mall, Columbus, 43232, 759-1155
3822 E. Broad St., Columbus, 43213, 237-5045

See description of All For One, which has the same merchandise and is owned by the same company. M-Sat 9:30-9, Sun 12-6.

KITCHEN COLLECTION
621 N. Memorial Dr., Lancaster, 43130, 687-1750
222 Scenic Crest Dr., Clay City Outlet Mall, Zanesville, 450-2529

Reconditioned small appliances can be found at savings of about 40off regular retail prices. You will also find Wearever cookery, Proctor Silex appliances, Anchor Hocking glassware, Bissell appliances, plus kitchen gadgets at more moderate savings of 15-30%. M-Sat 10-9, Sun 12-6.

KITCHEN PLACE
7675 New Market Center Way, New Market Mall, Columbus, 43235, 764-0318

This one stop kitchen source offers discounts of 20-40% off manufacturer's suggested retail prices on glassware, bakeware, shelf organizers, kitchen gadgets and even picture frames. You'll find such brands as Libbey, Ekco, Rubbermaid, Mikasa and Pyrex. The Lechters' stores (see listing elsewhere in this book), are owned by the same company and have similar stock. M-Sat 10-9, Sun 12-6.

LAKE ERIE FACTORY OUTLET CENTER
11001 Rt. 250 N., Milan, 44846, 1-800-344-5221

Here's your chance to buy direct at factory prices of 20-70% off regular retail, at Ohio's largest outlet center. There's 50 factory stores here including Farberware, Mikasa, Harve Benard, Bass Shoes, Jonathan Logan, Nilani, Leather Loft, Ribbon Outlet, Ruff Hewn, Wallet Works, American Tourister, Hanes, Toy Liquidators, Prestige Fragrances, Aileen, Olga/Warner's, Socks Galore, Bugle Boy, Izod, Manhatten, Swank, Van Heusen, Corning Revere, Hilda Of Iceland and other favorites. Call or write for information on special sales usually held once per month, where greater savings are available. M-Sat 10-9, Sun 10-6

LAKE STREET TRADING COMPANY (GOLDEN COUNTRY)
186 E. Winter St., Delaware, 43015, 363-3137

This unpretentious little shop offers small antique and collectible gift items, bric-a-brac, and used home decor at fair prices. M-Sat 11-5(winter), M-Sat 11-7(all other months), also open Sundays by chance.

LANCASTER GLASS CORPRATION
240 W. Main St., Lancaster, 653-0311

Utilitarian and decorative glassware are available at savings of 30-50% off retail prices. You'll find fruit designed baking dishes, crystal heart paperweights, lamps, lampshades, serving bowls, glass bells and colorful stemware. These are overstocks and discontinued items from the Lancaster Glass Company. The store also stocks Indiana Glass, Fostoria Glassware and Nelson McCoy Pottery (affiliates/former affiliates of the parent company). When the latter two were sold to the parent company, it also acquired the remaining inventory. Nostalgia buffs and collectible enthusiasts will enjoy purchasing these items, made in the 1980's, which are no longer in production. While the value on these pieces in books on collectibles, shows them to be still affordable, the prices will likely escalate in years to come. You should also note that when Fostoria was purchased, that the parent company purchased the right to use that name in future production, so there are items being sold in department and specialty stores using this trademarked name. However, they are not from the original Fostoria company. The stock is maintained in one small room and is mostly priced from $2-$10.

LECHTER'S
2752 Eastland Mall, Columbus, 43232, 866-8177
1717 Northland Mallway, Columbus, 43229, 267-0220

See description for the Kitchen Place which is under the same ownership and has the same merchandise. M-Sat 10-9, Sun 12-6.

LIQUIDATIONS NOW
1547 Lockbourne Rd., Columbus, 43207, 444-5333

Closeouts and buyouts of discontinued, odd lots, bankrupt, salvage and overstock merchandise are available at savings of 25-75% off regular retail prices. First quality and some irregular items (such as slightly misprinted garments which won't effect their durability) are found here. Household items, food, tools, fashion earrings at $1-$2 and moderate quality clothes can be found. Toys offered include such sought after brands as Playskool, Mattel and Parker Brothers. M-F 11-8, Sat 10-8. Accepts checks and cash only.

M&M THRIFT STORE
773 Parsons Avenue, Columbus, 43206, 338-0077

From trash to treasure at garage sale prices, you'll find some antiques, collectibles, curiosities and "what the heck is it" stuff. This is a tiny, hole in the wall store, but if you look carefully, you'll find some treasures. Don't be distracted by the bars on the windows and the no-frills atmosphere. Sat 10-2.

MS DISTRIBUTORS
2753 Westbelt Dr., Columbus, 43228, 777-1550

Several times during the year, this wholesale distributor opens its doors to the public. You'll save 30-50% off list price on such high end fireplace accessories as glass doors, gas logs, wooden baskets, fireplaces, tool sets, grates etc. Brands offered include Pilgrim, Rasmussen and others. The stock is sold "as is" and includes some scratch and dent items. The sales are usually held in the fall, October through December. Th/F 8-7, Sat 8-5.

MARIE'S ALTERATIONS AND GIFTS
3343 South Blvd., Columbus, 43204, 272-0263

Quality alterations are available at value prices. The owner's daughter makes beautiful porcelain dolls from molds, and the dolls' clothes from patterns of her own design. The dolls range in price from $12-$125 and come attired in Victorian, contemporary and other fashions. The prices are very reasonable, saving you about 30% off comparable quality items at other stores, as the middleman has been eliminated. M-Sat 9-6.

ME TOO
980 W. Broad St., Columbus, 43222, 228-7719

Find used, antique and collectible home furnishings including furniture and bric-a-brac at value prices. An area upstairs is set up like a Victorian parlor and also features similar items. Check out the business's adjacent storefront which is more like a garage sale than anything. Most of the bric-a-brac and what nots there are priced at under $5. M-Sat 11:30-8:30, Sun 12-6.

MID OHIO DOLL AND HISTORICAL MUSEUM
700 Winchester Pike, Canal Winchester, 4311, 837-5573

The museum has recently expanded its gift shop and now offers a larger selection of new, used, antique and collectible dolls at very reasonable prices. When the shop has the chance to purchase a doll at a great price, it passes on the savings to the customers. For example, a recent great purchase of a collectible doll, enabled the store to price it at about 40% less than its fair market value. The shop offers discounts on multiple doll purchases. The museum houses one of the most comprehensive doll collections in the country. You'll find dolls from the 1700's through Barbies and even G.I. Joe's. There's also cast iron toys and a wonderful miniature circus display. Admission is $3 children and animal welfare. W-Sat 11-5. Closed during holiday weeks and from January through April 1.

MUSIC BOX REVUE
2960 N. High St., Columbus, 43201, 263-2636

This museum houses the Midwest's largest collection of antique music boxes. Tours are available by appointment only, and are a wonderful trip through the past. The first floor of the building is dedicated to a gift shop which sells thousands of music boxes in all shapes, sizes and materials. Seventy percent of the shop's inventory consists of samples which offer savings of 25-50% off suggested retail prices. You'll find such brands as Schmid, Otagiri and others. This store is so packed with merchandise, that it is often hard to maneuver around the shelves, but you'll be pleasantly delighted with the selection. Generally Tu-Sat 11:30-5:30, but I suggest you call first.

MY COUSIN'S CLOSET
16-18 E. College Ave., Westerville, 43081, 899-6110

Nestled among the quaint shops in uptown Westerville, you will find this consignment shop for giftware and home decorating items. Furniture, artwork, vases, baskets, bath accessories, silver serving pieces, area rugs, dried flowers and other gently used items are available at savings of 25-70% off "if new" prices. This business is equally rewarding for the shopper as it is for the consignor. This is a great place to dispose of your quality household items which you no longer need. M-Sat 10-6, Sun 1-5. Accepts checks and cash only.

ODD LOTS

Eleven Columbus stores, plus Heath, Lancaster, Newark, Delaware, Circleville, Marion and Marysville

Closeouts, buyouts, discontinued goods, overstock and bankruptcy purchases result in a constantly changing inventory of automotive supplies, housewares, packaged and canned foods, toys, tools, hardware, gifts, linens, sporting goods, socks, office supplies and arts and crafts materials. The quality varies from budget to better. Savings are 30-75% off regular retail prices. On a recent visit, I purchased Columbia-Minerva yarns for 39 cents a skein (regularly $2.29), Playskool brand tools and Maybelline cosmetics for 89 cents (regularly $3.99), and Black and Decker drill for my husband for $48 (regularly $89). The Winchester Pike, Harrisburg Pike, North Wilson Road, Olentangy River Road and Marysville sites also feature frozen foods at similar savings. The Berwick Plaza and Morse Road locations carry a line of budget to moderate quality furniture at similar savings. Berwick Plaza also features the Dollar Zone, an area featuring thousands of items priced at only $1. A large area at the back of the Marion location, serves as a clearance outlet for area stores. In this section, you'll find overstock merchandise drastically reduced beyond their already low prices. Don't be discouraged by the no frills environment. This is truly a bargain hunter's delight. In cities over 60 miles out of Columbus, Odd Lots is called Big Lots. M-Sat 9-9, Sun 12-6.

ONLY $1/DOLLAR TREE
711 S. 30 St., Indian Mound Mall, Heath, 522-4774
1635 River Valley Circle, Lancaster, 653-0342

Closeouts, discontinued and liquidation merchandise is sold at only $1 each or several items for $1. You'll find tee shirts, toys, housewares, gift items, health and beauty aids, hair accessories, tools, automotive supplies, lunchbox snacks and other foods, in a constantly changing inventory. The first quality merchandise is budget to moderate quality. This is a great spot for party favors, every day needs and stocking stuffers. M-Sat 9-9, Sun 9-5.

ORDINARY MYSTERIES
245 W. Fifth Ave., Columbus 43201, 294-2000

New and used books, jewelry, stained glass, curiosities and metaphysical objects are value priced at this business. Free entertainment, lectures and other social events, many of them are of an off-beat nature, are also featured throughout the year. Tu-Sat 5-9, Sun 2-6.

ORTON GEOLOGICAL MUSEUM
155 S. Oval Mall, OSU, Columbus, 43210, 292-6896

The museum has been in this location since 1893! You'll see exhibits of fossils, meteorites, fluorescent minerals, a skeleton of a giant ground sloth and other interesting items. The museum has a small, but unusual gift shop offering a variety of mineral and gem specimens for fifty cents to two dollars, Ohio crude oil for fifty cents per vial and a few small gift items. Museum hours are Monday through Friday from 9-5 with occasional Saturday hours if a tour is scheduled. Gift shop hours vary because the manager may be out speaking to groups, so call first. Admission is free.

PIPES AND PLEASURES
4244 E. Main St., Columbus, 43213, 235-6422

While this store sells mostly new pipes, you'll find great deals on a large selection of "pre-smoked" or refurbished pipes. The better quality models are available in Meerschaum, Dunhill, Sheraton and other brands at savings of 25-55% less than "if new". M-F 9:30-6:30, Sat 9-6, Sun 1-5.

RED SQUARE IMPORTS
Northwest Columbus, 889-1373

Wholesaler of Russian art, jewelry and gifts sells to the public at wholesale prices. You'll find handpainted lacquered boxes $39-$750, paper mache and wooden flower pins for $5, mother of pearl pins for $35, Faberge type eggs jewelry at $59-$129, nesting dolls at $10-$400 and other items. By appointment only at the residence or call to find out at which show she will be exhibiting. This business is one of my personal favorites.

RED TRAILER
5290 W. Broad St., Columbus, 43228, 878-4458

This unpretentious business has several structures in which to shop for antique and used furniture as well as small collectibles. There is a small brick, stone front store as well as several red trailers featuring competitive prices. M-Sat 12-6.

ROBINSON-RANSBOTTOM POTTERY COMPANY
Roseville, 697-7355

You can take a free, self guided tour through the factory to observe the various steps in the pottery making process. The Pot Shop Outlet store is adjacent to the factory. Here you will find bird baths, ornamental garden statuary, cookware, mixing bowls and more at savings of 10-15% off regular retail prices. First quality and seconds are available. M-F 8:30-2:30.

SALEM WEST
1209 N. High St., Columbus, 43201, 421-7557

Save about 15-30% on jewelry crafts, beads and related paraphernalia of interest to magic enthusiasts. The owner takes a lower markup on his inventory so you can save. The back room, which operates as a community center, features pagan potlucks, Wicca workshops and Gnostic classes. Visit the regular Magickal Swap Meets where local artisans and others with magical interests sell their wares at fair prices. (Author's Comment: Please note that this business is included in the book because I feel it offers legitimate values for those who are interested in objects and events relating to this belief system. However, the philosophies represented in this store do not reflect my personal beliefs.) Tu-Sat 11-9, Sun 12-6.

SERVICE MERCHANDISE
2300 S. Hamilton Rd., Columbus, 43232, 868-0789
2680 Sawmill Place Blvd., Columbus, 43235, 792-5353
2727 Northland Plaza Dr., Columbus, 43231, 794-3434
4300 W. Broad St., Columbus, 43228, 275-3011

Save 10-40% off manufacturers' suggested retail prices on diamond and gold jewelry; watches by Casio, Armitron, Pulsar and Seiko; gift items such as crystal, silver plated serving pieces, and jewelry boxes; housewares by Farberware, Oneida and Pfaltzgraf such as pots, flatware, and dishes; small appliances by Eureka, Black and Decker and Kitchen Aid such as microwaves, waffle irons and blenders; sports equipment such as exercise machines and bicycles; children's toys, cribs and carriages; stereos, televisions, radios and keyboards; cameras, computers, bathroom accessories, small furniture and even lamps. M-Sat 10-9, Sun 11-6.

SILKCORP FACTORY OUTLET
1760 W. Lane Ave., Columbus, 43221, 488-3422
2621 Northland Plaza Dr., Columbus, 43231, 891-2666
6470 Consumer Sq. East, 43232, 868-1121
2855 Festival Lane, Dublin, 43017, 798-8388

You'll find a well displayed selection of potted silk flowers, trees, small bushes and hanging baskets at 50-70% off list prices. For example, a five to six foot ficus tree is regularly $80, but sells here for only $26, or a potted bush regularly $30 is only $11.99 here. This company, the Midwest's largest manufacturer of these types of florals, wholesales them to large chain and craft stores across the country. M-F 10-8, Sat 10-7, Sun 11-6.

STONEMAN GALLERY
1196 N. High St., Columbus, 43201, 297-7309

Antiques, collectibles, oddities, jewelry, artwork and small furniture are value priced at this small store. The atmosphere is very laid back so when someone drops in to serenade you with old folk music on his guitar, don't be surprised. I warned you. M-Sat 11-7.

TUESDAY MORNING
93 Westerville Sq., Westerville, 43081, 895-1444
5947 E. Main St., Carnaby Ctr., Columbus, 43213, 860-0271
1349 W. Lane Ave., Columbus, 43221, 487-1301
6524 Riverside Dr., Village Sq. Shpng. Ctr., Dublin, 43017, 791-0060

Save 50-80% on first quality famous maker closeouts and discontinued items many of which are available in limited quantities. You can find giftware, china, seasonal items, crystal, luggage, toys, collectibles, linens, clocks, fashion jewelry/accessories and toddler sized clothing. This nationwide chain operates 150 stores throughout the United States and is only open during certain times of the year. The sale dates are mid-February to mid-March, late April to mid-June, mid-August to late September and late October to late December. On my last visit I saw Silvestri collector porcelain dolls for $59 regularly $200, a Toscany crystal pitcher for $30 regularly $60, Royal Worcester Spode cake plates for $29.99 regularly $65, goose down pillows $39.99 regularly $80-$160 and Karastan oriental rugs for $200 regularly $400. Check out the red dot clearance areas where savings can be up to 90% off! The stores feature semi-annual sample sales in August and January which include one of a kind items from decorator showrooms and warehouse closings. Tuesday Morning stores are among my personal favorites. Be sure to sign up for their mailing list. M, Tu, W, F, Sat 9:30-6, Th 9:30-9, Sun 12-6.

WASSERSTROM'S RESTAURANT SUPPLY OUTLET
2777 Silver Dr., Columbus, 43211, 267-5288

Gourmet cooks and the general public will delight in the enormous selection of large bowls and pots, china, knives, gadgets, serving trays, stemware, onion soup bowls, kitchen chairs, janitorial supplies, even bar stools on display at savings of 20-40% off regular retail prices. If you don't see what you want, ask for it. Undoubtedly, the staff can order it for you at similar savings. M-F 8-5, Sat 8-12.

WATERFORD HALL
5911 Karric Sq. Dr., Dublin, 43017, 889-5141

Save about 25% off top quality home furnishings by Baldwin Brass, Frederick Cooper, Gorham, Steiff, Lenox China, Lladro, Herend, Pickard China, Sedgefield lamps, Wedgewood and others. You'll find furniture, original artwork by internationally recognized artists, lamps, flatware, collectibles and other decorative items. Special orders are similarly discounted. Although this store sells Waterford Crystal, it is not discounted. M-Th 10-8, F/Sat 10-6.

WRITE HOUSE INTERIORS/ E.&E. EXCLUSIVES
New Albany area, 861-2249
By appointment only

I am delighted with Eva Stein's extraordinary selection of top of the line gifts, designer reproductions, crystal, tapestry pillows and small accent pieces of furniture. Most of the business is conducted through special order. She has many books to choose from including Baker Knapp and Tubbs, Sweet Dreams, Swan Brass Beds, Eurodesigns, McGuire, Bernhardt, Reed and Barton, and others. Eva's skills as a professional interior designer can greatly help those who have difficulty in making choices. Eva can also get carpeting, china, window treatments, framed prints, as well as all types of furniture. The furniture will be delivered to your home. She also sells investment quality and promotional quality fine jewelry including gold, diamonds and pearls from a catalogue, with prices at 20% above wholesale. All styles are available, although she specializes in unique pieces. Custom imprinted stationery is offered at a 20-30% discount. Complete party and wedding planning services are also available. Savings on reproductions and accessories are usually 50-80% and furniture 30-50%. You'll find merchandise for the discriminating shopper, in all price ranges. Eva discourages recreational browsing. Only serious buyers should call. She's happy to provide your with a quote over the phone.

ZANESVILLE POTTERY AND CHINA
7395 E. Pike, Norwich, 872-3345

A large selection of Ohio and other pottery can be found at this business. The stock consists of first quality items at regular retail prices and a large selection of seconds at savings of 30-50%. Some of the potteries represented include Robinson Ransbottom, Homer Laughlin's new Fiesta line, Hartstone and Friendship. M-Sat 9-5:30, Sun 1-6.

ALSO SEE

All For One, Anew, Aurora Farms Factory Outlets, Babe Discovery Shop, Baggerie, Bath And Brass Emporium, Bexley Cancer Thrift Shop, Bloomingdeals, Burke Sales, Camp And Williams, Ci Bon, Drug Emporium, Dublin Music Boosters Giant Garage Sale, Dumontville Flea Market, Eddie Bauer Salvage Sales, Eddie Bauer Warehouse Outlet, Elegant Encore, Experienced Possessions, Extravaganza, Fabulous Finds, Gahanna Flea Market, Greater Columbus Antique Mall, Groll's Fine Furniture, Grove City Thrift Shop, Haggler's Day, Hartstone Pottery, Haas Furniture, In Review Thrift Shop, J.C. Penney Outlet, J.C. Penney Portfolio, Jeffersonville Outlet Center, Jo-Ann Fabrics, Kitchen Collection, Lake Erie Factory Outlet, Lancaster Colony, Lazarus Final Countdown, Leukemia Society Garage Sale, Libbey Glass Factory Outlet Store, Liberty Street Interiors, Lithopolis Antique Mall And Flea Market,

MPW, Marshalls, Mid America Antique Show and Flea Market, 99 Cent Shops, Odd Lots, Office America, Ohio Factory Shops, Old Worthington Market Day, Only $1, Otterbein Women's Thrift Shop, PM Gallery, Paul's Marine, Peddler's Village, Salesmen's Sample Sales, Salvation Army, Sam's Club, Saundra's Consignment And Specialty Shop, Schottenstein's, Sears Outlet, Second Impressions, Service Merchandise, Sharp's Grove City Auction, Sofa Express Outlet, Somewhere In Thyme In Old Gahanna, Star Beacon, Steinmart, Susan Budde, T.J. Maxx, Tag Sales, Target Greatland, 3 C Flea Market, Transformations, Tri-Village Trading Post, TWIG Attic, Urban Concern Garage Sale, Value City Department Stores, Village Swap Shop, Volunteers Of America, Worth Repeating, Worthington Thrift Shop and Westland Flea Market

HEALTH & BEAUTY/ EYEGLASSES

Did you know that supermarkets and stores which sell health and beauty aids generally place their most costly items at eye level? This method is used because they know that consumers are likely to purchase these items on impulse. I suggest that you look high and low on those shelves and compare the various brands before deciding on what you want to purchase.

ALL FOR ONE
2707 Northland Plaza Dr., Columbus, 43231, 899-7766
2835-2837 Festival Lane, Festival At Sawmill, Dublin, 43017, 798-0388
111 S. Third St., Columbus City Center, Columbus, 43215, 464-1185
4185 Westland Mall, Columbus, 43228, 274-8438
Stringtown Rd, Derby Square, Grove City, 43123, 539-1800
River Valley Mall, Lancaster, 687-4900

At one time, everything in this store was priced at only $1, but now, the store has added some merchandise at $10 and under. The store sells toys, housewares, gifts, jewelry, infant bottles and teething rings, cosmetics, hardware, stationery, gift items, health and beauty aids, snacks and who knows what. On my recent visit, I saw Chippendale underwear (regularly $3.50), Bain De Soleil tanning lotion (regularly $6), Max Factor makeup (regularly $4.50), Keebler cookies (regularly $2.50), decorative Neiman Marcus empty candy tins (valued at about $6), Snoopy hair clips (regularly $3) and many other wonderful items, Most of the merchandise is moderate to better quality. Savings are 50-90% below regular retail prices. All For One is operated by Consolidated Stores, the parent company of Odd Lots. Yet the display and type of merchandise is different. This chain has established its stores in upscale shopping centers as a way of reaching a different sort of clientele than its Odd Lots cousin. Don't overlook the Odd Lots description elsewhere in this book. Another Odd Lots cousin is the Itzadeal stores (see description elsewhere in this book). All For One has earned the distinction of being one of my personal favorites. M-Sat 9:30-9, Sun 12-6.

BARBER SCHOOL
6322 E. Livingston Ave., Reynoldsburg, 43068, 868-0668

This branch of the Ohio State School of Cosmetology, offers haircuts for $1.50-$3.95, perms for $15-$35, coloring for $20 and facials for $2-$2.50. Services are provided by students under the supervision of licensed individuals. No appointments are needed. Fridays and Saturdays are the busiest times, so if you don't want to wait long, try coming

Tuesday through Thursday. Tu/W 11-7:30, Th/F 8-4:30, Sat 8-4. Accepts checks and cash only.

BEAUTY WAREHOUSE
Worthington Sq. Mall, Worthington, 43085, 431-2221

Find your favorite brands of salon hair care products by Paul Mitchell, Nexus, Sebastian, Hayashi, Redken, Goldwell, Joice, KMS and others at prices about 15-30% less than in your local salon. M-Sat 9-9.

CENTRAL OHIO DIABETES ASSOCIATION
1803 W. 5 Ave., Columbus, 43212, 486-7124

Offers free blood tests for diabetes detection at various sites within the community. Call for details. M-F 9-5.

COLUMBUS FREE CLINIC
1043 E. Weber Rd., Columbus, 43211, 268-7531

Every Thursday from 6:30-8:30p.m., this clinic provides free simple health care checks for low income individuals. Shots will not be given. Call Dr. Howlison's office to schedule an appointment. M-F 9-5.

COLUMBUS WHOLESALE BARBER AND BEAUTY SUPPLY
962 N. High St., Columbus, 43201, 299-4000 or 299-2332

Shop where the professionals shop at this wholesale supplier of beauty and barbershop supplies and save 10-25% off comparable quality items. You'll find hair, skin, nail and scalp products including many hard to find items such as razor straps and professional shaving brushes. Colognes as well as bulk and large size products, are also available. Many of the brands cannot be purchased in regular health and beauty aid stores. Some items such as bleaches, color tints and perm supplies can only be sold to licensed cosmetologists. This store has been in business for over 50 years and is the only full service barber and beauty supply house in Central Ohio. Many of the customers are institutions, hospitals as well as country clubs. M-F 8-5, Sat 8-12.

DRUG EMPORIUM
Eight Columbus locations
789 Hebron Rd., Heath, 522-1767

This full service pharmacy and health and beauty aids store discounts all of its stock 10-50%. Designer fragrances are available at savings of 30-40% off manufacturers' suggested retail prices. American Greetings' Forget-Me-Not brand of candles, greeting cards, gift wrap and related items are sold at 40% off list price. Some of the stores offer a small selection of 14K gold necklaces, earrings and bracelets at 40-50% off regular retail prices. Save 30-60% on quality name brands of replacement contact lenses by Bausch & Lomb, Sola-Barnes Hind, Wesley-Jessen, Cibavision, Coopervision and Acuvue Disposable. Simply bring in your prescription and your contacts will be available within 48 hours. No appointments are needed. M-Sat 9a.m.-10p.m., Sun 10-8.

EYEGLASS FACTORY
2100 Morse Rd., Morse Center, Columbus, 43229, 848-7775
4636 W. Broad St., Columbus, 43228, 870-2121
893 S. Hamilton Rd., Columbus, 43213, 236-2400

You can buy one pair of eyeglasses or contacts and get one pair free at prices starting as low as $99.95. This 50 store national chain, based in Ferndale Michigan, sells manufacturers' overstocks and discontinued styles in such brands as Swank, Benelton, St. Moritz and Gazelle. M-F 10-6, Tu 10-8, Sat 9-5.

HEALTH LINE
645-2020

This call-in tape recorded information library, will provide you with free physical and mental health information. Topics include alcoholism, arthritis, birth control, cancer, dental health, diabetes, drug abuse, digestive disorders, eye care, hearing, heart problems, schizophrenia, pregnancy, respiratory ailments, skin disorders, smoking, women's health concerns, parenting and children's health issues. It is sponsored by the Columbus Metropolitan Library. M-Th 9-9, F and Sat 9-6, (Sun 1-5 Sept-May only).

KENNETH'S DESIGN GROUP
5151 Reed Rd., Columbus, 43220, 457-6111

You can be a model and earn a free haircut. No experience is necessary. This prominent hairstyling chain, offers the opportunity for their apprentice stylists (those still perfecting their skills but who have studied at a trade school) to demonstrate their expertise to management towards the achievement of a full fledged "hair stylist" designation. The apprentices will cut wedged, layered or bobbed styles for women and teens with some input from you. It is important that you are flexible to allow the apprentice to demonstrate the skills requested by her supervisor. All hair types and lengths are acceptable. These apprentice cutting sessions are held on Mondays. Call and leave your name. You will be contacted when a model is needed. M-F 8:30-8:30, Sat 8:30-4:30.

LENS CRAFTERS
1492 Morse Rd., Columbus, 43229, 846-4006
4427 Crossroads E. Shpng. Ctr., Columbus, 43232, 863-0199
771 S. 30 St., Indian Mound Mall, Heath, 43056, 522-3867
1635 River Valley Circle, River Valley Mall, Lancaster, 43130, 654-9734

Custom lenses are usually available in an hour as they are manufactured on premises. In avoiding the middleman, this business can pass the savings on to you at about 5-25% or about $10-$50 on a complete pair of glasses, as compared to comparable products at full price businesses. Lens Crafters also makes some of the frames themselves, while purchasing others. The stores also offers price incentives on the purchase of a second pair of glasses. M-Sat 9-8.

MEIJER
Five Columbus area locations plus Newark and Marion

This full service grocery and general merchandise business offers savings throughout the store. Save 50% off the Forget-Me-Not brand of greeting cards and invitations, 20-40% off Speidel and Timex watches and 20-60% off the list price on a select group of Nintendo cartridges. The large selection of health and beauty aids are discounted and/or value priced. Popular brands of basic and designer perfumes cost about 10-30% less than manufacturers' suggested retail prices. The book department features a 25% discount on New York Times best sellers and 10% off all paperbacks and magazines. Plus, there's a small bargain books section with closeouts at savings up to 70%. Pick up a free, preferred customer discount card in the shoe repair department, which will provide you with a 10% discount on all shoe repairs. If you are shopping with a young child, be sure to give him/her a ride on the mechanical horse in the outer lobby of the stores. This fun experience will only cost you one penny! Open 24 hours per day, 7 days per week.

NATIONWIDE BEAUTY ACADEMY
5050 N. High St., Columbus, 43214, 888-0790
3120 Olentangy River Rd., Columbus, 43202, 261-7588
898 S. Hamilton Rd., Columbus, 43213, 864-1544
88 N. Wilson Rd., Columbus, 43204, 275-0153

Hair and nail care is provided by students under instructor supervision. Savings are about 30-50% lower than standard salon prices. A haircut is $3.75, perm and a haircut is $25, haircoloring or frosting is $18.50-$21.50, facial massage is $3.50 and a manicure is $2.25-$3. Appointments are suggested although walk-ins are welcome. M-F 8:30-9, Sat 8-4.

OHIO STATE SCHOOL OF COSMETOLOGY
6320 E. Livingston Ave., Reynoldsburg, 43068, 868-1601
3717 S. High St., Columbus, 43207, 491-0492
4390 Karl Rd., Columbus, 43224, 263-1861
5970 Westerville Rd., Westerville, 43081, 890-3535

Beginning and advanced level students, under instructor supervision, provide hair and nail care services at savings of about 20-50% lower than at typical full price salons. Your cost depends on the skill level of the stylist. A haircut by a beginner is $4.95, or $6.25 by an advanced student. A beginner perm is $15-$25, or $20-$30 if done by an advanced student. Appointments are suggested. W/F 9-6, Th. 9-9, Sat 8-4:30. Accepts checks and cash only.

PERFUMANIA
126 Columbus City Center Mall, Columbus, 43215, 224-3779
Jeffersonville Outlet Center, 426-6063
Ohio Factory Shops, 948-2971

Popular brands of men's and women's perfumes and colognes are offered at savings of 20-60%. Sniff around and you'll find Gianfranco Ferre, Lauren, Carolina Herrera, White Diamonds, Fred Heyman, Calvin Klein, Poisson, Phantom, Joop, Zino Davidoff, Paco Rabanne, Khouros and other favorites. The Columbus City Center store is the smallest of the three sites. Monthly specials offer additional savings, as do the clearance areas. The stores will ship your purchase, simply call to place your order. M-Sat 10-9, Sun 12-6.

PHAR-MOR
2304 S. Hamilton Rd., Columbus, 43232, 864-2007
4131 W. Broad Plaza, Columbus, 43228, 275-4040
2605 Northland Plaza Dr., Columbus, 43231, 794-1722
6751 Dublin Ctr. Dr., Dublin Village Ctr., Dublin, 43017, 889-6411

The stores offer savings of 10-60% on a full line of health and beauty aids, snacks, soda, salad dressings, other food items, books and magazines, school/office supplies and toys. Prescriptions are filled with lots of extra opportunities for savings. There is a free co-pay, up to $3, on prescriptions covered by most insurance companies. The pharmacy area can also save you about 65% when you have your contact lens prescription filled. Their stock of decorative calendars arrives in November and is generally sold at 50-60% off while supplies last. In other stores, you usually have to wait until February before the calendars are reduced this much. Watches by Lorus and Timex are discounted 25% off manufacturers' suggested retail prices. Savings of 30-50% are available on all brands of greeting cards, gift wraps, bows and party invitations. If you use a lot of film, you'll find there perpetual sale of 50% off a Kodak seven pack to be a real deal. M-Sat 8-10, Sun 9-7.

ST. ANN'S HOSPITAL
500 S. Cleveland Ave., Westerville, 43081, 898-4095

Several free community health programs are offered each month which address such topics as living with arthritis, parenting in the 90's, sports nutrition/ injury prevention and other health topics of general interest. The programs are held weekdays in day and evening times. The programs are open to the general public. Call to be added to their mailing list.

SALLY BEAUTY SUPPLY

Ten Columbus area locations
1645 N. Memorial Dr., Lancaster, 43130, 653-7719
959 Hebron Rd., Heath, 43056, 522-8256
1013 Bechtel Ave., Springfield, 45502, (513) 322-9185

This national chain of 500 shops sells hair and nail care products, cosmetics and even decorative hair accessories. Many of these salon quality products are not available through regular retail outlets, but you will recognize some of the popular brands. Savings are 20-40% less then comparable quality products in other stores. If you like to have artistic or funky looking nails, try purchasing a nail art kit. Rhinestones or decorative designs can be easily applied at prices ranging from $3-$8 per kit. By doing it yourself, or having a friend help you, you can save 50-70% off the price of having this done at a beauty salon. The kits, in addition to other merchandise in the store, make great gifts or unusual stocking stuffers at Christmas. M-F 9-7, Sat 9-6, Sun 12-5.

STATE DISCOUNT
1782 N. High St., Columbus, 43201, 421-7555
1876 N. High St., Columbus, 43201, 299-2367

Health and beauty aids, CDs, OSU sweatshirts, vitamins and other similar products are sold at 10-50% off suggested retail prices. The merchandise is all first quality. M-F 9-9, Sat 10-6, Sun 12-5.

TRI-VILLAGE OPTICIANS
1442 W. 5 Ave., Columbus, 43212, 486-4871

Manufacturers closeouts and discontinued designer eyeglass frames by such brands as Oscar de la Renta, Joan Collins and Diane von Furstenberg, are sold here at savings of about 50-80% off suggested retail prices. Most of the frames are in the $25-$40 range but typically sell for $85-$250. Save an additional 20% on your second pair of glasses. Bring your prescription to be filled here, as examinations are not offered. Tu-F 10-6, Sat 10-2.

T'S DISCOUNT BEAUTY SUPPLY
3575 E. Livingston Ave., Columbus, 43227, 236-0758
973 Mt. Vernon Ave., Columbus, 43203, 252-0500

Popular brand name hair and beauty care products are available at savings of 20-30% off suggested retail prices. Cosmetologists and those in training, are offered additional discounts. Some of the brands featured include TCB, Carefree, Leisure Curl, Hawaiian Silky and others. The products are basically aimed at the ethnic customer. The 5th avenue location is open Monday to Saturday 10-7:30. Mt. Vernon Avenue is open Thursday to Saturday from 10-6. Livingston Avenue is open Friday through Sunday from 12-7. Accepts checks and cash only.

UNIVERSITY HOSPITAL, MOBILE MAMMOGRAPHY UNIT
293-4455

This travelling health care service will provide a mammogram for only $60 which is about 35-50% less than the fee charged by private physicians and clinics. The procedure takes about 10-15 minutes. This service is accredited by the American College of Radiology. A physician referral is needed. Call to find out about the locations which constantly change. M-F 9-5. Accepts checks and cash only.

ALSO SEE

All For One, Ask-A-Nurse, Aurora Farms Factory Outlets, Blockbuster Video, Central Ohio School Of Massage, Columbus Speech And Hearing Center, Drug Emporium, Health And Harmony Fair, It's Only $1.00, Itzadeal, Marshalls, Odd Lots, Ohio Affiliate/National Society To Prevent Blindness, Phar Mor, Revco Health And Beauty Expo, Sam's Club, Schottenstein's, Star Beacon, Vision USA Program

HOME IMPROVEMENT/ LIGHTING/FLOORING

HOME IMPROVEMENT

ARCHITECTURAL ANTIQUES
457-458 S. Ludlow St., Columbus, 43206, 221-8848 or 221-7374

If you need mantles, doors, staircases, sinks, tubs, tile, glass, hardware or related architectural antiques, then this no frills business is for you. Prices are very competitive. By appointment only.

BATH AND BRASS EMPORIUM
683 E. Lincoln Avenue, Columbus, 43229, 885-8420

Better quality bath fixtures and architectural hardware are offered at builder's discounts. Save on door and cabinet hardware, decorator mirrors, vanities and medicine cabinets, commodes and sinks, decorator faucets, shower curtains, unique accessories, bath and wall hardware, lighting fixtures as well as tub/shower doors. Savings are 15-30% on this first quality merchandise. M/Tu/Th/F 9-5, W 9-8, Sat 9-12.

BUILDERS SQUARE
5865 Chantry Dr., Columbus, 43232, 575-5780
3575 W. Dublin Granville Rd., Columbus, 43235, 791-2470
5850 Columbus, Sq. Shpng. Ctr., Columbus, 43231, 891-3450

A full line of hardware and home improvement supplies is a available at about 10-25% less than suggested retail prices. Carpet and linoleum remnants, in addition to a small but varied selection of quality desks, chairs, bar stools, computer tables, bookcases and end tables, are value priced. Throughout the year, the stores offer free do-it-yourself classes on wallpapering, ceramic tile installation and other home improvement topics. There are low prices on quality floor, hanging and table lamps, plus a large selection of ceiling fans, by such quality brands as Thomas, Hunter, Cheyenne and QualityMark. On a recent visit, I saw a five tiered swizzle stick chandelier with brass accents for $269 and a solid brass outdoor lamp for only $54. The stores also stock a large selection of replacement lamp globes. M-Sat 7a.m.-9p.m., Sun 9-6.

CAPITAL TOOL AND FASTENER
9009 Gemini Pkwy., Westerville, 43081, 846-3443

Find professional tools and related equipment by Makita, Senco, Delta, Hitachi, Porter Cable, Bosch and Emglo. You'll find compressors, miter saws, planers, belt sanders, framing nailers and more. Savings are about 15-30%. The business usually has a tent sale in late June where savings are even greater. M-F 7:30-5, Sat 8-12.

COLUMBUS JANITOR SUPPLY
575 E. 11 Ave., Columbus, 43211, 299-1187
1105 Hebron Rd., Heath, 522-8548

Save on industrial strength cleaning supplies which are sold in concentrated form. To the average consumer, it may not appear as if you're saving money, but the containers go a long way because the contents need to be diluted. M-F 7:30-5, Sat 8:30-12.

COLUMBUS PAINT DISTRIBUTORS
588 W. Schrock Rd., Westerville, 43081, 523-1030

Save 50-60% off custom order blinds by Levolor, Bali, Kirsch and Graeber. In-stock and special order wall coverings are discounted 30-80%. Choose from such popular brands as Waverly, Imperial and Schumacher. The first quality wallpaper consists of current and discontinued patterns. If you have questions about installing wallpaper which you have purchased from the store, call their wallpaper hotline at 523-1031 during regular business hours. New home buyers can stop in the store to pick up a VIP card which will entitle them to a savings of 20-30% off regular retail prices on paint purchases and 25% off supplies. Discounts do not apply to sale items or those already discounted. A free, in-home decorating service is also available. M-F 7:30a.m.-8p.m., Sat 8-5.

CONTRACTOR'S WAREHOUSE
4252 Groves Rd., Columbus, 43232, 863-3634

Offers complete assortments of lumber, doors and windows, moulding, roofing, tools, paint, lighting, hardware, building materials, plumbing, electrical supplies, kitchen cabinets and more at good values. All popular brands are offered including Stanley, Channelock, Kohler, Briggs, Nicholas and others. Tool rental is available at about 20% less than in other businesses. The store has a drive through lumber yard so you can load your purchase right into your vehicle. Inquire about the frequent buyer plan. M-F 5:30a.m.-9p.m., Sat 6a.m.-8p.m., Sun 8a.m.-7p.m.

FORTIN WELDING AND MANUFACTURING
1132 W. Third Ave., Columbus, 43212, 291-4342

Custom ironwork including railings, gates, furniture and garden trellis' are available from the manufacturer at value prices. Savings vary but could be as high as 30% depending on what you order. M-F 8-4:30.

GREYSTONE DESIGN
7395 E. Main St., Reynoldsburg, 43068, 759-7117

Save 50% off Starmark cabinetry, 30-40% off custom draperies, 20-30% off wall coverings, up to $4 per yard on carpeting, up to 25% on whirlpool baths, 50-60% on mini blinds, 35% on pleated shades and up to 50% off vertical blinds. The savings are based on manufacturers' suggested retail prices on these first quality products. M-Sat 10-7.

HABITAT FOR HUMANITY HOME STORE
3529 Cleveland Ave., Columbus, 43224, 267-8777

This business is operated by the Christian, nonprofit housing builder and is largely run by volunteers. The stock consists of building materials, hardware, appliances, furniture, plumbing supplies and related home improvement items, all of which have been donated by area businesses and individuals. The idea for the store came about as a result of Habitat's inability to utilize all of the enormous amount of items it received as donations to build homes for low income people, and the organization found that it was in turn donating the excess to other organizations. The shop has been in the planning stages for quite some time, and as we went to press, plans were not finalized as to an official opening date nor the pricing structure of its stock. However, you can bet that there will be great deals here.

HEATING AND COOLING OUTLET STORE
807 Parsons Ave., Columbus, 43206, 443-0288

Scratch and dent furnaces, central air conditioning, humidifiers, air cleaners and related machinery are offered at savings of 20-50%. Installation is available and the company is licensed, bonded, and insured. M-F 8:30-4, Sat 8:30-2.

HOME QUARTERS
3700 W. Dublin Granville Rd., Columbus, 43231, 798-1638
300 Wilson Rd., Columbus, 43228, 274-5117
3880 Morse Rd., Columbus, 43219, 475-1686

Find a full line of home improvement items, gardening tools, live and silk plants, paint, curtains, flooring, lighting and related products at savings of 10-30%. The stores feature free instructional clinics throughout the month including installing ceiling fans, repairing kitchen faucets, interior design, installing kitchen counters and more. You will also find free in-store child care, Kids Quarters, for ages 3-8. It includes a play and workshop area with toy tools, videotapes and books. M-Sat 8a.m-9p.m., Sun 10-6.

KINGWOOD LUMBER COMPANY
900 W. 3 Ave., Columbus, 43212, 294-3723

Check out the bargain barn at the back of the store, where savings are up to 75% off on seconds, returns and odd sizes of doors, lumber and formica counter tops. M-F 7-5.

LOWE'S
3600 Park Mill Run Dr., Hilliard, 43206, 529-5900
2888 Brice Rd., Columbus, 43232, 575-6000
230 Airport Pkwy, Heath, 43056, 522-3634
1921 River Valley Dr., Lancaster, 43130, 687-1235
233 American Blvd, Marion, 389-6002

Find a full line of home improvement items, gardening tools, and plants, paint, flooring, lighting, small and large appliances, wallpaper, the area's largest indoor lumber yard, special order window treatments and related items at value prices. The stores feature free how-to clinics such as hanging wall paper and borders, installing vinyl flooring, installing interior door units and installing a ceiling fan. M-Sat 7a.m-9p.m., Sun 9-6.

ROUSCH HARDWARE
609 S. State St., Westerville, 43081, 882-3623
373 W. Bridge St., Dublin, 43017, 764-8900

Both stores offer a free bag of popcorn, no purchase required, from 8a.m.-9p.m. on Saturdays, and 10-5 on Sundays throughout the year. The Dublin store also offers the popcorn on Fridays from 8a.m.-9p.m. Seniors can save 20% of all regularly priced merchandise in the stores on Mondays.

SPARTAN TOOL SUPPLY
1505 Alum Creek Dr., Columbus, 43207, 443-7607

Automotive, personal, industrial power and hand tools are offered at savings of 15-60% off suggested retail prices. There are over 10,000 different items in stock from 70 different companies. The merchandise consists of overstocks, liquidations and direct purchases of brands by AEG, Milwaukee, Black and Decker, Ingersoll-Rand, Bosch and Chicago Pneumatic. M-F 7:30a.m.-6p.m., Sat 8:30a.m.-2p.m.

STOUT SALES
6320 E. Main St., Reynoldsburg, 43068, 866-4933

Over twenty styles of kitchen and bath cabinets are available from one of the largest wholesale cabinet distributors in Ohio. You'll find raised panel, cathedral and flat panel doors, Eurostyle laminates as well as solid wood, at savings of 40-50% below the manufacturer's suggested retail price. This business also has custom countertops, whirlpool tubs and wood flooring at similar savings. The Handyman's Room contains discontinued, scratch and dent and slightly discolored items at 50-80% off regular retail prices. M/Tu/Th/F 8-5, W 8-8, Sat 9-1.

ALSO SEE

Amos Indoor Flea Market, Black And Decker USA, Columbus Stone Center, Department Of Defense, Extravaganza, Franklin County Home Weatherization Service, Franklin County Sheriff's Department, Franklin County Soil And Water Conservation District, Garage Sales, General Merchandise Sales, Greater Columbus Antique Mall, Higher A Firefighter, Liquidations Now, Majestic Paint Outlet, Majestic Paint Stores, Mendelson's Electronics, 99 Cent Shops, Odd Lots, Only $1, Panel Town And More, Sam's Club, Schottenstein's, Service Merchandise, Vaughn Paint And Wallcoverings

LIGHTING

CLASSIC LIGHTING COMPANY
6011 Columbus Pike (Rt. 23), Delaware, 43015, 548-5689

Save 20-40% off manufacturers' list prices on lamps and fans for the entire home. The top grade, first quality merchandise includes such brands as Quoizel and Wilshire. M/W/F 10-6, Tu/Th 10-8, Sat 10-4.

ELGEE LIGHTING
1030 W. 3 Ave., Columbus, 43212, 294-6261
440 S. Hamilton Rd., Columbus, 43213, 866-0123
1070 W. 3 Ave., Columbus, 43212, 294-6261

Quality lighting consisting of discontinued merchandise and first quality floor, table and ceiling lamps, is available at savings of 25-50% off manufacturers' suggested retail prices. Special orders and electrical supplies are available at similar savings. You'll find brass, stained glass, novelty as well as crystal lighting. The other two sites sell only electrical supplies. Hours vary per store.

HOME LIGHTING
6055 Cleveland Ave., Columbus, 43231, 794-0777

Lamps, mirrors, track lights, ceiling fans and chandeliers, from more than 200 manufacturers, are sold at 20-50% off regular retail prices. The store carries such brands as Frederick Cooper, Murray Fiess, Georgian Art, Tyndale, Casa Blanca, Remmington and others. M/F/Sat 10-6, Tu/W/Th 10-9, Sun 12-5.

JOHNSON'S LAMP SHOP
8518 Old National Rd., S. Vienna, 45369, (513) 568-4551

The Midwest's largest selection of lampshades for old and new lamps, features over 5,000 in stock. You'll find silks, linens, calicos, fringed, glass, parchments and more. It's best to bring your lamp base if your want to match up a shade. The store also carries a large selection of floor, wall, table and outdoor lighting. Mounting and repair work is available. The owner says he can make just about anything into a lamp! Antique lamp restoration is a specialty. A large selection of lamp parts is available for do it yourself jobs. Savings are about 20-40% on lamps, including stained glass lamps. Smaller discounts are available ion the shades. M 9-8, Tu-Sat 9-5.

LAMP AND SHADE GALLERY
4506 Cemetery Rd., Hilliard, 43026, 777-9386

Find a large selection of lamp shades at savings of 15-25% off manufacturer's suggested retail prices. Repair services are competitively priced. M/F/Sat 10-6, Tu/W/Th 11-8, Sun 2-5.

NORTHERN LIGHTING
5585 Westerville Rd., Westerville, 43081, 891-7600

Builder's discounts of 33% off list price, are offered to the general public on a broad selection of first quality floor, ceiling and tabletop lighting. You'll find traditional and contemporary styles by Murray Feiss, Quoizel, Kichler, Emerson, Georgean Art, Frederick Raymond, Rembrandt, Prism Industries, Toletek and others. Special orders are similarly discounted. M/F/Sat 10-6, Tu/W/Th 10-9.

ALSO SEE

Belair's Fine Furniture, Builders Square, Ci Bon, Cort Furniture Rental And Clearance Center, Experienced Possessions, Extravaganza, Furniture Liquidations Center, Glick's Outlet, Greater Columbus Antique Mall, Groll's Fine Furniture, Liberty Street Interiors, Model Home Furniture and Accessories Sale, J.C. Penney Portfolio, Schottenstein's, Service Merchandise , Sofa Express Outlet and Waterford Hall

FLOORING

A JACK FLOORING OUTLET
877 E. 11 Ave., Columbus, 43211, 299-5445

Countertops, ceramic tiles as well as vinyl and wood flooring are available at savings of about 10-20% at this wholesale distributor. You'll find all major brands such as Congoleum, Hart Company, Wilsonart and Marazzi. M-F 7:30-4:30, Sat 7:30N. Accepts checks and cash only.

BIG BOB'S USED CARPET
2556 S. Hamilton Rd., Columbus 43232, 863-0909
82 N. Wilson Rd., Columbus, 43204, 276-5800

Buys and sells new and used carpeting and area rugs from many sources including hotels, businesses and carpet mills. The stock consists of first quality, irregulars, trials, discontinued, closeouts, short rolls, factory returns, bankrupt stocks and one of a kinds. The store does not stock carpeting from pet owners. Rolls and remnants can be cut to fit your room and you'll only pay for what you need. The stores can arrange for an independent installer to lay the carpeting for you. Delivery charges vary but are reasonably prices. M-F 9:30-8:30, Sat 10-6, Sun 12-5.

BUDGET CARPET WAREHOUSE
4356 Indianola Ave., Columbus, 43214, 262-0765

Buyouts and short rolls of carpeting, vinyl and hardwood flooring are available at savings of about 25% off regular retail prices. Padding and carpet supplies can be purchased for those who wish to install the flooring themselves. Delivery, installation and binding are available. M-Th 10-5, F/Sat 10-3.

COLOR TILE
Five Columbus locations plus the following
789 Hebron Rd., Heath, 43056, 522-8551

In-stock and special order wallcoverings are discounted 20-50%. Blinds are discounted 30-50%. The stores feature free rentals of how-to videos on flooring installation and wallpaper hanging. Ask about the Tile Goof Proof Guarantee. M-F 8a.m.-9p.m., Sat 8-5, Sun 11-5.

DALTON MILLS CARPET OUTLET
1320 S.R. 37 W., Delaware, 43015, 369-6455

Carpet and vinyl flooring for commercial and residential use is available at this family owned business. All of the merchandise is first quality with brands such as Salem, Galaxy, Congoleum, Tarkett and others at savings of about 20-25%. M/Tu/Th/F 9-5:30, W 9-7:30, Sat 10-3.

DALTON MILLS RENMNANTS AND MORE
220 E. William St., Delaware, 43015, 363-7847

This store sells exclusively remnants of residential and commercial carpeting and vinyl flooring. You'll save about 50-70% off the manufacturer's suggested retail price. M-F 10-5:30, Sat 10-3.

DESIGN MATERIALS OF OHIO
43 W. Vine St., Columbus, 43215, 224-8453

Shop where the contractors shop! This direct importer of high quality marble and ceramic tiles sells Mexican Tile, Jasba Mosaics, Crossville, IAC Laufen and other brands at savings of 40-60% off regular retail prices. You will find handpainted tiles, unusual designs as well as basic tiles. A selection of hardwood flooring is available at similar savings. A free decorating service is also available. If you will be installing the tiles or flooring yourself, you can borrow their tools, videos and how-to manuals at no cost. Occasionally, the business offers free seminars. If you are redecorating or building a new home and want to make a strong decorating statement, this is the place to shop. Save some time so you can stop at the North Market and the Columbus Convention Center, both of which are within two blocks. M-F 7:30-4:30, Sat 9-1, and by appointment.

DIAL ONE, MARC'S CARPET SERVICE
1223 1/2 Cleveland Ave., Columbus, 43201, 299-2168 or 299-2167

First quality carpeting mill remnants, special purchases, short rolls, overstocks, irregulars and some special order seconds, are available at savings of 30-35% off typical retail prices. Please note that these seconds are "off color" being a different color than the manufacturers' sample, which will not affect its wearability. The store also sells some used carpeting at greater savings. Vinyl flooring and tiles are available at savings of 20-25% off regular retail prices. Popular brands such as Armstrong, Tarkett, Salem, Cabincraft, Congoleum and Mannington are available. M-F 10-4.

DIRECT CARPET MILLS OUTLET
4029 Morse Rd., Columbus, 43219, 471-1269
5181 N. High St., Columbus, 43214, 848-6560
401 S. Hamilton Rd., Columbus, 43213, 235-0800

Volume buying enables these locally owned stores to buy flooring directly from the mill, thereby avoiding the middleman. The values are passed on to you so you can save 20-30% off regular retail prices. The store carries first quality Monsanto, Stainmaster, Anso and other carpet brands and also sells wood flooring and tiles. Financing available. M-Th 10-8, F 10-5, Sat 10-8, Sun 12-6.

DURATILE TILES AND DISTRIBUTING
2930 Westerville Rd., Columbus, 43224, 261-0602

Approximately one half of the inventory is discounted 5-30% and includes first quality, overstocks, remnants and seconds in countertops, vinyl flooring and ceramic wall coverings. Brands offered include Kentile, Sunglow, Tarkett, Roppe and Cambridge. This family owned and operated business has been in existence since 1946. M-F 8-6, Sat 11-3.

EPRO/SURFACE STYLE
156 E. Broadway, Westerville, 43081, 899-6990

Manufacturer of upscale, handmade ceramic tiles sells its closeouts, discontinued, off-color and seconds year round by appointment only. However, during their annual warehouse sale (usually in September), you'll find an even bigger selection which also includes offerings from other companies such as Mannington, GTE, Laticrete, Italian imports and more. Tools and setting materials are available at typical retail prices. Savings are 30-60%. All sales are cash and carry. Epro also operates a business in the Short North called Surface Style.

EVANS CARPET JUNKYARD
546 S. Brehl Ave., Columbus, 43223, 469-9402

Full rolls, mill seconds, short rolls, irregulars, remnants, discontinued styles, used, new and scraps are found at this business. The company also offers a value priced binding service. Savings are 40-50% off regular retail prices. M-Sat 10-6.

FLOOR COVERINGS INTERNATIONAL
1813 Watertower Dr., Worthington, 43235, 764-1324

Unique shop at home carpet service saves you at least 20% off quality carpeting and padding. The distinctive carpet showroom on wheels, features a complete line of first quality, name brand carpeting from DuPont Stainmaster, Monsanto, and others. A definite plus to this service is the fact that you can match carpeting to your decor in its natural surroundings. The business is part of a franchise which buys mill direct and avoids the middle man's markup. The lack of overhead costs as a result of not having a storefront, also contributes to this business's ability to keep its prices low. A variety of financing plans are available as is quality installation. M-Sat 9-9.

METRO CARPET
3454 S. Hamilton Rd., Columbus, 43232, 833-4858

Flooring liquidator can save you 30-60% off carpeting and wood flooring from such companies as Dupont Stainmaster, Aladdin, World, Queen, Caladium, Monsanto and others. The stock consists of scratch and dent, short rolls, short widths, discontinued styles, unclaimed layaways and products which ended up a different color than anticipated during the dyeing process at the mill.   Carpeting prices start at $2.95 per yard, wooden flooring at $2.99 per square foot.   M-Th 10-8, F/Sat 10-5.

MR. B'S ADD-A-BUCK FLOOR STORE
4121 E. Main St., Columbus, 43213, 231-0040

Low overhead allows this flooring business to save you about 20% off manufacturers' list prices on a full line of carpet, vinyl flooring and ceramic tiles.   Some of the quality brands represented include World Carpet, Armstrong and Mannington.   M-Th 1-7, F 1-5:30, Sat 10-2.

OHIO REMCON, INC.
888 W. Goodale, Columbus, 43215, 224-0489

Residential and commercial carpet, tile, linoleum, ceramic and parquet flooring are available at savings of 20-25% off regular retail from this wholesale builder's carpet source.   Even greater savings can be found on closeouts and remnants.   Check the back room for area rugs priced at savings of 50% and more.   Now in its 20th year, this business stocks merchandise from twenty different mills including Philadelphia, Cabincraft, Armstrong-Salem, Mohawk Horizon, Galaxy and others.   M-F 9-5, Sat 9-1.

POOR OLD PEDDLERS CARPET BARN
6960 Long Rd., Canal Winchester, 43110, 837-8594

Save 20-40% off first quality carpet by Salem, World, Shaw Industries and Horizon. Oriental rugs, remnants as well as commercial and residential carpeting are available in a wide range of colors and patterns.   The prices are low because the store has personal connections to a Dalton, Georgia carpet mill.   M-Sat 9-6, Sun by appointment.

R.A.P. FLOORING DISTRIBUTORS
2544 Billingsley Rd., Columbus, 43235, 761-3766

Purchase carpet and area rugs at savings of 20-40% below wholesale prices at this wholesale distributor.   The first quality goods include closeouts and overruns, of plushes, textures and berbers by Stainmaster, Anso 5, Ultron, Wear Dated and others.   Imported area rugs from Mainland China and Bangladesh include Orientals, dhurries and other types. Carpeting is available for home, office or commercial use.   The store has an annual spring sample sale of one of a kind merchandise and discontinued styles at greater savings.   Open by appointment only.   Accepts checks and cash only.

RAINBOW FLOORS-THE REMNANT ROOM
5571 Westerville Rd., Westerville, 43081, 882-2430

Rolls and remnants of vinyl flooring and carpets are available at savings of 20-60% off regular retail prices.   This store carries such brands as Armstrong, Cabincraft, Mannington, Cornett, Galaxy and Salem.   The inventory consists of first quality, remnants, mill ends and overstocks.   90 days same as cash financing is available to qualified buyers.   M-Th 10-7, F 10-5, Sat 10-4.

RITE RUG CARPET OUTLET
45 Great Southern Blvd., Columbus, 43207, 261-6060

This site houses the clearance outlet for the area Rite Rug showrooms and also sells full price merchandise. You'll find bargains on area rugs including Orientals, remnants, mill seconds, short rolls, used, discontinued and special purchases of carpeting at savings of 30-50% off their regular low prices. Also sells odds and ends of tile and vinyl flooring remnants. M-F 10-9, Sat 9-6, Sun 12-6.

SCULPTURED RUGS BY ANN
457-4998

Custom sculptured area rugs, utilizing three dimensional effects, are available directly from the artist at savings of 30-50% less than through an interior designer. Prices start at about $300 and can go as high as several thousand dollars depending on the size and intricacy of the design. Rugs, which are made of nylon and are Scotchgarded, take about four to six weeks to complete. The finished rug is stronger than the original and carries a lifetime warranty. The artist described a situation in which a customer showed her an advertisement from a local, upscale furniture store, in which a rug was advertised for $2,800 (the artist thought this was high, even for a store). Ann was able to duplicate it for only $700. There's a large selection of designs to choose from, or Ann can match a design to your decor. By appointment only, in the comfort of your own home.

SKINNY SAM'S
864-8990

Save about 15-20% on special order carpet at this no frills operation. By appointment only.

ALSO SEE

Builders Square, Camp And Williams, Glick's Outlet, Greystone Design, Lazarus Final Countdown, Panel Town And More and Stout Sales

MUSICAL INSTRUMENTS/ RECORDS, TAPES & CDs

MUSICAL INSTRUMENTS

A.W. PIANO CENTER
3670 Parkway Lane, Suite J, Hilliard, 43026, 527-9000

New and used pianos are offered, but the best deals are on the used pianos. You'll be escorted to the back sales room which also doubles as the restoration area to see pianos in various stages of repair. Used pianos range from about $1,000-$1,800 and include a one year warranty on parts and labor. Most major brands have been available. M-Sat 10-6, Sun 12-5.

ACE IN THE HOLE MUSIC EXCHANGE
1153 Kenny Center, Columbus, 43220, 457-5666

Browse through a very large selection of used CDs, most priced at $4-$8. The store features about 700 in stock in all musical styles. This is the place to go to buy, sell or trade. M-Sat 11-8, Sun 12-5.

ARTS MIDWEST JAZZ LETTER
528 Hennepin Ave., Suite 310, Minneapolis, Minnesota, 55403

A free, bi-monthly jazz letter is available upon written request. It contains stories on topics which affect the development and continuation of jazz in the Midwest, in addition to reviews of recordings by regional artists and highlights of individual achievements. The jazz calendar provides a listing of jazz happenings in clubs, lectures and city jazz hotlines within the Midwest.

CD JUNGLE
1312 Mt. Vernon Ave., Marion, 389-3611

Find new and used CDs at this business which buys, sells and trades. The best deals are on the used CDs which are priced from 99 cents to $9.99 each. M-Sat 11-8, Sun 12-5.

COLUMBUS MUSIC CENTER
1010 Morse Rd, Columbus, 43224, 846-7744

Save 20-60% on new and used musical instruments and related items such as guitars, amplifiers, drums, PA systems, keyboards, recording gear etc. You'll find all popular brands including Gibson, Marshall, Tama, JBL, Korg and others. M-Th 11-8, F/Sat 11-5.

COLUMBUS PIANO LEASING
6493 Proprietor's Rd., Worthington, 43085, 436-2246

Save 40-60% on used pianos compared to new models. This business leases pianos and sells these and other models, all of which have been cleaned and reconditioned where needed. There are about twenty to forty models in stock including spinets, consoles, uprights and grandes. All popular brands have been offered including Steinway, Wurlitzer, Story and Clark, Becker and others. Prices start at $900. M/Tu 10-8, W/Th 10-6, F/Sat 10-4.

COWTOWN GUITARS
919 E. Dublin Granville Rd., Columbus, 43229, 436-4442

The store sells new, used and vintage musical instruments. The best deals are generally on the used models which can save you about 30-50%. M-Sat 10-7, Sun 12-5.

DURTHALER
1967 Lockbourne Rd., Columbus, 43207, 443-6867

The largest selection of pre-owned organs in Central Ohio is available at this business at savings of 30-50% off "if new" prices. Similar savings are available on pre-owned pianos and player pianos. M-Sat 10-6.

GRAN-RENTAL STATION
113 N. Prospect St., Granville, 587-4051

Find new Cds priced at slightly over wholesale and used Cds in the $5-$7 range. The business also sells previously rented videos and video games in the $5-$20 range. M-Th 10-9, F/Sat 10-10, Sun 12-8.

KINCAID'S MUSIC
1325 W. First St., Springfield, (513) 325-7071

This store offers value prices on new pianos and digital keyboards. The best deals, however, are on the used models where savings are 40-60% less than "if new". Uprights start at $650, baby grands at $2,700 and keyboards at $99. You'll find popular brands such as Kawai, Kimball, Wurlitzer and others. M 10-8, Tu-Th 12-8, F/Sat 10-5:30.

LANCASTER KEYBOARD CENTER
851 E. Main St., Lancaster, 43130, 654-5874

This business sells new and used pianos and organs. However the best buys are on the used/rebuilt models which sell for about 50% less than "if new". While the amount of inventory varies, most major brands have been available including Kimball, Story And Clark and others. M/Tu/Th./F 10-6, Sat 10-3.

MORSE ROAD MUSIC
2749 Morse Rd., Columbus, 43231, 475-6589

This family owned store has been in business for over 40 years. It is currently housed in a small garage, but don't be discouraged by its unpretentious appearance. The store sells used wind, percussion, brass and string instruments at about 50% off the cost of new instruments. They repair all instruments on premises, thereby avoiding the middleman, and saving you about 25-40%. The store also does not have a minimum charge on repairs, unlike most music stores. A complete clarinet overhaul would cost about $90 here, but could be about $120 elsewhere. According to the owner, the business is responsible for repairing about 80% of the instruments used by the City of Columbus Public Schools. The store also repairs government band instruments form across the United States. You can also purchase supplies such as reeds, for about 20-40% less than elsewhere. M-Th 12-9, F 12-6, Sat 9-4:30. Accepts checks and cash only.

MUSIC GO ROUND
Bethel Rd.(site to be determined), Columbus, 43214, 457-9328

This recently opened business buys, sells and trades all types of used instruments and related equipment except pianos. You'll find a large selection at fair prices. At the time we went to press for this book, the owner was looking at several locations on Bethel Road, but had not officially signed the lease. Hours to be determined.

MUSICIANS EXCHANGE
4095 Main St., Hilliard, 43026, 527-0022

This shop sells mostly used electric and acoustic guitars and related equipment by major manufacturers such as Fender, Gibson, Martin, Gretsch and others. You'll also find some new items at competitive prices. Tu-Th 11-7, F 11-5, Sat 11-4.

STRING SHOPPE
1704 N. High St., Columbus, 43210, 294-5296

Electric and acoustic guitars, amplifiers, synthesizers and recording equipment can be found here. Used merchandise sells for 40-60% less than "if new" and new items are 10-40% off manufacturer's list price. Some brands offered for sale include Gibson, Alvarez and Epiphone. M-Th 11-8, F 11-7, Sat 11-6.

UNCLE SAM'S PAWN SHOP
225 E. Main St., Columbus, 43215, 221-3711

An extensive selection of used and antique fine jewelry, watches, cameras, stereos, televisions, musical instruments, luggage, guns, Nintendo and Sega games as well as radios can be found at savings of about 20-40% off "if new" prices. You'll find such sought after brands as Pentax, Minolta, Seiko, Sony, Louis Vuitton and others. Much of the jewelry did not appear to have as much of a savings as the other items in the store, but you'll find some very unusual pieces not found in typical jewelry stores. Be sure to browse through all of their rooms. Offers 30 day warranties on mechanical items and cameras. M-Sat 9-5:30.

UPRIGHT PIANO SALES
Reynoldsburg, 43068, 866-7515

This business buys and sells used pianos. Prices start at $295 for the models which have all been cleaned and reconditioned. Although the selection is small, there is a very fast turnover, so there is always new merchandise. The owner will also scout around for what you want if he doesn't have it. All popular brands have been offered including Steinway, Kimball, Wurlitzer and others. If you decide later that you would like to trade up to a better piano, you'll get credit for the amount of your original purchase. Piano tuning services are also available. By appointment only.

USED PIANO WAREHOUSE
480 D East Wilson Bridge Rd., Worthington, 43085, 888-3441

A huge selection of quality new and used pianos is available. The used instruments are reconditioned before being sold and are priced at about 40-50% less than a comparable new piano. Provides a three year warranty on parts and a one year warranty on labor. M-Th 12-8, F 10-4, Sat 10-2.

RECORDS/TAPES/CDs

CD WAREHOUSE
1872 N. High St., Columbus, 43201, 291-9158

This store buys, sells and trades CDs. Used CDs sell from $5.99-$9.99. New CDs sell for $9.99-$12.99. The trade-in policy is that you can trade two of your unwanted used CDs for one of their used ones, or three used CDs for one of their new ones. Another option is that the store will buy your CDs outright for $4-$5 apiece. M-F 10-9, Sat 11:30-9, Sun 12-8.

COCONUTS MUSIC AND MOVIES
1277 Morse Rd., Columbus, 43229, 447-9800
3530 Soldano Blvd., Columbus, 43228, 276-0800

You'll find a large selection of used CDs here as these businesses buy, sell and trade them. They will pay you 50 cents to $5 each and price them between $2-$10 each. All musical styles are offered. The businesses also sell new CDs and videos at fair prices. M-Sat 10-9, Sun 12-6.

COLLEEN'S COLLECTIBLES
1482 Oakland Park Ave., Columbus, 43224, 261-1585

This store sells used CDs at $5-$10 each and used cassettes at $4-$6, in a variety of musical styles. The store also stocks used and collectible records priced according to condition and scarcity. Tu-Sat 11:30-5.

JOHNNY GO'S HOUSE OF MUSIC
1900 N. High St., Columbus, 43210, 291-6133

Step lively to this OSU campus record shop which is big on savings. Used cassettes are priced fifty cents to $2, and used CDs sell for $6.49-$7.99 and are available in all musical styles. M-Sat 11-8, Sun 12-5.

MAGNOLIA THUNDERPUSSY
1591 N. High St., Columbus, 43210, 421-1512

Find used CDs in all musical styles, starting at $1.99 each. Inquire about the store's trade-in policy. Save $2 on CDs on Tuesdays. M-Sat 11-8, Sun 12-5.

PAPPY'S PAWN SHOP
1873 Parsons Avenue, Columbus, 43207, 444-6400

General line of pawn shop merchandise including audio visual equipment, bicycles, televisions and Nintendo systems is available at a small savings of about 25% off new prices. The best deals here, however, include the large selection (about 350) of used CDs at $5-$8 each, in all musical styles, plus a small selection of used casettes at $2 apiece.

PAT'S RECORDS, CDs AND TAPES
31 N. Sandusky St., Delaware, 43015, 1-363-3198

A full line of CDs, records and cassettes by major recording artists, is sold at about $2-$4 lower than most other stores, according to the owner. Special orders are available at similar savings. The store is a TicketMaster outlet and also stocks a full line of Marvel and DC comics at regular retail prices. M-F 10-8, Sat 10-6, Sun 12-6.

QUICKSILVER CD'S AND TAPES
2610 Hilliard Rome Rd., Hilliard, 43026, 771-6277

This store buys, sells and trades new and used CDs and cassettes. You'll find a large selection in all musical styles. M-F 12-8, Sat 11-8, Sun 12-5.

RECORD CONNECTION
1403 S. Hamilton Rd., Columbus, 43227, 237-8821

Find about 500-600 used CDs priced at $4-$9, and about 300 used cassettes most at $2-$6. M-Sat 11-8, Sun 12-5.

ROBERT AND COMPANY
1910 Lockbourne Rd., Columbus, 43207, 444-9842

This store specializes in used LP records, but also offers other items of interest. There's a small selection of CDs priced at under $5, cassettes at $3.98-$9.98. The stock consists of new and used items in various price ranges and qualities. M-Sat 11-6.

SINGING DOG
1630 N. High St., Columbus, 43201, 299-1490

Buy or sell used records, cassettes and compact discs at this store. Purchases are at a savings of 20-50% off the new price. Cassettes and records sell for 99 cents-$4.99 each and CDs sell for $4.99-$9.99. You'll find an assortment of contemporary music including jazz, rock, soul and folk. M-Sat 11-9, Sun 12-7.

SOUR RECORDS, TAPES AND CD'S
24 E. College (rear), Westerville, 43081, 895-1965

This small business, located in an alley behind some buildings, is big on savings. New cassettes, and CDs are sold at 10-15% discount. Used CDs are priced at $8-$10, and used cassettes at $5 and under. M-F 11-7, Sat 12-6.

USED KIDS RECORDS
1992 N. High St., Columbus, 43201, 294-3833

A large selection of used records, CDs and cassettes are sold here at 50 cents and up which is a savings of 50-90% off the "if new" price. Used cassettes are priced at $1 to $4 and used CDs at $ to $9. New merchandise is also discounted about 10-20%. From Aerosmith to Garth Brooks, you'll find it here. The store opened an annex next door with more of the same great values. The stores are located below street level. The store's name is actually a misnomer, it does not sell children's records. M-Sat 10-8, Sun 12-6.

WORLD RECORD
1980 N. High St., Columbus, 43201, 297-7900

Although this store sells new CDs and cassettes, the best prices are on used CDs. These are marked in the $5 range. Their perpetual weekend sale features $2 off used CDs every Saturday and Sunday. New CD releases are only $10.99 during the first week they are out. Also, enjoy $2 off new and used CDs, cassettes and tee-shirts every Tuesday. M-Sat 10-10, Sun 12-7.

ALSO SEE

Book Warehouse, Extravaganza, Half Price Book Store, Incredible Universe, Outreach Christian Books And Records, Record Convention and Worthington Public Library

OFFICE SUPPLIES & EQUIPMENT/ STATIONERY

OFFICE SUPPLIES & EQUIPMENT

ARVEY PAPER AND SUPPLIES
431 E. Livingston Ave., Columbus, 43215, 221-0153

Volume buying for 50 stores in the U.S., allows this business to make purchases at far below typical wholesale prices. This translates into savings of 5-70% off list price on a full line of office, school and graphic arts supplies. The store also sells papers in all weights and colors at savings of about 20-30% off typical retail prices. M-F 8-5:30, Sat 9-1.

CAPITOL COPY
2309 W. Dublin Granville Rd., Worthington, 43085, 846-1510

Buy used copiers or fax machines which are trade-ins, repossessed, demonstrators and/or refurbished. You'll save about 50% from the cost of the new products, from such brands as Konica, Sharp, Minolta and Canon. M-F 8-5, Sat 9-12.

CHARLES HEADLEE
4160 Indianola Ave., Columbus, 43214, 263-1649

Several rooms of used office furniture can be found on the first level, in addition to a selection in the basement. You'll find top brands of upscale furniture by Atlantis, Kimball, Hon and others in woods, veneers and laminates. Savings on desks, chairs, filing cabinets, book cases, computer stands and other items are about 30-60% off new prices. The clearance area on the first level also has some overstocked and discontinued office supplies at similar savings. M-Sat 8-5.

CONTINENTAL'S OFFICE CENTER
1070 Morse Rd., Columbus, 43229, 436-7000

Find new and used upscale office furniture. While the new stock is competitively priced, the used and "as is" merchandise offers substantial savings of 50-80%. The annual tent sale is usually in May or June and features a large selection of new items at rock bottom prices. M-F 9-6, Sat 10-3.

COPIER RESOURCES
4324 N. High St., Columbus, 43214, 268-1268

This business specializes in used copiers, fax machines and computers, most appropriate for small and large businesses. Savings are 30-70% less than "if new" prices. Minolta, Sharp and other brands are available. Prices are in the $800-$2,500 range for used copiers with values to $8,000. M-F 8:30-5.

INTERIOR SERVICES
694 Harmon Plaza, Columbus, 43223, 443-0916

Quality re-manufactured modular office furniture by Steelcase, Herman Miller and Haworth can be found at savings of up to 50% off "if new" prices. The panels are reupholstered and otherwise cleaned up to look like new. CAD systems are used to develop custom floor plans at no cost. M-F 8-5.

NATIONAL OFFICE WAREHOUSE
500 W. Broad St., Columbus, 43215, 228-2233
637 E. Dublin Granville Rd., Columbus, 43229, 888-4177

The stores offer new and used office/computer furniture. Floor models, factory seconds, special buys, closeouts, discontinued and trade-ins are available at savings of 30-70%. Hours vary by store.

NEXT GENERATION WHOLESALERS
6625 Singletree Ave., Columbus, 43229, 888-5015

Find an enormous selection of commercial grade used, repossessed and forfeited copiers and fax machines. Copiers start at $150 and fax machines at $300. M-F 9:30-5.

OFFICE MAX
5825 Chantry Dr., Reynoldsburg, 43068, 577-0069
87 Huber Village Blvd.,Westerville, 43081, 899-6186
3614 Soldano Blvd., Consumer Sq. W., Columbus, 43228, 274-0087
6020 Sawmill Rd., Dublin, 43017, 791-2600

This business products superstore, offers 40-60% savings on popular brands of computers, peripherals, software, office supplies, office furniture and business machines. All popular brands are offered. The store also has a full service reproduction center which features ocmpetitive pricing. M-F 8a.m.-9p.m., Sat 9-9, Sun 12-6.

PEERLESS OFFICE SUPPLY
3465 Refugee Rd., Columbus, 43232, 239-9009

Business and commercial accounts can save 20-70% off regular retail prices on a full line of office supplies. Orders must be placed over the phone or by Fax and will be filled within 24 hours. Offers free delivery for orders over $20. M-F 9-5.

STAPLES
2800 S. Hamilton Rd., Columbus, 43232, 575-2801
1666 E. Dublin-Granville Rd., Columbus, 43229, 890-6619
4505 Kenny Rd., Columbus, 43220, 442-5554 or 442-5585

This full service store features an extensive selection of office supplies, office furniture and equipment, related books, lighting, luggage and portfolios at savings of 30-70%. You'll also find similar savings on a limited selection of art supplies for adults and kids. Membership is free and is open to the general public. Non-members pay 5% above the posted prices. The stores also feature in-house business centers which offer value pricing on photocopying, binding and other printing related needs. Offers one of the areas lowest prices on color copies at 99 cents per page. M-F 7a.m.-9p.m., Sat 9-9, Sun 11-6.

TORONTO BUSINESS SYSTEMS
1159 W. Broad St., Columbus, 43222, 272-5500

New IBM, Hewlett Packard, Casio and Royal typewriters, computers and calculators are discounted about 25%, and come with full manufacturer's warranties. Used items are sold at about 75% less than if they were new. The warranty will be in effect for 30 days. Toronto Business Equipment has been in business for over 30 years. M-F 8-5.

TRI-PRO
720 L Lakeview Plaza Blvd., Worthington, 43085, 841-1711

Save about 30-50% on used/rebuilt copiers compared to their new copiers. The shop specializes in copiers for business use by such brands as Panasonic, Sharp and Canon. Prices start at at about $500. M-F 8-5.

TYPEWRITER EXCHANGE
4554 Indianola Ave., Columbus, 43214, 784-8973

Save 35-50% on used, rebuilt or reconditioned word processors, electric typewriters and related electronics. You'll find popular brands including Smith Corona, Royal, Brothers and more. Used word processors begin at $249, used electric typewriters at $89. M-F 8-5.

ALSO SEE

Aaron Sells Furniture, Business Equipment Electronics, Columbus Metropolitan Library, Columbus Police Property Auction, Computer Success, Continental's Office Furniture Outlet, Cort Furniture Rental Resale Center, Department of Defense, Globe Furniture Rental, Kroger, Leather Direct, Mendelson's Electronics, Odd Lots, Phar Mor, Sam's Club and Sugarman Liquidators

STATIONERY

FACTORY CARD OUTLET
2630 Bethel Rd., Carriage Place Shp. Ctr., Columbus, 43220, 442-1788
6418 Tussing Rd., Consumer Sq., East, Columbus, 43232, 861-2111
4091 W. Broad St., Columbus, 43228, 351-0369

Save 20-50% on an extensive selection of paper party goods (napkins, plates etc). The store offer a large seelction of greeting cards priced at only 39 cents. Other gift items in the store are sold at regular retail prices. M-Sat 9-9, Sun 10-6.

HARLAN'S INVITATIONS AND CALLIGRAPHY
Northwest Columbus, 764-9624

Save 30% off custom imprinted invitations, 15% off matching stationery, 25% off groomsmen gifts (engraved marble clocks starting at $15) and comparable savings on aisle runners, candles and imprintables. Save 15% on a complete line off Beverly Clark and Lillian Rose bridal acessories including guest books, garters, flowergirl baskets and other items. Although most of the business is wedding related, this company can assist anyone who needs special occasion services. You can have the envelopes addressed in calligraphy by a laser printer which produces such beautiful work that it is difficult to tell that it has not been hand lettered. This laser calligraphy is about 50% less than paying a calligrapher to hand letter the envelopes. Personal service is stressed. By appointment only.

K. G. MARX PAPER PARTY OUTLETS
Eight Columbus locations

An extensive selection of paper and party goods is available at these stores. Save 35% on patterned paper and party goods. Save 25% on a complete line of custom wedding and special occasion invitations and 50% off greeting cards. Since the closing of their outlet store, all sites now have a selection of closeout and clearance merchandise at about 50% off. M-F 10-9, Sat 9-9, Sun 11-6.

1/2 OFF CARD SHOP
5777 Chantry Dr., Columbus, 43232, Reynoldsbrug, 43068, 755-4696
6090 Sawmill Rd., Dublin, 43017, 799-2240
3655 Fishinger Blvd., Hilliard, 43026, 527-9410

Offers 50% savings on first quality unpackaged greeting cards, and about 20-40% off paper party goods such as plates, napkins, bows etc. Save 40% off packaged invitations and thank you notes by Image Arts, Gallant, Paramount and Designer Greetings, plus 15-35% off party supplies. Other items in the store, including gift items, are not discounted. M-Sat 10-9, Sun 12-5.

PAPER PLUS
6297 Busch Blvd., Columbus, 43229, 846-7030

Writing, copying and printing grades of paper and stationery products are available at this no-frills warehouse. You'll find decorative and basic papers (but not art papers), such as linen and classic laid in small and large quantities. This business sells mostly to local printers, but will provide consumers with the same pricing. Obviously, the more you buy the more you'll save., In stock and special orders offer competitive pricing. I like to buy the blank stationery with envelopes so I can embellish them with my own collage work. M-F 7:30-5, Sat 9-1.

ALSO SEE

All For One, Arvey Paper, Columbus' Largest Garage Sale, Cub Foods, Drug Emporium, Meijer's, Odd Lots, 99 Cent Shops, Paper Plus, Phar Mor and Yankee Trader

PETS

CAPITAL AREA HUMANE SOCIETY
3015 Scioto Darby Executive Ct., Hilliard, 43026, 777-7387

Puppies, kittens and full grown animals can be adopted for $80 each. Take home a pet and you'll see how happy and even therapeutic it can be for you and your family. The Society also offers ongoing pet behavior classes and spaying/neutering at additional fees. M-F 12-7, Sat 12-5.

CAT WELFARE
736 Wetmore Rd., Columbus, 43224, 268-6096 or 262-8759

This shelter houses about 200 cats of all breeds (mixed and pure bred), sizes and ages. Your $30 fee includes the cost of spaying or neutering, the animal's first shots, worming and if appropriate, a rabies shot. Inquire about their low cost spay and neutering clinic for cats which were not purchased through this organization. The shelter also features a weekly sale of donated merchandise like you would find at a garage sale. It is featured on Saturdays from 9-2. Accepts checks and cash only.

DELAWARE COUNTY HUMANE SOCIETY
4920 State Rt. 37 E., Delaware, 43015, 548-7387

Many pets are available for adoption from this animal shelter. You'll find pedigrees as well as mixed breeds. Puppies or full grown dogs cost $55, kittens or full grown cats are $45. The fee includes spaying/neutering, the animal's first shots and worming. A low cost spaying/neutering clinic for animals which were not obtained at this shelter, is available at a cost of $20 for cats and $35 for dogs. Compare these to the prices charged at area veterinarian offices which can be $49-$160. M-F 9-4, Sat/Sun 12-4. Accepts checks and cash only.

GERMAN VILLAGE AQUARIUM
188 E. Whittier St., Columbus, 43206, 445-6000

This little German Village shop has a full line of fresh and saltwater fish and accessories at savings of 25-30%. M-Sat 11-7, Sun 12-6. Accepts checks and cash only.

JACK'S AQUARIUM AND PETS
6641 Dublin Ctr. Dr., Dublin, 43017, 764-8770
2631 Northland Plaza Dr., Columbus, 43231, 794-0184
6404 Tussing Rd., Consumer Sq. E., Reynoldsburg, 43068, 863-0290
3634 Soldano Blvd., Consumer Sq. W., Columbus, 43228, 278-2255

By joining the Fish Of The Month Club for a $1 annual fee, you will be entitled to one free fish per month from a choice of several, savings on purchases of additional fish from this pre-selected group, as well as a $5 credit toward the purchase of fish or live plants. Jack's prices are about 15-20% lower than in full price stores, on their entire inventory of fresh and saltwater fish, tanks and supplies, and about 10% lower on their cat and dog food. The frequent purchaser plan, called the Baker's Dozen Club, allows you to get your 13th bag of dog or cat food free. M-Sat 10-9, Sun 12-5.

PETSMART
2899 Morse Rd., Columbus, 43231, 475-3333
5781 Chantry Dr., Columbus, 43232, 575-2222
6010 Sawmill Rd., Dublin, 43017, 791-8200
240 N. Wilson Rd., Columbus, 43204, 275-0333

This full service pet food and supplies company sells premium brands at savings of 10-30%, most of which are not readily available in grocery store chains. Pet food, animal sweaters, bird feeders, bird seed, pet toys, cages, books, aquariums and supplies line the shelves. You'll find products by IAMS, Bil Jac, Mighty Dog, Kal Kan, Cat's Pride, Purina and other companies. Bring your pets and let them browse through the store, sample the products and choose their favorites. These stores are under new ownership and were once called Petzazz or Complete Petmart. Register your pet for the birthday club and it will receive a free toy valued at $3 and a gift certificate for 10% off your next purchase. Every other Sunday, the stores feature low cost dog and cat vaccination clinics. For example, the 7 in 1 shot for dogs is $20, a rabies shot is $6 for dogs or cats, feline leukemia shot is $11. Profits from the clinics are donated by area veterinarians to the Animal Foundation. M-F 9-9, Sat 10-6, Sun 12-5.

ALSO SEE

The Andersons General Store and Franklin County Soil And Water Conservation District

SENSATIONAL BIRTHDAY FREEBIES & VALUES

Birthdays can be lots of fun especially if other businesses provide you with an incentive to celebrate. From free desserts, to free admission to a movie, these are the businesses which are happy that you're a year older. This chapter is intended as a listing only, for details, see the descriptions of these companies elsewhere in this book.

Baskin Robbins, Bill Knapp's, Birthday Club Of America, Cinemark Movies 12, Denny's, Engine House No. 5, Flicker's Cinema, Ground Round, James Tavern, Lazarus-Club 61, Ohio Department of Aging, One More Time, Petsmart, Presidential Greetings Office, Shoney's, Video Universe and WTTE Channel 28 Kids Club

SERVICES

ASK-A-NURSE PROGRAM
293-5678

The OSU Children's Hospitals sponsor this free, 24 hour a day phone line, general health service, which is staffed by registered nurses. About 90,000 callers per year receive information on thousands of symptoms and 180 ailments. The medical information is accessed through a computer and is combined with the RN's knowledge to assist callers. The service cannot make a diagnosis.

ATTORNEY GENERAL'S OFFICE
Consumer Protection Division, 30 E. Broad St., Columbus, 43266-0410,
1-800-282-0515

This state agency enforces Ohio's consumer protection laws which were designed to protect the public from deceptive or unfair business practices. If you feel you have been victimized, call this office and you will be sent a complaint form to complete. In most instances, this agency will be able to assist you in resolving the problem by investigating your complaint and contacting the company or person you dealt with directly. You should expect a response within 30 days. The agency does not provide legal advice and will not act as your attorney. Services are provided free of charge without regard to income. M-F 9-5.

BETTER BUSINESS BUREAU OF CENTRAL OHIO
527 S. High St., Columbus, 43215, 221-6336

This local affiliate of a national consumer advocacy and awareness group, handles consumer complaints against area businesses. Call to request a complaint form. They also provide you with free single copies of consumer information booklets on such topics as buying a home computer, mail order profit mirages, buying tires, charitable giving, long distance phone services, tips on travel packages and more. The BBB also provides free mediation and /or arbitration of consumer/business disputes. M-F 8:30-4.

BIRTHDAY CLUB OF AMERICA
P.O. Box 211, Chillicothe, 1-800-568-2329 or 457-8118

Call or write to be added to their mailing list to receive coupons valid for freebies (with a purchase) or dollars off at participating merchants in your community. You'll receive you coupons near your birthday which are valid at restaurants and services.

BUCKEYE RANCH (FORMERLY BUCKEYE BOYS RANCH)
5665 Hoover Rd., Grove City, 43123, 875-2371

The E.P. Messham Center For Work Experience, offers troubled teenagers the opportunity to learn new skills and experience a sense of achievement. To accomplish this, the youths work in a commercial printing and graphics operation on site which offers binding, collating, folding, book stitching other printing services at very competitive prices. The Messham Center also features a recognition and awards development department which manufacturers and engraves flat plaques, trophies, awards and signage. Or you can have your own items engraved by the students, also at competitive prices. The center is staffed by professionals who ensure that high quality and efficiency are maintained. M-F 9-5.

CALLANDER CLEANERS
Eleven Columbus locations

Have your American or state of Ohio flag dry cleaned and pressed for free at any of their locations. The service usually takes two to three days. M-Sat 8-6.

CARPENTRY PROGRAM, HAYES TECHNICAL SCHOOL
Grove City, 43123, 878-0191 or 875-6249

Can you believe that the school has had difficulty finding families who want a home built at a savings of several thousand dollars? The carpentry program at the school has students who work under strict supervision to put up the framing for a new home. The family must arrange for the foundation, plumbing, electrical and finishing through subcontractors, but the end result, could literally save big bucks if you're not too concerned with the potential headaches associated with this sort of an arrangement. Only one home per year is built by the students, but there are generallyfew, if any people applying for the construction! Criteria for the program include: the home must be built in the southwestern City School District, the home must be constructed during the school year, the family must obtain architect's drawings, the family must reside in the home for two years, the residence must not be intended for commercial use or as a rental property, the family must prove they have enough funds to cover the cost of the framing and be willing to arrange for and oversee the work of subcontractors.

CENTRAL OHIO LUNG ASSOCIATION
4627 Executive Dr., Columbus, 43228, 457-4570

If you would like to quit smoking, purchase a self help kit for $5 from this organization, which includes a day to day plan for quitting. Accepts checks and cash only. M-F 9-5.

CENTRAL OHIO SCHOOL OF MASSAGE
1120 Morse Rd., Suite 250, Columbus, 43229, 841-0424

This school trains people to be licensed massage therapists or myofacial therapists under the approval of the Ohio State Medical Board and the American Massage Therapy Association. Students who have had six or seven months training, work under supervision in the student clinic to provide Swedish style massage, not a therapeutic massage. The cost is $20 here, but is generally $25-$45 by a licensed therapist. Day and evening appointments are available.

CLEANER IMAGE
523-6708

Basic housecleaning services are available at a cost $29.95 for four rooms and $5 for each additional room.   There is a surcharge for rooms which are above average in size or condition, as well as to clean windows, appliances or wash walls. You'll find the cleaner to be efficient and professional.   The company services Franklin county and the adjacent suburbs. Mention that you saw the business listed in this book, and you'll save $5 off your first visit!

COLUMBIA GAS OF OHIO
939 W. Goodale Blvd., Columbus, 43272, 460-2263

Seniors aged 62 and older are eligible to receive more than a dozen free services designed to save you time, energy and money from the Service For A Lifetime program.   The options available include modification of thermostat and appliance dials for the visually impaired; through the Warm Choice program, low income seniors can receive free home weatherization assistance and help in paying home heating bills; 30 day deferred payment option for gas bills if you are admitted to a hospital; the "Extra Protection Plan" guarantees that your service will not be disconnected in the winter months if you are late in your payments. Other "Service For A Lifetime" options are available. M-F 8-5.

COLUMBUS AND SOUTHERN ELECTRIC
231-7878

Free energy audit, weatherization and energy saving devices are provided by trained customers of Columbus and Southern. If you own your own home, have electric heat and/or use an electric hot water heater, you'll be eligible for any or all of the following energy conservation opportunities: electric water heater wrapping, wrapping up to six feet of piping, installation of low flow shower/bath/kitchen aerators, blower door test and weather strip caulking. The service is provided free of charge to Columbus and Southern customers without regard to income level.

COLUMBUS CANCER CLINIC
65 Ceramic Dr., Columbus, 43214, 263-5006

Low cost cancer screenings are available at various sites in the community through this clinic, in day and evening hours to suit your personal schedule.   The screenings are conducted by a physician and include a thorough physical, risk assessment and a brief education session. The cost is $10, but no one will be denied a screening if they are unable to pay. Appointments are needed. M-F 9-5.

COLUMBUS HEALTH DEPARTMENT
181 Washington Blvd., Columbus, 43215, 645-2437

Free, anonymous Aids and pregnancy testing, in addition to free education and counseling sessions are offered to residents of the City of Columbus. The clinic is open from 8-3:30 Monday, Tuesday, Wednesday and Friday, and 9-3:30 on Thursdays. By appointment only

COLUMBUS HOUSING LAW PROJECT
1066 N. High St., Columbus, 43201, 291-5076 and 221-2255

The "Landlord/Tenant Advice Only Clinic" operates at 11 a.m. on Mondays at 40 W. Gay Street in Columbus (at the Legal Aid office) and on Tuesdays at 6p.m. at the Third Avenue Community Church, 1066 N. High St. It is imperative that you arrive when they open as the lawyers will leave shortly thereafter if no one appears for their assistance. This free service is sponsored by the Columbus Housing Law Project.

COLUMBUS NEIGHBORS
239-4570

This unique service operates as a consumer advocacy group by maintaining a data bank of service providers which members can access by phone. You'll find the typical categories like plumbers and roofers, plus other categories such as alterations, clock repair, animal grooming and even window washing. There are over 100 categories with over 2,000 listings. The organization collects verbal reports from members who have used services and maintains this information, both good and bad. The referral service operates in such a way that you feel as if you are calling a friend for a recommendation. This business is one of my personal favorites. While new homeowners and newcomers to Columbus will benefit most from this service, apartment dwellers and long time residents can still anticipate a substantial gain. Your annual $30 membership fee entitles you to unlimited access to service providers who are reputable, conscientious and do not charge exorbitant rates. In fact, many of the service providers offer substantial savings compared to other businesses.

COLUMBUS POLICE CRIME PREVENTION UNIT
120 W. Gay St., Columbus, 43215, 645-4610

If you are concerned about security, members of this crime prevention unit can send a police officer to your home or business to provide an assessment. They will also suggest ways in which shoplifting and robberies can be discouraged and how you can better secure a building. To be eligible for this free service, you must live in or have a business in the City of Columbus, not within an incorporated area. M-F 8-5.

COLUMBUS SMALL BUSINESS DEVELOPMENT CENTER
c/o Columbus Chamber of Commerce, 37 N. High St., Columbus, 43215, 221-1321

Sponsored by the Columbus Chamber of Commerce, this free service provides technical assistance to small businesses and prospective small businesses. They have a network of over 160 volunteers who are business leaders willing to assist you in determining venture capital strategies, evaluating cash flow problems, developing accounting and record-keeping systems and more. You do not have to be a chamber member to participate. Call to request a packet of information. Several forms will need to be completed and mailed before your counseling session can be scheduled. M-F 8-5.

COLUMBUS SPEECH AND HEARING CENTER
4110 N. High St., Columbus, 43214, 263-5151(voice) or 263-5151(TTY)

Licensed audiologists will perform a free, ten minute hearing evaluation on Wednesdays from 1-4p.m. The center also offers free reading and writing enhancement classes for adults who are deaf, which uses a unique literacy program with American Sign Language to teach English as a second language.

COMMUNITY MEDIATION SERVICE OF CENTRAL OHIO
80 Jefferson Ave., Columbus, 43215, 228-7191

Free mediation assistance is provided to Franklin County residents, to help resolve disputes involving neighborhoods (noise, pets etc.), families, businesses (consumer/merchant disputes of faulty merchandise or service), employees/employers, school disputes (involving teachers, staff, students, parents) landlords/tenants etc.   This service is available to the entire community without regard to income including private citizens, businesses and community organizations.   The service helps to resolve disputes before they reach a level of seriousness requiring the use of courts, police or attorneys.   It can help you to improve valuable personal or professional relationships while helping you to participate in creating your own solutions to problems.   However, this service does not handle disputes involving serious violence or those needing legal assistance such as filing a lawsuit, criminal defenses, wills, etc.   This service has earned the distinction of being one of my personal favorites.

CONSUMER CREDIT COUNSELING SERVICE OF CENTRAL OHIO
697 E. Broad St., Columbus, 43215, 464-2227
399 E. Church St., Marion, 43302, 464-2227
121 W. Mulberry St., Lancaster, 43130, 464-2227
40 N. Sandusky St., suite 203, Delaware, 43015, 464-2227
1521 Maple Ave., Zanesville, 450-2227

This free service will advise you on ways in which you can repay your creditors and avoid filing for bankruptcy.   In most cases, your credit rating will not be affected.   After a repayment plan has been established, you will be protected from collection efforts by your creditors.   The Columbus phone number handles the scheduling for all of the branches except the one in Mansfield. M-F 9-5.

DEBTORS ANONYMOUS
341-7522

If your spending habits have become uncontrollable, this free self help group, which uses an approach similar to the "twelve steps", may be able to assist you.   Meetings are held every Monday from 7:30-8:30 p.m. at the Worthington United Methodist Church., 600 N. High St.   There are also additional meetings for newcomers which are held from 8:30-9:30 on the second and fourth Monday at the same location.

DUTCH GIRL CLEANERS
1963 Morse Rd., Columbus, 43229, 261-9677

Save on your dry cleaning bills.   All clothing items (except suede and leather) are $1.45 per piece prepaid, or $1.70 per piece if you pay at the time of pickup.   Draperies, blankets and other household dry cleaning is also value priced at $1.69 per pound. M-Sat 7a.m.-8p.m.

EARLY CHILDHOOD RESOURCE NETWORK
Columbus, 292-7714

This YMCA sponsored program, offers free developmental screenings to assess a child's physical (speech, language, motor, vision and hearing), social and mental development. The screenings are available for children up to age five and are offered twice a month at various Columbus sites.   The Network also serves as a referral agency to help families locate treatment for children having developmental difficulties. Call to schedule an appointment.

ENCORE PLUS
Columbus, 224-9121

The Columbus branch of the YWCA sponsors this free program for women aged 35-49 who do not have medical insurance and are income eligible. They will be offered a free mammogram and cervical screening at their choice of several locations in Franklin county. Women calling from outside the county, who meet the guidelines, may be referred to a site in their own county. The program also offers support groups for postsurgical women in recovery and those undergoing treatment. Childcare and transportation can be provided. M-F 9-5.

FRANKLIN COUNTY COOPERATIVE EXTENSION SERVICE
1945 Frebis Ave., Columbus, 43206, 443-6200

There is a wealth of free and low cost assistance available through this agency. If you enjoy gardening, sign up to receive the free monthly newsletter, Extension Garden News. It lists planting and pruning tips, horticultural happenings around town, plus special features such as plants and shrubs which will give good fall foliage color. The Expanded Food And Nutrition Program (EFNEP) is free to low income families with young children, who want to learn to improve the quality of their life. Participants are taught basic nutrition concepts, food buying skills, proper food management of available resources etc. You can receive a free subscription to the Home Living Newsletter, which provides helpful tips on cooking, cleaning and home maintenance. This agency also operates two hotlines, at 443-6419, which can provide you with instant information. The Horticulture Hotline is open from 8a.m.-12 noon Monday through Friday and can answer your questions about growing fruits and vegetables, lawn and garden care, the use of pesticides, holiday plant care etc. The Home Economics Hotline operates from 12:30-4 Monday through Friday and can answer your questions relating to stain removal, cooking, food poisoning, selecting toys for your child, balancing work and family and more. Free and low cost pamphlets are available by mail on a variety of related topics. This organization sponsors many workshops and seminars in the community on such subjects as how to start and operate a bed and breakfast, a homemaker's mini college (craft workshops, gardening, parenting, nutrition and other topics) a perennial plant seminar and others. The workshops cost about $3-$15, but there are also several which are free. M-F 9-5

FRANKLIN COUNTY ENGINEER'S OFFICE
970 Dublin Rd., Columbus, 43215, 462-3030

Provides free maps of Franklin county listing streets, highways, shopping centers, golf courses and heliports. Maps, which are revised every two years, must be picked up at their office. M-F 9-5.

FRANKLIN COUNTY HOME WEATHERIZATION SERVICE
c/o Mid Ohio Regional Planning Commission, 285 E. Main St., Columbus, 43215, 228-1825

MORPC provides free attic insulation, storm windows, caulking and weather stripping to eligible low income residents of Franklin county who live outside the city of Columbus.

Service is provided about 60 days after your request is received. Longer delays might exist if your request is made during the peak winter season. M-F 8-5.

FRANKLIN COUNTY SOIL AND WATER CONSERVATION OFFICE
1945 Frebis Ave., Columbus, 43206, 443-9416 or 443-2440

You can obtain a free soil survey with maps that identify, by location, the characteristics for all soils within Franklin county. Free soil suitability interpretations are provided upon request. This information can be used to determine subsurface and surface drainage conditions which are necessary in evaluating waste disposal options and possible flooding concerns. People interested in building a "home in the country", are urged to consult with this free service to avoid any unnecessary problems. Their annual spring fish sale provides you with the opportunity to purchase bass, blue gill, catfish and amur for pond stocking. The cost ranges from 25 cents each to 60 cents each for all but the white amur which costs $10 apiece. Orders should be placed in March and will be available for pickup in April. The Tree And Shrub Packet Program provides landowners with the chance to purchase a variety of trees and shrubs seedlings which are suited for wildlife habitat improvement, windbreak establishment, living hedges or screens or reforestation. There's no restrictions on where they may be planted. Austrian Pine, Colorado Blue Spruce, White Dogwood, Forsythia, Hardy Pecan, Black Walnut, Sycamore and other types are available at a cost of $8-$12 for 5-25 seedlings. Orders are placed in March for April pickup. M-F 8-4.

HANDYMAN CONNECTION
436-4944 Columbus

Retired craftsmen and other professionals offer low cost home repairs and remodeling services through this clearinghouse/agency of sorts. All workers have a minimum of ten years of experience in plumbing, carpentry, wallpapering, masonry, plastering, ceramic tile installation or general odd jobs. The business services residential customers by appointment. Free estimates can be provided after an on site visit to your home has occurred, as many factors can influence the estimate. Estimates are based on labor costs only, so as to allow the resident to be able to purchase and arrange for the needed materials. The company is insured and licensed.

HIRE A FIREFIGHTER, INC.
891-5670

A group of area firefighters have joined together in another sort of venture to provide quality home maintenance and repairs, odd jobs, and services such as accounting, airplane transport and more, at a savings! The skills and talents also include privacy and wood fences, roofing, electrical work and there's even a firefighter who makes and rents dunking machines! The notion behind hiring an employee of a trusted and well respected profession to help you out of other sorts of personal "trouble", is a powerful concept and one which seems to feel right inside of me. The company is licensed, bonded and insured, and maintains ethical business practices. While there is no service call fee, there is an hourly rate of about $25 which is charges. Materials are extra but are priced fairly. Services are available in Franklin and southern Delaware Counties. By the summer of '96, the company hopes to expand to other Central Ohio areas, and to publish a directory of firefighters who can perform various services.

MASSAGE AWAY SCHOOL OF THERAPY
663 Park Meadow Rd., Suite D, Westerville, 43081, 523-7430

Students who are pursuing a licensure in massage, provide a fifty minute, Swedish style rub down for only $20. This sort of technique has been known to relieve stress and improve circulation and relaxation. Appointments are available in day and evening times.

OHIO AFFILIATE/NATIONAL SOCIETY TO PREVENT BLINDNESS
1500 W. 3 Ave., Columbus, 43212, 464-2020

The society offers free glaucoma screenings every Thursday from 9:30-12 year round. No appointment is necessary. Glaucoma is one of the leading causes of irreversible blindness. It progresses without pain or symptoms in its early stages, but early detection can prevent further vision loss. The office is open M-F 9-5 to answer your questions.

OHIO DEPARTMENT OF AGING
Communications Dept., 50 W. Broad St., Columbus, 43266-0501, 466-3253

Senior citizens aged 100 and over, can receive a free certificate of congratulations on their birthday, which is signed by the Governor and the director of the Ohio Department of Aging. This treasured keepsake has a bright gold seal affixed to it and is the state's way of spreading birthday cheer on these landmark occasions. You can order the certificate over the phone or by mail. Allow 3-5 weeks for delivery. M-F 9-5.

OHIO TUITION TRUST AUTHORITY
1-800-233-6734, 589-6882 or 752-9200

College tuition costs are growing at nearly twice the cost of living index. The Guaranteed Tuition Program allows you to prepay college tuition at the current rate per credit hour so your child can attend any of the 35 public universities, community colleges or technical colleges in Ohio. The program was created in 1989 as a way for you to buy tomorrow's education at today's prices. The current cost is $41.50 per tuition credit. If your child decides to attend a private or out of state college, there is a refund policy which is available, details of which, can be obtained from OTTA. M-F 9-5.

1.50 CLEANERS
5424 Cleveland Avenue, Columbus, 43231, 890-0150

The first area business to offer such low prices on dry cleaning, features a cost of $1.50 per piece to clean and press you garment. Shirts can be laundered and pressed for 99 cents as well. The business will not clean household items, leather, suede or furs. It is your responsibility to ensure that the garment can in fact, be dry cleaned, so read the label first. All orders must be prepaid. M-F 7-7, Sat 8:30-5.

P.S. FIELD'S
225 S. 3 St., Marshall Field's, Columbus, 43215, 227-6352

Field's offers a free shopping service to the general public, P.S. Field's, by appointment only. A trained sales consultant will shop with you to help you find what you need, and you will get personalized attention, complete with private dressing suites and complimentary refreshments. Or if you prefer, the consultant can set aside certain items which you can evaluate at the store. You can use this service as your personal gift secretary. Staff members will phone you as special occasions draw near. They will even shop for you and mail out your purchase. This P.S. Field's service is available Monday through Friday 11a.m.-9p.m. and every other Saturday. Their direct phone line is 227-6352.

PRESIDENTIAL GREETINGS OFFICE
White House, Washington, D.C., 20500

The White House will send a free personal letter to any senior aged 75 and older to congratulate him/her on their birthday. The office will also send a congratulatory letter to parents on the birth of their child. Simply put your request in writing. Allow 6-8 weeks for delivery.

RIDESHARE
Mid Ohio Regional Planning Commission,(MORPC) 285 E.
Main St., Columbus, 43215, 1-800-875-POOL or 1-800-VAN-RIDE

The MORPC offers a free commuter assistance program which utilizes a computer based system to match you up with someone who lives and works near you, for the purpose of carpooling. The intake occurs by phone. Simply call 1-800-875-POOL and a representative will assist you. Within a few days, you will be sent a list of commuters who are interested in carpooling. A similar program, VanOhio, has a nominal fee and serves those who live 25 miles or more from work. You would meet a MORPC van at a central site and would be driven to your place of business or a convenient drop off spot. Phone 1-800-VAN-RIDE. Commuters using either of these pools, can average about a $25 per month savings over using their own car to commute to work. M-F 8-5.

SAGAR CLEANERS
5246 Cleveland Ave., Columbus, 43231, 882-5922

You'll be charged only $1.50 per item to have your sweaters, blazers, pants, nonpleated skirts or blouses dry cleaned. Dresses or overcoats cost $3.00 to clean. Add ten cents per pleat, plus the $1.50 to dry clean your pleated skirts. M-F 7-7, Sat 8-5.

SAM'S CLEANERS
5434 E. Livingston Save., Columbus, 43232, 864-2233
2480 E. Main St., Bexley, 43209, 231-9554
7123 E. Main St., Reynoldsburg, 43068, 759-4477
4235 Kimberly Pkwy., Columbus, 43232, 864-1188

Save on your drycleaning bills. The Bexley site charges $1.75 per garment and the other locations charge $1.99 per garment. Prices are for apparel only (suede and leather excluded), and do not include draperies nor other household items. M 8:30-6:30, Tu-F 11-6, Sat 9-5.

SCORE (SERVICE CORPS OF RETIRED EXECUTIVES)
85 Marconi Blvd., Columbus, 43215, 469-2357

If you are a potential small business owner, or currently operating a business, you can obtain free professional advice from this organization. A face-to-face meeting will provide you with answers to many of your questions from volunteers who are retired business executives. About four low cost business seminars are offered monthly on such topics as government contracts, record keeping, credit and collections, marketing etc. The classes are from 4-7 hours long and cost $10-$20. Pre-register so you can save $5 off the ticket price at the door. Classes are held at various sites. Call to be added to their mailing list. M-F 9-5. Accepts checks and cash only.

SEARS DISCOUNT TRAVEL CLUB; TRAVELLER'S ADVANTAGE
1-800-648-4037

Your one time only membership fee of $49 will provide you with many domestic and international savings opportunities. including half price at hotels, and substantial discounts of 10-50% on car rentals, Amtrak, airfares, all airlines, railroads, condo vacations, cruises and more. You'll have access to exclusive members only travel bargains including "brief notice" vacations offering deep discounts on trips booked 3-8 weeks in advance. You'll need to use your Discover card for these arrangements. Your membership fee is fully refundable at any time. As an option, you may request a 30 day free trial.

SENIOR MEDIATION SERVICES
645-7250

Do you need assistance resolving a dispute between neighbor, family member, business or landlord? Trained mediators will provide free assistance to seniors by identifying ways to resolve the issue and assisting with the negotiation of a settlement. Both parties must be present. No problem is too big or too small to be handled by this office. The service does not decide who is right or wrong, does not take sides and does not tell you how to resolve your dispute. The process is less time consuming than the traditional legal process. You can take other actions if not satisfied. The mediation remains private. The service is sponsored by the Ohio Commission on Dispute Resolution And Conflict Management and the City Of Columbus, Recreation And Parks Department's Central Ohio Area Agency On Aging. Appointments are suggested. M-F 9-5.

SIX ON YOUR SIDE
c/o WSYX TV, 1261 Dublin Rd., Columbus, 43215, 821-9799

Call the hotline number above and you will be sent a form to fill out on which you will describe the consumer related problem you are experiencing. Channel six will investigate the problem and try to resolve it for you. Very often, a business will respond quite readily to resolve the issue as they are afraid of televised publicity about the problem. "Six On Your Side" airs a featured problem/resolution weekly, but attempts to resolve all requests they receive. M-F 9-5

SKILLSBANK AT FIRSTLINK (FORMERLY CALLVAC SERVICES)
370 S. 5 St., Columbus, 43215, 464-4747

If you would like to become a volunteer, contact the Skillsbank at Firstlink, which is a computerized system that matches your interests and skills to the volunteer needs of more than 100 nonprofit organizations in Franklin county. Volunteering can help you advance a cause, improve services provided in your community, add a dimension of meaning to your life, help you avoid boredom and loneliness, help you to acquire new skills or refresh old ones, as well as help you make career, college and vocational decisions. The latter two are very helpful for personal growth and can assist you when listing experience on a job resume. Volunteer opportunities can be tailored to suit your personal schedule and may also include assisting at various festivals and special events. Other volunteer opportunities can include assisting people with their shopping needs who are terminally ill, have a disability or are elderly. Volunteerism is a no or low cost way to learn, grow, share and enjoy. M-F 8-5.

SWAN CLEANERS
42 area locations. Check the phone book.

You can have your American flag dry cleaned for free, year round, at any branch. No coupon is needed.

TOFYL DUTCHESS CLEANERS
2455 E. Main St., Bexley, 43209, 236-5785

Save money on your dry cleaning bills at this business. Winter coats and raincoats will be cleaned for $3.49 each and other clothing for $1.89 per piece prepaid. M-F 7-7, Sat 9-5.

U.S. $1.50 CLEANERS
3479 E. Broad St., Columbus, 43213, 237-1658

Dry cleaning doesn't have to be expensive. Although the store does not clean household items, just bring in your clothes (no suedes or leathers) and you'll be charged only $1.50 per piece prepaid. M-F 7a.m.-7p.m., Sat 7-5.

YELLOW JACKET REMOVAL SERVICE
792-BUGS (2847)

How about free removal of yellow jackets from your home or garden by a trained individual with eighteen years experience? If you had to pay a pest control company, it might cost you between $60-$125. The bugs are collected live and are used for their venom which helps in medical research and to create allergy shots. The insects will be trapped and removed with or without their nest, depending on the situation. While the company prefers nests which have not been sprayed, active/healthy critters are still able to be removed. The season for infestation and removal is typically late August through early October, depending on the weather. The business also occasionally removes hornets and bumble bees (but not honeybees). All bug removal is dependent on the need of the medical facility which uses the insects. The company primarily serves the Northwest and North sides of Columbus, but may service other areas if scheduling permits. Leave a message and it will be returned.

ALSO SEE

Cat Welfare, Entertainment '96/97/98 Book, Lazarus, Marshall Field's, Nu Look Factory Outlet, OSU Office of Women's Services, Pet Butler and Vacu-Medic Plus

SHOES/SPORTS

SHOES

Each manufacturer cuts their clothes and shoes differently. So don't be stubborn about trying on something which is several sizes smaller or larger than you usually wear. Carry a tracing of family members' feet with you, so that when you stumble upon an unexpected bargain in shoes, you'll know instantly if it will fit. When my children were younger, this was an excellent way of buying them shoes when they weren't with me. I admit, I received more than my share of giggles and stares from sales people. But I was the one who benefitted in the long run because I was prepared.

BOOT OUTLET
3775 Columbus Lanc. Rd. N.W., Carroll, 756-4072
3660 S. High St., Southland Expo Ctr., Columbus, 43207, 497-0200

Western leather boots by Laredo, Sage, Wrangler, Silverado, Tony Lama, Capezio and other brands are available for men and women at a cost of $69.99-$189.99. Children's western boots are sold at about $34.99. Savings are about 20-40% off regular retail prices. The Southland location operates under the name Thunderbird Trading Company and has a much smaller selection of boots than the Carroll site. M-Sat 10-7, Sun 10-6.

CAPEZIO FOOTWEAR
270 Graceland Blvd. (in the Burlington Coat Factory store), Columbus, 43214, 885-2628
1635 River Valley Cir., Lancaster, 687-6318

Save 20-40% off first quality men's, women's and children's dress, sport and casual shoes. You'll find such brands as Calvin Klein Sport, Capezio, Dexter, Eastland, Nunn Bush, Rockport, Cobblers and Arpegio in traditional and contemporary styles. M-Sat 10-9, Sun 12-5.

COMFORT SHOE WAREHOUSE
1157 Columbus Pike, Delaware, 369-2900

Save 30-50% on simply styled, comfort shoes for mature tastes by such companies as Naturalizer, Footsaver and others. You'll also find some athletic sneakers in popular brands at similar savings. M-Sat 10-9, Sun 12-6.

DESIGNER SHOE WAREHOUSE
6635 Dublin Center Dr., Dublin, 43017, 791-1115

This business has moved to larger quarters from a previous location next to the Lexus dealership on West Dublin Granville Road. Nationally recognized brands of moderate to designer quality women's and men's shoes plus purses and related accessories are sold at 20-60% off regular retail prices. The first quality merchandise, which sells for up to $170 in other stores, includes closeouts, overstocks and discontinued casual, career and dressy styles for discriminating tastes. You'll find traditional and the ultimate in chic contemporary styles in all widths for sizes 5-11. With their move to the new location, comes the addition of their golf shoe department. You'll find the types typically available in pro shops such as Foot-Joy and Etonic, at similar savings. Brand names can't be mentioned in print, but you'll instantly recognize them once inside the store. Designer Shoe Warehouse has 20,000 pairs of shoes in stock from 165 different designers, and offers the most unusual selection of quality women's shoes in Central Ohio. They also operate the leased shoe department at Schottenstein's. Membership in the frequent shoppers' club is free. It entitles you to an extra 10% off clearance items, plus 40% off socks, hose and water repellent. It has earned the distinction of being one of my personal favorites. M/W/Th/F/Sat 10-9, Sun 12-6. Closed Tuesday for restocking.

EL-BEE SHOE OUTLETS
52 Westerville Square, Westerville, 43081, 882-4809
2968 Derr, Springfield, (513) 390-3270
1475 Upper Valley Pike, Springfield, (513) 325-8142
3575 N. Maple Ave., Zanesville, 452-4259
771 S. 30 St., Indian Mound Mall, Heath, 522-4100

First quality, current and past season shoes for men, women and children are available at savings of 15-40%. The moderate to better quality merchandise includes traditional and contemporary styles in regular, narrow and wide widths by Calico, Evan Picone, Hush Puppies, Bass, Nunn Bush, Westies, Nike, Reebok, Vans, Fila, Eastland and others. The store is owned by Elder Beerman, which has recently closed many of their area El-Bee sites except these few. M-Sat 10-9, Sun 12-5.

FAMOUS FOOTWEAR
Seven Columbus locations, plus the following
1796 Columbus Pike, Delaware, 363-1794
957 Hebron Rd., Heath, 522-1618
1632 Marion Mt. Gilead Rd., Marion, 389-1708

Each store carries over 20,000 pairs of first quality national name brands for men, women and children such as Nike, Keds, Eastland, Nunn Bush, Jasmine, Bellini, Westies, Buster Brown, Reebok and more. Choose from dressy, casual or sport styles, including soccer shoes, at savings of 10-50% off regular retail prices. M-Sat 10-9, Sun 12-5.

FOOTSAVER SHOE OUTLET
1273 N. Memorial Dr., Lancaster, 687-3322

First quality and some irregular men's and women's leather shoes by Drew, Barefoot Freedom and Footsaver, are available at savings of 40-50% off regular retail prices. Women's shoes are in the $35-$50 range and consist largely of traditional styles in oxfords, sandals and pumps for the mature woman. The men's shoes are priced at about $35-$60 and include wing tips and casual styles. A small selection of inexpensive purses for mature tastes, is also available. The annual "Winter Warm-up Sale" is held from late November to late December and features savings of 25% off their already low prices. M-Sat 10-5.

JUST FOR FEET
3165 Dublin Center Dr., Dublin, 43017, 792-FOOT (3668)
2450 Park Crescent Drive E., Columbus, 43232, 861-7466

The world's largest athletic shoe store features such brands as Adidas, New Balance, Diadora, Rockport, Reebok, L.A. Gear, Etonic and other brands of athletic shoes, in addition to clothing such as warm ups, tee shirts, socks, sport bags and accessories. Even if you don't need any sneakers, you won't want to miss this multi level, high tech store which is equipped with an arcade, food concession as well as a basketball court. Street shoes are not allowed on this mini court, but kids, and even adults, will enjoy shooting a few baskets. The second level has a running track, which may be used to test your intended purchase or just for fun. Don't miss the clearance area at the front of the store, which offers a large selection of closeout and special purchase athletic shoes for the family, at savings of 30-70% off regular retail prices. Merchandise throughout the store is available for men, women and children at savings of about 15-40%. M-Sat 10-9:30, Sun 11-7.

MEGA SHOE OUTLET
3812 E. Broad St., Town And Country Shp. Ctr., Columbus, 43213, 231-7722

Save 50-75% off men's and women's sport, casual and dressy shoes, plus slippers collected from the corporation's 1,000 shoe stores or departments. The store stocks 100,000 pairs by Adidas, Dexter, Converse, Nunn Busch, Caressa, Connie, Impo, Reebok, Claiborne, Naturalizer and others. Prices start at $5 and go up to about $25. M-Sat 10-9, Sun 11-6.

ROCKY SHOE FACTORY OUTLET
39 E. Canal, Nelsonville, 45764, 753-9100 or 753-3130

The "Rocky" brand of men's and women's boots and shoes is manufactured in this factory. Find seconds and overstocks of Brooks merchandise at savings of 30-50% off retail, plus first quality athletic shoes from other companies at savings of 20% off retail. Stop by this outlet on your way to the Hocking Hills State Park and Old Man's Cave. M-Sat 9-7, Sun 11:30-5:30.

SHOE SENSATION
7640 New Market Center Way, Columbus, 43235, 764-0130
5766 Brice Outlet Mallway, Columbus, 43232, 868-0095
River Valley Mall, Lancaster, 653-6010
3575 Maple Ave., Zanesville, 453-9921
771 S. 30 St., Indian Mound Mall, Heath, 522-3797

Save 20-50% off regular retail prices on men's, women's and children's dress and casual shoes by Zodiac, Calico, Rockport, Fanfare, Evan Picone, Dexter, Nina, Bass, Eastland, Nike, Reebok, French Schriner, Bally and more. Coordinating purses are offered at similar savings. Narrow, regular and wide widths are available. The Zanesville site has a nearby Sports Sensation shop which offers better brands of athletic shoes and some apparel and similar savings. M-Sat 10-9, Sun, 12-6.

ZZ BOOTS
2264 S. Hamilton Rd., Columbus, 43232, 863-3320

Thousands of men's, women's and some children's boots are available at savings of 20-40% off manufacturers' suggested retail prices. You'll find rare and exotic leathers, studded, sequined and handpainted boots, calf, knee high and thigh highs in hunting, traditional, biker and contemporary styles. The first quality merchandise is available in all of the popular brands such as Tony Lama, Zodiac, Acme, Dan Post, J. Chisholm, Nocona and Laredo. The store also sells men's and women's leather coats and jackets at similar savings. M-Sat 9:30-9:30.

ALSO SEE

Burlington Coat Factory Warehouse, Eddie Bauer Outlet, Eddie Bauer Salvage Sale, Eddie Bauer Warehouse Sale At Veteran's Memorial, Extravaganza, General Merchandise Sales, Jeffersonville Outlet Center, Koenig Sports, Lake Erie Factory Outlet, Marshalls, Ohio Factory Shops, T.J. Maxx, J.C. Penney Outlet, Schottenstein's, Sears Outlet, Value City Department Stores

SPORTS

AMERICAN LUNG ASSOCIATION OF MID OHIO
1700 Arlingate Lane, Columbus, 43228, 279-1700

If you like golf, purchase a Golf Privilege Card for $35 from this nonprofit group. The card will permit you one round of golf during the current season, at 35 driving ranges and over 100 golf courses in Ohio such as Mohican Hills, Blackhawk, Bent Tree, Hickory, Grove Briar, Timberview and others. The usual price to play a round of golf is $12-$15, so if you used all of the coupons in the book, you would save about $400. The card is valid from March through October. Proceeds from this annual fundraiser will be used to help support an asthma camp for children, lung health education and pulmonary research. A portion of your purchase price may be tax deductible, so check with your accountant. M-F 8:30-4:30. Accepts checks and cash only.

AMERICAN YOUTH HOSTELS
P.O. Box 14384, Columbus, 43214, 447-1006

The name of this organization is actually a misnomer as membership is open to all ages. Over 5,000 inexpensive overnight accommodations are available throughout the United States and the world to members of this organization. These include lodging in a lighthouse in California, a tree house in Georgia, a rustic farmhouse in Ohio, a battleship in Massachusetts and other sites such as YMCA's. Membership is open to young and old alike at a cost of $10-$35 annually depending on the age of the individuals and type of membership. Workshops are available at low cost to members including canoeing, sailing, bicycle maintenance, back packing, mountain climbing and leadership skills. Low cost, outdoor equipment rentals as well as adventure trips are also available to members.

BERRY'S BARBELL AND EQUIPMENT
2997 E. Livingston Ave., Columbus, 43209, 236-8080

Save 30-40% off new prices on a selection of used exercise equipment such as stair steppers, rowers, treadmills, weight stations and other items. The store stocks only better brands such as Lifestyle, Body Solid, Biodyne, Precor, Diamond Back and Trotter and also sells these items at typical retail prices. M-Th 10-8, F/Sat 10-6.

BLACKHAWK GOLF PRO SHOP
8830 Dustin Rd., Galena, 43021, 965-1042

Enjoy savings of 20% on men's and women's golf clubs, shoes and accessories, by all popular brands such as Wilson, Cobra, Lynx, Ashworth, Izod Club, Titleist and Ping. 7a-Dusk, March-November.

BREAKAWAY CYCLING
17 W. William St., Delaware, 43015, 363-3232

Although this business sells mostly new bicycles, it stocks a small selection of better used bikes at savings of 30-50% less than their original new cost. The stock varies, but some of the brands you may find include Gary Fisher and Schwinn Paramount. Used bicycles are generally in the $100-$400 range with values up to $700. M-F 9-8, Sat 9-5.

CITY OF COLUMBUS SPORTS DEPARTMENT
c/o Columbus Recreation and Parks Dept.

Free adult volleyball and basketball clinics are offered at the Berliner and Anheuser Busch Athletic Complexes. Phone 645-3366. Free golf clinics are offered at various times. Phone 645-3300 for information. The department also offers a variety of other free and low cost sports instructional classes and activities through their community recreation centers and senior centers. Call 645-3300 for details.

COLORADO SKI AND SPORT
3018 E. Broad St., Bexley, 43209, 237-7541

Better brands of ski equipment and apparel are available at savings of 20-60% off manufacturer's suggested retail prices. M-Sat 10-6.

COLUMBUS CLIPPERS
1155 W. Mound St., Columbus, 43223, 462-5250

Certain games have themes, special appearances by costumed characters, giveaways such as pennants or autographed baseballs, low cost food such as "dime a dog" night" or even fireworks, several times during the season. Admission to these games is $4 for all seats. Games are held from April through August. The Clippers also feature a series of post game concerts where for one low price of $4-$8 per seat, you can enjoy the game and a performance with top name entertainment such as Frankie Valli and the Four Seasons, REO Speedwagon, Gary Puckett and the Union Gap, The Monkeys, Al Denson, Lee Greenwood and others.

DO IT AGAIN SPORTS
1225 Court St., Circleville, 474-2322

Find new and used sportswear, sporting goods and fitness equipment at savings of 25-60% less than "if new". The business buys, sells and consigns all major brands such as Solarfex and Nordic Trac, for young and old alike. You'll also find some value priced new items as well. M 12-7, Tu-F 10-7, Sat 10-5.

EXECUTIVE TOUR GOLFER'S CLUB
1429 King Ave., Columbus, 43212, 1-800-686-5555

Save over $2,000 (if you use every coupon in the book) on golf games, accessories and travel at courses, driving/practice ranges, miniature golf, private instruction , golf travel arrangements as well as purchases at golf pro shops. Membership costs $19.95 annually, plus $1.65 to ship the coupon book. During 1991, the plan includes a free round of 18 hole golf when you rent a cart or 50% off the green fees without a cart rental. In 1992, the plan will change to include free green fees with a cart rental or 25% off green fees without a cart rental. The participating courses are currently in Columbus and Central Ohio and include such favorites as the Bent Tree Golf Club, the Shamrock Golf Club and Turnbury. Miniature golf courses include Fantasy Golf, Putt Putt and Westerville Golf Center. In 1992, the owner of this club hopes to expand the offerings to include additional courses in other parts of the state. There's 100 coupons in the 1991 edition which include 2-5 passes at each course. The coupons are transferable to friends or relatives. About 70% of the coupons are valid weekdays before 4p.m. Others are valid on weekends after 1p.m. Call anytime.

FINISH LINE OUTLET
6420 Tussing Rd., Consumer Sq. E., Reynoldsburg, 43068, 863-0421

Nationally recognized athletic wear by Champion, Umbro, Ocean Pacifac, Adidas, Nike, Converse and other brands, is available at savings of about 30-60% below retail. The first quality merchandise includes athletic shoes, sweat shirts, swimwear, nylon jackets and tennis wear, most of which are available in sizes for men, women and children. You'll find past season and discontinued items from their Central Ohio stores. M-Sat 10-9, Sun 12-5.

GLOBAL GOLF
59 S. State St., Westerville, 43081, 523-7407

Compare the quality of putters, shafts and grips to name brand products to save about 50%. Offers custom fit/custom made clubs in an extensive selection from which to choose. Also offers ready to assemble kits for do-it-yourself jobs. The business sells first quality golf bags by Bennington, Fila, Miller and Unimax at about 25-35% off list price. A catalog is available. M/W 9-8, Tu/Th/F 9-6, Sat 9-3.

GOLF PAK
2338 S. Hamilton Rd., Suite 200, Columbus, 43232, 866-4000 or (800) 434-4900

Twelve of Central Ohio's finest golf courses await your visit where you can save up to $1,200 by using all the coupons in this special booklet. Your $49.50 fee includes shipping and enables you to save on greens fees, gold cart rentals, items at gold shops and lessons from professionals. The featured courses are within an hour form Columbus and have included Apple Valley, Granville, Blackhawk, Bent Tree, Steeplechase and others.

GRANDVIEW CYCLE SHOP
1472 W. Fifth Ave., Columbus, 43212, 488-4500

This store has a large selection of 60-75 gently used bicycles in the basement. Ask a sales clerk to escort you down there. Choose from quality brands such as Piranha, Schwinn, Jazz, Murata, Trek, Pro-Flex, Univega and others. Most prices are in the $60-$190 range, with values up to $700. The business stocks only top of the line bikes for finicky tastes. The bikes will be cleaned and repaired, if necessary, prior to leaving the store. The shop also stocks used lawn mowers by Toro and other brands at comparable savings. M/W/Th 11-7, F 11-6, Sat 10-5. Seasonal hours may vary.

HACKER'S HELPER
630 W. Schrock Rd., Westerville, 43081, 899-6969
6720 Riverside Dr., Powell, 43065, 793-0660
2768 S. Hamilton Rd., Columbus, 43232, 755-4449

Everything for the golfer is under one roof here at savings of 20-50% off suggested retail prices. You will find golf bags by Professional, Hogan, Spaulding and Hot-Z, golf shoes by Foot Joy, Etonic, Reebok and Nike, as well as clothes and accessories. Junior clubs for 5-14 year olds are also available. All of the merchandise is first quality, current season and year. Golf club regripping is $3-$5 per club. M-Sat 10-8, Sun 10-6.

HANDY BIKES CORPORATION
1055 W. Fifth Ave., Columbus, 43212, 299-0550

New mopeds, Scooters and bicycles for adults and children are sold at savings of about 25% off regular retail prices through this distributor. Used items are priced about 40-50% less than "if new". The merchandise includes such brands as Pugh, Hercules, Columbia, Quentin, Sach, Yamaha, Motorbecane and Victoria. Parts and service are offered at prices which are about 10-15% lower than in other retail stores. M-Sat 9-6.

IT'S DIVE TIME
961 E. Dublin Granville Rd., Columbus, 43229, 785-0959

The business offers savings of 20-50% on a full line of scuba gear by such sought after brands as Thunderwear, Oceanic, Uwatec, Padi and Scubapro. You'll also find a large selection of used and reconditioned gear at savings of 40-50% off new prices. On site repairs of equipment are competitively priced. A staff member can arrange for great travel deals for scuba diving trips across the country and abroad. Instructional classes are also offered. M-Sat 12-8.

KIDS DISCOVER FITNESS
Driving Pk. Recreation Ctr. 1100 Rhoads Ave., Columbus, 43206, 645-3328
Linden Recreation Ctr., 1254 Briarwood Ave., Columbus, 43211, 645-3067
Marion-Franklin Recreation Ctr., 2801 Lockbourne Rd., Columbus, 43207, 645-3160
Thompson Recreation Ctr., 1189 Dennison Ave., Columbus, 43201, 645-3082
Westgate Recreation Ctr., 455 S. Westgate Ave., Columbus, 43204, 645-3264

This exciting program is sponsored by the City of Columbus, Recreation and Parks Department, and is offered during the summer time, as well as during the spring and Christmas school breaks. Youths aged 6-12 can enjoy a variety of fitness related programs in addition to off site trips. The program is ideal for working parents as it is offered from

7a.m.-6p.m. on specified weekdays. The cost to attend the six full day Christmas break program was only $18, which comes to a mere $3 per day. The summer fee is $15 weekly or $105 for the entire seven week term. Register early as the program fills up quickly.

NEWARK GOLF COMPANY FACTORY OUTLET
99 S. Pine St., Newark, 43055, 1-800-222-5639 or 344-6915

Sells golf clubs, balls, clothing, golf bags and shoes by such popular brands as Ram, PGA Tour, Brunswick, Miller, Nike, Etonic, Dunlop and others. Golf bags are priced at $35-$99, shoes start at $43, and 12-15 golf ball packs start at $15. Savings on this first quality merchandise for adults and kids is 40-60% off regular retail prices. Quality, custom built clubs is their specialty. The store offers free custom fitting of golf equipment utilizing their practice rooms and swing computers. M-F 8-6, Sat 9-6.

O.D.N.R. DIVISION OF WATERCRAFT
Fountain Sq., Bldg. C-2, Columbus, 43224, 265-6480

A free home study course, Ohio Boating Basics-A Small Craft Primer, is available from the Ohio Department of Natural Resources. Successful completion will earn you an Ohio Boating Basics Certificate, and possibly enable you to be eligible for a 5-20% discount on your boat insurance. Low cost boating and watercraft safety courses are also offered throughout Central Ohio. Call for details. M-F 9-5.

O.D.N.R. RENT-A-CAMP-PROGRAM
Fountain Sq., Bldg. C-3, Columbus, 43224, 265-7000

Twenty-three Ohio State parks are available as Rent-A-Camp sites through the Ohio Department of Natural Resources' popular seasonal program. For only $17 per night, an entire family can enjoy a fully equipped campsite with a 10x12 foot lodge type tent erected on a wooden platform, a picnic table, twelve foot square dining fly shelter, two cots, two foam sleeping pads, 60 quart cooler, a propane stove, camplight, fire extinguisher, broom and a dustpan. Rentals must be made after March 1, for the May 1-September 30 season. A $10 deposit must accompany your registration. Call M-F 8-5.

ONCE RIDDEN BIKES
350 E. Hudson St., Columbus, 43211, no phone

Choose from over forty used adult and children's bicycles by Huffy, Schwinn, Murray and other brands. You'll find all sizes and types, including some racing bicycles. Condition varies from gently used to those which need some tender loving care. Prices are in the $30-$75 range, offering savings of about 40-60% off "if new" prices. The store also offers a value priced repair service and accepts trade-ins. M-Sat 10-6.

PAUL'S MARINE-THE DOCK SHOPPE
2300 E. Dublin-Granville Rd., Columbus, 43229, 899-1616

A large selection of boat accessories are available at savings of 15-25% off regular retail prices. Nautical inspired gifts such as jewelry and clothes, are sold at full retail prices. M-Sat 10-8, Sun 12-5.

PLAY IT AGAIN SPORTS
7420 Sawmill Rd., Columbus, 43235, 791-9344

1153 Columbus Pike, Rt. 23, Delaware, 43015, 363-2664

5673 Emporium Sq., Columbus, 43231, 890-2110

5111 E. Main St., Columbus, 43213, 868-0018

2177 Eakin Rd., Columbus, 43223, 279-7529

4714 Cemetery Rd., Hilliard, 43026, 529-9100

7412 Sawmill Rd., Columbus, 43235, 791-9344

1144 N. Memorial Dr., Lancaster, 654-9555

1608 Upper Valley Pike, Springfield, (513) 324-1144

959 Hebron Rd., Heath, 522-5376

Save about 50% off regular retail prices, compared to new prices, on gently used sports equipment for baseball, softball, hockey, football, scuba diving, golf, weight lifting, tennis, camping, roller skating, water-skiing, wind surfing, fishing, soccer, lacrosse and every other sport. This franchised operation sells such brands as McGregor, Spaulding, Wilson, Cooper and Rawlings. A limited amount of new merchandise is sold at about 10-20% off retail. The inventory is a combination of consigned and purchased merchandise for adults and children. Accepts trade-ins. Hours vary by store.

PRO GOLF DISCOUNT
2009 E. Dublin Granville Rd., Columbus 43229, 436-8714

6495 Sawmill Rd., Dublin, 43017, 792-3553

1359 Brice Rd., Reynoldsburg, 43068, 864-0110

3712 Riverside Dr., Columbus, 43221, 459-4111

Savings are about 20% off the price of first quality, current merchandise. You'll find clubs, balls, bags, shoes and clothes for the golf enthusiast. Offers low markups on a full selection of nationally recognized brands such as Ping, Hogan, Powerbilt, Wilson, PGA Tour and others. M-F 10-8, Sat 10-6, Sun 11-4.

SOUTHWEST COMMUNITY CENTER INDOOR POOL
3500 First Ave., Grove City, 43123, 875-1880

This large indoor pool has been recently renovated. The annual membership fee is $50 per year per person, plus $25 for each additional family member. Seniors aged 55 and over, pay $30 per year. Another option is to pay $1 per person per visit instead of the annual fee. As of the time this book went to press, the pool had not confirmed its year round operating hours. It is open to the entire community and you do not have to reside in Grove City.

SPECIAL-TEE GOLF-TENNIS-RACQUETBALL
1870 W. Henderson Rd., Columbus, 43220, 457-3238

886 S. Hamilton Rd., Columbus, 43213, 868-0794

1668 E. Dublin Granville Rd., Columbus, 43229, 891-4653

6350 Sawmill Rd., Dublin, 43017, 761-2447

4056 W. Broad St., Columbus, 43228, 272-7888

Top quality brands of golf, tennis and racquetball clothing, shoes and equipment are sold at savings of 20-30% off manufacturer's suggested retail prices. The merchandise is first quality, current and past season goods, as well as some used merchandise. Brands offered include Ping, Hogan, Spaulding, Etonic and others. Adult and children sizes are available. This family owned business operates sixteen stores in Ohio. M-Sat 10-9, Sun 11-5:30.

SPORTS EXCHANGE
1244 Hill Rd. N., Pickerington, 43147, 575-0177

Many different types of used sports equipment, soccer shoes, baseball gloves, ice skates and related items are offered in this business which buys, sells, trades and consigns these items. You'll also find exercise equipment at similar savings. M-F 11-8, Sat 10-6.

SPORTS SALES
1750 Idlewild Dr., Columbus, 43232, 268-7463

Custom imprinted and embroidered shirts, jackets and shorts for teams or clubs are available at savings of about 20% according to the owner. From design to conception, Sports Sales can emblazon anything made out of fabric for adults and children. This business also has a "no minimum order", unlike most custom businesses. M-F 9-6.

SUB-AQUATICS
8855 E. Broad St., Reynoldsburg, 43068, 864-1235

Save 10-20% on a full line of brand name ski apparel and accessories. You'll find Elan, Head, Tyrolia, Rachilie, Fera, Hot Finger, Pre, Dolomite, Geze, Obermeyer, Oakley, Oneal and other brands. M-Sat 10-7.

SUNSPORTS
2620 Bethel Rd., Columbus, 43220, 326-1427

This store buys and sells used snowboarding equipment at savings of 20-50% less than new prices. M-F 10-9, Sat 10-7, Sun 12-5.

SUPREME GOLF SALES, INC.
6421 Busch Blvd., Columbus, 43229, 888-8815
2256 S. Hamilton Rd., Columbus, 43232, 868-0754

All price ranges of first quality golf clothes and related accessories are discounted by about 25% off suggested retail prices. Merchandise is available for children as well as adults. M-F 10-8, Sat 10-6, Sun 10-4.

UPPER ARLINGTON HIGH SCHOOL NATATORIUM
1950 Ridgeview Rd., Columbus, 43221, 487-5213

Open swim time is from 2-4p.m. every Sunday during the school year. The fee is $1 per person. Lifeguards are on hand at all times at this large indoor pool. You do not need to be a resident of Upper Arlington to use the facility. Showers and lockers are also available. M-F 9-4 for inquiries.

ALSO SEE

Agler Davidson Annual Sale, Blackhawk Golf Pro Shop, Columbus Police Property Auction, Extravaganza, Famous Footwear, Fore Love-Garage Sale, General Merchandise Sales, J.C. Penney Outlet Store, Jeffersonville Outlet Center, Just For Feet, Koenig Sports, Koval Knives, Meijer, Ohio Factory Shops, Q's Sportswear, Sam's Club, Sammie's Card Shop, Sears Outlet, Schottenstein's, Service Merchandise, Skiswap at the Skismith, Ultimate Garage Sale, Urban Concern Garage Sale

SPECIAL EVENTS &
SPECIAL SALES

In this section, you'll find special sales which don't have a year round walk-in location as well as special events lasting for one or several days. Other special events can be found in the entertainment chapter. Follow the newspapers or call the sponsoring organization for the exact dates of these sales and events. The listings in this chapter offer quality, low cost entertainment options and/or the opportunity to purchase artwork and other items at excellent prices. Refer to the description of the Ohio Arts Council in the arts and crafts chapter for pertinent information about arts festivals. Don't overlook attending some of the smaller shows and even church bazaars. Sometimes the prices will be lower than in the larger shows. Often, an artist who is just creating art as a hobby may not be prepared for the rigid entry requirements of some of the bigger arts festivals. However, it does not necessarily mean that their work is inferior. Also, artists have more overhead at larger, more prominent arts fairs and so their prices may be higher as a result, but not always. Remember that holidays are a popular time for stores to run large sales-President's Day, Memorial Day and the like. I have tried to list as many of the special events and special sales as possible, but due to space limitations, I have not been able to include all of them.

JANUARY

ACORN WAREHOUSE SALE
Four day event where end of season better women's apparel is reduced 40-60% and merchandise for the upcoming season is on sale for 40% off. The inventory is consolidated from 40 stores. Sale sites vary. Free. 764-8868

AGLER DAVIDSON ANNUAL 40% OFF SALE
Once a year in early January, the entire inventory is reduced 40% off their selling price for one day only at their five Columbus area stores. You'll find sporting goods, athletic apparel and footwear for the family. 457-1711.

BUCILLA'S BRIDAL ANNUAL SALE
This two day annual sale, features the chance to save 40-75% on a large selection of quality apparel and accessories such as Moonlight, Alfred Angelo, Jasmine, Galina and Bridal Originals. Bridesmaid gowns start at $10, bridal gowns at $75, prom gowns at $10 plus accessories and shoes at $10 and up. The sale also ties in with a fashion show and the opportunity to meet area caterers, florists and photographers. Many of the items in the sale are samples, so you'll find an abundance of sizes 8, 10 and 12, although the sale will

feature items up to size 44. The event is generally held at the Hyatt Regency Hotel in Columbus. 871-4152.

COLUMBUS CD AND RECORD SHOW
One day event held in January and April, where you can buy, sell or trade new, used and collectible albums, CDs and cassettes. You'll find music from the 1950's to the 1990's in all musical styles. There are many great deals here! The events are held at Veteran's Memorial Auditorium and a North Columbus hotel. Admission is $3 for adults and kids are admitted for free. 261-1585.

FABRIC FARMS ANNUAL WINTER SALE
20-60% savings throughout the store off their already discounted prices on quality home decorating and garment fabrics. (also held in July) 3590 Riverside Dr., 451-9300

J. CREW WAREHOUSE SALE
The annual warehouse sale, from the popular mailorder company, offers savings of 50-70% on first quality apparel for men and women. On my last visit to the sale, sweaters were priced at $12-$35, flannel shirts at $9, button down shirts at $14-$18, men's shorts at $5. Additional markdowns are taken during the sale based on the type of merchandise remaining on various days. Items at the sale are all from the catalogue, but intermittent markdowns may have been taken in the catalogue. Sales are usually at Veterans Memorial Auditorium down, and are also held in Cincinnati and Toledo. The four day events are held from Thursday through Sunday. The catalogue customer relations phone number is 800-932-0043.

MARTIN LUTHER KING JR. CELEBRATION
Annual celebration featuring a march through downtown, performance by nationally recognized group and lectures. Held on the third Monday in January. Free, but ticket is required. 645-7410.

NORTHCOAST GOLF SHOW
Three day event features deals on name brand golf equipment and apparel, seminars, golf clinics, contests, raffles, discounted gold vacations and exhibits. Your $6.50 admission allows you to participate in all activities at no additional cost. Usually held at Veteran's Memorial Auditorium in Columbus. (216) 963-6963 or (614)221-4341

NOWHERE MUSIC FEST
Two day event held at a different Campus bar each year, in which underground bands have the opportunity to perform alternative, folk and other types of music. $3. 294-4006.

PERCUSSION DAY
Local, regional and nationally recognized jazz musicians present concerts, workshops and lectures. Co-sponsored by Coyle Music and held at OSU's Weigel Hall. Free. 885-2729 or 292-8050

SIDEWALK SALES
January is a popular month for shopping malls to have these indoor sales where savings are 30-80%.

TALBOTT'S FAMOUS SEMI-ANNUAL SALE
See June description

VISION USA PROGRAM
The Ohio Optometric Association offers an annual program for low income families during Save Your Vision Week, the first week of March. Participating optometrists will provide free exams for working Ohioans who do not have health insurance to cover the eyecare. Potential candidates may enroll from January 15-31 only by calling 1-800-766-4466. Qualified applicants are then matched with a volunteer optometrist in their community. This free service includes an eye exam and free glasses, if necessary.

WHITE SALES
January and August are popular times for department and specialty stores to feature their white sales (special sales on linens, towels, bedspreads and similar items). Savings can be 30-50% off and sometimes even higher.

FEBRUARY

AFRICAN AMERICAN HISTORY MONTH CELEBRATION
Sponsored by the U.S. Postal Service, this annual Columbus event features entertainment with local and nationally recognized performers, unveiling of the newest Black Heritage stamp, a theatrical performance and discussions by prominent area leaders. The two hour program is generally held at the Fawcett Center. Free. 469-4521.

AMERICAN MUSIC FESTIVAL
Five days of free lectures and low cost concerts (about $6) on early and contemporary American music with local, regional and nationally acclaimed performing artists. Sponsored by OSU School Of Music. 292-2354.

ART STUDIO CLEARANCE SALE
About 100 exhibitors from across the country feature quality handcrafted items at savings of 30-60%(and sometimes more). Presented by the Ohio Designer Craftsmen, the organization which sponsors Winterfair, you'll find jewelry, clothing, sculpture, gifts and other items in most media. 1996 was the first year for this event which provided artists with an opportunity to sell prototypes, discontinued, overstocked and some seconds/irregular works. Artists represented feature upscale, quality items. The annual event will be featured on Saturday and Sunday February 1-2, 1997 and will likely be held this time each year at Veterans Memorial Auditorium in Columbus. This show is one of my personal favorites. Admission is $3. 486-4402

CHOCOLATE FANTASY FAIR
Enjoy free samples of candy, pastries and ice cream by local and national companies and chocolatiers at this one day event. Continuous entertainment, demonstrations and specialty boutiques. If you stay until half an hour before closing, all remaining samples are generally given away to attendees, so come with several empty shopping bags. Benefits Central Ohio Lung Association. Columbus Convention Center. $5 adults, $2 children. 457-4570 or 1-800-592-8563.

GRANDVIEW LIBRARY BOOK SALE
see library description in the chapter on entertainment

INTERNATIONAL GEM AND JEWELRY SHOW
Three day sales and exhibition event featuring loose gems and semi-precious stones, 14K gold and gemstone jewelry, costume jewelry and gift items. Held at Veteran's Memorial Auditorium. $5. 221-4341.

MCDONALD'S VALENTINE'S PROMOTION

From February 1-14, selected locations sell children's coupon books which can be redeemed from February 13-March 31. For only $1, your child will get twelve coupons good for various freebies such as sampler sized ice cream sundaes, boxes of McDonaldland cookies, ice cream cones and beverages. While it is not necessary to purchase another item in order to use your coupons, only one coupon per child may be used per visit. When all of the coupons are used, the value is about $9.

NOW MUSIC FESTIVAL

see Capital University description in the chapter on entertainment

UNITED BLACK WORLD WEEK CELEBRATION

Ohio State University celebration in observance of Black history month includes soul food luncheons, lectures, videos, children's activities, Igbajo Ball and other festivities. Most programs are free. 292-6584.

MARCH

BABY BARGAIN BOUTIQUE

New and used children's clothes, toys, furniture and even maternity clothes are offered by your neighbors who rent a table to sell their items. Table space rents for only $5 for non-commercial vendors and $10 for commercial vendors. This sale is presented twice a year in March and September at the Westerville Senior Center, 310 W. Main St., Westerville from 10-2.

BELLEPOINTE SALE

Manufacturer's warehouse sale of first quality better women's novelty themed sweaters, skirts, and knit tops. Current season and upcoming season's merchandise is available at savings of 50-60% off regular retail prices. The stock is priced at about $15-$75 at the sale. The four to ten day sales also feature daily specials and bargain tables. This company manufactures for Pappagallo, Talbott's, the Acorn and other upscale boutiques and department stores nationwide. The sales are held three times a year. 26 Israel Street, Westerville. Free. 895-8268.

DECORATORS' SHOW HOUSE

A different Columbus area home is tastefully decorated every two by some of the top interior designers in the area providing you with valuable decorating ideas. You can also shop at the adjacent tag sale featuring new decorators' scratch and dent pieces and donated new and used giftware and home furnishings. Tag sale savings are 30-60% off store prices. At the end of the Show House, the items used in its decoration are sold at about 30-60% off regular retail prices. Benefits Columbus Museum Of Art. Month long event from late April to late May. $6 admission. 888-2917.

EXTRAVAGANZA

Buy furniture, fine jewelry, toys, audio/stereo systems, clothes, gifts, hardware, athletic wear, ski equipment, luggage and leather goods, Warner Brothers/Disney merchandise, sequin tops, electronics, vacuum cleaners, leather apparel, video games, socks, watches, oil paintings, handmade sheepskin and alpaca rugs, ties, computers, CDs, ski equipment, tools, books, shoes, spas, musical instruments and more. Savings are 20-80% on popular brands from local and national companies. Vendors vary from show to show. Held three times a year at the Ohio State Fairgrounds, including a Holiday Extravaganza show. Free show admission, but $3 site parking fee. 644-3247 or (517) 332-3053.

MONEY TALKS EXPO

Ohio's largest financial exposition features two days of free workshops, seminars and exhibits. Nationally recognized portfolio managers and industry experts discuss retirement, starting a business, investing in international markets, selecting mutual funds, long term health care and insurance, creative uses of trusts and estate plans that work, tax shelters annuities, charitable giving, surfing the Internet to make money and other topics. You may attend as many seminars as you like. Sponsored by the International Association For Financial Planning, Nationwide Insurance , the Columbus Dispatch and other businesses. Usually held at the Columbus Convention Center. Admission is free. 451-4245 or 249-7111 ext. 3091.

NEW HOUSE SEMINAR

Displays of house plans by area builders and discussions by industry experts relating to building a new home. Order free tickets by mail or pick them up at the Columbus Dispatch. 461-5204.

SANCTUARY RE-RUN SALE

Now in its fifteenth year, this semi-annual sale is also held in September. You'll find gently used children's clothing in newborn to size fourteen, toys, furniture and related items at garage sale prices. The merchandise is sold by your friends and neighbors who set up tables to sell their children's items, with a portion of the proceeds going to maintenance projects on the structure. The Sanctuary is actually a church which is on the National Register of Historic Places, and now is used as a community recreation center. This three hour event is open to adults only, so please make babysitting arrangements for your children! 82 N. High St., Gahanna. 337-3737 ext. 1696 or 868-5353.

SHRINE CIRCUS

Clowns, animal acts, acrobatics and more will delight young and old alike. This eight day event begins in late March and last through early April. Ohio State Fairgrounds. Adults $4-$7, children under twelve, $2-$3.50. Pick up discount tickets at Big Bear supermarkets. 475-0058 or 644-3247.

SUPER BOWL OF GARAGE SALES

Find rock bottom prices on donated merchandise such as clothing, books, tools, household and gift items, small appliances, toys, linens and small furniture,. This day long event benefits the Delaware City Schools and is sponsored by the President's Advisory Council. Held from 8-2 at the Delaware Joint Vocational School, 1610 State Rt. 521, Delaware. 363-4499 or 369-6250.

APRIL

ACORN WAREHOUSE SALE

Four day sale of first quality, previous season women's apparel, consolidated from 41 stores, at savings of 60-70% off regular retail prices. There's also a selection of special purchase current season clothes at 40% off . Sale site varies. 451-4909.

CCAD STUDENT ART SHOW AND SALE
The Columbus College Of Art And Design annual student event is held one day and features artwork in all media.   This is a great chance to purchase quality artwork by tomorrow's prominent artists, at prices less than you would pay at area galleries. 224-9101

CENTRAL OHIO, GEM, MINERAL AND FOSSIL SHOW
Two day event featuring educational exhibits, lectures, sales, demonstrations, silent auctions, free gem identification and children's activities.   Sponsored by the Columbus Rock and Mineral Society and the Licking County Rock and Mineral Club.   Held at Veteran's Memorial Auditorium. $4 adult admission, $1 for children aged 6-16, under six admitted free. 221-4341.

COLUMBUS BOOKFAIR
One day event at the Aladdin Temple Shrine featuring 35 dealers in rare, used and collectible books, prints and other paper items. $2. 263-2903.

COLUMBUS CD AND RECORD SHOW
One day event held in January and April, where you can buy, sell or trade new, used and collectible albums, CDs and cassettes. You'll find music from the 1950's to the 1990's in all musical styles.   There are many great deals here! The events are held at Veteran's Memorial Auditorium and a North Columbus hotel. Admission is $3 for adults and kids are admitted for free. 261-1585.

COLUMBUS MICRO SYSTEMS WAREHOUSE SALE
Save 30-60% on scratch and dent, used and discontinued computer hardware and software at these sales.   The one day events are held twice a year in April or May and again in October. You'll find all the popular brands. 5087 Westerville Rd., Westerville, 794-1981.

EARLY CHILDHOOD SALE (ECS SALE)
This sale of gently used children's toys, clothing and accessories is held in the spring, generally in April. You'll find rock bottom prices on popular brands such as Fischer Price, Coleco, Oshkosh, Polly Flinders, Tickle Me and others. Held at the Leo Yassenoff Jewish Center, 1125 College Ave., Columbus, 231-2731.

GOLDEN HOBBY SHOW
1996 marked the 48th year for this event which showcases the artistic talent of seniors.   Art demonstrations, continuous performances, lectures and an art exhibition, highlight this family event. Held at the Martin Janis Senior Center in Columbus. Free. 644-7492.

KITE FESTIVAL
Held on the third Saturday of April, this event features kite flying for all ages, kitemaking competitions, children's kitemaking classes, stunt kite demonstrations, vendors and kite flying lessons. Free admission to all programs. Held at the Park of Roses. 645-7464.

OSU FRIENDS OF THE LIBRARY BOOK SALE
Two day event features great bargains on books and magazines, most priced at $1 and under. Held at the OSU Main Library. 292-3387.

OSU JAZZ FESTIVAL
One day event featuring local, regional and nationally known performers. Free. Held at Weigel Hall Auditorium. 292-2787.

TWIG ATTIC

A giant garage sale of new and used donated merchandise is held yearly as a fundraiser to benefit Children's Hospital. From trifles to treasures, you'll find household decor, clothes from local retailers, toys, gifts, jewelry and miscellaneous items. Prices are dirt cheap, with many being $5 and under. Admission is $1 for this one day event held at the Aladdin Temple Shrine, 3850 Stelzer Rd., Columbus, 475-2609 or 475-6042.

URBAN CONCERN GARAGE SALE

Two enormous buildings house new and used items such as adult and children's clothing, electronics, sporting goods, antiques and collectibles, hardware, linens, toys, baked goods, records, books and home decor which have been donated. The one day sale benefits a non-profit group which works with inner city residents to break the cycle of poverty in the South Linden area. It is a part of the ministry of the Xenos Christian Fellowship. The sale is held from 9-3. Located at 888 Freeway Dr. N., Buildings 11-12, Columbus, 784-8600.

USED BOOK SALE

The TWIGS group of the Licking Memorial Hospital, sponsors a four day sale of used books. Prices start at $2 the first day, the second and third day prices drop to $1 a book, and the last day it is $1 a bag. A small selection of collectible books may be initially priced somewhat higher, but still at a good deal. Located at the Centenary United Methodist Church, 102 E. Broadway, Granville, 587-3451.

MAY

DELAWARE ARTS FESTIVAL

Large juried show and sale of fine arts and crafts on the streets of downtown Delaware. Live entertainment. Free. 363-2695.

FUN FAIR

Two day children's event featuring games, face painting, performances and other free activities. Columbus Metropolitan Library, 96 S. Grant Avenue. 645-2770.

GASLIGHT REVUE

Vocal and dance performances by employees of Columbus Gas. 1996 is the 55th year for this event, which is held at Veteran's Memorial Auditorium. Free. 460-2000.

GERMAN VILLAGE VALUABLES SALE

One day community wide yard sale at over 100 homes and businesses throughout the Village. Pickup a free map at the German Village Society Office, 624 S. 3 St. 221-8888.

HERB AND CRAFT FESTIVAL

Sale of live medicinal and cooking herb plants, baked goods and craft items in Gahanna. One day event. Free. 471-4219.

INTERNATIONAL FAIR

Two day festival of dancing, foods, costumes and entertainment by Central Ohio ethnic groups. Held on the square in Sunbury. Free. 965-3901.

JOHNSTOWN LION'S CLUB FLEA MARKET
Held on Memorial Day on the village square in Johnstown. You'll find antiques, collectibles, new and used items. Prices and quality vary from vendor to vendor. 9-5. 967-1279.

LITHOPOLIS FLEA MARKET
Held on Memorial Day on Columbus Street. About sixty vendors sell antiques, collectibles, crafts as well as new and used items. Prices and quality vary from dealer to dealer. 7-5. 965-2684.

MEDIEVAL AND RENAISSANCE FESTIVAL
Step into living history during this unusual event featuring musical and other performances, jousting, human chess game, period crafts for sale and other activities in this re-created medieval fair. One day outdoors event at OSU. Free. 292-2324.

OHIO CAMERA COLLECTORS SOCIETY SHOW AND SALE
Two day event over Memorial Day weekend, featuring collectible and used cameras and equipment. Some new items are offered. $3 admission. 885-3224.

OHIO'S LARGEST GARAGE SALE
One day sale features 130 vendors offering new and used merchandise including antiques, collectibles, tools, furniture, toys, food, clothes, CDs and cassettes and other items. From trash to treasure, you'll find it here,. Look carefully to discover the best deals. Admission is $1 to the event, sponsored by the Lion's Club, held at the Knox County Fairgrounds in Mt. Vernon. 393-1301 or 392-1627.

POWELL VILLAGE ANTIQUE AND FLEA MARKET
Three times a year (May, July and September) the village is the site of an antique and collectible flea market. Vendors hawk their wares along the main thoroughfares and alleys. While prices vary from dealer to dealer, it's possible to get some great deals. 885-6034.

RECORD CONVENTION
One day event featuring albums, 45s, CDs and tapes bought, sold and traded. Held at Veteran's Memorial Auditorium. Free. 261-1585.

SUNBURY FLEA MARKET
Held on the square on Memorial Day. You'll find about 300 vendors selling new and used items, collectibles, antiques and what nots. Prices and quality vary from vendor to vendor. 7-5. 965-2684.

WHITE ELEPHANT SALE
1996 is the 32nd year for this two day garage sale which offers new and used merchandise such as clothing, sporting goods, toys, housewares, live plants etc., donated by businesses and community members. Held at Veteran's Memorial Auditorium to benefit the Columbus Cancer Clinic. Free. 235-5184 or 263-5006.

JUNE

COLUMBUS ARTS FESTIVAL STREET FAIR
Features over 300 artists from across the United States, selling their work, continuous entertainment on several stages, children's activities, demonstrations, food concessions by

local chefs and fine restaurants. One of the top 25 arts festivals in the country. Don't miss this event. Three day festival on downtown riverfront. Free. 224-2606.

FORE LOVE-GARAGE SALE
Gently used golf and tennis equipment, memorabilia, clothes, shoes, trophies, CDs and tapes, jewelry and other items are sold to benefit the local chapter of the American Cancer Society. The annual sale of donated items, held in the North end of Columbus, is featured during a two day weekend generally at the Lakes Golf and Country Club and the Wedgewood Golf and Country Club. If you have merchandise to donate and can't stop by the drop off site, a volunteer can arrange to pick it up at you home. 228-8466 or 792-0755

HERB DAYS
Gahanna is known as the herb capital of Ohio. Three day event features herbal cooking programs, prominent area chefs, live entertainment, demonstrations (herb bonsai, herb wreaths, potpourri) plus other festivities. This free family event takes place at the practice field of Gahanna Lincoln High School. 475-3342 or 471-6009.

POWELL DAYS
95 artists and antique/collectible dealers sell wares on the street. Entertainment is also featured. Free. 841-0990.

ROSE FESTIVAL
The peak of the rose season features a celebration with entertainment, arts and crafts, plant sales and the opportunity to see and smell 9,000 roses in the largest municipal rose garden in the U.S. Three day event at the Park of Roses. Free. 645-3300

SENIOR SALUTE
Columbus Symphony Orchestra concert, exhibits by area agencies serving seniors and a movie are featured during this annual event. Optional box lunches are available for $4. Tickets to this free event must be obtained in advance form the Franklin County Office On Aging, and are restricted to senior citizens only. The event is held at the Palace Theater, 34 W. Broad Street, Columbus. 462-5230.

TALBOTT'S SEMI-ANNUAL SALE
see January write-up

TUESDAYS AT TRINITY
Summer music series throughout the month at the Gloria Dei Worship Center of the Trinity Lutheran Seminary in Bexley. Features popular, classical and contemporary vocal and instrumental performances. Free. 235-4136.

WHITE ELEPHANT SALE
The Westerville Civic Symphony League sponsors this afternoon fundraiser which features garage sale prices on new and used items. You'll find home decor, gifts, toys, books and miscellaneous items. Held outside of the Otterbein College Library. 794-0401 or 890-3000.

YELLOW SPRINGS STREET FAIR
Arts and crafts fair and flea market features new and used merchandise, entertainment and food concessions in this quaint town. 45 minutes from Dublin. Free. (513) 767-2686.

JULY

ANDERSONS GENERAL STORE
Bring in your dog for a free flea dip. This event is held in July and August and would cost you $20-$25 if it were done at an area veterinary clinic. Be sure to bring an old towel so you can dry off your dog. Dogs must be on a leash and collar, be handled by an adult and must be at least three months old. Area nonprofit organizations will be available to assist . Your optional donation benefits these groups. Held at 5800 Alshire Rd. (864-8800) and 7000 Bent Tree Blvd. (766-9500) locations. 9-2.

FABRIC FARMS ANNUAL SUMMER SALE
See January description. 3590 Riverside Drive 451-9300

HAGGLER'S DAY
About 75 vendors sent up along the streets of Olde Worthington and sell new and used trash to treasure. You'll find antiques, collectibles, miscellaneous household items clothing, gifts, books, toys, furniture and what-nots. This day long event is sponsored by the Olde Worthington Business Association. Admission is free. Held on High Street and W. Dublin Granville Rd. 436-3100.

JAZZ AND RIB FEST
Ribs prepared by local restaurants, rib tasting contests, continuous jazz performances by local groups, plus headliners such as Chick Corea Band. Held in conjunction with the riverfront Jazz Festival. Three day event held on the last weekend of July along the downtown riverfront. Free. 221-1321 or 645-3300.

KIDS EXPO
Features appearances by costumed characters, continuous entertainment, exhibitor booths, samples of products. Held the last weekend in July at the Columbus Convention Center. Sponsored by WTTE 28 Kids Club. Free. 895-2800.

KROGER SENIOR EXPO
Two day event presents exhibitor booths with information on a wide variety of products and services of interest to seniors, product samples, health screenings and seminars. Local, regional and nationally recognized entertainment, such as the Guy Lombardo Orchestra, will perform throughout the expo. Free admission to Golden Buckeye cardholders. $2 for all others. Held at the Columbus Convention Center. 221-6700.

LANCASTER FESTIVAL
In mid July, this eleven day music, art, theater and dance festival highlights some of the most noted regional, national and internationally acclaimed artists. Over 50 public performances and exhibitions are held in various Lancaster sites and include programs for adults, families and children, many of which are free. Ben Vereen, Tony Randall, Christopher Reeve, Roberta Flack, the Chicago Brass Quintet have appeared as guest artists. Call to be added to their mailing list. Held at various sites in Lancaster. 687-4808 or 653-8251.

POWELL VILLAGE ANTIQUE AND FLEA MARKET
See May description.

RED, WHITE AND BOOM
On July 3, there's entertainment from noon to midnight with prominent local, regional and nationally recognized performers. A children's entertainment area, parade at 7p.m. and fireworks highlight this event. Held on the downtown riverfront. Free. 645-3300.

SIDEWALK SALES
July is a popular time for malls and strip shopping centers to have sidewalk sales where savings are 30-80% off regular retail prices. Lane Avenue Shopping Center, Arlington Square, New Market mall and other shopping spots typically have these sales during the second week of July. Watch the newspapers.

WESTERVILLE MUSIC AND ART FESTIVAL
Held on the second weekend in July on the Otterbein College campus. Features over 160 fine art and crafts artists exhibiting and selling their works, demonstrations, continuous entertainment and a children's activity area. Free. 882-8917.

AUGUST

ANDERSONS GENERAL STORE
Bring in your dog for a free flea dip. This event is held in July and August and would cost you $20-$25 if it were done at an area veterinary clinic. Be sure to bring an old towel so you can dry off your dog. Dogs must be on a leash and collar, be handled by an adult and must be at least three months old. Area nonprofit organizations will be available to assist . Your optional donation benefits these groups. Held at 5800 Alshire Rd. (864-8800) and 7000 Bent Tree Blvd. (766-9500) locations. 9-2.

ARTS AND CRAFTS FESTIVALE
Enjoy the picturesque setting of a European street at the Continent as you browse amongst 75 booths where arts and crafts are being sold. Two day event with strolling entertainment. Free. 846-0418. (Continent sidewalk sale is the third weekend)

DESANTIS FLORIST ANNUAL GARAGE SALE
This clearance sale features savings of up to 50% on dried and silk floral arrangements, planters, baskets and miscellaneous items. This two day sale is held on a weekend from 9-5. 865 DeSantis Court, Columbus, 451-4414.

DUBLIN MUSIC BOOSTERS GIANT GARAGE SALE
Day long garage sale features merchandise from 150 families and includes household, clothing, books, CDs, tools, toys, sporting goods, furniture and what-nots at rock bottom prices. Proceeds benefit the Dublin Music Boosters, a non-profit organization supporting music programs in the Dublin Schools. Held at the Dublin Coffin High School, 6780 Coffman Rd., Dublin, 889-9905 or 761-8466.

HEALTH AND HARMONY FAIR
Sales booths, demonstrations and workshops on earth consciousness, holistic products and services, spiritual awareness, healing modalities, healthy foods, crystals and more. Held in mid August at the Murphy Archeological site in Newark. $3 for adults and $1 for kids. 587-3361

NATIONAL BARGAIN HUNTING WEEK
Debbie Keri-Brown, the author of Bargain Hunting In Central Ohio, is the founder of this week, which has it's inaugural celebration August 5 through 11, 1996. It will be take place the first Monday through the following Thursday in August every year. Listed in the book, Chase's Annual Events, this week is a time when businesses and shoppers can celebrate the thrill of the hunt for those bargains and the triumph of the find through their own personal celebrations, sales and special ways of saying "I am proud to be a bargain hunter" or "this deal's for you". Write to me and let me know what you are planning or what you have done to celebrate National Bargain Hunting Week. For a free list of suggested activities, send a self addressed stamped envelope to Lotus Press, P.O. Box 8446, Westerville, Ohio, 43086-8446.

OHIO STATE FAIR
Commercial, agricultural and international exhibits and vendors, entertainment on several stages and in all musical styles, demonstrations, celebrity appearances are all included in your $6 admission fee for adults or $4 for ages 3-4, seniors $2. Admission to the opening night is only $3 as some exhibitors will not be open. The fair has special days set aside where additional savings or free admission are available: free admission for veteran's, family value days, junior sports day, disabilities day and others. An additional $10 fee lets you enjoy unlimited midway rides which is a marked savings over individual ticket prices. Nationally recognized entertainment (such as Bob Hope, Wayne Newton, the Statler Brothers) perform in the 12,000 seat Celeste Center at an additional fee of $6-$10. Parking is $3. 644-3247.

WHITE SALES
White sales are typically held in August and January and provide the opportunity for you to purchase linens, blankets, bedspreads, towels and similar items at substantial savings. The department and specialty stores typically offer 30-60% savings on many items in their inventory.

WORTHINGTON FOLKLIFE CELEBRATION
see Worthington Arts Council description in the entertainment chapter.

SEPTEMBER

ACORN WAREHOUSE SALE
see January description

ARTISTS-IN-SCHOOLS PREVIEW NIGHT
The Greater Columbus Arts Council's program holds an annual showcase of over 125 professional artists which includes displays, demonstrations and ongoing sample performances in music, theater, dance, video and multi-arts. While the event provides facilities/organizations which present performances, the opportunity to evaluate the artists before contracting with them, The general public is welcome to attend and will find this quite enjoyable. Held at the Galbreath Pavilion of the Ohio Theater. Free. 224-2606.

BABY BARGAIN BOUTIQUE
See March description. The sale is held twice a year.

DUBLIN FESTIVAL OF THE ARTS

Over 125 artists exhibit and sell their works, entertainment, food concessions and kid's activities are also featured. Sponsored by the Dublin Women's Club on the second Sunday in September in historic Dublin. Free. 766-585.

The main branch of the Columbus Metropolitan Library features this very large sale of used and collectible books over a two day weekend. Most books are priced at 50 cents to $5. Admission is free. Consider attending the pre-sale party where admission is $3 for Friends of the Library members and $5 for nonmembers. The party includes entertainment and special happenings, plus the chance to get first pick at the books. The library is at 96 S. Grant Avenue. 645-2800

EXTRAVAGANZA

Buy furniture, fine jewelry, toys, audio/stereo systems, clothes, gifts, hardware, athletic wear, ski equipment, luggage and leather goods, Warner Brothers/Disney merchandise, sequin tops, electronics, vacuum cleaners, leather apparel, video games, socks, watches, oil paintings, handmade sheepskin and alpaca rungs, ties, computers, CDs, ski equipment, tools, books, shoes, spas, musical instruments and more. Savings are 20-80% on popular brands from local and national companies. Vendors vary from show to show. Held three times a year at the Ohio State Fairgrounds, including a Holiday Extravaganza show. Free show admission, but $3 site parking fee. 644-3247 or (517) 332-3053.

FAMOUS SPORTSWEAR TWO DAY SALE

see description on page 50

FRIENDS OF THE LIBRARY BOOKSALE

The main branch of the Columbus Metropolitan Library features this very large sale of used and collectible books over a two day weekend. Most books are priced at 50 cents to $5. Admission is free. Consider attending the pre-sale party where admission is $3 for Friends of the Library members and $5 for nonmembers. The party includes entertainment and special happenings, plus the chance to get first pick at the books. The library is 96 S. Grant Avenue. 645-2800

GAHANNA FLEA MARKET

Held on the third Sunday in September, this event features over 300 booths of new and used merchandise in addition to antiques and collectibles. Mill Street in Old Gahanna. 9-5. $1 admission. 471-1657 or 478-2749.

GREEK FESTIVAL

The Annunciation Greek Orthodox Cathedral, 555 North High Street, is the site of a four day celebration of Greek culture over the Labor Day weekend. You'll find entertainment, demonstrations, arts and crafts, dancing, travel films and food concessions. Adults $3 for three days, seniors $2.50 for three days, kids under twelve are free. Admission is free for everyone on Friday from 11-3. 224-9020.

GROVE CITY ARTS IN THE ALLEY

100 artists sell their work, entertainment and kids activities are included. Free two day event. 871-9049.

HOT TIMES IN OLD TOWN EAST

Community arts festival and streetfair featuring music, exhibits, entertainment and kids activities. Two day event is held along Parsons Avenue. Free. 221-4411.

KIDSPEAK KIDSFEST
Children's festival with entertainment on five stages, costumed characters, rides, parade, puppet shows, fireworks, contests, vendor booths, games and more. One day event is held at Franklin Park. Sponsored by the Columbus Recreation and Parks Department. Free. 645-3380.

LEUKEMIA SOCIETY'S GARAGE SALE
One day sale in late September, features new and used household decor, tools, books and toys. It benefits research, patient assistance and educational programs for the Leukemia Society. of course, you won't want to miss the One More Time's racks for great deals on men's and women's apparel and accessories. Held at One More Time, an upscale consignment store, 1521 W. Fifth Avenue, Grandview, 486-0031.

NORTHWEST ARTS AND CRAFTS FAIR
Over 65 artists sell their work at this one day event on the first weekend of September. Held at the Bethel Center Shopping Center. Free. 451-2908 or 442-1957.

OHIO RENAISSANCE FESTIVAL
Pick up your free passes to the festival at area Majestic Paint Stores. You'll get one free pass for every $25 you spend. This thirty acre festival will transport your back to the time of Elizabethan England. There's period performances, costumed arts and crafts vendors, jousting, and other continuous festivities. Regular admission fee is $11.95 for adults and $5 for children. Located sixty miles South of Columbus near Waynesville (and the two outlet malls). Held for five weekends from early September through mid October. (513) 897-7000.

OLD WORTHINGTON MARKET DAY
Hop aboard the free shuttle from Thomas Worthington High School to this wonderful hodge podge of stuff, unless of course you're lucky enough to find nearby parking. The eclectic mix of merchandise includes arts and crafts, sidewalk sales by downtown vendors and a flea market with new and used items. The event also includes free games and crafts for kids, musical entertainment, plus food for purchase. The night before is the free, Sunsplash Fest featuring Arnett Howard and the Creole Funk Band in concert. Running concurrently with the Market Day, the Worthington Public Library (805 Hartford Street, 885-3185) will hold a book sale with paperbacks at fifty cents and hardbacks at $1, plus upscale magazines such as Connoisseur for only a quarter. Held in downtown Worthington at High Street and W. Dublin Granville Rd. One day event from 9-5. Free. 888-3040.

POWELL VILLAGE ANTIQUE AND FLEA MARKET
See May listing.

SANCTUARY RE-RUN SALE
See March description

UPPER ARLINGTON LABOR DAY ARTS FESTIVAL
see Upper Arlington Cultural Arts Commission listing in the entertainment chapter

WOMEN'S HEALTH DAY
Grant Medical Center and other corporate sponsors team up to present a day of free health and wellness events. Educational presentations, health displays and screenings, entertainment and a nationally recognized keynote speaker are featured. Advance tickets are needed to attend the keynote speaker's program. The event site is divided into different

pavilions, each focusing on an area of interest; new discoveries, for women only, women in motion, mind-body connection, caring for our families, feeling great from the inside out and women's health for a lifetime. Childcare is available on site at a nominal fee and includes activities and snacks. COTA offers free round trip passes for the event. Generally held at the Greater Columbus Convention Center, 400, N. High St., Columbus, 444-7268.

OCTOBER

BARGAIN BOX
Giant garage sale of new and used household items, furniture, clothing, antiques and collectibles, toys and sporting goods donated by merchants and families. Held on the first weekend of October to benefit the Junior League. This is Central Ohio's largest garage sale. Two day event held at Veteran's Memorial Auditorium. Free. 464-2717 or 221-4341.

CIRCLEVILLE PUMPKIN SHOW
Pumpkins and pumpkins products are on display and for sale, parades, contests, food concessions and arts and crafts are also featured. Held over four days, the third weekend in October in downtown Circleville. Free. 474-4224 or 474-7000.

COLUMBUS MICRO SYSTEMS WAREHOUSE SALES
See April listing for these twice a year sales

COLUMBUS USA WEEKEND
Arts festival, midway with rides, family games, local/regional/nationally recognized entertainment, fireworks and a parade. Three day event held the first weekend in October along the downtown riverfront. Free. 481-7534.

FIRST COMMUNITY VILLAGE OKTOBERFEST
Celebrate Oktoberfest with a fashion show and German music at this free, community event. An optional German luncheon will be served for a nominal fee. 18800 Riverside Dr., Columbus, 486-9511.

GIANT COLUMBUS FANTASTIC CAMERA SHOW AND COMPUTER SWAP
Sixty dealers buy, sell and trade new and used cameras and computer equipment and related items, computer programs, photographs, stereo cards and books. Free appraisals of old photographic items. One day event at the Aladdin Temple. $4. 475-2609.

HERB FAIR
The Central Ohio Unit of the Herb Society Of America co-sponsors this one day event at Inniswood Metro Gardens in Westerville. There's herbal cooking programs, crafts demonstrations, entertainment and a sale of herb plants at fair prices. You'll enjoy the breathtaking beauty of this park, which is my favorite among all those in the Metro Park system. Admission is free. 901-0700.

INTERNATIONAL GEM AND JEWELRY SHOW
Three day event. See February description.

OTTERBEIN COLLEGE BOOK SALE
This one day sale of used books, benefits the scholarship fund. Held at the Courtright Memorial Library at the college in Westerville, from 9-3. 823-1215.

REVCO HEALTH AND BEAUTY EXPO
Health information, beauty tips, product samples, demonstrations, appearances by nationally recognized speakers and Hollywood celebrities, plus beauty makeovers await you at this two day event. Admission is free to the event which is generally held at the Columbus Convention Center. 235-3024 or 645-5000.

SECRET SANTA HOLIDAY HOUSE CRAFT SHOW
Seventy artists exhibit and sell their works at the Wellington School in Upper Arlington. $2. 487-2499.

SKI SWAP AT THE SKISMITH
One weekend in mid October, you'll find great deals on used ski equipment and clothing, consigned by your neighbors. Proceeds from the event benefit the Columbus Ski Club. Held at The Skismith, 4550 Kenny Rd., Columbus, 457-1868.

UNIVERSAL LIGHT EXPOSITION
Expand your horizons at this enlightening, metaphysical expo which features entertainment/demonstrations, over 150 booths of products and services relating to healthy lifestyles, natural foods, jewelry, gems, healing, adornment and other areas. Continuous lectures, demonstrations and workshops feature about 100 experts form across the country and Europe. Topics include book discussions by noted authors, pet healing, devic gardening, aromatherapy, UFOs, astrology, dreams, crystals, past lives, angels and other topics. A small portion of these carry an extra fee of about $10 per program, but the majority are free with your admission price of $6. This two day event is usually held at Veteran's Memorial Auditorium in Columbus. 262-5793 or 262-0146.

YELLOW SPRINGS STREET FAIR
see June listing

NOVEMBER

BELLEPOINTE WAREHOUSE SALE
see March description

CAMPUS COMMODITIES
Generally once a year, and sometimes twice, this wholesale business offers quality apparel at a special sale to the public, where you can save about 40% off regular retail prices. Campus is a licensee of college logo emblazoned apparel and accessories. It designs its own lines which are sold to college bookstores such as Conrad's Gifts, Buckeye Corner, Long's College Book Company and others across the nation. The business also sells similar items with custom imprinting or embroidered logos to resort and sports stores as well as to catalogue companies. The goods are generally sold under the TD Sportsline brand. Located at 101 Stover Dr., Delaware. 369-9559.

COLUMBUS ARTS AND CRAFTS FAIR
Over 150 artists sell quality, handmade works in all media. Two day event held in late November at the Aladdin Temple. $2 admission. 486-4991 or 268-4554.

COLUMBUS INTERNATIONAL FESTIVAL
Food, music, dancing and vendors representing the rich ethnic culture found in Ohio, are featured in this two day spectacular event at Veteran's Memorial Auditorium. Don't miss this event! 228-4010.

COLUMBUS RECORD CONVENTION
Columbus' original record convention offers new and used records, cassettes and sheet music for sale or trade. Held on the first Saturday in November at Veterans Memorial Auditorium. $2.50 admission. 261-1585.

EDDIE BAUER WAREHOUSE SALE
Over $8 million in overstocked and discontinued items from their national catalogue and 180 stores is available at savings of 50-60% (higher discounts towards the end of the sale). You'll find linens, towels, specialty foods, luggage, travel accessories, men's and women's apparel/outerware/shoes in traditional, rugged and keyed contemporary styles. There is a very limited selection of kids clothes. This month long sale is held at Veteran's Memorial Auditorium in downtown Columbus. 224-3100.

EXTRAVAGANZA
Buy furniture, fine jewelry, toys, audio/stereo systems, clothes, gifts, hardware, athletic wear, ski equipment, luggage and leather goods, Warner Brothers/Disney merchandise, sequin tops, electronics, vacuum cleaners, leather apparel, video games, socks, watches, oil paintings, handmade sheepskin and alpaca rugs, ties, computers, CDs, ski equipment, tools, books, shoes, spas, musical instruments and more. Savings are 20-80% on popular brands from local and national companies. Vendors vary from show to show. Held three times a year at the Ohio State Fairgrounds, including a Holiday Extravaganza show. Free show admission, but $3 site parking fee. 644-3247 or (517) 332-3053.

FESTIVAL OF THE TREES
Spectacular display of over 100 professionally decorated holiday trees and wreaths, children's activities, handmade gingerbread houses by area chefs, arts and crafts for sale and non-stop entertainment. Trees are auctioned in a private patron preview party before the event officially opens to the public. Held on the Monday through Sunday of Thanksgiving, including Thanksgiving Day, at the Columbus Convention Center. Special Family Days are Monday through Wednesday where groups of five are admitted at a bargain price of only $10 and $1 for each additional person. Don't miss this event regardless of what is your religious belief. $5 adult admission, $3 for kids. 722-2996.

JEWISH BOOKFAIR
A week-long celebration of Jewish culture features author visits, luncheons, craft workshops and performances for all ages. Nationally recognized writers such as Belva Plain, Letty Pogrebin, Molly Katz, Allen Zweibel and Lawrence Kushner have appeared in the past. Luncheon/lecture programs are $8-$10, craft workshops are $1-$5, and entertainment is free to $10. Books are also available at typical retail prices. Childcare is available at a nominal fee. Leo Yassenoff Jewish Center, 1125 College Avenue, Columbus, 231-2731.

NORTHWEST MULTI COURSE CHRISTMAS SALE
Seven area golf courses join to offer a clearance sale of apparel, golf clubs, golf shoes and related accessory items at 30-70% off. You'll find such brands as Ashworth, Aureus, Maxi, Spaulding, Izod, Reebok, Ping, Pro Group, Foot Joy, Aurea, Hogan and others. The three day sale is featured at the Shamrock Golf Club, 4436 Powell Rd. 792-6630.

TWIG BAZAAR
Five acres of handcrafted items, antiques, homemade baked goods, toys and gifts are featured at the world's largest one day bazaar. Benefits Children's Hospital. Held on the second Sunday in November at the Ohio State Fairgrounds. Free. 644-3247.

ULTIMATE GARAGE SALE
Golf apparel and related paraphernalia is available at savings of 40-70%. Three area golf shops (Royal American Links, Bent Tree Golf Club and Black Hawk Golf Club) have joined forces to sell off about $250,000 in excess inventory. One day event is held at the Royal American Links banquet Hall, 3300 Miller Paul Rd., Galena, 965-1215 or 965-5122.

DECEMBER

FIRST NIGHT COLUMBUS
Alcohol free, family oriented New Year's Eve celebration is a good value compared to other area festivities and dining where you could expect to pay $25-$125 per person. The event includes arts and crafts workshops, a grand procession, 400 performance artists to entertain you, a teen dance and fireworks display held at several downtown Columbus sites. While 90% of the events are indoors, you'll still have to brave the elements to go from site to site. Free hot chocolate, balloons and popcorn are available. Area restaurants will offer food at fair prices. Volunteer at the event and you'll enjoy it all for free! Your $6 admission to the event also includes free COSI admission from 3-5 that day. Purchase tickets at Krogers and Ticketmaster locations. Held from 3p.m. to midnight on New Year's Eve. 575-9777.

HILLIARD HOLLYFEST
82 arts and crafts booths, continuous entertainment, Santaland, and display of professionally designed wreaths are featured in this three day holiday event. Held on the first weekend of December at the Hilliard High School. $2 admission. 876-7666.

HOLIDAY CHOIRFEST
Hundreds of senior citizens from Franklin county choruses perform holiday and popular tunes at the Martin Janis Senior Center, 600 East 11th Avenue. There will be dancing to recorded music before and after the concert. Free. 645-3106

SANTA'S SURPLUS
This store is only open seasonally from early November through the end of December, and offers closeouts, overstocks and discontinued toys, gifts, Christmas and home decor items. The quality varies form budget to better, and includes popular brands such as Hasbro and Playskool. Savings are 20-65%. The business operates one or more temporary sites in Columbus, which change each year. Check the newspapers or directory assistance in mid November.

WHITE LIGHTS OF CHRISTMAS
Tour of the downtown holiday lights aboard gaily decorated COTA busses. Tours leave from the COTA terminal at Columbus City Center from the first Monday in December until a few days after Christmas. Tours are Monday through Thursday 5:45-10:15p.m. and Friday/Thursday 5:45-11p.m. The coach does not operate December 24 and 25. Admission is free, but pick up your tickets in advance at the special booth on the street level of the parking garage from 10a.m. to 9p.m. Monday through Saturday. 228-4101.

TOYS

AMAZING TOY STORE
30 Westerville Square, Westerville, 43081, 899-7204
1768 Columbus Pike, Delaware, 43015, 363-9634

Save 30-70% on toys at these strip shopping center sites. While not as large as a Toys R Us, the stores nonetheless, have a generous selection of first quality closeouts, overstocks and discontinued items in a cozy and non-overwhelming atmosphere. You'll find all your favorite brands including Playskool, Hasbro, Fischer Price, Coleco and others. You'll also find baseball cards and educational books. The stores are planning interactive play areas where kids can have fun while mom and dad shop. Watch for fun special events which are now in the planning stages. M-Sat 10-8, Sun 12-5.

DROWSY DRAGON
34 Maplewood Avenue, Columbus, 43213, 231-8534

A large selection of unusual chess games can be found at fair prices. The store specializes in role playing games, board games, lead and pewter miniatures and historical games. Offers a 10% discount on TSI products. The far corner of the store has a sizeable offering of similar types of used games at least 40% off the new price. M/W 11-6, Tu/Th 11-9, F/Sun 10-3.

KAYBEE TOYS AND HOBBY SHOPS
1719 Northland Mallway, Columbus, 43229, 267-8120
2715 Eastland Mall, Columbus 43232, 863-6800
4337 Westland Mall, Columbus, 43228, 272-8254
157 Columbus City Center Dr., Columbus, 43215, 221-9258
264 Southland Mall, Marion, 389-6266
1635 River Valley Mall., Lancaster, 687-0313
3575 N. Maple Ave., Zanesville, 452-6563
771 S. 30 St., Heath, 522-4100

Half of the inventory consists of first quality prior season and discontinued toys which are available at savings of about 20-60%. You will find all of the highly sought after brands such as Fisher-Price, Playskool, Coleco, Buddy-L and others. Nintendo games are also available at similar savings. M-Sat 10-9, Sun 12-5.

MAGIC COLLECTION
6663F Huntley Rd., Columbus, 43229, 848-8749

Although this store sells mostly new magical tricks and illusions, you'll find a small selection of used items at savings of 30-60% off the new price. There's also a showcase filled with new, discontinued and clearance items at a 20% savings. Instructional videos may be rented at a cost of $5 per week. M-F 12-7, Sat 10-4.

MINIATURES UNLIMITED
6130 Busch Blvd., Columbus, 43229, 846-MINI (6464)

This store purchases inventories from retailers who are going out of business, discontinued merchandise and manufacturer closeouts. While the majority of the merchandise is first quality, there is some slightly damaged merchandise which is clearly marked and usually in a separate area of the store. You can save 10-40% off dollhouses, furniture, dollhouse wallpaper, building and electrical supplies for dollhouses, as well as Erna Meyer dolls. You'll also find a large selection of decorative kites at value prices. M-Sat 10-7, Sun 12-5.

SAMMIE'S CARD SHOP
50 W. Olentangy St., Powell, 43065, 431-5152

Located in an old church in the heart of Powell, this store boasts an extensive selection of sport cards for avid and novice collectors at very competitive prices. M-F 3-7, Sat 12-3.

TOYS R US
4340 W. Broad St., Columbus,. 43228, 274-3389
4285 Groves Rd., Columbus, 43232, 866-9163
1265 Morse Rd., Columbus, 43229, 268-3586
6547 Sawmill Rd., Dublin, 43017, 792-9194

This store features a large clearance section of discontinued, overstock and boxed damaged toys at savings of 30-80% off regular retail prices. Special values and reduced merchandise are also scattered throughout the store. You'll find a large selection of toys, games, children's furniture, bicycles, sporting goods, carriages, infant clothes and accessories from all major manufacturers at everyday low cost of about 10-20% less than manufacturer's suggested retail prices. M-Sat 10-9, Sun 12-5.

YANKEE TRADER
463 N. High St., Columbus, 43215, 228-1322

This store offers a large selection of paper and party goods, novelties, gags, seasonal and holiday items, decorations and carnival type prizes. Closeouts, buyouts, discontinued stock and volume buying enable this business to offer savings of 10-50% on many items. If you purchase a dozen of the same product, you'll be entitled to a further savings of about 15%. This is a fun store to purchase prizes for kids' parties as well as stocking stuffers. M-F 8:30-5:30, Sat 8:30-3:30.

ALSO SEE

All For One, Baby Bargain Boutique, Baby Superstore, Bearly Worn Clothes, Berwick Corner Outlet, Columbus' Largest Garage Sale, Columbus Metropolitan Library, Doll

House, Dublin Music Boosters Giant Garage Sale, Early Childhood Sale, Extravaganza, Family Dollar, Garage Sales, Golden Hobby Shop, Grove City Thrift Shop, Guys And Dolls, It's Only $1.00, Itzadeal, J.C. Penney Outlet Store, Jefersonville Outlet Center, Just For Kids, Kids And Moms Again, Kids Choice And Alterations By Gosia, Kids Kastle, Kinderduds, Lake Erie Factory Outlet Center, Leukemia Society's Garage Sale, Lil Rascals, Liquidations Now, Little People-Wear It Again, 99 Cent Shops, Nearly New Shop, Odd Lots, Ohio Factory Shops, Old Worthington Market Day, Once Upon A Child, Only $1, Outreach Christian Books And Records, Radio Shack Outlet Store, Sam's Club, Sanctuary Re-Run Sale, Schottenstein's, South Drive In Theater, Springfield Antique Show and Flea Market, Trader Tots, Treasure Trunk, Tuesday Morning, Twig Attic, Uptown Kids, Urban Concern Garage Sale, Video Trader and Warehouse Club

BARGAIN HUNTING TERMINOLOGY

BAIT AND SWITCH
How many times have you seen an ad in a newspaper or advertised on the radio and have gone to the store to purchase the item, only to find that it is supposedly sold out? Or perhaps you were told that the advertised product was inferior and that a different, higher priced product in the store would be a better value? This bait and switch tactic is illegal! Insist on seeing the advertised item.

BANKRUPT STOCK
A business which is in financial trouble, will sell their inventory to another business at prices below wholesale, to pay off their creditors. The business which purchases the inventory, is able to resell it to the public at far below regular retail prices. Bankrupt stock is also referred to as liquidations or liquidation merchandise. Schottenstein's buys bankrupt stock in addition to other types of merchandise.

BETTER QUALITY
Quality workmanship, durability and unique styling, characterize this merchandise.

BUDGET QUALITY
Inexpensive components, simple styling and often imprecise workmanship, characterize this type of merchandise. However, in some cases, you might be inclined to purchase these products due to their low cost or short term need.

BUYOUTS
This is a broad term which can refer to the act of purchasing all of the inventory of a business or all of a particular type of merchandise such as a buyout of bankrupt stock, a buyout of overruns etc.

CANCELLED GOODS (CANCELLATIONS)
Due to late delivery, financial difficulties or a variety of other reasons, a retailer may decide not to accept delivery of an order which was placed with a manufacturer. This merchandise, if it cannot be resold to another retailer at the regular wholesale price, becomes surplus merchandise which is sold to another retailer below wholesale. This business then resells it to the public at a percentage below its regular retail price.

CLOSEOUTS
A small amount remaining of a certain style or model is sold below wholesale in order to make room for new merchandise at manufacturer. This is sometimes also refereed to as

odd lots. This term is additionally used to refer to styles or models which will be discontinued by the manufacturer. A business which purchases this inventory, will resell it to the consumer at a percentage below its retail price. It is important to consider whether parts will be available in the future for your purchase if needed.

COMBINATION PRICING

This method is used to encourage you to buy a group of related items at a fixed price, such as a patio set consisting of two lounge chairs, a table and an umbrella. Check to ensure that this combination price is really offering you a savings, and that it is not merely the sum of the prices for each individually marked item. Be sure that you can use all of the items in the group before you decide to make your purchase.

DIRECT IMPORT PRICES

Similar to "factory direct" or "manufacturer direct" prices in that the middleman has been eliminated by importing directly, in this case, from the overseas company.

DISCONTINUED MERCHANDISE

This term is used to refer to models or styles which will no longer be manufactured. A business which purchases this inventory, will sell it to you at a percentage below its retail price. You should inquire as to whether parts will be available for your purchase in the future.

DISCOUNT

A percentage or dollar amount off the regular retail price.

FACTORY DIRECT

You have seen this phrase many times, but does it mean a good value? Not always. To most people, the term implies that the retailer has purchased inventory directly from the factory or manufacturer and has eliminated the middleman's markup. This happens frequently in big volume purchases. This phrase also implies that you are being offered savings from regular retail prices. In many instances, this is the case. However, some unscrupulous businesses will use that phrase to mislead you into believing that you will be saving money. There are many manufacturers who always sell their products directly to retailers at traditional wholesale prices. So the phrase, factory direct, does not always indicate a good value. When in doubt, ask the store's staff.

FACTORY OUTLET MALL OR FACTORY OUTLET SHOPPING CENTER

A group of stores under one roof, in one strip shopping center or in a specified area (such as the Aurora Farms Factory Outlets) which are supposed to be factory outlets or manufacturers' outlets (see description above). Most consumers expect that all of the stores in this shopping facility will provide good values on all of their products. But this is not always so! Often, there will be businesses intermingled among the true outlets, which do not discount at all, just to give a good tenant mixture. These malls provide an opportunity to visit many stores in one easy trip. Find out about the outlet malls' special seasonal sales which offer even greater savings.

FACTORY OUTLET OR MANUFACTURER'S OUTLET

In this business, you can purchase merchandise in a retail store which is often owned and operated by the manufacturer. Sometimes these retail businesses are located within, or adjacent to, the manufacturing facility. In another instance, there may be one or more factory outlets , owned by the same manufacturer, in other parts of town or even in other cities. The factory outlet generally provides you with the opportunity to see the manufacturer's full line of goods. This is not always possible in other stores as businesses tend to stock only those items which sell best and often like to have a variety of products from several manufacturers. The factory outlet does not always provide a discount on their first quality, current merchandise. If it does, savings can vary from 10-60% depending on the store. The outlet may also carry discontinued, past season, overstocks, seconds and otherwise blemished goods at savings of up top 90% depending on the store. Perhaps only a small portion of the factory outlet's stock is discounted, as is the case with Krema Products. However, since it is difficult to find their full line of peanut butters at any one grocery, the outlet store is a good option if you are loyal to the Krema brand. Many factory outlets also provide the opportunity to purchase food products almost right out of the oven. Each factory outlet operates differently. Some businesses will use the words, factory outlet, to let you know that they are the only store in a certain geographic area to sell a certain product. The store may sell items from one or more different manufacturers. This does not imply that the store is offering you a savings off the retail price. By understanding the nature of these outlets, you can be a more informed shopper.

FIRST QUALITY
Merchandise which has no visible or hidden defects or flaws in workmanship, design, material or pattern.

FLOOR SAMPLE OR "DEMO"
A demonstration model or style of merchandise which is displayed in the store. These sometimes get a little dirty or may be come scratched due to customer use. Savings on floor samples/demos vary from store to store, but are generally 20-60%. Be sure to inquire about the floor sample's/demo's warranty prior to making your purchase. Often, you will be compromising on a warranty in exchange for this lower price. Floor samples are also referred to demonstration models. Automobiles can often be purchased at substantial savings through car dealers, if they have been "demos".

FREIGHT DAMAGED OR SALVAGE
All or part of a shipment from a manufacturer may be chipped, dented or otherwise damaged in transit. The entire shipment will then be marked "freight damaged", and sold to a business way below wholesale even though there are likely to be many undamaged items. The savings are then passed on to you.

FREQUENT BUYER PROGRAMS
This is a popular program, which unfortunately is not widely advertised. You'll need to ask your favorite stores if they have this opportunity. Each time you make a purchase of a particular item or a certain dollar amount, a card is punched or marked off to record the transaction. You keep the card with you and present it when making your purchases. After you have reached a pre-determined amount, you are entitled to a bonus of some sort: a free item, a gift certificate in the store, a discount on your next purchase etc. Another similar method which some stores use is that you have to save your receipts and when a certain dollar amount is accumulated, you are entitled to one of the items mentioned above.

GRADED SECONDS OR SELECTED SECONDS
The merchandise has been hand sorted to extract only that which has minor flaws which will probably not affect the performance or appeal of the product.

IRREGULARS
Merchandise with minimal imperfections which are hardly noticeable and may not affect its performance or durability. Some seconds, however, are marked irregular.

JOBBER
The wholesaler who serves as the middleman between the retailer and the manufacturer. Not all manufacturers deal through jobbers. When you read the advertisements which state "factory direct" or "no middleman", the jobber is the one who is supposedly out of the picture.

KNOCKOFFS
This phenomenon runs rampant in the garment industry in which; less costly copies are created of the expensive clothes.

LIQUIDATIONS
See bankrupt stock

LOSS LEADER
This is an item which is priced very low, often at a loss for the retailer, as a way of enticing you into the store. The business anticipates that once inside, you will not only purchase the low priced item, but will also impulsively purchase more expensive items (which have a higher profit margin). The solution is to stock up on as many of those loss leaders as you will reasonably use. Don't be led into buying items which you do not need and which are not good values.

MANUFACTURER'S OUTLET
See factory outlet.

MANUFACTURER'S SUGGESTED RETAIL PRICE
Sometimes a manufacturer will pre-ticket his merchandise with the price he is suggesting it to be sold at in the stores. At other times, a manufacturer may recommend a retail price for his merchandise as depicted in a wholesale catalogue. Different sorts of merchandise have different markups or profit margins for the retailer. Some businesses will take a lower markup for a variety of reasons, and then pass the savings on to you, resulting in a good value.

MARKUPS
See manufacturer's suggested retail price

MULTIPLE PRICING
Retailers will subtly encourage you to purchase more than you need by offering several items at a single price, such as five for $1, instead of 20 cents each. Therefore, it may appear as a better deal to you, when in fact, it may not be. On the other hand, businesses may legitimately offer a discount for buying several of an item such as 20 cents each or ten for $1.50. In multiple pricing, you do not always have to buy more than you need. Often you can purchase one of an item at a pro-rated price.

NO FRILLS ENVIRONMENT
The bare minimum of store decoration usually assists in keeping the prices low to the consumer. Such is the case with the Warehouse Club.

ODD LOT
This is a very small amount of remaining inventory in a particular style, size or color, at the wholesale level. The wholesaler will sell this merchandise cheaply to another business which in turn offers the consumer a price which is lower than the suggested retail price. The store, Odd Lots, is a fine example of this.

OFF PRICE OR O.P. RETAILER
These businesses generally purchase goods during the season they are to be used by the consumer, as opposed to pre-season, which is typical with most retailers. This in-season buying helps the manufacturer to unload surplus inventory which is still in the stores at the proper timing for consumer use. Off price retailers may also purchase samples, overruns, seconds or discontinued items. Sometimes the O.P. retailer will remove the labels from the merchandise so as to hide the manufacturer's name from the consumer. Marshalls and T.J. Maxx are off price retailers.

OUTLET
Webster's New Collegiate Dictionary describes this as "a market for a commodity", "an agency (as a store or dealer) through which a product is marketed at retail". The word, outlet, is being used very frequently in a business' name and/or advertising to denote a place where there are good values or items sold at a discount. Another frequently used reason is to denote a retail operation (often a cash and carry) of a wholesaler. You may or may not be getting a savings off retail in these places. However, this allows you to have a bigger selection of that company's products under one roof and/or the opportunity to purchase freshly baked or prepared products .

OVERRUNS
A manufacturer may create more merchandise than needed to account for damages and faulty construction, which sometimes can occur. These are sold below wholesale to a business which then passes the savings on to the consumer. This merchandise is sometimes referred to as surplus or overstocks.

OVERSTOCK
See surplus goods.

PAST SEASON MERCHANDISE
Items which have been created or manufactured for a previous season.

PSYCHOLOGICAL PRICING
A common practice is to price items at one penny or one dollar less than the next larger whole number. For example, a $99 item is only $1 less than $100, but it appears as if it costs much less than it does, although after paying sales tax and/or service charges, your item can cost over $100.

REMNANT
This term is usually used to refer to carpet and flooring, wallpaper and fabric. It refers to ends of rolls which are leftovers. Sometimes these are short lengths. The terms, mill ends or bolt ends, are used interchangeably with the term, remnant.

SAMPLE
An item which a salesperson shows to a prospective purchaser for the purpose of taking orders for the product. The sample is created as a result of a plan or a pattern. As potential problems may not be realized until the sample is actually created and/or tested, the sample item may be slightly different than the item actually shipped to a store. For instance, maybe the crotch was cut too short, or the neckline too tight, or perhaps the pocket should be on the right side instead of the left. Although samples tend to be first quality, some are slightly soiled. Some samples on the other hand, are exactly the way the merchandise will be shipped to the stores.

SECONDS
Merchandise which has more than just a minor blemish or flaw which may, in some instances, affect its performance or appeal. Some of these imperfections can be easily repaired. The Hanes L'eggs mail order company mentioned in this book, offers seconds of pantyhose which has variations in color or a different weave in the knit panty than intended. Seconds are sometimes erroneously referred to as irregulars.

SURPLUS OR OVERSTOCK
An amount of merchandise which is more than a manufacturer or dealer needs

VALUE PRICED OR GOOD VALUE
Your money is well spent by purchasing one of these items as the quality might be better than you would expect for the price, the size may be bigger than usual, the warranty may be longer than usual etc. In these cases, the merchandise is not necessarily discounted, but by comparing the cost of the product to what you are getting, the value is great. Low markups by retailers often result in good values. The MCL Cafeteria, mentioned in this book, is a fine example of value priced food.

WHOLESALE OR WHOLESALE PRICE
This is the cost which retailer s pay for their merchandise.

LOTUS PRESS

The **Lotus** is attributed to Nepthys. the Egyptian goddess of tranquility. The flower represents the ideas of continuity, placidity and inner peace through meditation.

INDEX

C

G

H

I

J

ORDER FORM

PLEASE SEND ME:

TITLE	# OF COPIES	COST
Bargain Hunting In Central Ohio $12.95 + .74 tax= $13.69	_____	_____

Shipping is free

TOTAL COST_____

TERMS

Allow 3-6 weeks for delivery. Payment may be made by check or money order made payable to Lotus Press. There will be a $20 fee assessed for each check returned by your bank for any reason. If not completely satisfied with your purchase, you may return it for a refund.

SHIP TO:

NAME_____

ADDRESS _____

CITY, STATE, ZIP _____

AREA CODE & PHONE _____

MAIL ORDER TO:

LOTUS PRESS
P.O. BOX 8446
WESTERVILLE, OHIO 43086-8446

238

ABOUT THE AUTHOR

Debbie Keri-Brown was born in Brooklyn, New York on January 8, 1953. Having extensive family ties to the New York garment industry, has enabled her to learn from behind the scenes since she was very young. She is a 1973 cum laude graduate from Long Island University with a B.A. in speech pathology and has made Columbus her home since 1980. She is happily married to David Brown whom she drags around on her shopping expeditions since her grown children, Jason and Janelle, have learned how to say, "no".

She is currently an antique dealer with several locations in Central Ohio and also spends her time as a freelance writer while working on other books. 1996 marks the inaugural year of a national holiday she founded, National Bargain Hunting Week. Listed in the book, Chase's Annual Events, it will be held every year on the first Monday through the following Sunday in August. Debbie is the former owner of the Potpourri Boutique and Fantasy Designs Gallery in the Ohio Center, Columbus. She is the founder and former executive director of Arts Alive, a nonprofit organization providing opportunities in the visual and performing arts for people with disabilities. The Columbus Dispatch has honored her with two awards for advancement in the cultural arts and Arts Alive was the recipient of another. For the past fifteen years, she has been the producer and host of a weekly radio show addressing the arts and community affairs on the Central Ohio Radio Reading Service.

Debbie, a professional artist who creates jewelry using beads, handmade paper and mixed media, maintains memberships in several art leagues including the Ohio Designer Craftsmen and the Central Ohio Bead Society. She has taught many classes in wearable art, bargain hunting and publicity through most area adult education programs. As a public relations and marketing professional by vocation, she was responsible for these areas on a local, regional and national basis for the Columbus Cultural Arts Center. Debbie has provided consultancies in public relations and marketing to many organizations and individuals and may be contacted at: Lotus Press, P.O. Box 8446, Westerville, Ohio, 43086-8446.